Patterns in Literary Arts Series

The Art of Narration: THE SHORT STORY
A. Grove Day

The Art of Narration: THE NOVELLA
A. Grove Day

Themes in the One-Act Play
R. David and Shirley Cox

The Bible as Literature
Alton C. Capps

The Comic Vision
Peter J. Monahan

Dramatic Tragedy
William McAvoy

The Hero and Anti-Hero
Roger B. Rollin

The Black Experience
Nettye Goddard

Dramatic Comedy
Harry Shanker

Classical Literature
George Kearns

Non-Fiction
George Kearns

Dramatic Tragedy

Dramatic Tragedy

Edited by

WILLIAM McAVOY

Professor of English
St. Louis University

WEBSTER DIVISION
McGRAW-HILL BOOK COMPANY

New York St. Louis San Francisco Dallas Atlanta Toronto

ISBN 07-044790-X

Editorial Development, Bob Towns; Editing and Styling, Dorothy Donovan; Design, John Keithley; Production, Dick Shaw

Contents

Development of Dramatic Tragedy

It is impossible to know when man began to produce drama, but authorities all agree that the germ of what came to be drama is as old as mankind. It is likely that our earliest forefathers indulged in mimicry in some form or other, imitating a friend, an animal, or other things in nature. This practice is so widespread among all races, races which could have had no contact with each other, that we can reasonably say that this inclination to mimicry is innate in man. Man had only to add two more elements to his mimicry, dialogue and action (in the sense of plot), and he had the three essentials of all drama.

The plays in this volume were written over a very long period of time, from about 420 B.C. to the middle of the present century, and the subject they deal with has haunted men in every age. Every man that has ever lived has asked himself at some time or other the same question that each of the authors in this volume is concerned with: Why is there evil in the world? This question and the attempt to answer it are the very essence of literary tragedy. Whether it was Sophocles in the fifth century before Christ, Shakespeare in the early seventeenth century, or Arthur Miller in our own day, each was attempting to give an answer to this question. Thus we can say that tragedy is the art form which attempts to account for the presence of evil in the world. The many answers given in tragedy have varied widely; but, no matter how different the answers, the question has remained the same. The answers given by the various artists are different not because of the differing arts of their authors, but because of the different worlds which the minds of the artists inhabit.

It was in Greece, a small country and the cradle of western civilization, that tragedy had its beginnings. *Oedipus Rex,* which Sophocles wrote in the fifth century B.C., is an example of the working out of earlier primitive Greek thought in tragic drama. In order to understand the tragedy of Oedipus, therefore, it is necessary to grasp some of the characteristic Greek ways of looking at the world before the fifth century B.C.

First, the cult of the hero was of the utmost importance. The Greeks cherished a vision of the greatness of their own past and saw in their forefathers men who were heroic, superhuman. From their admiration of such men, the Greeks derived the ideals of human life. According to these ideals, a man should live for honor and reknown. Such a life was one of action—action which was courageous and glorious—action played out in a world of notable men. This hero's life would reach its climax in a great and noble death. Originally, the hero's reknown was earned by actions which benefitted himself, and there was little thought of service or sacrifice for others. But as time passed and the Greeks formed themselves into city states, it came to be the high destiny of the hero to gain honor and reknown in the service of his city. The Greek hero, then, was a man out of the ordinary, a man wholeheartedly devoted to the pursuit of honor—and this goal could be accomplished by a great sacrifice for his people.

The second major characteristic of the earlier Greek world view lies in its picture of what we would call the supernatural world. This other world for the Greeks was not separate from the world of man; the Greek gods occupied the same world as the Greeks themselves. The gods interfered in the lives of individual men, too, and played an integral part in human history. And it was the gods who were believed to send suffering and evil into the life of man. For Sophocles it was thus the gods who brought about the downfall of the tragic hero. But in his very greatness the Greek tragic hero helped to bring about his own misfortune: the qualities of intelligence and courage and honor, so important to the hero, contributed to his tragedy. He freely co-operated in his own destiny. Sophoclean tragedy therefore presents the spectacle of the hero undone by his own honorable actions and the action of malignant divine forces—forces which are far more powerful than man. It clearly demonstrates the tension between free will and necessity, or fate, which lies at the heart of tragedy.

The Greeks had long brooded on the problem of *why* the gods sent suffering into the life of man. For Sophocles, suffering brings knowledge, and through tragical self-knowledge man was to come to a sublime knowledge. Oedipus came to such self-knowledge in his suffering, but he attained much more: he became aware of the shadowy nothingness of human strength (even heroic human strength) and the fragility of human happiness. He came to see the greater world which exists beyond mere human concerns, the terrifying, often malignant, greater reality.

A hundred years after Sophocles wrote *Oedipus Rex,* Aristotle composed his *Poetics.* In the *Poetics* he dealt with poetry in general. When he came to deal with the theory of poetry and drama, he collected all the known facts about drama. He attempted to explain how an audience could obtain pleasure from observing terrible and tragic events on the stage. By searching the works of the writers of Greek tragedy, Aeschulus, Euripides, and especially those of Sophocles (whose *Oedipus Rex* he considered the finest of all Greek tragedies), Aristotle came up with what we know as his "definition of tragedy." This definition, or explanation, of tragedy has had a profound influence for more than twenty centuries on those attempting to write tragedies. Tragedy existed before Aristotle, but a large number of the tragedies written after he wrote his *Poetics* have been composed within the framework of his thought.

Aristotle began his consideration of tragedy by describing the effect such a work had on its audience as a *katharsis,* a purging of the emotions. He decided that the *katharsis* was primarily the purging of two emotions: pity and fear. He went on to ask what it was in tragedy that would produce such a *katharsis.*

> . . . pity is aroused by someone who undeservedly falls into misfortune, and fear is evoked by our recognizing that it is someone like ourselves who encounters this misfortune . . . This would be a person who is neither perfect in virtue and justice, nor one who falls into misfortune through vice and depravity; but rather, one who succumbs through some miscalculation. He must also be a person who enjoys great reputation and good fortune, such as Oedipus . . . and other illustrious men from similar families. . . . It is necessary, furthermore, . . . to illustrate a change of fortune not from bad fortune to good but, rather, the very opposite . . . and for this to take place not because of depravity but through some great miscalculation on the part of the type of person we have described . . .[1]

Notice that the change in the hero's fortune takes place because he has made a miscalculation. He has committed an offense because he is in ignorance of a material fact, and not from wickedness or depravity. The word Aristotle uses (which is translated above as *miscalculation*) is *hamartia*. *Hamartia* has often been spoken of as "the tragic flaw." For many years, moralizing critics sought some moral fault in the tragic hero which could be identified as the tragic flaw. Belatedly, many critics came to the realization that in Greek tragedy *hamartia* did not represent a moral shortcoming; it was, rather, an offense committed in ignorance. (Oedipus, for example, is ignorant of his true parentage.)

Aristotle wrote his description of tragedy with Greek tragedy as his only model, and long before Christianity (with its teachings of sin and Divine Providence) changed the course of thinking in western civilization. According to the Greeks, evil and suffering are sent to men through the agency of the gods. The advent of Christianity was to change this picture of tragedy.

After the golden age of Greek tragedy in the fifth century, of which we have been speaking, no great tragedy was written until the Renaissance. Although the Medieval literature of all civilized western nations is full of dramatizations of biblical stories and the lives of the saints, none of them developed into dramatic tragedy. For the men of the Medieval period, the universe was ruled by an all-powerful God; and the force of evil, though it existed, was not stronger than man assisted by God's grace. Thus the Medieval period found its answers to the presence of evil in its theology and its theologically-based philosophy. Medieval drama was not in any true sense tragic; for the Christian hero, even though he was beset by great difficulties, could eventually find his place with God.

The Medieval drama *Everyman* is included in this volume as an example of the teaching of Christian theology through the use of drama. It is the story of the moral evaluation which every man must face at the time of death. It therefore serves to demonstrate the Medieval conception of the human condition. It is representative of a type of play which exerted a strong influence on Renaissance drama. There are elements within it which occur again in the tragedy of the Renaissance; it combines humor with very serious matter and it shows the use of irony and satire that later became an out-

[1] Aristotle, *Poetics*, trans. Leon Golden (New Jersey: Prentice-Hall, 1968) pp. 21-22.

standing characteristic of Renaissance drama.

With the passing of the Medieval period, dramatists turned again to the art of tragedy. Renaissance Tragedy existed in a Christian setting and made extensive use of Christian theology in dealing with the presence of evil in the world. Greek tragedy itself, however, reached the Renaissance primarily through Roman versions of the earlier Greek writers.

The first of the plays of the Renaissance which combines the influences of the classical world and the Middle Ages is Christopher Marlowe's *Doctor Faustus.* In structure it is classical; in theme it is an expanded and advanced form of the morality play. It also solves the difficulty for anyone attempting to write tragedy in a Christian culture. For the writer undertaking to write tragedy in a Christian setting, there always remains the fact of heaven and the question of how he is to deal with it. No matter how severe the hero's suffering or how terrible his death, if he goes to heaven for all eternity, there really is, in the long view, no real tragedy. Marlowe solves this difficulty in a very simple manner: his hero is really a tragic character because he ends up in hell.

The essential tragic tension between human will and necessity, or fate, is very much present in *Faustus,* but the reality of the world beyond man is not that of the Greek world view. For the Greeks, the world beyond man was inhabited by gods who were responsible for the hero's suffering. Marlowe's hero, on the other hand, sins and is driven on by his own overweening ambition. He is brought down because he has willfully violated divine law.

William Shakespeare dealt with what were basically the same tragic problems, but his solutions differed from those of his predecessors. Shakespeare, therefore, wrote tragedies which are different in some essentials from the others we have discussed. First, in the tragedies of Shakespeare we find a thorough and acute analysis of human behavior in terms of Elizabethan psychology. Shakespeare's analysis of the workings of human nature and the springs of human action prepared the way for the tragedies of the modern period. Second, Christian ideas such as that of sin are very much present, and Shakespeare deals with them as part of his psychology. Sin is a psychological as well as a moral evil, and causes suffering before death as well as after.

The English tragic dramatists of the first half of the seventeenth century, relying heavily on the revenge tradition (of which *Hamlet* is the most important example) and on the tragedy of blood generally, gave to the theater the greatest age of tragedy since that of ancient Greece. They had about dried up the well of inspiration, however, by 1642, when the Puritan revolutionaries closed the public theaters.

With the reopening of the English theaters at the time of the restoration of King Charles II in 1660, tragedy failed to regain either its artistic depth or its theatrical popularity. The age of the Restoration and, later, the eighteenth century, had little relish for high tragedy. In the eighteenth century, tragedies continued to be written, but all followed the same design, not only of plot, but of character and diction. The story of tragedy during this period is not one of decline; it is the story of the death of the species. Tragedy died because the age found its answer to the problem of evil not in theology, not in any art form, but in denying its very existence. The poetic statement of this position is exemplified in the lines of Alexander Pope:

> All Nature is but Art, unknown to thee;
> All Chance, Direction, which thou canst not see;
> All Discord, Harmony not understood;
> All partial Evil, universal Good:
> And, spite of Pride, in erring Reason's spite,
> One truth is clear, WHATEVER IS, IS RIGHT.[2]

If we take this kind of logic as exemplifying the intellectual attitude of the age—and with certain notable exceptions it does—there is no need for tragedy to explain the problem of evil. Evil and the problems surrounding it really do not exist.

The nineteenth century was a time of great actors rather than of great tragedies. Its complacency, hypocrisy, and squeamishness forced its dramatists to observe an unreal cautiousness in dealing with such matters as profanity and sex. Too, the overwhelming mood of self confidence which grew from the intellectual attitudes of the eighteenth century and from the scientific and industrial revolutions was not compatible with the tragic view of life.

Both the child of the nineteenth century and one of its most violent critics, Henrik Ibsen ran head on into its prudery and its smug view of itself. Ibsen's fiercely realistic plays inspired almost unparalleled critical abuse; but, in spite of this, he continued to produce one after another. The social issues Ibsen dealt with, and his bitter attacks on many of society's most cherished notions, scandalized the intellectual world on the Continent as well as in England. Each play in its turn was violently attacked on moral grounds by conservative critics.

In Ibsen's plays, as in *Oedipus Rex* and *Hamlet,* we are confronted by crime, punishment, and high tragedy, but this time the subject is the common man. Ibsen dealt with the same problems as Sophocles and Shakespeare, but always depicted these problems in the setting of everyday life. He treated the problem of evil in the framework of middle-class society. His approach, consequently, was radically different than that of the earlier tragic dramatists.

> Reality was now a matter of careful scientific observation . . . Against the back drop of . . . extensive investigations into the nature of contemporary society, man emerged as the puny victim of tremendous forces beyond his control . . . Society was the culprit, and in the long run a better designed society would evolve.[3]

The tragic tension between human will and necessity is present in Ibsen, but there is an important change. The larger reality of the Greek's supernatural world has disappeared. Gone, too, are the necessities imposed by

[2]Alexander Pope, *Essay on Man,* Epistle I, ll. 289–294.
[3]H. D. Piper and J. K. Clark, *Dimensions in Drama* (New York: Charles Scribner's Sons, 1964), p. xii.

divine law in the Elizabethan world view. In Ibsen's thought, human society itself is the seed ground of those malignant forces which move against the individual man. Ibsen's tragic hero is pitted as an adversary against the evil forces Ibsen saw in society. Such a tragic hero embraces an individual moral responsibility, and this responsibility takes the form of not bowing to current ideals and commonly accepted moral codes. The questioning of these moral codes is made explicit by Ibsen. This questioning is indeed one of the central aspects of his thought.

The tradition which Ibsen set in motion spread over Europe and the English-speaking world, especially America. The final two selections in this volume, Tennessee Williams' *The Glass Menagerie* and Arthur Miller's *All My Sons,* show the strong influence of the Norwegian master.

Obviously both Williams and Miller have brought new and different approaches of their own to the theater, but both are in the Ibsen tradition of realism in two important ways: (1) each mirrors contemporary society in realistic terms, not in the way society would like to see itself, and (2) each asks questions about contemporary social values, questions which expose these values to a critical appraisal. The social realism of Williams' and Miller's dramas is by no means the only kind of drama found on the modern stage, but it is certainly a part of the most significant, consequential, and durable dramatic tradition of this century.

There is a very genuine and recognizable realism in Tennessee Williams' *The Glass Menagerie.* Williams follows Ibsen when he maintains that "plays in the tragic tradition offer us a view of certain moral values in violent juxtaposition." He also stands with Ibsen in his explicit questioning of contemporary values. As he himself says, he brings to his works a "distinct moral attitude." His attitude toward the presence of evil in the world, and his ideas on the irrational aspects of life are distant echoes of the earlier Greek views. When he faces evil in the world, Williams "finds life a mysterious and terrifying experience."

A comparison of Miller's view of tragedy with Aristotle's shows both the relationship of modern American tragedy to classical tragedy and the immense distance which separates them. Miller rejects Aristotle's theory that the tragic hero must be a man of high estate:

> . . . the common man is as apt a subject for
> tragedy in its highest sense as kings were.[4]

The arguments Miller advances to support his use of the common man as the tragic hero illustrate both the continuing strength of the Greek view of tragedy and the nature of the changes imposed by realism. In abandoning the man of high estate, Miller abandons the Greek idea of the hero itself. Miller's hero is not the man set apart by courage, grace, and intelligence; his hero is a man of commoner stamp. His rejection of the hero involves him in a difficulty, however. How is he to give his common hero the necessary qualities of character which would make him and his fate large enough for

---

[4]Arthur Miller, "Tragedy and the Common Man," *The New York Times,* February 27, 1947, Sec. 2, pp. 1–3.

tragedy? Miller's solution to this problem reveals the core of his beliefs about tragedy.

Miller says his tragic hero is moved by a compulsion to evaluate himself justly, to gain his true place in society. The hero's effort to establish his dignity brings about his destruction because of a wrong or evil in the environment. But in making his effort, in his questioning, in his "stretching and tearing apart of the cosmos," the hero gains in size and takes on tragic stature, no matter how lowly his origins.

Witnessing such a tragic struggle, even though it ends in destruction, arouses feelings of exaltation in the audience. As Miller sees it, however, exaltation is not the only emotion aroused by tragedy—tragedy also arouses feelings of terror. These feelings of terror Miller ascribes to tragedy's revolutionary questioning of the environment—the attempt of the tragic dramatist to enlighten by pointing out the enemies of man's freedom.

Modern American tragedy, then, contains elements drawn from centuries of exploration into the nature of evil. Although our tragic horizons are now bounded by realism, we are haunted by Greek visions. Our hero now is everyman, and his adversaries no longer include the devil of the Medieval period or the gods of the ancient Greeks: we ourselves are the adversary. We may find this too restricted and narrow a tragic view; the tragedy of the future may again find room for an irrational larger world.

In the plays that follow we are shown the nature of evil through tragedy. We glimpse the struggles of men to come to terms with the questions inevitably raised by our humanity. The great writers of tragedy, by searching into the dark places of the human heart with such intensity, by giving so much value to the passions and desires that move the human will, have attempted to answer the question with which we began: Why is there evil in the world? The answers have varied with different ages and different men, but the question remains the same.

Oedipus Rex

Introduction

Sophocles was born at Colonus, near Athens, early in the fifth century B. C. He may have written as many as one hundred twenty-three plays, but only one hundred twelve of these can be identified and only seven still exist in their entirety. In the fifth century, Greek dramatists competed for prizes at great religious and civic events. These festivals were held annually in March. Each playwright submitted four plays in the judging, three tragedies and a ribald comedy known as a *satyr play.* There are two significant factors in this situation which determined the form of these Greek tragedies. First, the plays were composed as part of a religious festival. They were therefore deeply concerned with the fundamental relations of the gods with man. Second, the playwrights used Greek myths from an earlier more primitive period as the stories or plots of their plays. These myths were familiar to the audience in their general outlines. The use of these myths as the framework for the relationships between gods and men made Greek tragedy the most completely symbolical of all of the world's drama. While the characters of the old myths, heroes like Oedipus, for example, are certainly individuals in their own right, the fact that they are also symbols carries us beyond the incidents of their own particular lives into much larger, deeper dimensions of life and thought. This Greek use of symbols enabled them to present objectively on a stage ideas and passions which are very difficult to grasp or to think about clearly. (We will see another such striking use of symbols in a later play in this volume, *Doctor Faustus.*)

Oedipus Rex (Oedipus the king) is one of the stories in a three-part myth—the so-called "Theban cycle." These myths deal with the fate of the royal house of Thebes, one of the chief cities in Boeotia. (Boeotia was an ancient republic in east central Greece.) Sophocles wrote three plays in his version of the Theban cycle. While it forms but one part of the cycle, the tragedy of *Oedipus Rex* is complete in itself.

Greek plays were given in large open-air theaters. There was an area in front of the stage called the *orchestra* in which the chorus moved and danced as they chanted the choral odes. There were no curtains—the play was presented as a whole, with no act or scene divisions. There was usually a building at the back of the stage containing a central doorway. In *Oedipus Rex* this doorway represents the entrance to the palace at Thebes. There were two other stage entrances, one at the left end of the stage, the other at the right. One entrance customarily represented the country, and a character entering from there was supposed to be coming from the country, and the other represented the city.

The chorus in the plays of Sophocles usually consisted of fifteen persons; in the case of *Oedipus Rex* they are the Elders of Thebes, the men of the

noblest families in the city. As the play opens there are a group of suppliants (petitioners) on stage—this is not the chorus proper, and the suppliants are only present during the prologue, or first part of the play.
Oedipus Rex is divided into several parts: the prologue, or introduction,
the parados, or entrance of the chorus, and four episodes, separated from
one another by stasimons, or choral odes. These odes are lyric poetry, lines
chanted or "sung" as the chorus moved rhythmically across the orchestra.
(The entire *Oedipus Rex* was written as poetry. The English translation in
this volume, however, is in prose.) The movement of the chorus across the
orchestra in one direction, and the lines of the ode chanted during this
movement, are called the *strophe*. The return movement, and the lines
which accompany it, are called the *antistrophe*. The meter (rhythm or
pattern) of the verse in the strophe is the same as that in the antistrophe. A
choral ode might well contain more than one strophe and more than one
antistrophe.

The chorus itself was such a vital part of a Greek tragedy that these
tragedies were often called *choruses*. The chorus members are characters
in the play and, at the same time, they are commentators on the action. In
Oedipus Rex the chorus of Theban Elders not only are worried representa-
tives of a city ravaged by plague, but they comment philosophically on the
destruction of Oedipus as thoughtful spectators might. The chorus thus
serves to draw the audience "into" the play—they are the bridge between
actors and audience.

Oedipus Rex is concerned with the first part of the Theban myth. The
city of Thebes had been founded by Cadmus, son of Agenor. Polydorus,
the son of Cadmus, in turn had a son named Laius. Laius married Jocasta,
and they learned from an oracle (prophet) of the god Apollo that a son born
to them would kill Laius and marry Jocasta.

When a son was born to them, therefore, Laius and Jocasta determined to
do away with the child. They turned him over to one of their servants with
orders to abandon him in the mountains. But the servant, filled with compassion for the child, gave it instead to a shepherd of Corinth whom he
met in the mountains. The shepherd returned with the child to Corinth, a
city in east central Greece ruled by Polybus and his wife Meropè. They
were childless, and because they were taken with the child, decided to
raise him as their own son.

Oedipus (the name given him by Polybus and Meropè) grew up thinking
that the rulers of Corinth were his true parents. After he was grown, however, he heard by chance a rumor that they were not his parents. He resolved
to visit the shrine of Apollo at Delphi and consult the oracle there as to his
true parentage. At Delphi he learned only that he was fated by Apollo to
kill his father and marry his mother. Believing that Polybus and Meropè
were his parents, Oedipus resolved to stay away from Corinth so as to avoid
his ghastly fate. As he travelled away from Delphi he met Laius (whom he of
course did not know) in a lonely spot where three roads met. In a roadside
quarrel Oedipus killed Laius, thus fulfilling the oracle of Apollo. Oedipus
then moved on in the direction of Thebes. When he approached that city,

however, he found the way guarded by a great monster, the Sphinx. The Sphinx challenged Oedipus with a riddle. No one had yet been able to answer the riddle, and many Thebens had perished in the human tax the monster had laid upon the city. Oedipus successfully answered the riddle and freed Thebes from the Sphinx. In gratitude the Thebans elected him their king, and he married Jocasta, widow of Laius and his own mother. Years passed, and Oedipus ruled Thebes in peace. He and Jocasta had four children, two sons and two daughters. But Apollo was not content that the unconscious crimes of Oedipus should go unnoticed. He brought a great plague on Thebes. The Thebans, desperately seeking deliverance from famine, pestilence, and death, dispatched Jocasta's brother, Creon, to consult the oracle of Apollo at Delphi. As the play opens, the citizens of Thebes, and Oedipus their king, await Creon's return.

In *Oedipus Rex* Sophocles seems to say that man has within him the freedom to make choices and through these choices to come to self-knowledge. Much of what happens in his life is brought about by Oedipus' own actions; but, just as in our own lives, much happens over which he has no control. Oedipus is partly responsible for the tragic fate of himself and others. But many events come about because the gods willed them, and Oedipus has no possible way of controlling these events. They were for him, just as they are for us, part of the mystery of life. Sophocles has the chorus comment on the ultimate fall of Oedipus when they say

> Dwellers in our native Thebes, behold, this is Oedipus,
> who knew the famed riddle, and was a man most mighty;
> on whose fortunes, what citizen did not gaze with envy?
> Behold, into what a stormy sea of dread trouble he has
> come!
>
> Therefore, while our eyes wait to see the destined final
> day, we must call no one happy who is of mortal race, until
> he has crossed life's border free from pain.

Oedipus Rex

SOPHOCLES

Characters in the Play

OEDIPUS   *King of Thebes*

PRIEST OF ZEUS

CREON   *brother of Jocasta*

CHORUS   *of Theban Elders*

TEIRESIAS   *a blind prophet*

JOCASTA   *Queen of Thebes; wife of Oedipus, widow of Laius, the late King of Thebes*

MESSENGER   *from Corinth*

HERDSMAN   *formerly in the service of Laius*

SECOND MESSENGER

MUTE PERSONS   *a train of Suppliants (old men, youths, children)*

THE CHILDREN   *Antigone and Ismene, daughters of Oedipus and Jocasta*

Oedipus Rex

Scene: Before the royal palace of Oedipus at Thebes.[1] *In front of the large
central doors there is an altar; a smaller altar stands also near each of
the two side-doors. Suppliants—old men, youths, and young children—
are seated on the steps of the altars. They are dressed in white tunics
and cloaks,—their hair bound with white fillets. On the altars they
have laid down olive-branches wreathed with fillets of wool. The Priest
of Zeus, a venerable man, is alone standing, facing the central doors of
the palace. These are now thrown open. Followed by two attendants,
who place themselves on either side of the doors, Oedipus enters, in the
robes of a king. For a moment he gazes silently on the groups at the
altars, and then speaks.*

OEDIPUS. My children, latest-born to Cadmus[2] who was of old,
why are you set here thus with wreathed branches of suppliants,[3]
while the city reeks with incense, rings with prayers for health and
cries of woe? I judged it unbecoming, my children, to hear these
things from the mouths of others, and have come hither myself, I,   5
Oedipus highly acclaimed by all.

Tell me, then, venerable man—since it is natural for you to speak
for these—in what mood are you placed here, with what dread or
what desire? Be sure that I would gladly give all aid. I would be hard
of heart if I did not pity such suppliants as these.   10

PRIEST OF ZEUS. Nay, Oedipus, ruler of my land, you see of what
years we are who beset your altars,—some, nestlings still too tender
for long journeys,—some, bowed with age, priests, as I of Zeus,[4]—
and these, the chosen unmarried youths; while the rest of the
people sit with wreathed branches in the market-places, and before   15
the two shrines of Pallas,[5] and where Ismenus gives answer by fire.[6]

For the city, as you see yourself, is now too sorely vexed, and can
no more lift her head from beneath the angry waves of death; a

1 *Thebes:* an old city in Boeotia, an ancient republic in east central Greece.
2 *Cadmus:* legendary founder and guardian genius of Thebes, great-great grandfather of Oedipus.
3 *wreathed branches of suppliants:* suppliants customarily carried branches decorated
with wool, which were placed upon the altar.
4 *Zeus:* chief of the Greek gods and the protector of suppliants.
5 *two shrines of Pallas:* There were two temples of Pallas Athena (daughter of Zeus,
goddess of civilization and its arts) at Thebes.
6 *where . . . fire:* An altar of Apollo by the river Ismenus in Thebes. Divination (the
discovery of hidden knowledge) by burnt offerings was practised there.

blight is on her in the fruitful blossoms of the land, in the herds among the pastures, in the barren pangs of women;[7] and above all the fire-carrying god, the malign plague, has swooped on us, and ravages the town; by whom the house of Cadmus is made waste, but dark Hades[8] rich in groans and tears.

It is not as judging you ranked with gods that I and these children are suppliants at your hearth, but as judging you to be first among men, both in the events of life and the intervention of the deities: seeing that you came to the town of Cadmus, and did free us from the tax[9] that we rendered to the hard songstress;[10] and this, though you knew nothing from us that could help you, nor had been schooled; but rather by a god's aid, 'tis said and believed you did uplift our life.

And now, Oedipus, king glorious in all eyes, we beseech you, all we suppliants, to find for us some help, whether by the inspiration of a god you know it, or perhaps as in the power of man; for I see that, when men have been proved by their past deeds, the results of their counsels, too, most often have effect.

On, best of mortals, again save our State! On, guard your fame,[11] —since now this land calls you saviour for your former zeal; and never be it our memory of your reign that we were first restored and afterward cast down: rather, lift up this State in such a way that it fall no more!

With good omen you gave us that past good fortune; now also show yourself the same. For if you are to rule this land, even as you are now its lord, 'tis better to be lord of men than of a dead city: since neither walled town nor ship is anything, if it is void and no life dwells within it with you.

OEDIPUS. O my piteous children, known, well known to me are the desires which you have come with: well know I that you all are deathly sick; yet, sufferers as you are, there is not one of you who

---

7 *blight . . . women:* the crops and flocks of the Thebans were blighted, and women failed to give birth to live children or else died in childbirth.

8 *Hades:* the underworld, haunt of the dead.

9 *tax:* tribute of human victims.

10 *hard songstress:* the Sphinx, a winged creature who had the body of a lion and the upper part of a woman. It was the personification of a force which ordinarily men could not master, but Oedipus had been made king of the Thebans for solving the riddle of the Sphinx: "What animal in the morning walks on four feet, at noon on two, and in the evening three?" Oedipus answered: man. Man in his infancy (morning) crawls on all four; in his manhood (noon) man walks on two feet; in his old age (evening), man walks with a staff—his third "foot." In a more tragic sense the answer to the riddle is Oedipus himself; he has been an infant, is now a man in the fullness of his powers, and will soon be broken and aged beyond his years by his tragic destiny.

11 *guard your fame:* As a hero the only concern of Oedipus should be the growth of his fame—no thought of personal risk to him is considered here.

is as sick as I. Your pain comes on each one of you for himself   50
alone, and for no other; but my soul all at once mourns for the city,
and for myself, and for you.

I have not been sleeping: no, be sure that I have wept full many
tears, and have given much thought. And the sole remedy which,
well pondering, I could find, this I have put into act. I have sent   55
the son of Menoeceus, Creon, my own wife's brother, to the
Pythian house of Phoebus,[12] to learn by what deed or word I might
deliver this town. And already, when the lapse of days is reckoned,
I wonder what he is doing; for he delays strangely, beyond the
time needed for the journey. But when he comes, then shall I be   60
no true man if I do not do all that the god shows.

PRIEST. Nay, in season have you spoken; at this moment they
signal to me that Creon draws near.[13]

OEDIPUS. O king Apollo, may he come to us in the brightness of
saving fortune, even as his face is bright!   65

PRIEST. Indeed, to all appearances, he brings comfort; else
would he not be coming crowned thus thickly with berry-laden
bay.[14]

OEDIPUS. We shall know soon: he is within hearing distance.—

[Enter Creon.]

Chieftan, my kinsman, son of Menoeceus, what news have you   70
brought us from the god?

CREON. Good news: I tell you that even terrible troubles,—if by
chance all goes well,—will end in perfect peace.

OEDIPUS. But what is the oracle? So far, your words make me
neither bold nor yet afraid.   75

CREON. If you wish to hear while these are present, I am ready
to speak; or else to go within.

OEDIPUS. Speak before all: the sorrow which I bear is for these
more than for my own life.

CREON. With your permission, I will tell what I heard from the   80
god. Phoebus our lord bids us plainly to drive out a polluted person,
which (he says) has been harboured in this land, and not to harbour
it, so that our land can be healed.

---

12 *Pythian . . . Phoebus:* an epithet for the famous oracular shrine of Apollo (Phoebus)
at Delphi. Such use of an epithet (a complimentary descriptive term) is conventional
in Greek tragedy, and occurs frequently in *Oedipus Rex.* The shrine at Delphi
was given the epithet *Pythian* because it was the site of the Pythian Games, held to
celebrate Apollo's victory over the serpent Python. Creon was sent to consult the
oracle (prophet) of Apollo at Delphi.

13 *they . . . near:* some of the suppliants have indicated to the priest that Creon is
approaching.

14 *berry-laden bay:* The bay laurel worn here as a wreath indicates that Creon brings
a favorable reply from the oracle of Apollo.

OEDIPUS. By what rite shall we rid ourselves of it? What is the defilement? 85

CREON. By banishing a man, or by bloodshed in expiation of bloodshed, since it is that blood which brings the tempest on our city.

OEDIPUS. And who is the man whose fate he thus reveals?

CREON. Laius, king, was lord of our land before you were governor 90 of this State.

OEDIPUS. I know it well—by hearsay, for I never saw him. ←

CREON. He was slain; and the god now bids us plainly to take revenge on his murderers—whoever they be.

OEDIPUS. And where are they upon the earth? Where shall the 95 dim track of this old crime be found?

CREON. In this land,—said the god. The one sought for can be caught; only that which is not watched escapes.

OEDIPUS. And was it in the house, or in the field, or on strange soil that Laius met his bloody end? 100

CREON. 'Twas on pilgrimage to Delphi, as he said, that he had left our land; and he did not come home, after he had once set forth.

OEDIPUS. And was there none to tell? Was there no comrade with him who saw the deed, from whom information might have been gained, and used? 105

CREON. All perished, except one who fled in fear, and could tell for certain only one thing of all that he saw.

OEDIPUS. And what was that? One thing might be the clue to many, could we get but a small beginning for hope.

CREON. He said that many robbers met and fell on them, not 110 with the strength of one man, but with very many hands.

OEDIPUS. How, then, unless there was some dealing in bribes from here,[15] should a single robber have dared thus far?

CREON. Such things were surmised; but, once Laius was slain, new troubles arose and we had no avenger. 115

OEDIPUS. But, when royalty had fallen thus, what trouble could possibly have hindered a full search?

CREON. The riddle-singing Sphinx had made us let dark things go, and was inviting us to think of our present troubles.

OEDIPUS. Well, I will start afresh, and once more make dark 120 things plain. Right worthily has Phoebus, and worthily have you, bestowed this care on the cause of the dead; and so, as is suitable, you shall find how I stand by you in seeking vengeance for this land, and for the god besides. On behalf of no far-off friend,[16] no, but in my own cause, shall I dispel this taint. For whoever was the 125

15 *unless . . . here:* unless someone in Thebes paid for the killing. Oedipus begins to suspect a plot in the killing of Laius.
16 *far-off friend:* Laius; Oedipus is of course ignorant of the fact that Laius was his own father and not a far-off friend.

slayer of Laius might wish to take vengeance on me also with as fierce a hand. Therefore, in doing right to Laius, I serve myself.

Come then my children, rise from the altar-steps, and lift these suppliant boughs; and let someone else go and summon hither the folk of Cadmus,[17] warned that I mean to leave nothing untried; for   130 our health (with the god's help) shall be made certain—or our ruin.

PRIEST. My children, let us rise; we came at first to seek what this man promises of himself. And may Phoebus, who sent these oracles, come to us at once, our saviour and deliverer from the pestilence.   [Exeunt Oedipus, Priest, and Suppliants.]   135

[Enter Chorus of Theban Elders.][18]

CHORUS. *(singing) Strophe*[19] *1.* O sweetly-speaking message of Zeus, in what spirit have you come from golden Pytho[20] to glorious Thebes? I am on the rack, terror shakes my soul, O Delian healer[21] to whom wild cries rise, in holy fear of you, what thing you will work for me: new plagues in punishment for fresh impieties, or in   140 retribution for some old defilement. Tell me immortal Voice,[22] born of Golden Hope!

Antistrophe[23] *1.* First I call on you, daughter of Zeus, divine Athena, and on your sister, guardian of our land, Artemis,[24] who sits on her throne of fame, above the circle of our Agora,[25] and on   145 Phoebus the great bowman: O shine forth on me, my three-fold help against death![26] If ever before in stopping ruin coming upon the city, you drove a fiery pest beyond our borders, come now also!

Strophe 2. Woe is me, countless are the sorrows that I bear; a plague is on all our host, and thought can find no weapon for   150

17 *folk of Cadmus:* the inhabitants of Thebes.
18 *Theban Elders:* men of noble birth; the "folk of Cadmus" whom Oedipus has just summoned.
19 *Strophe:* the stanza of a Greek choral ode sung as the chorus moved across the orchestra in one direction.
20 *golden Pytho:* the temple of Apollo at Delphi, which had a temple treasury, where it was possible to deposit gold as in a bank.
21 *Delian healer:* Apollo, the healer, came from the island of Delos.
22 *immortal Voice:* Apollo's answer (not yet known to the Elders) is personified here as a voice.
23 *Antistrophe:* "the counter turn," the stanzas of the Greek choral ode which were sung as the chorus returned across the orchestra. These stanzas are metrically equal to the stanzas of the strophe.
24 *Artemis:* sister of Athena and Apollo, Artemis was the goddess of wildlife and the growth of the field. As the guardian of very young animals, she was also thought to preside over human birth.
25 *Agora:* the place of assembly in a Greek city.
26 *three-fold help against death:* Athena, Artemis, and Apollo (Phoebus) were the guardians of Thebes.

defence. The fruits of the glorious earth grow not; by no birth of
children do women surmount the pangs in which they shriek; and
life on life may you see sped like bird on nimble wing, aye, swifter
than resistless fire, to the shore of the western god.[27]

Antistrophe 2. By such deaths, past numbering, the city perishes: 155
unpitied, her children lie on the ground, spreading pestilence, with
none to mourn: and meanwhile young wives and grey-haired
mothers with them, moaning at the steps of the altars, some here,
some there, entreating for their weary woes. The prayer to the
Healer rings clear, and blent therewith, the voice of lamentation: 160
for these things, golden daughter of Zeus,[28] send us the bright
face of comfort.

Strophe 3. And grant that the fierce god of death,[29] who now with
no brazen shields, yet amid cries as of battle, wraps me in the flame
of his attack, may turn his back in speedy flight from our land,   165
borne by a fair wind to the great deep of Amphitrite,[30] or to those
waters in which none find haven, even to the Thracian wave;[31] for
if night leave anything undone, day follows to accomplish this. O
you who wield the powers of the fire-fraught lightning, O Zeus
our father, slay him beneath your thunderbolt!   170

Antistrophe 3. Lycean King,[32] gladly would I see your shafts also
from your bent bow's string of woven gold, go abroad in their
might, our champions in the face of the foe; yea, and the flashing
fires of Artemis[33] wherewith she glances through the Lycean hills.
And I call him whose locks are bound with gold, who is named   175
with the name of this land, ruddy Bacchus[34] to whom Bacchants[35]
cry, the comrade of the Maenads,[36] to draw near with the blaze of
his blithe torch, our ally against the god unhonoured among gods.[37]

[Oedipus enters during the closing strains of the choral prayer.]

27 *the western god:* Pluto; the West was the region of the dead.
28 *golden daughter of Zeus:* Athena.
29 *the fierce god of death:* Ares, customarily the god of war, is here the destroyer.
30 *the great deep of Amphitrite:* the Atlantic; Amphitrite was the wife of Poseidon
and goddess of the sea.
31 *waters . . . wave:* the Black Sea.
32 *Lycean King:* the epithet of Apollo as god of light.
33 *flashing . . . Artemis:* the torches with which Artemis was represented.
34 *Bacchus:* Bacchus (Dionysus), the god of wine, was known as *the Cadmeian king.*
35 *Bacchants:* the frenzied worshippers of Bacchus.
36 *Maenads:* also called *Bacchae,* were the female followers of Bacchus, and ac-
companied him on his wanderings.
37 *god . . . gods:* Ares, as the cause of destruction, was hated by Zeus.

OEDIPUS. You pray: and in answer to your prayer,—if you will give a loyal welcome to my words and minister to your own disease, —you may hope to receive aid and relief from woes. I now have heard this story for the first time, for I was not living here when the murder was committed. I should not be far on the track, if I were tracing it alone, without a clue. But as it is,—since it was only after the time of the deed that I was enrolled a Theban among Thebans, —to you, the Cadmeans all, I do thus proclaim. 180

185

Whoever of you knows by whom Laius son of Labdacus was slain, I bid him to declare all to me. And if he is afraid, I tell him to remove the danger of the charge from his path by denouncing himself; for he shall suffer nothing else unlovely, but only leave the land, un-hurt. Or if any one knows an alien, from another land, as the assassin, let him not keep silence; for I will pay his reward, and my thanks shall rest with him besides. 190

But if you keep silence[38]—if any one, through fear, shall seek to screen friend or self from my behest—hear you what I then shall do. I charge you that no one of this land, of which I hold the sovereignty and the throne, give shelter or speak word unto that murderer, whoever he be. I forbid anyone to make him partner of his prayer or sacrifice, or serve him with the lustral rite;[39] but that all ban him their homes,[40] knowing that *this* is our defiling thing, as the oracle of the Pythian god has newly shown me. I then am in this way the ally of the god and of the slain. And I pray solemnly that the slayer, whoever he be, whether his hidden guilt is his alone or has partners, evilly, as he is evil, may wear out his unblest life.[41] And for myself I pray that if, with my knowledge, he should become an inmate of my house, I may suffer the same things which even now I called down upon others. And on you I lay it to make all these words good, for my sake, and for the sake of the god, and for our land's, thus blasted with barrenness by angry heaven. 195

200

205

For even if the matter had not been commanded by a god, it was not fitting that you should leave the guilt thus unpurged, when one so noble, and he your king, had perished; rather were you bound to search it out. And now, since 'tis I who hold the powers which once he held, who possess his bed and the wife who bare children to him; and since, had his hope of issue not been frustrated, children 210

215

---

38 *But . . . silence:* Oedipus here begins to pronounce a solemn and dreadful curse on the unknown murderer of Laius, and on anyone who would shield him.

39 *lustral rite:* purifying rite; in the opening moments of sacrifice offered in the home, those present and the altar were purified by being sprinkled with consecrated water.

40 *ban . . . homes:* the murderer is shut out not only from communal worship but from family life itself.

41 Oedipus is actually calling down his curse upon his own head.

born of one mother would have made ties between him and me—
but, as it was, fate swooped upon his head; by reason of these
things will I uphold this cause, just as though it were the cause of
my own father,[42] and will leave nothing undone in seeking to find
him whose hand shed that blood, for the honour of the son of　　220
Labdacus and of Polydorus and elder Cadmus and Agenor who
was of old.[43]

And for those who obey me not, I pray that the gods send them
neither crops of the earth nor fruit of the womb, but that they be
consumed by their lot that now is, or by one that is still worse. But　　225
for all you, the loyal folk of Cadmus to whom these things seem
good, may Justice, our ally, and all the gods be with you graciously
for ever.

LEADER OF THE CHORUS. As you have put me on my oath, on my
oath, O King, I will speak. I am not the slayer, nor can I point to　　230
him who slew. As for the question, it was for Phoebus, who sent
it, to tell us this thing—who can have wrought the deed.

OEDIPUS. Justly said; but no man on the earth can force the gods
to what they will not.

LEADER. I would gladly suggest what seems to me the next best　　235
method of procedure after this plan of asking Apollo, which you
say is impracticable.

OEDIPUS. If there is yet a third course, do not hesitate to show it.

LEADER. I know that our lord Teiresias[44] is the seer most like
to our lord Phoebus; from whom, O King, a searcher of these　　240
things might learn them most clearly.

OEDIPUS. Not even this have I left out of my cares. On the hint
of Creon, I have twice sent a man to bring him; and this long
while I wonder why he is not here.

LEADER. Indeed (his skill apart) the rumours are but faint and old.　　245

OEDIPUS. What rumours are they? I look to every story.

LEADER. Certain wayfarers were said to have killed him.

OEDIPUS. I, too, have heard it, but none sees him who saw it.

LEADER. Nay, if he knows what fear is, he will not stay when he
hears your curses, so dire as they are.　　250

OEDIPUS. When a man shrinks not from a deed, neither is he
scared by a word.

LEADER. Well, here is one to put him to the test.[45] For here they
bring at last the godlike prophet, in whom alone of men the truth
lives.　　255

---

42 Oedipus lays a horrifying though unwitting emphasis upon those very things
which are the results of the unspeakable crimes he himself has committed.
43 *Labdacus . . . old:* the male ancestry of Oedipus: Agenor, Cadmus, Polydorus,
Labdacus, Laius, Oedipus.　　44 *Teiresias:* the blind Theban prophet.
45 *to . . . test:* to convict him.

[Enter Teiresias,[46] led by a boy.]

OEDIPUS. Teiresias, whose soul understands all things, the lore that may be told and the unspeakable, the secrets of heaven and the low things of earth,—you feel, though you cannot see, what a plague haunts our State,—from which, great prophet, we find in you our protector and only saviour. Now, Phoebus—if indeed you   260
know it not from the messengers—sent answer to our question that riddance could come from this pest only if we learn aright the slayers of Laius, and slay them, or send them into exile from our land. Do not, then, withhold either voice of birds or any other way of seer-lore that you have,[47] but rescue yourself and the State,   265
rescue me, rescue all that is defiled by the dead. For our hopes of deliverance are in your hands; and man's noblest task is to help others by his best means and powers.

TEIRESIAS. O how dreadful to have wisdom where it profits not the wise! Indeed, I knew this well, but let it slip out of mind; other-   270
wise I would never have come here.

OEDIPUS. What now? How sad you have come in!

TEIRESIAS. Let me go home; most easily will you bear your own burden to the end, and I mine, if you will consent.[48]

OEDIPUS. Your words are strange, nor kindly to this State which   275
nurtured you, when you deprive the city of this oracle.

TEIRESIAS. No, I see that you, on your part, speak inopportunely: therefore I speak not, that I also may not have your misfortune.

OEDIPUS. For the love of the gods, turn not away, if you have knowledge, all we suppliants implore you on our knees.   280

TEIRESIAS. Aye, for you are all without knowledge; but never will I reveal my griefs—that I may not tell yours.

OEDIPUS. What do you say? You know the secret, and will not tell it, but are minded to betray us and to destroy the State?

TEIRESIAS. I will pain neither myself nor you. Why rashly ask   285
these things? You will not learn them from me.

OEDIPUS. Why so harsh and unyielding?—for you would anger a very stone,—will you never speak out? Can nothing touch you? Will you never make an end?

TEIRESIAS. You blame my mood, but you do not see that to which   290
you are wedded: no, you find fault with me.

OEDIPUS. And who would not be angry to hear the words with which you now slight this city?

---

46 There are now two "blind" men present: Teiresias, who is blind physically, and Oedipus, who is blind to the facts of his own situation.
47 Teiresias uses divination by the voice of birds and, when that fails, he uses divination by fire.
48 Knowing the truth about Oedipus Teiresias feels that no good will come of the disclosure and wants no part in it.

TEIRESIAS. Since the future will come of itself, there is no need of my saying these things. 295

OEDIPUS. Then, seeing that it must come, you on your part should tell me of it.

TEIRESIAS. I will speak no further; rage, then, if you will, with the fiercest wrath your heart knows.

OEDIPUS. Aye, indeed, I will not spare—so angry I am—to speak 300 all my thought. Know that I think you even helped in plotting the deed, and to have done it, short of slaying with your hands. If you had eyesight, I would have said that the doing, also, of this thing was yours alone.

TEIRESIAS. Indeed?—I charge you that you abide by the decree 305 of your own mouth, and from this day speak neither to these nor to me: *you are* the accursed defiler of this land.

OEDIPUS. So brazen with your blustering taunt? And how do you trust to escape your due?

TEIRESIAS. I have escaped: for I have truth as my fortress. 310

OEDIPUS. Who taught you this? It was not, at least, your art.

TEIRESIAS. You: for you did spur me to speak against my will.

OEDIPUS. What speech? Speak again that I may learn it better.

TEIRESIAS. Did you not understand me? Or are you tempting me to speak more? 315

OEDIPUS. No, I did not understand you so that I can say that your remark was perfectly intelligible. Speak again!

TEIRESIAS. I say that you are the slayer of the man whose slayer you seek.

OEDIPUS. Now you shall be sorry that you have twice said words 320 so dire.

TEIRESIAS. Would you have me say more, that you may be more angry?

OEDIPUS. Speak as much as you wish; it will be said in vain.

TEIRESIAS. I say that you have been living in unguessed shame 325 with your nearest kin, and see not to what woe you have come.

OEDIPUS. Do you indeed think that you shall always speak thus without being punished?

TEIRESIAS. Yes, if there is any strength in truth.

OEDIPUS. Indeed, there is,—for all except you; for you that 330 strength is not, since you are maimed in ear, and in mind, and in eye.

TEIRESIAS. Aye, and you are a poor wretch to utter taunts which every man here will soon hurl at you.

OEDIPUS. Night, endless night has you in her keeping, so that you can never hurt me, or any man who sees the sun. 335

TEIRESIAS. No, your doom is not to fall by *me:* Apollo is enough, whose care it is to work that out.

OEDIPUS. Are these Creon's plots, or yours? [49]

---

[49] Having already begun to unravel the suspected murder plot, Oedipus now lays it at Creon's door.

TEIRESIAS. No, Creon is no plague to you; you are your own.

OEDIPUS. O wealth, and empire, and skill surpassing skill in   340
life's keen rivalries,[50] how great is the envy that cleaves to you, if
for the sake, yea, of this power which the city has put into my hands,
a gift unsought, Creon the trusty, Creon my old friend, has crept on
me by stealth, yearning to thrust me out of it, and has suborned
such a scheming magician as this, a tricky quack, who has eyes   345
only for his gains, but in his art is blind!

Come, now, tell me, where have you proved yourself a seer?
Why, when the Watcher[51] was here who wove dark song, did you
say nothing that could free this folk? Yet the riddle, at least, was
not for the first comer to read; there was need of a seer's skill;   350
and no such skill were you found to have either, by help of birds,
or as known from any god: no, I came, I, Oedipus, the ignorant,
and made her mute, when I had seized the answer by my wit,
untaught of birds. And it is I whom you are trying to oust, thinking
to stand close to Creon's throne. I think that you and the plotter of   355
these things will regret your zeal to purge the land. Indeed, if you
were not an old man you would have learned at your cost how bold
you are.

LEADER. To our thinking, both this man's words and yours,
Oedipus, have been said in anger. Not for such words is our need,   360
but to seek how we shall best discharge the mandates of the god.

TEIRESIAS. King though you are, the right of reply, at least, must
be judged the same for both; of that I too am lord. Not at all am I
servant to you, but to Loxias;[52] and so I shall not stand enrolled
under Creon for my patron.[53] And I tell you—since you have   365
taunted me even with blindness—that you have sight, yet do not
see what misery you are in, nor where you dwell, nor with whom.
Do you know to what family you belong? And you have been an
unwitting foe to your own kin, in the grave, and on the earth above;
and the double lash of your mother's and your father's curse shall   370
one day drive you from this land in dreadful haste, with blindness
then on the eyes that now see clearly.

And what place will possibly be a haven to your shrieks, will not
all Cithaeron[54] ring with it soon, when you have learned the meaning of the marriage entered upon, within that house, in which you   375
found a fatal haven, after a voyage so fair? And a throng of other

50 *skill . . . rivalries:* Oedipus is commenting upon his own skills and intelligence,
which surpass those of other men. The possession of these traits, and the rewards
which they bring, are a source of bitter envy among lesser men.
51 *the Watcher:* the Sphinx.
52 *Loxias:* the epithet of Apollo as the god of prophecy and guardian of seers and
prophets.
53 Teiresias denies being Creon's tool.
54 *Cithaeron:* a range of mountains between Attica and Boeotia; the place where the
infant Oedipus had been left to die.

ills of which you can not guess, will make you level with your true self and with your own brood.[55]

Therefore heap your scorns on Creon and on my message: for no one among men shall ever be crushed more miserably than you.   380

OEDIPUS. Are these taunts to be indeed borne from *him?*—Hence, ruin take you! Go, this instant! Back!—away!—go away from these doors!

TEIRESIAS. I would never have come, not I, if you had not called me.   385

OEDIPUS. I knew not that you were about to speak folly, or I would have delayed long before I called you to my house.

TEIRESIAS. Such am I,—as you think, a fool; but for the parents who conceived you, sane.

OEDIPUS. What parents? Stay . . . and who is my father?   390

TEIRESIAS. This day shall show your birth and shall bring your ruin.

OEDIPUS. What riddles, what obscure words you always speak.

TEIRESIAS. Nay, are you not most skilled in unraveling obscure speech?

OEDIPUS. Yes, taunt me in that[56] in which you will find me   395
great.[57]

TEIRESIAS. Yes, 'twas just that fortune that undid you.

OEDIPUS. But, if I delivered this town, I care not.

TEIRESIAS. Then I will go: so do you, boy, take me hence.

OEDIPUS. Aye, let him take you: while here, you are a hindrance,   400
a trouble; when you have vanished, you will vex me no more.

TEIRESIAS. I will go when I have done my errand, fearless of your frown. For you can never destroy me. And I tell you—the man of whom you have for a long time been in search, uttering threats, and proclaiming a search into the murder of Laius—that man is here,   405
—in appearance an alien sojourner, but soon, he shall be found a native Theban, and shall not be glad of his fortune. A blind man, he who now has sight, a beggar, who now is rich, he shall make his way to a strange land, feeling the ground before him with his staff. And he shall be found at once brother and father of the   410
children with whom he lives; son and husband of the woman who bore him; heir to his father's bed, shedder of his father's blood.

So go in and think on that; and if you find that I have been at fault, say, thenceforth that I have no understanding in prophecy.

[Teiresias is led out by the boy. Oedipus enters the palace.]

CHORUS. *(singing) Strophe 1.* Who is he of whom the divine voice   415
from the Delphian rock[58] has spoken, as having wrought with red

---

55 *level . . . brood:* Oedipus and his own children are alike (level) in that they are all children of Jocasta.
56 *that:* the skill shown by Oedipus in reading riddles.
57 It is his skill in reading riddles which has brought Oedipus honour.
58 *Delphian rock:* the platform of rock on which stood the town and temple of Delphi.

hands horrors that no tongue can tell?

It is time that he flee on feet stronger than the feet of storm-swift steeds: for the son of Zeus[59] is springing on him, all armed with fiery lightnings, and with him come the dread, unerring Fates.   420

Antistrophe 1. Yea, newly given from snowy Parnassus,[60] the message has flashed forth to make all search for the unknown man. Into the deadly forests, among caves and rocks he is roaming, fierce as a bull, wretched and forlorn on his joyless path, still seeking to put from him the doom spoken at Earth's central shrine:[61] but that   425
doom ever lives, ever flits around him.

Strophe 2. Dreadly, indeed, dreadly does the wise augur[62] move me, who approve not, nor am able to deny.[63] How to speak, I know not; I am flustered with forebodings; neither of the present have I clear vision, nor of the future. Never in past days, nor in these,   430
have I heard how the house of Labdacus or the son of Polybus[64] had, either against the other, any quarrel I could bring as proof in assailing the public fame of Oedipus, and seeking to avenge the line of Labdacus for the undiscovered murder.

Antistrophe 2. Nay, Zeus indeed and Apollo are keen of mind,[65]   435
and know the things of earth; but that mortal seer wins knowledge above mine,[66] of this there can be no sure tests; though man may surpass man in knowledge of omens. Yet, until I have real evidence, never will I affirm men right when they blame Oedipus. Before all eyes, the winged maiden[67] came against him of old, and he was seen   440
to be wise; he survived the test by actual trial, in welcome service to our State; never, therefore, by the verdict of my heart shall he be adjudged guilty of crime.

[Enter Creon.]

CREON. Fellow-citizens, having learned that Oedipus the king lays dire charges against me, I come here, indignant. If, in the   445

---

59 *son of Zeus:* Apollo.

60 *snowy Parnassus:* a mountain; the temple of Apollo at Delphi was on its southern slope. The Thebans would see Parnassus to the west of Thebes.

61 *Earth's central shrine:* Delphi; it was the ancient belief that Delphi stood exactly in the center of the earth.

62 *wise augur:* Teiresias.

63 *approve not . . . deny:* The Elders do not approve of Teiresias' words, but cannot totally disbelieve them. An ominous note.

64 *son of Polybus:* Oedipus, who was brought up as his son by Polybus, king of Corinth. The Elders obviously think that Oedipus is the real son of Polybus.

65 *are keen . . . mind:* have complete knowledge.

66 *mortal seer . . . mine:* Teiresias knows more of the mysterious, hidden things than the Elders.

67 *winged maiden:* the Sphinx.

present troubles, he thinks that he has suffered from *me,* by word or deed, or by anything that tends to harm, in truth I crave not even to go on living, when I must bear such blame as this. The wrong of this rumour touches me not in one point alone, but has the largest scope,[68] if I am to be called a traitor in the minds of the public, a traitor also by you and by my intimate friends. 450

LEADER OF THE CHORUS. But this taunt came under stress, probably, of anger, rather than really from the heart.

CREON. And the saying was uttered, that *my* counsels won the seer to utter his falsehoods? 455

LEADER. Such things were said—I know not with what meaning.[69]

CREON. And was this charge laid against me with steady eyes and steady mind?[70]

LEADER. I know not; I see not what my masters do:[71] but here comes our lord forth from the house. 460

[Enter Oedipus.]

OEDIPUS. Sirrah, how did you come here? Are you so bold that you have come to my house, you, the proved assassin of its master,— the palpable robber of my crown? Come, tell me, in the name of the gods, was it cowardice or folly that you saw in me, that you plotted to do this thing? Did you think that I would not note this deed of yours creeping on me by stealth, or, aware, would not ward it off? Now is not your foolish attempt,—to seek, without followers or friends, a throne,—a prize which followers and wealth must win? 465

CREON. Mark me now,—in answer to your words, hear a fair reply, and then judge for yourself on the basis of knowledge. 470

OEDIPUS. You are skillful in speech, but I am ill-disposed toward your lessons, since I have found you my malignant foe.

CREON. Now first hear how I will explain this very thing[72]—

OEDIPUS. But one thing do not explain—that you are not false.

CREON. If you think that stubbornness without sense is of any value, you are not wise. 475

OEDIPUS. If you think that you can wrong a kinsman and escape the penalty, you are not sane.

CREON. Justly said, I grant thee: but tell me what is the wrong that you say you have suffered from me. 480

---

68 *the largest scope:* Creon is touched in all his relationships, both as a man and as a citizen, by the charge of treason laid against him.

69 *with what meaning:* The Elders do not know whether Oedipus spoke idly or had received some private information.

70 *with steady eyes and steady mind:* sanely; Creon is asking whether Oedipus showed any sign of madness.

71 The Theban Elders are cautious—they do not "see" any lapse in their master.

72 Creon will explain by showing that he had no motive.

OEDIPUS. Did you advise, or did you not, that I should send for that reverend seer?

CREON. And now I am still of the same mind.

OEDIPUS. How long is it, then, since Laius—

CREON. Since Laius . . . ? I do not understand you . . .   485

OEDIPUS. —was swept from men's sight by a deadly violence?

CREON. The time of that is far in the past.

OEDIPUS. Was this seer, then, practicing his craft in those days?[73]

CREON. Yes, skilled as now, and of equal honour.

OEDIPUS. Made he, then, any mention of me at that time?   490

CREON. Never, certainly, when I was within hearing.

OEDIPUS. But did you not hold an investigation into the murder?

CREON. Due search we held, of course—and learned nothing.

OEDIPUS. And how was it that this sage did not tell his story *then?*

CREON. I'll make no guess on this point; where I am not certain,   495 'tis my custom to be silent.

OEDIPUS. Thus much, at least, you know, and could declare with certainty enough.

CREON. What is that? If I know it, I will not deny.

OEDIPUS. That, if he had not conferred with you, he would never   500 have named *my* slaying of Laius.

CREON. If he says so, you know it best; but I claim to learn from you as much as you now have learned from me.

OEDIPUS. Learn your fill: I am no murderer.

CREON. Say, then—you have married my sister?   505

OEDIPUS. I do not deny this.

CREON. And you rule the land as she does with like sway?

OEDIPUS. She obtains from me all she desires.

CREON. And do not I rank as a third peer of you two?[74]

OEDIPUS. Yes indeed; it is from this very point of view that you   510 are seen as a false friend.

CREON. You would not say so if you would reason with your own heart as I with mine. And first consider this,—whether you think that any one would choose to rule amid terrors rather than in unruffled peace,—granting that he is to have the same powers. I am   515 not one of those who prefer the name of king to kingly power; nor would any other man in his right senses. For now I receive all favors from you without fear; but, were I ruler myself, I should be doing much even against my own pleasure.[75]

How, then, could royalty be sweeter for me to have than painless   520 rule and influence? I am not yet so misguided as to desire other

---

73 The reference to the skill of Teiresias by Oedipus is contemptuous. Notice the contrast between Creon's calm and the violent anger of Oedipus during this episode.
74 Creon asks if he is not virtually of the same rank as Oedipus and Jocasta.
75 *against my own pleasure:* for the public good.

honours[76] than those which profit. Now, all wish me joy; now every man has a greeting for me; now, those who have requests to you desire to speak with me, since therein is all their hope of success. Then why should I resign these things, and take those? No mind will become false, while it is wise. Nay, I am no lover of such policy, and, if another put it into practice, I could never bear to act with him.

And, in proof of this, first, go to Pytho, and ask if I brought you true word of the oracle; then next, if you find that I have planned anything in concert with the soothsayer, take and slay me, by the sentence not of one mouth, but of two—by my own, no less than yours. But judge me not guilty on weak suspicion's unproved surmise. It is not right to adjudge bad men good at random, or good men bad. I count it a like thing for a man to cast off a true friend as to take away the life in his own bosom, which most he loves. But, you will learn these things with sureness in time, for time alone shows a just man; but you could discern a knave even in one day.

LEADER. Well has he spoken, O King, he has given good advice to anyone who shuns a fall: the quick in counsel are not sure.

OEDIPUS. When the stealthy plotter is moving on me quickly, I, too, must be quick with my counterplot. If I await him in repose, his ends will have been gained, and mine missed.

CREON. What do you want then? To cast me out of the land?

OEDIPUS. Not so: I desire your death—not your banishment—that you may show forth what kind of thing envy is.

CREON. You speak as one resolved not to yield or to believe?

OEDIPUS. No; for you do not persuade me that you are worthy of belief.

CREON. No, for I find you not sane.

OEDIPUS. Sane, at least, in my own interest.

CREON. But you should be so in mine also.

OEDIPUS. No, you are false.

CREON. But if you understand nothing?

OEDIPUS. Yet must I rule.

CREON. Not if you rule ill.

OEDIPUS. Hear him, O Thebes!

CREON. Thebes is for me also[77]—not for you alone.

LEADER. Be still, Princes! I see Jocasta coming from her palace—and in good time. With her help you should be able to settle your present feud.

[Jocasta enters from the palace.]

JOCASTA. Misguided men, why have you raised such foolish strife of tongues? Are you not ashamed, while the land is thus sick, to stir up troubles of your own? Come, go into the house,—and you Creon,

525

530

535

540

545

550

555

560

---

76 *other honours:* honours which carry with them the heavy burden of responsibility.
77 *Thebes . . . also:* As a citizen Creon has rights in Thebes also.

to your home,—and forbear to make so much of a petty grief.

CREON. Sister, your lord wishes to do one of two terrible things   565
to me—either to banish me from the land of my fathers or to slay me.

OEDIPUS. Yea; for I have caught him, lady, working evil, by ill
arts, against my person.

CREON. Now may I see no good, but perish accursed, if I have
done anything of what you charge me!   570

JOCASTA. O, for the gods' love, believe it, Oedipus—first, for the
awful sake of this oath to the gods,—then for my sake and for theirs
who stand before you!

*[The following lines are sung as answers and replies between the Chorus and
Oedipus and between the Chorus, Jocasta, and Oedipus.]*

CHORUS. *Strophe 1.* Consent, reflect, hearken, O my king, I pray
you!   575

OEDIPUS. What grace, then, would you have me grant you?

CHORUS. Respect him who before was not foolish, and who, now,
has sworn a strong oath.

OEDIPUS. Now do you know what you crave?

CHORUS. Yes.   580

OEDIPUS. Declare, then, what you mean.

CHORUS. That you should never use an unproved rumour to cast
a dishonouring charge on a friend who has bound himself with an
oath.[78]

OEDIPUS. Then be very sure that, when you seek this, for me   585
you are seeking destruction, or exile from this land.

CHORUS. *Strophe 2.* No, by him who stands in the front of all
the heavenly host, no, by the Sun![79] Unblest, unfriended, may I die
by the uttermost doom, if I have that thought! But my unhappy soul
is worn by the withering of the land, and again by the thought that   590
our old sorrows should be crowned by sorrows springing from you
two.

OEDIPUS. Then let him go, though I am surely doomed to death,
or to be thrust dishonoured from the land. Your lips, not his, move
my compassion by their utterance of grief, but he, wherever he be,   595
shall be hated.

CREON. You appear as sullen in yielding as vehement in the excesses of your wrath; but such natures are justly most difficult for
themselves to bear.

OEDIPUS. Will you not leave me in peace, and be gone?   600

CREON. I will go my way; I have found you ignorant of my case,
but in the eyes of these I am just.   *[Exit Creon.]*

---

78 *who . . . oath:* Because he has bound himself with an oath, Creon is liable to a
curse if he proves false.

79 *by . . . Sun:* The Sun, the source of light, brings light to hidden things.

CHORUS. *Antistrophe 1.* Lady, why do you delay to take yonder man into the house?

JOCASTA. I will do so, when I have learned what has happened. 605

CHORUS. Blind suspicion, bred of talk, arose; and, on the other part, injustice wounds.

JOCASTA. It was on both sides?

CHORUS. Both.

JOCASTA. And what was the story? 610

CHORUS. It is enough, I think, enough—when our land is already vexed—that the matter should rest where it ceased.

OEDIPUS. Do you see to what you have come, for all your honest purpose, in seeking to relax and blunt my zeal?[80]

CHORUS. *Antistrophe 2.* King, I have not said it only once—be 615 sure that I would have been out of my senses, bankrupt in sane counsel, if I put you away—you, who gave a true course to my beloved country when distraught by troubles—you, who now also are like to prove our prospering guide.

JOCASTA. In the name of the gods, tell me also, O King, on what 620 account you have conceived this steadfast wrath.

OEDIPUS. That I will do; for I honour you, lady, above yonder men:—the cause is Creon, and the plots that he has laid against me.

JOCASTA. Speak on—if you can tell clearly how the feud began.

OEDIPUS. He says that I stand guilty of the blood of Laius. 625

JOCASTA. Of his own knowledge? Or on hearsay from another?

OEDIPUS. No, he has made a rascal prophet his mouthpiece; as for himself, he keeps his own lips clear of any guilt.

JOCASTA. Then absolve yourself of the things of which you speak; listen to me, and learn for your comfort that there is no mortal who 630 can claim the gift of prophecy.[81] I will give you solid proof of that.

An oracle came to Laius once—I will not say from Phoebus himself, but from his ministers—that the doom should overtake him to die by the hand of his child, who should be the offspring of him and me. 635

Now Laius,—as, at least, the rumour says,—was murdered one day by foreign robbers at a place where three highways meet.[82] And the child's birth was not three days old, when Laius pinned its ankles

80 Oedipus rebukes the Elders indignantly; he feels that they have been led by their sympathy for Creon to an attempt to hush up the terrible charge of murder laid against Oedipus himself, their king. Oedipus feels he should be cleared instead.
81 *no mortal . . . prophecy:* the gods have foreknowledge but they do not share it with any man, not even Apollo's Delphic oracles.
82 As Jocasta speaks of the place where three highways meet, Oedipus recalls with growing apprehension that he himself killed a man in just such a place.

together, and had it thrown, by others' hands, on a trackless mountain.[83]   640

So, in that case, Apollo did not bring it about that the babe should become the slayer of his father, or that Laius should die—the dread thing which he feared—by his child's hand. Thus did the messages of the prophet map out the future.[84] Do not pay any attention to them. Whatever needful things the god seeks, he himself will easily bring to light.   645

OEDIPUS. What restlessness of soul, lady, what tumult of the mind has just come upon me since I heard you speak!

JOCASTA. What anxiety has startled you, that you say this?

OEDIPUS. I thought I heard this from you,—that Laius was slain   650 where three highways meet.

JOCASTA. Yes, that was the story; it has not died out yet.

OEDIPUS. And where is the place where this happened?

JOCASTA. The land is called Phocis; and branching roads lead to the same spot from Delphi and from Daulia.[85]   655

OEDIPUS. And what is the time that has passed since these things took place?

JOCASTA. The news was published to the town shortly before you were first seen in power over this land.

OEDIPUS. O Zeus, what have you decreed to do to me?   660

JOCASTA. And why, Oedipus, does this thing weigh upon your soul?

OEDIPUS. Ask me not yet; but tell me what was the stature of Laius, and how old he was.

JOCASTA. He was tall,—the silver just lightly strewn among his   665 hair; and his appearance was not greatly unlike yours.

OEDIPUS. Unhappy that I am! I think that I have been unwittingly laying myself even now under a dread curse.

JOCASTA. How say you? I tremble when I look on you, my king.

OEDIPUS. I have dread misgivings that the seer can see. But you   670 will make it clearer if you will tell me one thing more.

JOCASTA. Indeed—though I tremble—I will answer all that you ask, when I hear it.

83 Laius fastened the infant's ankles together by driving a pin through them. This pinning was intended to cripple the child so that no one could raise it if it somehow survived being exposed on the mountain.

84 Jocasta lost all faith in any human prophecy when the killing of her own child did not save Laius.

85 In Phocis, a coastal region of northern Greece, there is a wild and desolate spot where the road from Daulia (an ancient city at the foot of Mount Parnassus) crosses the road from Delphi and a third road from the south. At the time of the killing, Oedipus was coming from the direction of Delphi and Laius was on the road from Daulia.

OEDIPUS. Did he go in small force, or with many armed followers, like a chieftain? 675

JOCASTA. Five they were in all,—a herald one of them; and there was one carriage,[86] which bore Laius.

OEDIPUS. Alas! 'Tis now clear indeed.—Who was he who gave you these tidings, lady?

JOCASTA. A servant—the sole survivor who came home. 680

OEDIPUS. Is he by chance at hand in the house now?

JOCASTA. No, truly; so soon as he came thence,[87] and found you reigning instead of Laius, he took me by the hand and begged me to send him to the fields, to the pastures of the flocks, that he might be far from the sight of this town. And I sent him; he was worthy, 685 for a slave, to win even greater favor than that.

OEDIPUS. Would, then, that he could return to us without delay!

JOCASTA. It is easy: but why do you command this?

OEDIPUS. I fear, lady, that my own lips have been unguarded; and therefore am I eager to behold him. 690

JOCASTA. Indeed, he shall come. But I too, I think, have a claim to learn what lies heavy on your heart, my king.

OEDIPUS. Yes, and it shall not be kept from you, now that my forebodings have advanced so far. Who, indeed, means more to me than you, to whom I should speak in passing through such a fortune 695 as this?

My father was Polybus of Corinth,—my mother, the Dorian Meropè;[88] and I was held the first of all the folk in that town, until something happened to me, worthy, indeed, of wonder, though not worthy of my own anger concerning it. At a banquet, a man full of 700 wine cast it at me in his cups that I was not the true son of my father. And I, vexed, restrained myself for that day as best I could; but on the next I went to my mother and father, and questioned them; and they were angry with him who had taunted me so. So on their part I had comfort; yet the thing was ever rankling in my heart; for it was 705 still strongly rumored about. And, unknown to mother or father, I went to Delphi; and Phoebus sent me forth disappointed of that knowledge for which I came, but in his response set forth other things, full of sorrow and terror and woe; even that I was fated to defile my mother's bed; and that I should show to men a brood 710 which they could not endure to behold; and that I should be the slayer of the father who conceived me.

---

86 *carriage:* in this case, a four-wheeled vehicle drawn by colts.
87 *so . . . thence:* The servant did not return to Thebes and come to Jocasta until Oedipus was reigning in Thebes. It may be that Sophocles did not notice the fact that had the servant returned immediately to Thebes after the murder, Oedipus could not have been reigning there.
88 *the Dorian Meropè:* The epithet *Dorian* carried a great honour; Meropè claimed descent from an ancient and honourable house.

And I, when I had listened to this, turned to flight from the land of Corinth, thenceforth knowing of its region by the stars alone, to some spot where I should never see fulfillment of the infamies forecast for me. And on my way I came to the region where you say that this prince perished. Now, lady, I will tell you the truth. When in my journey I was near to those three roads, I met a herald and a man seated in a carriage drawn by colts, as you have described; and he who was in front, and the old man himself, were for thrusting me rudely from the path. Then, in anger, I struck him who pushed me aside—the driver; and the old man, seeing it, watched the moment when I was passing, and, from the carriage, brought his goad[89] with two teeth down directly upon my head. Yet was he paid with interest; by one swift blow from the staff in this hand he was rolled right out of the carriage, on his back; and I slew every man of them.[90]

If any relationship existed between this stranger and Laius, who is now more wretched than the man before you? What mortal could prove more hated of heaven? Whom no stranger, no citizen, is allowed to receive in his house; whom it is unlawful that any one accost; whom all must repel from their homes! And this—this curse—was laid on me by no mouth but my own! And I pollute the bed of the slain man with the hands by which he perished. Say, am I vile? O, am I not utterly unclean?—seeing that I must be banished, and in banishment see not my own people, nor set foot in my own land, or else be joined in wedlock to my mother, and slay my father, even Polybus, who begat and reared me.[91]

Then would not he speak aright of Oedipus, who judged these things sent by some cruel power above man?[92] Forbid, forbid, you pure and awful gods, that I should see that day! No, may I be swept from among men, before I behold myself visited with the brand of such a doom!

LEADER OF THE CHORUS. To us, indeed, these things, O King, are fraught with fear; yet have hope, until at last you have gained full knowledge from him who saw the deed.

OEDIPUS. Hope, in truth, rests with me in this alone; I can await the man summoned from the pastures.

JOCASTA. And when he has appeared—what would you have of him?

715

720

725

730

735

740

745

89 *goad:* a stick or pole with two sharpened points on one end, used for driving animals.

90 Oedipus does not appear to notice that one of the servants escaped.

91 Oedipus now believes that he is the killer of Laius, but does not yet know that he is also the son of Laius.

92 *Some cruel power above man:* some cruel daimon. In early Greek thought the daimon represented a superhuman power. Each man has a daimon who attaches himself to the individual at birth. A man's daimon was thought to determine his fate or destiny.

OEDIPUS. I will tell you. If his story be found to tally with yours, 750
I, at least, shall stand clear of disaster.[93]

JOCASTA. And what of special note did you hear from me?

OEDIPUS. You were saying that he spoke of Laius as slain by robbers. If, then, he still speaks, as before, of several, I was not the
slayer: a solitary man could not be held the same with that band. But 755
if he names one lonely wayfarer, then beyond doubt this guilt is
upon me.

JOCASTA. Be assured that thus, at least, the tale was first told; he
cannot revoke that, for the city heard it, not I alone. But even if he
should diverge somewhat from his former story, never, King, can 760
he show that the murder of Laius, at least, is truly in keeping with the
prophecy; of whom Loxias plainly said that he must die by the hand
of my child. Nevertheless that poor innocent never slew him, but
perished first itself. So henceforth, for what touches divination, I
would not give it a second thought. 765

OEDIPUS. You judge well. But nevertheless send some one to fetch
the peasant, and do not neglect this matter.

JOCASTA. I will send without delay. But let us come into the house:
I will do nothing except at your good pleasure.

[Jocasta and Oedipus go into the palace.]

CHORUS. *(singing) Strophe 1.* May destiny still find me winning 770
the praise of reverent purity in all words and deeds sanctioned by
those laws of range sublime, called into life throughout the high
clear heaven, whose father is Olympus alone; their parent was no
race of mortal men, no, nor shall oblivion ever lay them to sleep;
the god is mighty in them, and he grows not old. 775

Antistrophe 1.[94] Pride[95] breeds the tyrant; Pride, once vainly
surfeited on wealth that is not suitable nor good for it, when it has
scaled the topmost ramparts,[96] is hurled to a dire doom, wherein no
service of the feet can serve.[97] But I pray that the god never quell
such rivalry as benefits the State; I will ever hold the god for our 780
protector.

---

93 *disaster:* the killing of Laius.   94 *Antistrophe 1:* This *antistrophe,* and *strophe*
which follows it, deal with the fall of a tyrant. Some critics feel that the substance of
these two puzzling choric songs was based upon an earlier *Oedipus* written by
Aeschylus. There is scant justification in the Sophoclean *Oedipus* for anyone seriously
considering Oedipus a tyrant or in danger of becoming one.

95 *Pride:* this is the modern translation of the Greek word *hybris,* meaning pride in
the sense of arrogance.

96 *it . . . ramparts:* when pride has reached its climax in wanton violence, when the
outrageously proud man has arrived at the belief that there is no difference between
him and the gods.

97 *is hurled . . . serve:* The proud man is cast headlong to a destruction so complete
and so deep that there is no safe resting place for his feet.

Strophe 2. But if any man walks haughtily in deed or word, with no fear of Justice, no reverence for the images of gods, if he will not win his vantage fairly, nor keep him from unholy deeds, but must lay profaning hands on sanctities, may an evil doom[98] seize him for his ill-starred pride.　　　　785

Where such things are, what mortal shall boast any more that he can ward the arrows of the gods from his life? In fact, if such deeds are in honour, why should we join in the sacred dance?[99]

Antistrophe 2. No more will I go reverently to earth's central and inviolate shrine, no more to Abae's temple[100] or Olympia,[101] if these oracles[102] do not prove true, so that all men shall point at them with the finger. Nay, King,—if you are rightly called,—Zeus all-ruling, may it not escape you and your ever-deathless power!　　　　790

The old prophecies concerning Laius are fading; already men are setting them at nought, and nowhere is Apollo glorified with honours; the worship of the gods is perishing.　　　　795

[Jocasta comes forth, bearing a branch, wreathed with festoons of wool, which, as a suppliant, she is about to lay on the altar of the household god, Lycean Apollo, in front of the palace.]

JOCASTA. Princes of the land, the thought has come to me to visit the shrines of the gods, with this wreathed branch in my hands, and these gifts of incense. For Oedipus is mentally bewildered with all manner of alarms, nor, like a man of sense, judges the new things by the old, but is at the will of any speaker if he speaks of any kind of disaster.　　　　800

Since, then, by counsel I can do no good, to you, Lycean Apollo, for you are nearest, I have come, a suppliant with these symbols of prayer, that you may find us some riddance from uncleanness. For now we are all afraid, seeing *him* affrighted, just as they who see fear in the helmsman of their ship.[103]　　　　805

[While Jocasta is offering her prayers to the god, a Messenger, evidently a stranger, enters and addresses the Elders of the Chorus.]

MESSENGER. Might I learn from you, strangers, where is the house of the King Oedipus? Or, better still, tell me where he himself is— if you know.　　　　810

98 *an evil doom:* an evil daimon.
99 If proud men can abuse religion, making themselves equal with the gods, why should the Elders perform the old religious rites?
100 *Abae's temple:* an old town in Phocis in which Apollo had an ancient oracular shrine.
101 *Olympia:* A plain in the Peloponnesus, where there was a well-known temple of Zeus. Divination was practised at the altar of this temple.
102 *these oracles:* that Laius would be killed by his son.
103 Jocasta, in this tragic prayer, begs aid from the very god who means to destroy Oedipus.

LEADER OF THE CHORUS. This is his dwelling, stranger, and he himself is within; and this lady is the mother of his children.

MESSENGER. Then may she be ever happy in a happy home, since she is his heaven-blest queen.   815

JOCASTA. Happiness to you also, stranger! It is the due of your fair greeting. But say what you have come to seek or to tell.

MESSENGER. Good tidings, lady, for your house and for your husband.

JOCASTA. What are they? And from whom have you come?   820

MESSENGER. From Corinth: and at the message which I will soon speak you will rejoice—doubtless; yet perhaps grieve.

JOCASTA. And what is it? How does it have a double possibility?

MESSENGER. The people wish to make him king of the Isthmian land,[104] as it was said there.   825

JOCASTA. How then? Is the aged Polybus no more in power?

MESSENGER. No, truly: for death holds him in the tomb.

JOCASTA. What are you saying? Is Polybus dead, old man?

MESSENGER. If I do not speak the truth, I am content to die.

JOCASTA. O handmaid, away with all speed, and tell this to thy   830
master! O you oracles of the gods, where do you stand now![105] This is the man whom Oedipus feared so and fled so, lest he should slay him; and now this man has died by another fate, not by his hand.

[Oedipus enters from the Palace.]

OEDIPUS. Jocasta, dearest wife, why have you summoned me   835
forth from these doors?

JOCASTA. Hear this man, and judge, as you listen, to what the awful oracles of the gods have come.

OEDIPUS. And he—who may he be, and what news has he for me?   840

JOCASTA. He is from Corinth, to tell that your father Polybus lives no longer, but has perished.

OEDIPUS. How, stranger? Let me have it from your own mouth.

MESSENGER. If I must first make these tidings plain, know indeed that he is dead and gone.   845

OEDIPUS. By treachery, or by visit of disease?

MESSENGER. A light thing in the scale brings the aged to their rest.

OEDIPUS. Ah, he died, it seems, of sickness?

MESSENGER. Yea, and having reached an advanced age.   850

OEDIPUS. Alas, alas! Why, indeed, my wife, should one look to

---

104 *Isthmian land:* Corinth.
105 Jocasta's contempt is not of course for the gods, but for the seers, whose prophecies she thinks are again proved false.

the hearth of the Pythian seer,[106] or to the birds that scream above
our heads,[107] on whose showing I was doomed to slay my father?
But he is dead, and hid already beneath the earth; and here I am, and
I have not touched a spear. Nor did I slay him. Unless, perhaps,   855
he was killed by longing for me: thus, indeed, I should be the cause
of his death. But the oracles as they stand, at least, Polybus has
taken with him to his rest in Hades: they are worth nothing.

JOCASTA. Nay, did I not predict this to you long ago?

OEDIPUS. You did: but I was misled by my fear.   860

JOCASTA. Now no more take any of those things to heart.

OEDIPUS. But surely I must needs fear my mother's bed?

JOCASTA. Nay, what should mortal fear, for whom the decrees
of Fortune are supreme, and who has clear foresight of nothing?[108]

It is best to live at random, as one may. But be not frightened   865
concerning wedlock with your mother. Many men before now have
so fared in dreams also: but he to whom these things are as nothing
bears his life most easily.

OEDIPUS. All these bold words of yours would have been well,
were not my mother living; but as it is, since she lives, there is   870
every reason to fear—though you speak reassuringly.

JOCASTA. Nevertheless your father's death is a great sign to cheer
us.

OEDIPUS. Great, I know; but my fear is of her who lives.

MESSENGER. And who is the woman about whom you fear?   875

OEDIPUS. Meropè, old man, the wife of King Polybus.

MESSENGER. And what is it in her that excites your fear?

OEDIPUS. A heaven-sent oracle of dread import, stranger.

MESSENGER. Can you tell me about it, or are you sworn to silence?

OEDIPUS. Certainly I can tell you. Loxias[109] once said that I was   880
doomed to marry my own mother, and to shed with my own hands
my father's blood. Therefore I have long kept clear of my home in
Corinth; with a fortunate outcome,[110] indeed,—yet it would still
have been sweet to see the face of parents.

MESSENGER. Was it indeed for fear of this that you were an exile   885
from that city?

OEDIPUS. And because, old man, I did not wish to be the slayer
of my father.

---

106 *Pythian seer:* the oracle of Apollo at Delphi.
107 *birds . . . heads:* a scornful reference to the auguries (divinations) of the seer
Teiresias. Note, however, that Teiresias only says that the birds scream when their
omens are not clear. There is irony in the fact that the auguries of Teiresias will
prove to be true, and it is Oedipus who is fatally confused.
108 Jocasta is not denying that the gods rule the world, but she points out that men
do not have the power to foresee the future.   109 *Loxias:* Apollo.
110 *fortunate outcome:* Oedipus' being made ruler in Thebes.

MESSENGER. Then why have I not freed you, King, from this
fear, seeing that I came with friendly purpose?   890

OEDIPUS. Indeed you should have reward due from me.

MESSENGER. Indeed it was chiefly for this that I came—that, on
your return home, I might reap some good.

OEDIPUS. No, I will never go near my parents.

MESSENGER. Ah, my son, it is plain enough that you know not   895
what you do.

OEDIPUS. How, old man? For the gods' love, tell me.

MESSENGER. If for these reasons you shrink from going home.

OEDIPUS. Aye, I dread lest Phoebus prove himself true for me.[111]

MESSENGER. You dread to be stained with guilt through your   900
parents?

OEDIPUS. Even so, old man—this it is that always frightens me.

MESSENGER. Do you know, then, that your fears are wholly
groundless?

OEDIPUS. How so, if I was born of those parents?   905

MESSENGER. Because Polybus was nothing to you in blood.

OEDIPUS. What do you say? Was Polybus not my father?

MESSENGER. No more than he who speaks to you, but just so
much.

OEDIPUS. And how can my father be equal with him who is as   910
nothing to me?

MESSENGER. Indeed, he did not beget you, any more than I.

OEDIPUS. Why then did he call me his son?

MESSENGER. Know that he had received you as a gift from my
hands long ago.   915

OEDIPUS. And yet he loved me so dearly, who came from another's hand?

MESSENGER. Yes, his former childlessness brought him to love you.

OEDIPUS. And you—had you bought me or found me by chance,
when you gave me to him?   920

MESSENGER. I found you in Cithaeron's winding glens.[112]

OEDIPUS. And why were you roaming in those regions?

MESSENGER. I was there in charge of mountain flocks.

OEDIPUS. What, you were a shepherd—a wandering worker?

MESSENGER. But your preserver, my son, in that hour.   925

OEDIPUS. What was my condition when you took me in your
arms?

MESSENGER. Your ankles should tell you that.

OEDIPUS. Ah me, why do you speak of that old trouble?

MESSENGER. I freed you when you had your ankles pinned to-   930
gether.

---

111 *lest Phoebus . . . me:* lest Apollo send the daimon promised in his oracles.
112 *Cithaeron's winding glens:* the secluded winding valleys of the Cithaeron range.

OEDIPUS. Aye, it was a dread brand of shame that I took from my cradle.

MESSENGER. From that happening you were called by the name which is still yours.[113]   935

OEDIPUS. O, for the gods' love—was I wounded by my mother or by my father? Speak!

MESSENGER. I know not who wounded thee; he who gave you to me knows that better than I.

OEDIPUS. What, you got me from another? You did not find me yourself?   940

MESSENGER. No: another shepherd gave you to me.

OEDIPUS. Who was he? Can you tell me clearly?

MESSENGER. I think he was called one of the household of Laius.

OEDIPUS. The king who ruled this country long ago?   945

MESSENGER. The same: it was in his service that the man was a shepherd.

OEDIPUS. Is he still alive, that I might see him?

MESSENGER. Indeed, you people of the country should know best.

OEDIPUS. Is there any of you here present that knows the shep-   950
herd of whom he speaks—that has seen him in the pastures or the town? Answer! The hour has come when these things should be finally revealed.

LEADER OF THE CHORUS. It seems to me that he speaks of no other than the peasant whom you are already eager to see; but our   955
lady Jocasta might best tell of that.

OEDIPUS. Lady, do you know of him whom we lately summoned? Is it of him that this man speaks?

JOCASTA. Why ask of whom he spoke? Regard it not . . . waste not a thought on what he said . . . it would be foolish to remember.[114]   960

OEDIPUS. It must not be that, with such clues in my grasp, I should fail to bring my birth to light.

JOCASTA. For the gods' sake, if you have any regard for your own life, give up this search! My anguish is enough.

OEDIPUS. Be of good courage; though I be found the son of a   965
slave mother,—aye, a slave for three generations,—you will not be proved base-born.[115]

JOCASTA. Yet hear me, I implore you: do not do it.

OEDIPUS. I must not hear of not discovering the whole truth.

JOCASTA. Yet I wish you well—I advise you for the best.   970

OEDIPUS. Then these best counsels vex my patience.

---

113 The name *Oedipus* literally means "swollen foot."
114 Jocasta obviously now realizes the whole gastly truth, but she puts off answering to spare Oedipus the ordeal of that knowledge.
115 Oedipus thinks that Jocasta'a reluctance to carry the search further arises from fear of exposing his possibly ignoble birth.

JOCASTA. Ill-fated one! May you never come to know who you are!

OEDIPUS. Go, someone, bring me the herdsman hither,—and leave that woman to brag of her royal stock.

JOCASTA. Alas, alas, miserable!—that word alone can I say to 975 you, and no other word henceforth for ever.

[She rushes into the palace.]

LEADER. Why has the lady gone, Oedipus, in a transport of uncontrollable grief? I fear a storm of sorrow will break forth from this silence.

OEDIPUS. Let come what will! Be my race never so lowly, I still 980 wish and will continue to wish to learn it. That woman—for she is proud with more than a woman's pride[116]—perhaps thinks shame of my base birth. But I, who hold myself son of Fortune that gives good, will not be dishonoured.[117] She is the mother from whom I spring; and the months, my kinsmen,[118] have marked me sometimes 985 lowly, sometimes great. Such being my lineage, never more can I prove false to it, or spare to search out the secret of my birth.

CHORUS. *(singing) Strophe.*[119] If I am a seer or wise of heart, O Cithaeron, you shall not fail—by yonder heaven, you shall not!— to know at tomorrow's full moon that Oedipus honours you as 990 native to him, as his nurse, and his mother, and that you are celebrated in our dance and song, because you are well-pleasing to our prince. O Phoebus to whom we cry, may these things find favour in your sight!

Antistrophe. Who was it, my son, that of the race whose years 995 are many that bore you in wedlock with Pan, the mountain-roaming father? Or was it a bride of Loxias that bore you? For dear to him are all the upland pastures. Or perchance it was Cyllene's lord,[120] or the Bacchants' god,[121] dweller on the hill-tops, that received you, a new-born joy, from one of the Nymphs of Helicon,[122] with whom 1000 he most has pleasure.

OEDIPUS. Elders, if it is proper for me to guess, who have never met with him, I think I see the herdsman of whom we have long

---

116 *more than woman's pride:* Women had a lowly and unimportant place in the Greece of Sophocles' day.

117 Oedipus, with faith in the goodness of his "mother," Fortune, will not fear to seek the truth.   118 Fortune was also regarded as the mother of the months.

119 *Strophe:* Sophocles substitutes a short choral ode here for the more usual stasimon. Both the content of this ode and its manner (a lively dance song) demonstrate the joyous expectancy of the Elders that Oedipus will turn out to be begotten of the gods on Cithaeron. The contrast with the terrible discovery to come is intense.

120 *Cyllene's lord:* Hermes, messenger of the gods, guide of the dead, bringer of good luck.   121 *the Bacchants' god:* Bacchus (Dionysus).

122 *Helicon:* a famous range of mountains in Boeotia, sacred to Apollo and the Muses.

been in quest; for in his venerable age he tallies with yonder stranger's years, and besides I know those who bring him, I think, as   1005
servants of my own. But perhaps you may have the advantage of
me in knowledge, if you have seen the herdsman before.

LEADER. Yes, I know him, be sure; he was in the service of
Laius—faithful, if anyone was faithful.

[The herdsman is brought in.]

OEDIPUS. I ask you first, Corinthian stranger, is this he whom   1010
you mean?

MESSENGER. The very man whom you see.

OEDIPUS. Ho, you, old man—I would have you look this way,
and answer all that I ask you. You were once in the service of
Laius?   1015

HERDSMAN. I was—a slave not bought, but reared in his house.

OEDIPUS. Employed in what labour, or what way of life?

HERDSMAN. For the best part of my life I tended flocks.

OEDIPUS. And what were the regions that you mainly frequented?

HERDSMAN. Sometimes it was Cithaeron, sometimes the neighbour-   1020
ing ground.

OEDIPUS. Have you seen this man[123] in those parts—

HERDSMAN. Doing what? . . . What man do you mean? . . .

OEDIPUS. This man here—or have you ever met him before?

HERDSMAN. Not that I could speak at once from memory.   1025

MESSENGER. And no wonder, master. But I will refresh his memory. I am sure that he well knows of the time when we abode in the
region of Cithaeron,—he with two flocks, I, his comrade, with one—
three full half-years, from spring to Arcturus;[124] and then for the
winter I used to drive my flock to my own fold, and he took his to   1030
the fold of Laius. Did any of this happen as I tell it, or did it not?

HERDSMAN. You speak the truth—though it is long ago.

MESSENGER. Come, tell me now—do you know of having given
me a boy in those days, to be reared as my own foster-son?

HERDSMAN. What now? Why do you ask the question?   1035

MESSENGER. Yonder man, my friend, is he who then was young.

HERDSMAN. Plague take you—be silent once for all![125]

OEDIPUS. Ha! chide him not, old man—your words need chiding
more than his.

HERDSMAN. And wherein, most noble master, do I offend?   1040

OEDIPUS. In not telling of the boy about whom he asks.

123 *this man:* the Messenger.
124 *from spring to Arcturus:* roughly from the middle of March to the middle of
September.
125 The good old servant, faithful to Jocasta, wishes nothing more to be said on a
subject which is bound to bring great suffering.

HERDSMAN. He speaks without knowledge—he is busy to no purpose.

OEDIPUS. You do not want to speak with a good grace, but you shall or be punished.   1045

HERDSMAN. No, for the love of the gods, do not misuse an old man!

OEDIPUS. Ho, some one—bind him by the arms this instant!

HERDSMAN. Alas, why? what more would you learn?

OEDIPUS. Did you give this man the child of whom he speaks?   1050

HERDSMAN. I did,—and I wish that I had perished that day!

OEDIPUS. Well, you will come to that, unless you tell the honest truth.

HERDSMAN. No, I am much more lost, if I speak.

OEDIPUS. The fellow is bent, it seems, on more delays . . .   1055

HERDSMAN. No, no!—I said before that I gave it to him.

OEDIPUS. From where had you got it? In your own house, or from another?

HERDSMAN. I assure you the child was not mine; I had received it from a man.   1060

OEDIPUS. From whom of the citizens here? from what home?

HERDSMAN. Give up, for the gods' love, master, refrain from asking more!

OEDIPUS. You are lost if I have to question you again.

HERDSMAN. It was a child, then, of the house of Laius.   1065

OEDIPUS. A slave? or one born of the king?

HERDSMAN. Ah me—I am now at the point of having to say the very worst.

OEDIPUS. And I of hearing; yet must I hear.

HERDSMAN. You must know, then, that it was said to be his own   1070
child—but your lady within could best say how these things are.

OEDIPUS. How? She gave it to you?

HERDSMAN. Yes, O King.

OEDIPUS. For what purpose?

HERDSMAN. That I should make away with it.

OEDIPUS. Her own child—the wretched mother did so?   1075

HERDSMAN. Yes, from fear of evil prophecies.

OEDIPUS. What were they?

HERDSMAN. It was said that the boy must slay his father.

OEDIPUS. Why, then, did you give him up to this old man?   1080

HERDSMAN. Through pity, master, because I thought that he would bear him away to another land, from which he himself came; but he saved him for the direst woe. For if you are what this man says, know that you were born to misery.

OEDIPUS. O, O! All brought to pass—all true! O light, may I   1085
now look my last on you—I who have been found accursed in birth, accursed in wedlock, accursed in the shedding of blood!

[He rushes into the palace.]

CHORUS. *(singing) Strophe 1.* Alas, you generations of men, how mere a shadow do I count your life! Where, where is the mortal who wins more of happiness than just the seeming, and, after the semblance, a falling away? Yours is a daimon that warns me,—yours, yours, unhappy Oedipus—to call no earthly creature blest. 1090

Antistrophe 1. For he, O Zeus, having sped his arrow to the loftiest flight, and won the prize of an all-prosperous fortune; he slew the maiden with crooked talons and the riddling speech; he arose for our land as a tower against death. And from that time, Oedipus, you have been called our king, and have received the highest honors, bearing sway in great Thebes. 1095

Strophe 2. But now whose story is more grievous in men's ears? Who is a more wretched captive to fierce plagues and troubles, with all his life reversed? 1100

Alas, renowned Oedipus! The same bounteous place of rest sufficed you, as child and as father also, that you should make thereon your marriage bed. O, how can the soil wherein your father sowed have suffered you, unhappy one, in silence so long? 1105

Antistrophe 2. All-seeing time has detected and passed sentence on the unwitting crime: he judges[126] the monstrous marriage wherein both sire and son have long been one.

Alas, you child of Laius, would, would that I had never seen you! I wail as one who pours a dirge from his lips;[127] truth to tell, it was you that gave me new life,[128] and through you darkness has fallen upon my eyes.[129] 1110

[Enter Second Messenger from the palace.]

SECOND MESSENGER. You who are ever most honoured in this land, what deeds shall you hear, what deeds behold, what burden of sorrow shall be yours, if, like kinsmen you still care for the house of Labdacus! For I believe that neither Ister nor Phasis[130] could wash this house clean, so many are the hidden evils that will soon be brought to light,—ills wrought not unwittingly, but on purpose.[131] And those griefs smart most which are seen to be of our own choice.[132] 1115

1120

126 *judges:* punishes.   127 Oedipus is to the speaker as one dead.
128 *gave . . . life:* by answering the Sphinx.
129 The Elders feel that their well-being perishes with that of Oedipus.
130 *Ister nor Phasis:* the great rivers Danube and Rion.
131 *not unwittingly, but on purpose:* There seems to be a clear distinction here between conscious crimes and acts committed in ignorance.
132 *those griefs . . . choice:* The griefs of our own choice cannot be blamed on the gods and are therefore more painful.

LEADER. Indeed those evils which we already know require great lamentation: besides them, what do you announce?

SECOND MESSENGER. This is the shortest tale to tell and to hear: our royal lady Jocasta is dead.

LEADER. Oh, most miserable woman! How?   1125

SECOND MESSENGER. By her own hand. The worst of all that has happened is spared us, for there was no one there to see. Nevertheless, so far as I am able to recount it, you shall learn that unhappy woman's fate.

When frantic, she had passed within the vestibule, she rushed   1130
straight towards her marriage bed, clutching her hair with the fingers of both hands; once within the chamber, she slammed the doors together behind her; then called on the name of Laius, long since dead, mindful of that son, begotten long ago, by whom the father was slain, leaving the mother to breed accursed offspring   1135
with his own.

And she bewailed the wedlock wherein, wretched, she had borne a two-fold brood, husband by husband, children by her child. And how thereafter she perished, is more than I know. For with a shriek Oedipus burst in,[133] and did not permit us to watch her   1140
woe unto the end; on him, as he rushed around, our eyes were set. To and fro he went, asking us to give him a sword,—asking where he should find the wife who was no wife, but a mother whose womb had borne alike himself and his children. And, in his frenzy, a power above man was his guide;[134] for it was none of us   1145
mortals who were near. And with a dread shriek, as though some one beckoned him on, he sprang at the double doors, and from their sockets forced the bending bolts, and rushed into the room.

There we saw the woman hanging by the neck in a twisted noose of swinging cords. But he, when he saw her, with a dread,   1150
deep cry of misery, loosed the halter by which she hung. And when the hapless woman was stretched upon the ground, then was the sequel most horrible to see. For he tore from her raiment the golden brooches[135] with which she was decked, and lifted them, and struck directly on his own eye-balls, uttering words like   1155
these: 'No more shall you behold such horrors as I have suffered and have caused! Long enough have you looked on those[136] whom you ought never to have seen, failed in knowledge of those[137] whom I yearned to know—henceforth you shall be dark!'

To such dire refrain, not once alone but oft he struck his eyes   1160

133 *Oedipus burst in:* into the vestibule.
134 *in his frenzy . . . guide:* Oedipus' daimon guided him.
135 *brooches:* Jocasta's brooches had long sharp pins.
136 *those:* his mother and his children.   137 *those:* his parents.

with lifted hand; and at each blow the bloody eye-balls dripped on his beard. They did not send forth sluggish drops of gore, but all at once a dark shower of blood came down like hail.

From the deeds of two, such ills have broken forth, not on one alone, but with mingled woe for man and wife. The old happiness   1165
of their ancestral fortune was once happiness indeed; but today— lamentation, ruin, death, shame, all earthly ills that can be named —all, all are theirs.

LEADER. And has the sufferer now any relief from pain?[138]

SECOND MESSENGER. He cries for some one to unbar the gates   1170
and show to all the Cadmeans his father's slayer, his mother's—the unholy word must not pass my lips,—as purposing to cast himself out of the land, and abide no more, to make the house accursed under his own curse. However, he lacks strength, and one to guide his steps; for the anguish is more than man may bear. And he will   1175
show this to you also; for lo, the bars of the gates are withdrawn, and soon you shall behold a sight which even he who abhors it must pity.

[The central door of the palace opens and Oedipus comes forth, leaning on attendants. Bloody stains are still upon his face. The following lines between Oedipus and the Chorus are chanted responsively.]

CHORUS. Strophe 1. O dread fate for men to see, O most dreadful of all that have met my eyes! Unhappy one, what madness has   1180
come on you? Who is the unearthly foe[139] that, with a bound of more than mortal range, has made your ill-starred life his prey?[140]

Alas, alas, you hapless one! No, I cannot even look on you, though there is much that I would eagerly ask, eagerly learn, much that draws my wistful gaze,—with such a shuddering do you fill me!   1185

OEDIPUS. Woe is me! Alas, alas, wretched that I am! Whither, whither am I borne in my misery?[141] How is my voice swept abroad on the wings of the air?[142] Oh my daimon, how far have you sprung!

CHORUS. To a dread place, dire in men's ears, dire in their sight.

OEDIPUS. O horror of darkness that enfolds me, daimon un-   1190
speakable, resistless, sped by a wind too fair!

Ay me! and once again, ay me!

How is my soul pierced by the stab of these goads, and above

---

138 pain: his agony.
139 unearthly foe: daimon.
140 who was the daimon which leaped far into your already doomed destiny?
141 Whither . . . misery? Oedipus speaks in the tones of a person who is rushed along in the currents of passion without any self-control or sense of direction.
142 my voice . . . air? Oedipus not only feels lost in his agony, but because he cannot see his hearers he also feels that his voice is carried from him.

all by the memory of sorrows![143]

CHORUS. Yea, amid woes so many a twofold pain may well be   1195
yours to mourn and to bear.

OEDIPUS. *Antistrophe 1.* Ah, friend, you still are steadfast in
your care of me,—you still have patience to care for the blind man!
Ah me! Your presence is not hid from me—no, blind though I am,
yet I know your voice very well.[144]   1200

CHORUS. Man of dread deeds, how could you in such a manner
take away your vision? What more than human power urged you?

OEDIPUS. *Strophe 2.* Apollo,[145] friends, Apollo was he that
brought these my woes to pass, these my miserable, miserable
woes: but the hand that struck the eyes was none save mine,[146]   1205
wretched that I am! Why was I to see, when sight could show me
nothing sweet?

CHORUS. These things were even as you say.

OEDIPUS. Say, friends, what can I more behold, what can I love,
what greeting can touch my ear with joy? Haste, lead me from the   1210
land, friends, lead me hence, an utterly lost one, the thrice accursed, yea, the mortal most abhorred of heaven!

CHORUS. Wretched alike for your fate and for your sense of it,[147]
would that I had never so much as known you![148]

OEDIPUS. *Antistrophe 2.* Perish the man, whoever he was, that   1215
freed me in the pastures from the cruel shackle on my feet, and
saved me from death, and gave me back to life,—a thankless deed!
Had I died then, to my friends and to your own soul I would not
have been so sore a grief.

CHORUS. I also would have had it thus.   1220

OEDIPUS. Then I would not have come to shed my father's
blood, nor have been called among men the spouse of her from
whom I sprang: but now I am forsaken of the gods, son of a defiled
mother, successor to his bed who gave me my own wretched

---

143 With his present agony the recollection of past sorrows is mingled. This would
come with most force to a blind man, who has no object of vision to take his attention
from his inner visions. Thus his eyes and his mind have both been pierced when he
put out his eyes.
144 Oedipus begins to pull himself together again. His frenzy is passing, though his
anguish remains.   145 *Apollo:* Oedipus identifies his daimon as Apollo.
146 *the hand . . . mine:* Sophocles here widens his picture of the springs of human
passion. Oedipus blinds himself, it is true, but he does so when his mind is filled
with passion—the passion urged on him by his daimon, Apollo. There is no clear
separation here between conscious, voluntary acts and unwitting ones.
147 *your sense of it:* Oedipus apprehends his fate clearly and completely.
148 *would . . . you!* This cry of sympathy is wrenched from the Chorus.

being: and if there be yet a woe surpassing woes, it has become a   1225
part of the suffering of Oedipus.

CHORUS. I know not how I can say that your remedy was good:
for you would be better dead than living and blind.

OEDIPUS. Do not advise me further that these things are not best
done thus: give me counsel no more.[149] For, if I had sight, I do not   1230
know with what eyes I could even have looked on my father, when
I came to the place of the dead, or indeed on my miserable mother,
since against both I have sinned such sins as strangling could not
punish fully. But do you think that the sight of children, born as
mine were born, would have made me glad to look upon? No, no,   1235
not lovely to my eyes forever! No, nor could I remain in this town
with its towered walls, nor with its sacred statues of the gods, since I,
thrice wretched that I am,—I the noblest son of Thebes,—have
robbed myself of ever knowing these again, by my own command
that all should expel that one whom the gods should show to be a   1240
defilement in the house of Laius!

After learning of such a stain on me, was I to look with steady
eyes on my people? No, in truth, no. Were there yet a way to end
my power of hearing, I would not hesitate to make a complete
prison of this wretched carcas of mine, so that I might know   1245
neither sight nor sound; for it is sweet for thought to dwell in her
own world apart from evils.

Alas, Cithaeron, why did you have a shelter for me? When I was
given to you, why did you not slay me immediately, that thus I
might never have revealed my origin to men? Ah, Polybus,—ah,   1250
Corinth, and you that were called the ancient house of my fathers,
how fair in appearance was I your nurseling, and what ills were
festering beneath! For now I am found evil, and of evil birth. O
you three roads, and you secret glen,—you woodland grove and
narrow way where three paths met—you[150] who drank from my   1255
hands that father's blood which was my own,—you remember,
perchance, what deeds I wrought for you to see,—and then, when
I came here, what fresh deeds I went on to do?

O marriage-rites, you gave me birth, and when you had brought
me forth, again you bore children to your child, you created an   1260
incestuous kinship of fathers, brothers, sons,—brides, wives,
mothers,—yea, all the foulest shame that is wrought among men!
But, indeed, it is unfitting to name what it is unfitting to do:—
hasten, for the gods' love, hide me somewhere beyond the land,
or slay me, or cast me into the sea, where you shall never behold   1265
me more! Approach,—consent to lay your hands on a wretched
man;—hearken, fear not,—my plague can rest on no other mortal.

149 Oedipus is now more his old, commanding self.
150 *you:* the earth at the meeting place of the three roads.

[Enter Creon.]

LEADER. No, here is Creon, at an opportune time for your requests, be they for action or advice; for he alone is left to guard the land in your place.   1270

OEDIPUS. Ah me! how indeed shall I meet him? What ground of confidence can he have in me? For in the past I have been found wholly false to him.

CREON. I have not come in mockery, Oedipus, nor to reproach you with any bygone fault. *[To the attendants.]* But you, if you   1275
respect the children of men no more, revere at least the all-nurturing flame of our lord the Sun,—cease showing thus nakedly a pollution such as this,—one which neither earth can welcome, nor the holy rain, nor the light.[151] No, take him into the house as quickly as you can; for it best accords with piety that kinsfolk alone   1280
should see and hear a kinsman's woes.

OEDIPUS. For the gods' love—since you have done a gentle violence to my prediction, you who have come in a spirit so noble to me, a man most vile—grant me a favor:—for your good I will speak, not for my own.   1285

CREON. And what favor are you so eager to have from me?

OEDIPUS. Cast me out of this land with all speed, to a place where no mortal shall be found to greet me again.

CREON. This would I have done, be sure, but that I wished first to learn all my duty from the god.   1290

OEDIPUS. No, his command has been set forth in full,—to let me perish, the parricide, the unholy one, that I am.

CREON. Such was the purport;[152] yet, seeing to what a pass we have come, it is better to learn clearly what should be done.[153]

OEDIPUS. Will you, then, seek a response on behalf of such a   1295
wretch as I am?

CREON. Yes, for you yourself will now surely put faith in the god.

OEDIPUS. Yes; and on you I lay this charge, to you I will make this entreaty:—give to her who is within such burial as you yourself would; for you will fittingly render the last rites to your own.   1300
But for me—never let this city of my father be condemned to have me dwelling in it while I live:[154] no, let me abide on the hills, where yonder is Cithaeron, famed as mine,—which my mother and father, while they lived, set for my appointed tomb,—that thus I may die by the decree of them who sought to slay me. How-   1305
ever, of this much am I sure,—that neither sickness nor anything

---

151 The pollution of Oedipus is so great that he must not remain in the presence of the elements.   152 *the purport:* the meaning of the oracle of Apollo.
153 Creon intends to consult the oracle again.
154 It is plain that Oedipus still works to lift the plague from Thebes by fulfilling the terms of the oracle.

else can destroy me;[155] for I would never have been snatched from death, but in reserve for some strange doom.

No, let *my* fate go whither it will: but concerning my children,—I pray you, Creon, take no thought for the care of my sons;[156] they are men, so that, wherever they may be, they can never lack the means to live. But my two girls, poor unfortunate ones,—who never knew my table laid with food without their father's presence, but ever in all things shared my daily bread,—I pray you, care for *them;* and—if you can—let me touch them with my hands and indulge my grief. Grant it, prince, grant it, you noble heart! Ah, could I but once touch them with my hands, I should think that they were with me, even as when I had sight. . . . 1310

1315

[Creon's attendants lead in the children Antigone and Ismene.]

Ha? O you gods, can it be my loved ones that I hear sobbing,—can Creon have taken pity on me and sent me my children—my darlings? Am I right? 1320

CREON. Yes: it is of my contriving, for I knew your joy in them of old,—the joy that now is yours.

OEDIPUS. Then blessed be you, and, for reward of this act, may heaven prove to you a kinder guardian than it has to me! My children, where are you? Come here,—here to the hands of him whose mother was your own, the hands whose acts have brought it about that your father's once bright eyes should be such orbs as these,—his, who seeing nothing, knowing nothing, became your father by her from whom he sprang! For you also do I weep—behold you I cannot—when I think of the bitter life in days to come which men will make you live. To what gathering of the citizens[157] will you go, to what festival, from which you shall not return home in tears, instead of sharing in the holiday? But when you come to a marriageable age, who shall he be, who shall the man be, my daughters, that will hazard accepting the reproaches which will be injurious alike to my offspring and to yours? What possible misery is lacking? Your father slew his father, he had children by her who bore him, and begot you at the sources of his own being! Such are the taunts that will be cast at you; and who will then wed you? The man does not live, no, it cannot be, my children, but you must wither in barren maidenhood. 1325

1330

1335

1340

Ah, son of Menoeceus,[158] hear me—since you are the only father left to them, for we, their parents, are lost, both of us,—do not

155 Oedipus has regained his former stature as a man set apart from others, and his achievement is all the greater because of the agony in which he moves.
156 Oedipus had two sons, Eteocles and Polynices.
157 *gathering of the citizens:* the only type of occasion on which Athenian women could appear in public.   158 *son of Menoeceus:* Creon.

allow them, who are your kinswomen, to wander poor and unwed; 1345
nor abase them to the level of my woes.[159] No, pity them, when you
see them at this tender age so utterly forlorn, except for you. Ratify
your promise, generous man, by shaking hands! To you, my children, I would have given much counsel, were your minds mature;
but now I would have this to be your prayer—that you live where 1350
occasion permits, and that the life which is your portion may be
happier than your father's.

CREON. Your grief has had large enough scope: now pass into
the house.

OEDIPUS. I must obey, though it is in no way sweet. 1355

CREON. Yes: for it is in season that all things are good.

OEDIPUS. Do you know, then, on what conditions I will go?

CREON. You shall name them; thus I shall know them when I
hear.

OEDIPUS. See that you send me to dwell beyond this land. 1360

CREON. You ask me for that which only the god can give.

OEDIPUS. No, to the gods I have become most hateful.

CREON. You shall have your wish of banishment presently.

OEDIPUS. Do you consent?

CREON. It is not my habit to speak idly what I do not mean. 1365

OEDIPUS. Then it is time to lead me hence.

CREON. Come, then,—but let your children go.

OEDIPUS. No, do not take these from me!

CREON. Do not desire to be master in all things: for the mastery
which you did win has not followed you through life. 1370

CHORUS. *(singing)* Dwellers in our native Thebes, behold, this is
Oedipus, who knew the famed riddle, and was a man most mighty;
on whose fortunes what citizen did not gaze with envy? Behold
into what a stormy sea of dread trouble he has come!

Therefore, while our eyes wait to see the destined final day, 1375
we must call no one happy who is of mortal race, until he has
crossed life's border, free from pain.

159 Oedipus asks Creon to take on the position of guardian to his daughters.

Everyman

Introduction

As is the case with so many Medieval works, the authorship of *Everyman* is unknown. The date of its composition is debatable, but we may safely assume that it was written before the close of the fifteenth century. Even the date of its first printing is not certain, but the evidence argues that it was very likely first printed around 1519. It was one of the first plays to be printed in England. Three more printings before 1535 attest to its popularity (in no age have printers been known to publish what they foresee will not sell).

Everyman is a morality play: a dramatized allegory in which the abstract virtues and vices appear in personified form. Like all the mystery plays (Medieval religious plays based upon Biblical history) and the other moralities, it is primarily religious in purpose and is openly intended for religious instruction as well as for entertainment.

Printed at the end of the Renaissance, at the opening of the Reformation, *Everyman* is nevertheless completely the product of the Medieval world. Scholars are still waging academic war over which version of the play came first, the English *Everyman* or the Dutch *Elckerlijc,* but the controversy is of little consequence because this morality play is rather the product of Medieval Christian Europe than of any one country. *Everyman* has nothing of the Renaissance or Reformation about it. It tells how man, at the time of death, fortified by Confession and Holy Communion and joined only by his good deeds, successfully commends his soul into the hands of his Maker. Thus it is, strictly speaking, not tragedy, but the story of the moral evaluation which the Medieval world thought every man had to face at the time of his death.

Although the best known and by far the finest of the moralities, *Everyman* differs slightly from other plays in the category. The other moralities generally present the struggle of virtue and vice for the soul of man during life, but *Everyman* concerns itself solely with the moment of death. It also lacks much of the rough humor frequently found in the moralities. *Everyman's* chief humor lies in the speed with which all except Good Deeds leave him. It is not, however, lacking in the irony and satire which Medieval drama so frequently used to comment on the life around it.

Everyman

The Players' Names

GOD	CONFESSION
EVERYMAN	BEAUTY
DEATH	STRENGTH
GOOD FELLOWSHIP	DISCRETION
KINDRED	FIVE WITS
COUSIN	MESSENGER
GOOD DEEDS	ANGEL
KNOWLEDGE	DOCTOR

Everyman

*Here beginneth a treatise how the High Father of Heaven sendeth death to
summon every creature to come and give account of their lives in this
world, and is in manner of a moral play.*

[Enter Messenger as a Prologue.]

MESSENGER. I pray you all give your audience,
   And hear this matter with reverence,
   By figure[1] a moral play.
   The *Summoning of Everyman* called it is,
   That of our lives and ending shows,   5
   How transitory we be all day.
   This matter is wonder precious,[2]
   But the intent of it is more gracious,
   And sweet to bear away.[3]
   The story saith: Man, in the beginning,   10
   Look well, and take good heed to the ending,
   Be you never so gay.
   Ye think sin in the beginning full sweet,
   Which in the end causeth thy soul to weep,
   When the body lieth in clay.   15
   Here shall you see how Fellowship and Jollity,
   Both Strength, Pleasure, and Beauty,
   Will fade from thee as flower in May;
   For ye shall hear how our Heaven King
   Calleth Everyman to a general reckoning.   20
   Give audience, and hear what he doth say.   *[Exit.]*

[God speketh from above.]

GOD. I perceive here in my Majesty,
   How that all creatures be to me unkind,
   Living without dread in worldly prosperity:
   Of ghostly[4] sight the people be so blind,   25
   Drowned in sin, they know me not for their God.
   In worldly riches is all their mind,
   They fear not my rightwiseness, the sharp rod;
   My love that I showed, when I for them died,

1. *By figure:* in design.   2. *precious:* moral.
3. But our purpose is to give you pleasure.   4. *ghostly:* spiritual.

They forget clean, and shedding of my blood red; 30
I hanged between two,[5] it cannot be denied;
To get them life I suffered to be dead;
I healed their feet, with thorns hurt was my head:
I could do no more than I did truly,
And now I see the people do clean forsake me. 35
They use the seven deadly sins damnable;
As pride, covetise, wrath, and lechery,
Now in the world be made commendable;
And thus they leave of angels the heavenly company;
Every man liveth so after his own pleasure, 40
And yet of their life they be nothing sure:
I see the more that I them forbear
The worse they be from year to year;
All that liveth appaireth[6] fast,
Therefore I will in all the haste 45
Have a reckoning of every man's person;
For, if I leave the people thus alone
In their life and wicked tempests,
Verily they will become much worse than beasts;
For now one would by envy another up eat; 50
Charity they all do clean forget.
I hoped well that every man
In my glory should make his mansion,
And thereto I had them all elect;[7]
But now I see, like traitors deject 55
They thank me not for the pleasure that I to them meant,
Nor yet for their being that I them have lent;
I proffered the people great multitude of mercy
And few there be that asketh it heartly;
They be so cumbered with worldly riches, 60
That needs on them I must do justice,
On every man living without fear.
Where art thou, Death, thou mighty messenger? *[Enter Death.]*
DEATH. Almighty God, I am here at your will,
Your commandment to fulfil. 65
GOD. Go thou to Everyman,
And show him in my name
A pilgrimage he must on him take,
Which he in no wise may escape;
And that he bring with him a sure reckoning 70
Without delay or any tarrying.
DEATH. Lord, I will in the world go run over all,
And cruelly out-search both great and small; *[God withdraws.]*

5. The two thieves between whom Christ was crucified.
6. *appaireth:* degenerates.　7. *elect:* chosen.

Every man will I beset that liveth beastly,
Out of God's laws, and dreadeth not folly: 75
He that loveth riches I will strike with my dart,
His sight to blind, and from heaven to depart,[8]
Except that alms be his good friend,
In hell for to dwell, world without end.
Lo, yonder I see Everyman walking;   80
                 [Everyman enters at a distance.]
Full little he thinketh on my coming;
His mind is on fleshly lusts and his treasure;
And great pain it shall cause him to endure
Before the Lord, Heaven's King.
Everyman, stand still; whither art thou going   85
Thus gaily? Hast thou thy Maker forgot?   *[Everyman halts.]*
EVERYMAN. Why askest thou?
Wouldest thou wit?[9]
DEATH. Yea, sir, I will show you;
In great haste I am sent to thee   90
From God out of his Majesty.
EVERYMAN. What, sent to me?
DEATH. Yea, certainly:
Though thou have forgot him here,
He thinketh on thee in the heavenly sphere,   95
As, ere we depart, thou shalt know.
EVERYMAN. What desireth God of me?
DEATH. That shall I show thee;
A reckoning he will needs have
Without any longer respite.[10]   100
EVERYMAN. To give a reckoning longer leisure I crave;
This blind[11] matter troubleth my wit.
DEATH. On thee thou must take a long journey;
Therefore thy book of count[12] with thee thou bring;
For turn again thou cannot by no way,   105
And look thou be sure of thy reckoning;
For before God thou shalt answer, and show
Thy many bad deeds and good but a few;
How thou hast spent thy life, and in what wise,
Before the chief lord of paradise.   110
Hurry now that thou were on that way,
For, wit thou well, thou shalt make none attorney.[13]
EVERYMAN. Full unready I am such reckoning to give:
I know thee not; what messenger art thou?

8. *depart:* separate.
9. What would you know?   10. *respite:* delay.   11. *blind:* obscure.
12. *count:* sins and good works.
13. For know you well you shall have no attorney.

DEATH. I am Death, that no man dreadeth;[14]   115
  For every man I arrest, and no man spareth;
  For it is God's commandment
  That all to me should be obedient.
EVERYMAN. O Death! thou comest when I had thee least in mind;
  In thy power it lieth me to save,   120
  Yet of my goods will I give thee, if thou will be kind,
  Yea, a thousand pounds shalt thou have,
  And[15] thou defer this matter till another day.
DEATH. Everyman, it may not be by no way;
  I set not by gold, silver, nor riches,   125
  Ne by pope, emperor, king, duke, ne princes;
  For, and I would receive gifts great,
  All the world I might get;
  But my custom is clean contrary.
  I give thee no respite; come hence, and not tarry.   130
EVERYMAN. Alas, shall I have no longer respite?
  I may say Death giveth no warning:
  To think on thee, it maketh my heart sick,
  For all unready is my book of reckoning:
  But if twelve years I might have living,   135
  My counting-book I would make so clear,
  That my reckoning I should not need to fear.
  Wherefore, Death, I pray thee, for God's mercy,
  Spare me till I be provided of remedy.
DEATH. Thee availeth not to cry, weep, and pray: 140
  But haste thee lightly that thou wert gone this journey;
  And prove[16] thy friends if thou can.
  For, wit you well, the tide abideth[17] no man,
  And in the world each living creature
  For Adam's sin must die of nature.[18]   145
EVERYMAN. Death, if I should this pilgrimage take,
  And my reckoning surely make,
  Show me, for Saint Charity.
  Should I not come again shortly?
DEATH. No, Everyman; and thou be once there,   150
  Thou mayest never more come here,
  Trust me verily.
EVERYMAN. O gracious God! in the high seat celestial,
  Have mercy on me in this most need.
  Shall I have no company from this vale terrestrial   155
  Of mine acquaintance that way me to lead?

---

14. that fears no man.
15. *and:* here and elsewhere *and* frequently means *if.*   16. *prove:* test.
17. *tide abideth:* time awaits.   18. *of nature:* according to the law of nature.

DEATH. Yea, if any be so hardy,
    That would go with thee and bear thee company.
    Hie thee that thou were gone to God's magnificence,[19]
    Thy reckoning to give before his presence.   160
    What, weenest[20] thou thy life is given thee,
    And thy worldly goods also?
EVERYMAN. I had ween'd so, verily.
DEATH. Nay, nay; it was but lent thee;
    For, as soon as thou art gone,   165
    Another awhile shall have it, and then go therefrom,
    Even as thou hast done.
    Everyman, thou art mad; thou hast thy wits five,
    And here on earth will not amend thy life;
    For suddenly I do come.   170
EVERYMAN. O wretched caitiff,[21] whither shall I flee,
    That I might escape this endless sorrow?
    Now, gentle Death, spare me till to-morrow,
    That I may amend me
    With good advisement.[22]   175
DEATH. Nay, thereto I will not consent,
    Nor no man's life will I prolong,
    But to the heart suddenly I shall smite
    Without any advisement.
    And now out of thy sight I will me hie;[23]   180
    See thou make thee ready shortly,
    For thou mayst say this is the day
    That no man living may 'scape away.   *[Exit Death.]*
EVERYMAN. Alas! I may well weep with sighs deep;
    Now have I no manner company   185
    To help me in my journey, and me to keep;
    And also my writing[24] is full unready.
    How shall I do now for to excuse me?
    I would to God I had never be got![25]
    To my soul a full great profit it had be;   190
    For now I fear pains huge and great.
    The time passeth; Lord, help, that all wrought![26]
    For though I mourn, it availeth nought.
    The day passeth, and is almost a-go;
    I wot[27] not well what for to do.   195
    To whom were I best my complaint to make?
    What if I to Fellowship thereof spake,
    And showed him of this sudden chance?

---

19. Hurry up and go to God's magnificence.   20. *weenest:* thought.
21. *caitiff:* base person.   22. *advisement:* deliberation, consideration.
23. *hie:* hurry.   24. *my writing:* account of my life.   25. *be got:* been born.
26. *that all wrought:* who made all.   27. *wot:* know.

For in him is all mine affiance;[28]
We have in the world so many a day   200
Be good friends in sport and play.
I see him yonder, certainly;
I trust that he will bear me company;
Therefore to him will I speak to ease my sorrow.

[Enter Fellowship.]

Well met, good Fellowship, and good morrow!   205
FELLOWSHIP. Everyman, good morrow by this day.
  Sir, why lookest thou so piteously?
  If any thing be amiss, I pray thee, me say,
  That I may help to remedy.
EVERYMAN. Yea, good Fellowship, yea,   210
  I am in great jeopardy.
FELLOWSHIP. My true friend, show to me your mind;
  I will not forsake thee, to my life's end,
  In the way of good company.
EVERYMAN. That was well spoken, and lovingly.   215
FELLOWSHIP. Sir, I must needs know your heaviness;
  I have pity to see you in any distress;
  If any have you wronged, ye shall revenged be,
  Though I on the ground be slain for thee,—
  Though that I know before that I should die.   220
EVERYMAN. Verily, Fellowship, gramercy.[29]
FELLOWSHIP. Tush! by thy thanks I set not a straw.
  Show me your grief, and say no more.
EVERYMAN. If my heart should to you break,[30]
  And then you to turn your mind from me,   225
  And would not me comfort, when you hear me speak,
  Then should I ten times sorrier be.
FELLOWSHIP. Sir, I say as I will do in deed.
EVERYMAN. Then be you a good friend at need:
  I have found you true here-before.   230
FELLOWSHIP. And so ye shall evermore;
  For, in faith, if thou go to hell,
  I will not forsake thee by the way.
EVERYMAN. Ye speak like a good friend; I believe you well;
  I shall deserve[31] it, if I may.   235
FELLOWSHIP. I speak of no deserving, by this day.
  For he that will say and nothing do
  Is not worthy with good company to go.
  Therefore show me the grief of your mind,
  As to your friend most loving and kind.   240

28. *affiance:* trust.
29. *gramercy:* many thanks.   30. *break:* open.   31. *deserve:* repay.

EVERYMAN. I shall show you how it is.
  Commanded I am to go a journey,
  A long way, hard and dangerous,
  And give a strait count[32] without delay
  Before the high judge Adonai.[33]   245
  Wherefore I pray you, bear me company,
  As ye have promised, in this journey.
FELLOWSHIP. That is matter indeed![34] Promise is duty,
  But, if I should take such a voyage on me,
  I know it well, it should be to my pain: 250
  Also it me makes afeard, certain.
  But let us take counsel here as well as we can,
  For your words would fear a strong man.
EVERYMAN. Why, ye said, if I had need,
  Ye would me never forsake, quick ne dead,[35]   255
  Though it were to hell truly.
FELLOWSHIP. So I said certainly;
  But such pleasures be set aside, the sooth[36] to say:
  And also, if we took such a journey,
  When should we come again?   260
EVERYMAN. Nay, never again till the day of doom.[37]
FELLOWSHIP. In faith, then will not I come there!
  Who hath you these tidings brought?
EVERYMAN. Indeed Death was with me here.
FELLOWSHIP. Now by God that all that bought,[38]   265
  If Death were the messenger,
  For no man that is living to-day
  I will not go that loathsome journey,
  Not for the father that begat me!
EVERYMAN. Ye promised other wise, pardy.[39]   270
FELLOWSHIP. I wot well I said so truly;
  And yet if thou wilt eat, and drink, and make good cheer,
  Or haunt to women the lusty company,[40]
  I would not forsake you, while the day is clear,
  Trust me verily!   275
EVERYMAN. Yea, thereto ye would be ready.
  To go to mirth, solace,[41] and play,
  Your mind will sooner apply[42]
  Than to bear me company in my long journey.

---

32. *strait count:* strict accounting.   33. *Adonai:* God Almighty.
34. That is indeed important!   35. *quick ne dead:* alive or dead.
36. *sooth:* truth.   37. *doom:* judgment.   38. *that bought:* who all redeemed.
39. *pardy:* by God, indeed.   40. Or seek women who are gay company.
41. *solace:* entertainment.   42. *will sooner apply:* would rather turn to.

FELLOWSHIP. Now, in good faith, I will not that way.   280
   But, if thou wilt murder, or any man kill,
   In that I will help thee with a good will!
EVERYMAN. O that is a simple advice indeed!
   Gentle fellow, help me in my necessity;
   We have loved long, and now I need,   285
   And now, gentle Fellowship, remember me.
FELLOWSHIP. Whether ye have loved me or no,
   By Saint John, I will not with thee go!
EVERYMAN. Yet I pray thee, take the labor,[43] and do so much for me
   To go along the way, for Saint Charity,   290
   And comfort me till I come without the town.
FELLOWSHIP. Nay, and thou would give me a new gown,
   I will not a foot with thee go;
   But and thou had tarried, I would not have left thee so.
   And as now, God speed thee in thy journey!   295
   For from thee I will depart, as fast as I may.
EVERYMAN. Whither away, Fellowship? will you forsake me?
FELLOWSHIP. Yea, by my fay,[44] to God I send thee.
EVERYMAN. Farewell, good Fellowship; for thee[45] my heart is sore;
   Adieu for ever, I shall see thee no more.   300
FELLOWSHIP. In faith, Everyman, farewell now at the end;
   For you I will remember that parting is mourning.
                             [Exit Fellowship.]
EVERYMAN. Alack! shall we thus depart indeed?
   O! Lady, help! Without any more comfort,
   Lo, Fellowship forsaketh me in my most need: 305
   For help in this world whither shall I resort?
   Fellowship here before with me would merry make;
   And now little sorrow for me doth he take.
   It is said, in prosperity men friends may find,
   Which in adversity be full unkind.   310
   Now whither for succor shall I flee,
   Since that Fellowship hath forsaken me?
   To my kinsmen I will truly,
   Praying them to help me in my necessity;
   I believe that they will do so,   315
   For kind will creep, where it may not go.[46]
   I will go say,[47] for yonder I see them go.
   Where be ye now, my friends and kinsmen?
                     [Enter Kindred and Cousin.]
KINDRED. Here be we now at your commandment.
   Cousin, I pray you show us your intent   320

43. *labor:* trouble.   44. *fay:* faith.   45. *for thee:* because of you.
46. For kinsmen creep through where it is impossible to go.
47. *say:* try, attempt.

In any wise, and not spare.
COUSIN. Yea, Everyman, and to us declare
  If ye be disposed to go any whither,
  For wot ye well, we will live and die together.
KINDRED. In wealth and woe we will with you hold,   325
  For over his kin a man may be bold.[48]
EVERYMAN. Gramercy, my friends and kinsmen kind.
  Now shall I show you the grief of my mind.
  I was commanded by a messenger,
  That is an high king's chief officer;   330
  He bade me go a pilgrimage to my pain,
  And I know well I shall never come again;
  Also I must give a reckoning straight;
  For I have a great enemy,[49] that hath me in wait,
  Which intendeth me for to hinder.   335
KINDRED. What account is that which ye must render?
  That would I know.
EVERYMAN. Of all my works I must show
  How I have lived and my days spent;
  Also of ill deeds that I have used   340
  In my time, since life was me lent;
  And of all virtues that I have refused.
  Therefore, I pray you, go thither with me,
  To help to make mine account, for Saint Charity.
COUSIN. What, to go thither? Is that the matter?   345
  Nay, Everyman, I had liefer fast on bread and water
  All this five year and more.
EVERYMAN. Alas, that ever I was bore!
  For now shall I never be merry
  If that you forsake me.   350
KINDRED. Ah, sir; what, ye be a merry man!
  Take good heart to you, and make no moan.
  But one thing I warn you, by Saint Anne,
  As for me, ye shall go alone.
EVERYMAN. My Cousin, will you not with me go?   355
COUSIN. No, by our Lady; I have the cramp in my toe.
  Trust not to me, for, so God me speed,
  I will deceive you in your most need.
KINDRED. It availeth not us to entice.
  Ye shall have my maid with all my heart;   360
  She loveth to go to feasts, there to be nice,
  And to dance, and abroad to start:[50]
  I will give her leave to help you in that journey,
  If that you and she may agree.

48. For of his relatives a man may be confident.
49. *a great enemy:* the devil.   50. *abroad to start:* to gad abroad.

EVERYMAN. Now show me the very effect[51] of your mind. 365
   Will you go with me, or abide behind?
KINDRED. Abide behind? yea, that I will and I may!
   Therefore farewell until another day.   *[Exit Kindred.]*
EVERYMAN. How should I be merry or glad?
   For fair promises to me they make; 370
   But when I have most need, they me forsake.
   I am deceived; that maketh me sad.
COUSIN. Cousin Everyman, farewell now,
   For verily I will not go with you;
   Also of mine own an unready reckoning 375
   I have to account; therefore I make tarrying.
   Now, God keep thee, for now I go.   *[Exit Cousin.]*
EVERYMAN. Ah, Jesu, is all come hereto?
   Lo, fair words maketh fools fain;[52]
   They promise and nothing will do certain. 380
   My kinsmen promised me faithfully
   For to abide with me steadfastly,
   And now fast away do they flee:
   Even so Fellowship promised me.
   What friend were best me of to provide? 385
   I lose my time here longer to abide.
   Yet in my mind a thing there is:
   All my life I have loved riches;
   If that my Goods now help me might,
   He would make my heart full light. 390
   I will speak to him in this distress.—
   Where art thou, my Goods and riches?
           [Enter Goods from behind boxes and bags.]
GOODS. Who calleth me? Everyman? What haste thou hast.
   I lie here in corners, trussed and piled so high,
   And in chests I am locked so fast, 395
   Also sacked in bags, thou mayst see with thine eye
   I cannot stir; in packs lo! where I lie!
   What would ye have, quickly me say.
EVERYMAN. Come hither, Goods, in all the haste thou may,
   For of counsel I must desire thee.   *[Goods comes forward.]* 400
GOODS. Sir, if ye in the world have trouble or adversity,
   That can I help you to remedy shortly.
EVERYMAN. It is another disease[53] that grieveth me;
   In this world it is not, I tell thee so;
   I am sent for another way to go, 405
   To give a straight account general
   Before the highest Jupiter of all;
   And all my life I have had my pleasure in thee.

---

51. *effect:* tenor.   52. *fain:* happy.   53. *disease:* annoyance, trouble.

Therefore I pray thee go with me;
For, peradventure,[54] thou mayst before God Almighty   410
My reckoning help to clean and purify;
For it is said ever among,[55]
That money maketh all right that is wrong.

GOODS. Nay, nay, Everyman, I sing another song,
I follow no man in such voyages;   415
For, and I went with thee,
Thou shouldst fare much the worse for me:
For because on me thou did set thy mind,
Thy reckoning I have made blotted and blind,[56]
That thine account thou cannot make truly;   420
And that hast thou for the love of me.

EVERYMAN. That would grieve me full sore,
When I should come to that fearful answer:
Up, let us go thither together.

GOODS. Nay, not so; I am too brittle, I may not endure: 425
I will follow no man one foot, be ye sure.

EVERYMAN. Alas, I have thee loved, and had great pleasure
All my life-days on goods and treasure.

GOODS. That is to thy damnation without lying
For my love is contrary to the love everlasting.   430
But if thou had me loved moderately during,[57]
As to the poor give part of me,
Then shouldst thou not in this dolor have be,
Nor in this great sorrow and care.

EVERYMAN. Lo, now was I deceived ere I was aware,   435
And I may blame it on my wasting time.

GOODS. What, weenest thou[58] that I am thine?

EVERYMAN. I had went so.

GOODS. Nay, Everyman, I say no;
As for a while I was lent thee,   440
A season thou hast had me in prosperity;
My condition is man's soul to kill;
If I save one, a thousand I do spill;
Weenest thou that I will follow thee?
Nay, not from this world, verily.   445

EVERYMAN. I had weened otherwise.

GOODS. Therefore to thy soul Goods is a thief;
For when thou art dead, this is my guise[59]
Another to deceive in the same wise,
As I have done thee, and all to his soul's reprefe.[60]   450

---

54. *peradventure:* perhaps.   55. *ever among:* again and again.
56. *blind:* obscure, dark.   57. *during:* during your life.
58. *weenest thou:* do you imagine (suppose).   59. *guise:* custom, practice.
60. *reprefe:* shame.

EVERYMAN. O false Goods, cursed may thou be!
  Thou traitor to God, that hast deceived me,
  And caught me in thy snare.
GOODS. Marry, thou brought thyself this care,
  Whereof I am glad.   455
  I must needs laugh, I cannot be sad.
EVERYMAN. Ah, Goods, thou hast had long my hearty love;
  I gave thee that which should be the Lord's above.
  But wilt thou not go with me in deed?
  I pray thee truth to say.   460
GOODS. No, so God me speed,
  Therefore farewell, and have good day.   *[Exit Goods.]*
EVERYMAN. Oh, to whom shall I make my moan
  For to go with me in that heavy journey?
  First Fellowship said he would with me gone;   465
  His words were very pleasant and gay,
  But afterward he left me alone.
  Then spake I to my kinsmen all in despair,
  And also they gave me words fair,
  They lacked no fair speaking,   470
  But all forsake me in the ending.
  Then went I to my Goods that I loved best,
  In hope to have comfort; but there had I least;
  For my Goods sharply did me tell
  That he bringeth many in hell.   475
  Then of myself I was ashamed,
  And so I am worthy to be blamed:
  Thus may I well myself hate.
  Of whom shall I now counsel take?
  I think that I shall never speed[61]   480
  Till that I go to my Good Deeds;
  But alas; she is so weak,
  That she can neither go nor speak;
  Yet will I venture on[62] her now.—
  My Good Deeds, where be you?   485

[Good Deeds speaks up from the ground.]

GOOD DEEDS. Here I lie cold in the ground;
  Thy sin hath me sore bound,
  That I cannot stir.
EVERYMAN. O, Good Deeds, I stand in fear;
  I must you pray of counsel,   490
  For help now should seem right well.
GOOD DEEDS. Everyman, I have understanding
  That ye be summoned account to make

---

61. *speed:* succeed, prosper.   62. *venture on:* take a chance on, gamble on.

Before Messias, of Jerusalem King;
  And you do my way, that journey with you will I take.   495
EVERYMAN. Therefore I come to you, my moan to make;
  I pray you, that ye will go with me.
GOOD DEEDS. I would full fain,[63] but I cannot stand verily.
EVERYMAN. Why, is there anything on you fall?
GOOD DEEDS. Yea, sir, I may thank you for all;   500
  If ye had comforted me,
  Your book of account now full ready had be.
                              [Shows him his account books.]
  Look, moreover, at the books of your works and deeds;
  Behold now they lie under the feet,
  To your soul's heaviness.   505
EVERYMAN. Our Lord Jesus, help me!
  For I cannot see one letter here.
GOOD DEEDS. There is a blind[64] reckoning in time of distress!
EVERYMAN. Good Deeds, I pray you, help me in this need,
  Or else I am for ever damned indeed;   510
  Therefore help me to make reckoning
  Before the Redeemer of all thing,
  That king is, and was, and ever shall.
GOOD DEEDS. Everyman, I am sorry of your fall,
  And fain would I help you, and I were able.   515
EVERYMAN. Good Deeds, your counsel I pray you give me.
GOOD DEEDS. That shall I do verily:
  Though that on my feet I may not go.
  I have a sister, that shall with you also,
  Called Knowledge, which shall with you abide,   520
  To help you to make that dreadful reckoning.

                      [Enter Knowledge.]

KNOWLEDGE. Everyman, I will go with thee, and be thy guide,
  In thy most need to go by thy side.
EVERYMAN. In good condition I am now in every thing.
  And am wholly content with this good thing;   525
  Thanked be God my Creator.
GOOD DEEDS. And when he hath brought thee there,
  Where thou shalt heal thee of thy smart,
  Then go thou with thy reckoning and Good Deeds together
  For to make thee joyful at heart   530
  Before the blessed Trinity.
EVERYMAN. My Good Deeds, gramercy.
  I am well content, certainly,
  With your words sweet.

63. *full fain:* quite happily.
64. *blind:* difficult, that is, a sinful person finds his record of good deeds dark or dim
and, therefore, difficult to see.

KNOWLEDGE. Now go we together lovingly, 535
   To Confession, that cleansing river.
EVERYMAN. For joy I weep: I would we were there;
   But, I pray you, give me by instruction,
   Where dwelleth that holy man, Confession.
KNOWLEDGE. In the house of salvation:[65] 540
   We shall find him in that place.
   That shall us comfort by God's grace.

[Knowledge leads Everyman to Confession.]

   Lo, this is Confession; kneel down and ask mercy,
   For he is in good conceit[66] with God Almighty.
EVERYMAN. O glorious fountain; that all uncleanness doth clarify, 545
   Wash from me the spots of vices unclean,
   That on me no sin may be seen;
   I come with Knowledge for my redemption,
   My heart repentant and full of contrition;
   For I am commanded a pilgrimage to take, 550
   And great accounts before God to make.
   Now, I pray you, Shrift,[67] mother of salvation,
   Help my good deeds for my piteous exclamation.[68]
CONFESSION. I know your sorrow well, Everyman;
   Because with Knowledge ye come to me, 555
   I will you comfort as well as I can,
   And a precious jewel I will give thee,
   Called penance, voider of adversity;
   Therewith shall your body chastised be,
   With abstinence and perserverance in God's service: 560
   Here shall you receive that scourge[69] of me
            [Gives Everyman a scourge.]
   Which is penance strong that ye must endure.
   Remember thy Saviour was scourged for thee
   With sharp scourges, and suffered it patiently;
   So must thou, ere thou pass thy pilgrimage. 565
   Knowledge, keep him in his voyage,
   And by that time Good Deeds will be with thee.
   But in any case be sure of mercy,
   For your time draweth fast. If ye will saved be,
   Ask God mercy, and He will grant truly; 570
   When with the scourge of penance man doth him bind,
   The oil of forgiveness then shall he find.
EVERYMAN. Thanked be God for his gracious work!
   For now I will my penance begin;
   This hath rejoiced and lighted my heart, 575

---

65. *house of salvation:* the church.
66. *conceit:* esteem.   67. *Shrift:* Confession.   68. *exclamation:* utterance.
69. *scourge:* punishment by whipping.

Though the knots[70] be painful and hard within.
KNOWLEDGE. Everyman, look your penance that ye fulfil,
  What pain that ever it to you be,
  And I shall give you counsel at will,
  How your account ye shall make clearly.   580
EVERYMAN. O eternal God! O heavenly figure!
  O way of rightwiseness! O goodly vision!
  Which descended down in a virgin pure,
  Because he would Everyman redeem,
  Which Adam forfeited by his disobedience;   585
  O blessed Godhead! elect and high Divine,
  Forgive me my grievous offense;
  Here I cry thee mercy in this company.
  O ghostly treasure! O ransomer and redeemer!
  Of all the world hope and conductor,   590
  Mirror of joy, and founder of mercy,
  Which illumineth heaven and earth thereby,
  Hear my clamorous complaint, though it late be;
  Receive my prayers out of thy mercy;
  Though I be a sinner most abominable,   595
  Yet let my name be written in Moses' table;[71]
  O Mary! pray to the Maker of all thing
  Me for to help at my ending,
  And save me from the power of my enemy;
  For Death assaileth me strongly;   600
  And, Lady, that I may, by means of thy prayer,
  Of your Son's glory to be partner.
  By the means of his passion,[72] I it crave,
  I beseech you, help me my soul to save.
  Knowledge, give me the scourge of penance;   605
  My flesh thereby shall give me acquittance;
  I will now begin, if God give me grace.
KNOWLEDGE. Everyman, God give you time and space!
  Thus I bequeath you in the hands of our Saviour,
  Thus may you make your reckoning sure.   610
EVERYMAN. In the name of all the Holy Trinity,
  My body punished sore shall be:
  Take this, body, for the sin of the flesh;
                  [He begins to scourge himself.]
  Also thou delightest to go gay and fresh,
  And in the way of damnation thou did me bring;   615
  Therefore suffer now strokes and punishing.

70. *knots:* knotted whip.
71. The two tables given to Moses on Mount Sinai were regarded by Medieval theologians as symbols of penance and baptism. Everyman is begging to be numbered among those who have done penance for their sins.
72. *passion:* Christ's sufferings on the cross.

Now of penance I will wade the water clear
To save me from purgatory, that sharp fire.
GOOD DEEDS. I thank God, now I can walk and go;
   And am delivered of my sickness and woe.   620
   Therefore with Everyman I will go, and not spare;
   His good works I will help him to declare.
KNOWLEDGE. Now, Everyman, be merry and glad;
   Your Good Deeds cometh now; ye may not be sad;
   Now is your Good Deeds whole and sound,   625
   Going upright upon the ground.
EVERYMAN. My heart is light, and shall be evermore;
   Now will I smite faster than I did before.
GOOD DEEDS. Everyman, pilgrim, my special friend,
   Blessed be thou without end;   630
   For thee is prepared the eternal glory.
   Ye have me made whole and sound,
   Therefore I will bide by thee in every stound.[73]
EVERYMAN. Welcome, my Good Deeds; now I hear thy voice,
   I weep for very sweetness of love.   635
KNOWLEDGE. Be no more sad, but evermore rejoice;
   God seeth thee living in his throne above;
   Put on this garment to thy behove,[74]
   Which with your tears is now all wet,
   Lest before God it be unsweet;   640
   When you to your journey's end come shall.
EVERYMAN. Gentle Knowledge, what do you it call?
KNOWLEDGE. It is the garment of sorrow:
   From pain it will you protect;
   Contrition it is,   645
   That getteth forgiveness;
   It pleaseth God passing well.
GOOD DEEDS. Everyman, will you wear it for your heal?[75]
            [Everyman puts on the robe.]
EVERYMAN. Now blessed be Jesu, Mary's Son!
   For now have I on true contrition.   650
   And let us go now without tarrying.
   Good Deeds, have we clear our reckoning?
GOOD DEEDS. Yea, indeed I have it here.
EVERYMAN. Then I trust we need not fear;
   Now, friends, let us not part in twain.   655
KNOWLEDGE. Nay, Everyman, that will we not, certain.
GOOD DEEDS. Yet must thou lead with thee
   Three persons of great might.
EVERYMAN. Who should they be?

73. *stound:* trial, hard time.
74. *behove:* advantage.   75. *heal:* recovery, (spiritual health).

GOOD DEEDS. Discretion and Strength they hight,[76]   660
  And thy Beauty may not abide behind.
KNOWLEDGE. Also ye must call to mind
  Your Five Wits as for your counselors.
GOOD DEEDS. You must have them ready at all hours.
EVERYMAN. How shall I get them hither?   665
KNOWLEDGE. You must call them all together,
  And they will hear you immediate.
EVERYMAN. My friends, come hither and be present!
  Discretion, Strength, my Five Wits, and Beauty!

   [Enter Discretion, Strength, Five Wits, and Beauty.]

BEAUTY. Here at your will we be all ready;   670
  What will ye that we should do?
GOOD DEEDS. That ye would with Everyman go,
  And help him in his pilgrimage,
  Consider now, will ye with him or not in that voyage?
STRENGTH. We will bring him all thither,   675
  To his help and comfort, ye may believe me.
DISCRETION. So will we go with him all together.
EVERYMAN. Almighty God! loved may thou be,
  I give Thee laud that I have hither brought
  Strength, Discretion, Beauty, and Five Wits; lack I nought;   680
  And my Good Deeds, with Knowledge clear,
  All be in my company at my will here;
  I desire no more for my business.
STRENGTH. And I, Strength, will by you stand in distress,
  Though thou wouldest in battle fight on the ground.   685
FIVE WITS. And though it were through the world round,
  We will not depart for sweet nor sour.
BEAUTY. No more will I until death's hour,
  Whatsoever therof befall.
DISCRETION. Everyman, advise you first of all;   690
  Go with a good advisement and deliberation;
  We all give you virtuous admonition
  That all shall be well.
EVERYMAN. My friends, heark what I will tell:
  I pray God reward you in His heavenly sphere.   695
  Now hearken, all that be here,
  For I will make my testament
  Here before you all present:
  In alms half my good I will give with my hands twain
  In the way of charity, with good intent,   700
  And the other half still shall remain
  In queth[77] to be returned where it ought be;
  This I do in despite of the fiend of hell,

76. *hight:* are called.   77. *queth:* legacy.

To go quite out of his peril
  Ever after this day.   705
KNOWLEDGE. Everyman, hearken what I will say:
  Go to priesthood, I you advise,
  And receive of him in any wise[78]
  The holy sacrament[79] and ointment[80] together;
  Then shortly see ye turn again hither;   710
  We will all await you here.
FIVE WITS. Yea, Everyman, hurry that ye ready were,
  There is no emperor, king, duke, ne baron,
  That of God hath commission,
  As hath the least priest in the world being;   715
  For of the blessed sacraments pure and benign
  He beareth the keys, and thereof hath cure
  For man's redemption, it is ever sure,
  Which God for our soul's medicine
  Gave us out of his heart with great pain,   720
  Here in this transitory life, for thee and me.
  The blessed sacraments seven there be,
  Baptism, confirmation, with priesthood good,
  And the sacrament of God's precious flesh and blood,
  Marriage, the holy extreme unction, and penance;   725
  These seven be good to have in remembrance,
  Gracious sacraments of high divinity.
EVERYMAN. Fain would I receive that holy body[81]
  And meekly to my ghostly father[82] I will go.
FIVE WITS. Everyman, that is the best that ye can do: 730
  God will you to salvation bring,
  For priesthood exceedeth all other thing;
  To us Holy Scripture they do teach,
  And converteth man from sin, heaven to reach;
  God hath to them more power given   735
  Than to any angel that is in heaven;
  With five words[83] he may consecrate
  God's body in flesh and blood to take,
  And handleth his Maker between his hands,
  The priest bindeth and unbindeth all bands,   740
  Both in earth and in heaven;
  Thou ministers all the sacraments seven;
  Though we kiss thy feet, thou were worthy;
  Thou art the surgeon that cureth sin deadly:
  No remedy we find under God,   745

---

78. *in any wise:* at all costs.
79. *holy sacrament:* sacrament of the Lord's Supper.
80. *ointment:* Extreme Unction administered to one in danger of death.
81. *holy body:* the Body of Christ.   82. *ghostly father:* spiritual father (the priest).
83. *five words:* For This is My Body.

Except in the priesthood.
Everyman, God gave priests that dignity,
And setteth them in his stead among us to be;
Thus be they above angels in degree.
                    [Everyman exits to receive the last sacraments.]
KNOWLEDGE. If priests be good, so it must be,   750
  But when Jesu hang on the cross with great smart,
  There he gave us, out of his blessed heart,
  The same sacrament in great torment.
  He sold them not to us, that Lord Omnipotent.
  Therefore Saint Peter the apostle doth say   755
  That Jesu's curse have all they
  Which God their Saviour do buy or sell,
  Or they for any money do take or tell.[84]
  Sinful priests giveth the sinners example bad;
  Their children sitteth by other men's fires, I have heard;[85] 760
  And some haunteth women's company,
  With unclean life, as lusts of lechery:
  These be with sin made blind.
FIVE WITS. I trust to God, no such may we find;
  Therefore let us priesthood honour,   765
  And follow their doctrine for our souls' succor;
  We be their sheep, and they our shepherds be,
  By whom we all be kept in surety.
  Peace, for yonder I see Everyman come,
  Which hath made true satisfaction.   *[Everyman re-enters.]* 770
GOOD DEEDS. Methinketh it is he indeed.
EVERYMAN. Now Jesu be our alder speed.[86]
  I have received the sacrament for my redemption,
  And then mine extreme unction:
  Blessed be all they that counselled me to take it!   775
  And now, friends, let us go without longer respite;
  I thank God that ye have tarried so long.
  Now set each of you on this rod[87] your hand,
  And shortly follow me:
  I go before, there I would be; God be our guide.   780
STRENGTH. Everyman, we will not from you go
  Till ye have gone this voyage long.
DISCRETION. I, Discretion, will stay with you also.
KNOWLEDGE. And though this pilgrimage be never so strong,
  I will never part you from;   785
  Everyman, I will be as sure by thee
  As ever I was by Judas Maccabee.[88]

84. *tell:* count (refers to selling that which is sacred).
85. They have illegitimate children.   86. *alder speed:* greatest support.
87. *rod:* cross.
88. *Judas Maccabee:* a leader of the Jews, noted for his bravery and strength.

[They proceed together to the grave.]

EVERYMAN. Alas, I am so faint I may not stand,
My limbs under me do fold;
Friends, let us not turn again to this land,   790
Not for all the world's gold.
For into this cave must I creep.
And turn to the earth and there to sleep.
BEAUTY. What, into this grave? alas!
EVERYMAN. Yea, there shall you decay more and less.[89]   795
BEAUTY. And what, should I smother here?
EVERYMAN. Yea, by my faith, and never more appear.
In this world live no more we shall,
But in heaven before the highest Lord of all.
BEAUTY. I cross out all promise; adieu by Saint John;   800
I take my tap in my lap and am gone.[90]
EVERYMAN. What, Beauty, whither will ye?
BEAUTY. Peace, I am deaf; I look not behind me,
Not if thou wouldst give me all the gold in thy chest.
                                        [Exit Beauty.]
EVERYMAN. Alas, whereto may I trust?   805
Beauty doth fast away hie;
She promised with me to live and die.
STRENGTH. Everyman, I will thee also forsake and deny;
Thy game liketh me not at all.
EVERYMAN. Why, then ye will forsake me all.   810
Sweet Strength, tarry a little space.
STRENGTH. Nay, sir, by the rod of grace
I will hie me from thee fast,
Though thou weep till thy heart brast.
EVERYMAN. Ye would ever bide by me, ye said.   815
STRENGTH. Yea, I have you far enough conveyed;
Ye be old enough, I understand,
Your pilgrimage to take on hand;
I repent me that I hither came.
EVERYMAN. Strength, you to displease I am to blame;   820
Yet promise is debt; this ye well wot.
STRENGTH. In faith as for that, I care not;
Thou art but a fool to complain,
You spend your speech and waste your brain;
Go, thrust thee into the ground.   *[Exit Strength.]*   825
EVERYMAN. I had thought surer I should you have found.
He that trusteth in his Strength
She him deceiveth at the length.

89. *more and less:* completely.
90. *tap:* a bunch of flax, fiber or wool. Thus for a woman to "take her tap in her lap"
was proverbial for "take up her things and go."

Both Strength and Beauty forsaketh me,
Yet they promised me fair and lovingly. 830
DISCRETION. Everyman, I will after Strength be gone;
As for me, I will leave you alone.
EVERYMAN. Why, Discretion, will ye forsake me?
DISCRETION. Yea, in faith, I will go from thee,
For when Strength is gone before, 835
I follow after evermore.
EVERYMAN. Yet, I pray thee, for the love of the Trinity,
Look in my grave once piteously.
DISCRETION. Nay, so near will I not come.
Now farewell, fellows everyone! *[Exit Discretion.]* 840
EVERYMAN. O all thing faileth, save God alone;
Beauty, Strength, and Discretion;
For when Death bloweth his blast,
They all run from me full fast.
FIVE WITS. Everyman, my leave now of thee I take; 845
I will follow the other, for here I thee forsake.
EVERYMAN. Alas! then may I both wail and weep;
For I took you for my best friend.
FIVE WITS. I will no longer with thee stay;
Now farewell, and here an end. *[Exit Five Wits.]* 850
EVERYMAN. Now, Jesu, help! all hath forsaken me!
GOOD DEEDS. Nay, Everyman, I will abide with thee,
I will not forsake thee indeed;
Thou shalt find me a good friend in need.
EVERYMAN. Gramercy, Good Deeds; now may I true friends see; 855
They have forsaken me every one;
I loved them better than my Good Deeds alone.
Knowledge, will ye forsake me also?
KNOWLEDGE. Yea, Everyman, when ye to death do go:
But not yet for no manner of danger. 860
EVERYMAN. Gramercy, Knowledge, with all my heart!
KNOWLEDGE. Nay, yet I will not from hence depart,
Till I see where ye shall be come.
EVERYMAN. Methinketh, alas that I must be gone,
To make my reckoning, and my debts pay; 865
For I see my time is nigh spent away.
Take ensample, all ye that this do hear or see,
How they that I loved best do forsake me,
Except my Good Deeds that waiteth truly.
GOOD DEEDS. All earthly things is but vanity: 870
Beauty, Strength, and Discretion, do man forsake,
Foolish friends and kinsmen, that fair spake,
All fleeth save Good Deeds, and that am I.
EVERYMAN. Have mercy on me, God most mighty;
And stand by me, thou Mother and Maid, Mary. 875

GOOD DEEDS. Fear not, I will speak for thee.

EVERYMAN. Here I cry, God mercy!

GOOD DEEDS. Short our end, and minish our pain;[91]
Let us go and never come again.

EVERYMAN. Into thy hands, Lord, my soul I commend;　　　　880
Receive it, Lord, that it be not lost;
As thou me boughtest, so me defend,
And save me from the fiend's boast,[92]
That I may appear with that blessed host
That shall be saved at the day of doom:　　　　885
In manus tuas, of might most,
For ever *commendo spiritum meum.*[93]
　　　　[Everyman and Good Deeds descend into the grave.]

KNOWLEDGE. Now hath he suffered that we all shall endure;
The Good Deeds shall make all sure.
Now hath he made ending;　　　　890
Methinketh that I hear angels sing
And make great joy and melody,
Where Everyman's soul received shall be.

ANGEL. Come, excellent elect spouse to Jesu;
Hereabove thou shalt go　　　　895
Because of thy singular virtue:
Now the soul is taken thy body from;
Thy reckoning is crystal clear.
Now shalt thou into the heavenly sphere,
Unto the which all ye shall come　　　　900
That liveth well before the day of doom.

　　　　[Enter Doctor as an epilogue.]

DOCTOR. This memory all may have in mind;
Ye hearers, take it of worth, old and young,
And forsake pride, for he deceiveth you in the end,
And remember Beauty, Five Wits, Strength, and Discretion,　　　　905
They all at the last do Everyman forsake,
Save his Good Deeds, them he there doth take.
But beware, for, if they be small,
Before God he hath no help at all.
None excuse may be there for Everyman;　　　　910
Alas, how shall he do them?
For after death amends may no man make
For then mercy and pity doth him forsake.
If his reckoning be not clear when he do come,
God will say—*ite, maledicti, in ignem aeternum.*[94]　　　　915
And he that hath his account whole and sound,

91. Shorten our end and diminish our pain.　　92. *fiend's boast:* devil's boast.
93. Into thy hands I commend my spirit.　　94. Go, you accursed, into eternal fires.

High in heaven he shall be crowned;
Unto which place God bring us all thither,
That we may live body and soul together.
Thereto help the Trinity;   920
Amen, say ye, for Saint Charity.

Doctor Faustus

Introduction

Most scholars agree that Christopher Marlowe's *Doctor Faustus* was probably written between 1588 and 1592. It is attributed to Marlowe on the title page of the first edition still in existence—that of 1604. The present editor, well aware that some authorities argue that Marlowe is not the sole author, nevertheless treats *Doctor Faustus* as a unified work written by Christopher Marlowe.

The legend of a man who sells his soul to the devil—the legend which forms the basis of Marlowe's *Doctor Faustus*—is found in Jewish literature before the birth of Christ, and it is widespread at least from the sixth century A.D. in Christian literature. The historical Johannes Faustus, however, a magician and necromancer (one who conjures up the spirits of the dead), flourished in Germany in the first half of the sixteenth century, and it was he who became the nucleus around whom many of the earlier legends and tales gathered. His fame spread, especially after his death, and he was mentioned in England as early as 1572. A German version of the story of Faustus was published, and was translated into English. It was this English translation that most probably served as Marlowe's source for *Doctor Faustus*.

Whatever religious beliefs Christopher Marlowe may or may not have held personally, in *Doctor Faustus* he produced a perfectly orthodox limited-scope morality play (one which deals with a single vice or problem or a situation applicable to a certain person). It is the natural descendant of *Everyman, Mankind,* and the other earlier moralities. Just as *Everyman* demonstrated how man attains eternal bliss, *Doctor Faustus* shows how man comes to the most tragic of ends in the loss of his eternal soul. In dramatizing how the human soul is lost, Marlowe treated tragedy in the least sophisticated and least complicated way open to him in a Christian culture and environment. He does this by presenting two choices open to Faustus— the Devil or Christ.

No amount of refinement can make any story really tragic for the Christian if the hero attains eternal happiness. Thus beginning with the tragic ending of Faustus, Marlowe's only need was to demonstrate *how* he came to be damned. He did this by showing over and over that repentance was always open to Faustus, even at the very end of his life. At that moment Faustus beholds the face of Christ:

See, see where Christ's blood streams in the firmament!
One drop would save my soul—half a drop. Ah, my Christ!

But he is unable to withstand even for a few moments the torture inflicted by the devils around him, and turning to the devils he cries out:

Ah, rend not my heart for naming of my Christ!
Yet will I call on him!

Unable still to bear the physical pains the devils are inflicting on him, he changes his call to Christ to:

O, spare me, Lucifer!

This was Faustus' final opportunity for salvation. When he turns back to where a moment before he had beheld the bleeding face of Christ, he finds it has gone:

Where is it now? Tis gone.

In its place he sees

. . . where God
Stretcheth out his arm, and bends his ireful brows!

Then Marlowe demonstrates how Doctor Faustus has chosen to damn himself eternally.

The most amazing thing about this play is that, although Faustus has time and again deliberately chosen evil over good, Christopher Marlowe's genius enables him to make his audience, then and now, sympathize with Doctor Faustus, even at the very final moment—that moment when Faustus himself consciously choses Lucifer, the devil, over Christ, the savior. We sympathize because each man in his own way is confronted with the same kind of problem—the choice between good and evil. As we will see, this same choice is handled differently in *Hamlet, The Glass Menagerie,* and *All My Sons.*

The Tragical History of Doctor Faustus

CHRISTOPHER MARLOWE

Names of Characters

THE POPE

CARDINAL OF LORRAIN

EMPEROR OF GERMANY

DUKE OF VANHOLT

FAUSTUS

VALDES ⎫
⎬ *friends to*
CORNELIUS AGRIPPA ⎭ *Faustus*

WAGNER   *servant to Faustus*

CLOWN

ROBIN

RAFE

VINTNER

HORSE-CORSER

KNIGHT

OLD MAN

SCHOLARS, FRIARS, *and* ATTENDANTS

DUCHESS OF VANHOLT

LUCIFER

BELZEBUB

MEPHISTOPHILIS

GOOD ANGEL

EVIL ANGEL

THE SEVEN DEADLY SINS

DEVILS

SPIRITS *in the shapes of Alexander the Great, of his Paramour, and of Helen of Troy*

CHORUS

Chorus

[Enter Chorus.]

Not marching now in fields of Thrasimene,
Where Mars did mate[1] the Carthaginians,
Nor sporting in the dalliance of love,
In courts of kings where state is overturned,
Nor in the pomp of proud audacious deeds,   5
Intends our Muse to daunt[2] his heavenly verse.
Only this, gentlemen: we must perform
The form[3] of Faustus' fortunes, good or bad.
To patient judgments we appeal our plaud,[4]
And speak for Faustus in his infancy.   10
Now is he born, his parents base of stock,
In Germany, within a town called Rhodes;
Of riper years to Wertenberg[5] he went,
Whereas[6] his kinsmen chiefly brought him up.
So soon he profits in divinity,   15
The fruitful plot of scholarism graced,
That shortly he was graced with doctor's name,
Excelling all whose sweet delight disputes
In heavenly matters of theology;
Till swollen with cunning,[7] of a self-conceit,   20
His waxen wings did mount above his reach,
And, melting, heavens conspired his overthrow,
For, falling to a devilish exercise,
And glutted now with learning's golden gifts,
He surfeits upon curséd necromancy.   25
Nothing so sweet as magic is to him,
Which he prefers before his chiefest bliss.
And this the man that in his study sits!

                                                            [Exit.]

---

1 *mate:* enter into alliance with.   2 *daunt:* wear out.   3 *form:* course.
4 *plaud:* approval.
5 *Wertenberg:* Wittenberg, city in eastern Germany on the Elbe River. Famous for its
university and as the home of the Reformation.   6 *Whereas:* where.
7 *cunning:* learning.

SCENE 1

[Enter Faustus in his study.]

FAUST. Settle thy studies, Faustus, and begin
  To sound the depth of that thou wilt profess.   30
  Having commenced,[1] be a divine in show;
  Yet level at the end[2] of every art,
  And live and die in Aristotle's works.
  Sweet analytics,[3] 'tis thou hast ravished me!
[Reads.] *"Bene disserere est finis logices."*   35
  Is "to dispute well logic's chiefest end?"
  Affords this art no greater miracle?
  Then read no more; thou hast attained the end.
  A greater subject fitteth Faustus' wit.
  Bid *Oncaymaeon*[4] farewell. *[Puts down Aristotle and takes up*   40
  Galen.][5] Galen, come,
  Seeing *"Ubi desinit Philosophus, ibi incipit Medicus."*[6]
  Be a physician, Faustus, heap up gold,
  And be eternized[7] for some wondrous cure.
[Reads.] *"Summum bonum medicinae sanitas:"*   45
  "The end of physic is our body's health."
  Why, Faustus, hast thou not attained that end?
  Is not thy common talk sound aphorisms?[8]
  Are not thy bills[9] hung up as monuments
  Whereby whole cities have escaped the plague,   50
  And thousand desperate maladies been eased?
  Yet art thou still but Faustus, and a man.
  Wouldst thou make man to live eternally,
  Or, being dead, raise them to life again?
  Then this profession were to be esteemed.   55
  Physic, farewell.—Where is Justinian?[10]

[Puts down Galen, takes up Justinian, and reads.]

---

1 *commenced:* graduated.   2. *level at the end:* aim at the perfection.
3 *analytics:* logic.   4 *Oncaymaeon:* being and not being.
5 *Galen:* Greek physician who settled in Rome (164 A.D.). Of his many treatises on medicine, about 100 are still in existence.
6 *Ubi . . . Medicus:* Where the philosopher leaves off, the physician begins.
7 *eternized:* immortalized.   8 *sound aphorisms:* scientific medical maxims.
9 *bills:* prescriptions.
10 *Justinian:* ruler of the Eastern Roman Empire from 527–565 A.D. He was responsible for preserving in writing Roman laws and statutes.

"Si una eademque res legatur duobus, alter rem, alter valorem rei," [11]
etc.

    A pretty case of paltry legacies!
[Reads.] "Exhaereditare filium non potest pater nisi—" [12]   60
    Such is the subject of the Institute[13]
    And universal Body of the Law.
    Its study fits a mercenary drudge,
    Who aims at nothing but external trash,
    Too servile and illiberal for me.   65
    When all is done, divinity is best.
    Jerome's Bible,[14] Faustus, view it well.

        [Puts down Justinian, takes up the Vulgate, and reads.]

"Stipendium peccati mors est." Ha! *"Stipendium,"* etc.:
    "The reward of sin is death." That's hard.
[Reads.] "Si peccasse negamus, fallimur, et nulla est in nobis veritas:"   70
    "If we say that we have no sin,
    We deceive ourselves, and there's no truth in us."
    Why then, belike,
    We must sin and so consequently die.
    Ay, we must die an everlasting death.   75
    What doctrine call you this? *Che sera, sera:*
    "What will be, shall be." Divinity, adieu!

        [Puts down the Vulgate and takes up his book of magic.]

    These metaphysics of magicians
    And necromantic books are heavenly;
    Lines, circles, scenes, letters, and characters,   80
    Ay, these are those that Faustus most desires.
    O, what a world of profit and delight,
    Of power, of honor, of omnipotence
    Is promised to the studious artisan![15]
    All things that move between the quiet poles   85
    Shall be at my command. Emperors and kings
    Are but obeyed in their several provinces,
    Nor can they raise the wind or rend the clouds;
    But his dominion that exceeds[16] in this
    Stretcheth as far as doth the mind of man.   90
    A sound magician is a mighty god.
    Here, Faustus, try thy brains to gain a deity.—

11 *Si . . . rei:* If one and the same thing is willed to two persons, one gets the thing
and the other its value.
12 *Exhaereditare . . . nisi:* A father cannot disinherit the son unless—
13 *Institute:* textbook for law students compiled under the direction of Justinian.
14 *Jerome's Bible:* St. Jerome's Latin translation of the Bible (the Vulgate).
15 *studious artisan:* liberal arts student.   16 *exceeds:* excels.

[Enter Wagner.]

Wagner! Commend me to my dearest friends,
The German Valdes[17] and Cornelius;[18]
Request them earnestly to visit me.   95
WAG. I will, sir.   *[Exit.]*
FAUST. Their conference will be a greater help to me
Than all my labors, plod I ne'er so fast.

[Enter the Good Angel and the Evil Angel.]

GOOD A. O Faustus, lay that damnéd book aside,
And gaze not on it lest it tempt thy soul,   100
And heap God's heavy wrath upon thy head!
Read, read the Scriptures. That is blasphemy.
EVIL A. Go forward, Faustus, in that famous art
Wherein all Nature's treasury is contained.
Be thou on earth, as Jove is in the sky,   105
Lord and commander of these elements.   *[Exeunt Angels.]*
FAUST. How am I glutted with conceit[19] of this!
Shall I make spirits fetch me what I please,
Resolve me of all ambiguities,[20]
Perform what desperate enterprise I will?   110
I'll have them fly to India[21] for gold,
Ransack the ocean for orient pearl,
And search all corners of the new-found world
For pleasant fruits and princely delicates;
I'll have them read me strange philosophy   115
And tell the secrets of all foreign kings;
I'll have them wall all Germany with brass,
And make swift Rhine circle fair Wertenberg;
I'll have them fill the public schools with silk,
Wherewith the students shall be bravely clad;   120
I'll levy soldiers with the coin they bring,
And chase the Prince of Parma[22] from our land,
And reign sole king of all our provinces;
Yea, stranger engines for the brunt of war
Than was the fiery keel[23] at Antwerp's bridge,   125

---

17 *Valdes:* no such person is known as an associate of the historical Faustus.
18 *Cornelius Agrippa:* a famous scholar associated with the historical Faustus.
19 *conceit:* thought.   20 *ambiguities:* uncertainties.
21 *India:* American Indies.
22 *Prince of Parma:* Spanish Governor-General of the Netherlands 1579–1592. He was interested in bringing large portions of Europe under Spanish rule.
23 *fiery keel:* the burning ship used by the defenders of Antwerp in 1583 to blow up the barrier which Parma had built across the Scheldt River during a blockade of the city.

I'll make my servile spirits to invent.
Come, German Valdes and Cornelius,
And make me blessed with your sage conference.

       [Enter Valdes and Cornelius.]

Valdes, sweet Valdes, and Cornelius,
Know that your words have won me at the last   130
To practice magic and concealéd arts—
Yet not your words only, but mine own fantasy,
That will receive no object,[24] for my head
But ruminates on necromantic skill.
Philosophy is odious and obscure;   135
Both law and physic are for petty wits;
Divinity is basest of the three,
Unpleasant, harsh, contemptible, and vile.
'Tis magic, magic, that hath ravished me!
Then, gentle friends, aid me in this attempt;   140
And I that have with concise syllogisms
Graveled[25] the pastors of the German church,
And made the flow'ring pride of Wertenberg
Swarm to my problems,[26] as the infernal spirits
On sweet Musaeus[27] when he came to hell,   145
Will be as cunning as Agrippa was,
Whose shadows[28] made all Europe honor him.
VALD. Faustus,
These books, thy wit, and our experience
Shall make all nations to canonize us.   150
As Indian Moors[29] obey their Spanish lords,
So shall the subjects[30] of every element
Be always serviceable to us three.
Like lions shall they guard us when we please;
Like Almain rutters[31] with their horsemen's staves,   155
Or Lapland giants, trotting by our sides;
Sometimes like women or unwedded maids,
Shadowing[32] more beauty in their airy brows
Than has the white breasts of the Queen of Love;

---

24 *object:* solid realities   25 *Graveled:* silenced.
26 *problems:* lectures.
27 *Musaeus:* a mythical singer, son of Orpheus; the latter charmed the inhabitants of
hell with his music.
28 *shadows:* Cornelius Agrippa, German author, was credited with being able to call
up the shadows of the dead. The power of Agrippa had become proverbial by
Marlowe's time.   29 *Indian Moors:* dark-skinned American Indians.
30 *subjects:* spirits.   31 *Almain rutters:* German cavalry.
32 *Shadowing:* sheltering.

From Venice shall they drag huge argosies,[33]   160
And from America the golden fleece
That yearly stuffs old Philip's treasury,[34]
If learned Faustus will be resolute.
FAUST. Valdes, as resolute am I in this
As thou to live; therefore object it not.[35]   165
CORN. The miracles that magic will perform
Will make thee vow to study nothing else.
He that is grounded in astrology,
Enriched with tongues, well seen in[36] minerals,
Hath all the principles magic doth require.   170
Then doubt not, Faustus, but to be renowned,
And more frequented for this mystery
Than heretofore the Delphian oracle.
The spirits tell me they can dry the sea,
And fetch the treasure of all foreign wracks,   175
Ay, all the wealth that our forefathers hid
Within the massy entrails of the earth.
Then tell me, Faustus, what shall we three want?
FAUST. Nothing, Cornelius! O, this cheers my soul!
Come, show me some demonstrations magical,   180
That I may conjure in some lusty[37] grove,
And have these joys in full possession.
VALD. Then haste thee to some solitary grove,
And bear wise Bacon's[38] and Albanus'[39] works,
The Hebrew Psalter and New Testament;   185
And whatsoever else is requisite
We will inform thee ere our conference cease.
CORN. Valdes, first let him know the words of art,
And then, all other ceremonies learned,
Faustus may try his cunning by himself.   190
VALD. First I'll instruct thee in the rudiments,
And then wilt thou be perfecter than I.
FAUST. Then come and dine with me, and after meat
We'll canvass every quiddity[40] thereof;
For ere I sleep I'll try what I can do.   195
This night I'll conjure though I die therefor.   *[Exeunt.]*

33 *argosies:* fleets of ships.
34 *Old Philip's treasury:* the treasury of Philip II of Spain.
35 *object it not:* do not oppose it.   36 *well seen in:* well versed in.
37 *lusty:* pleasant.
38 *Bacon's:* Roger Bacon, English philosopher, who was at one time accused of dealing in black magic.
39 *Albanus':* perhaps Pietro d'Albano, an Italian alchemist who lived during the thirteenth century.   40 *quiddity:* essential element.

SCENE 2   *Before Faustus' house.*

[Enter two Scholars.]

1 SCH. I wonder what's become of Faustus that was wont to make our schools ring with *sic probo?*[1]

2 SCH. That shall we know, for see here comes his boy.

[Enter Wagner.]

1 SCH. How now, sirrah! Where's thy master?   200

WAG. God in heaven knows!

2 SCH. Why, dost not thou know?

WAG. Yes, I know. But that follows not.

1 SCH. Go to, sirrah! Leave your jesting, and tell us where he is.

WAG. That follows not necessary by force of argument, that you,   205
being licentiate,[2] should stand upon't; therefore, acknowledge your error and be attentive.

2 SCH. Why, didst thou not say thou knew'st?

WAG. Have you any witness on't?

1 SCH. Yes, sirrah, I heard you.   210

WAG. Ask me fellow if I be a thief.

2 SCH. Well, you will not tell us?

WAG. Yes, sir, I will tell you; yet if you were not dunces, you would never ask me such a question, for is not he *corpus naturale*,[3] and is not that *mobile?*[4] Then wherefore should you ask me such a   215
question? But that I am by nature phlegmatic, slow to wrath, and prone to lechery (to love, I would say), it were not for you to come within forty foot of the place of execution,[5] although I do not doubt to see you both hanged the next sessions. Thus having triumphed over you, I will set my countenance like a precisian,[6] and begin to   220
speak thus: "Truly, my dear brethren, my master is within at dinner with Valdes and Cornelius, as this wine, if it could speak, would inform your worships; and so the Lord bless you, preserve you, and keep you, my dear brethren, my dear brethren."   *[Exit.]*

1 SCH. Nay, then, I fear he has fallen into that damned art for   225
which they two are infamous through the world.

2 SCH. Were he a stranger, and not allied to me, yet should I grieve for him. But come, let us go and inform the rector,[7] and see if he by his grave counsel can reclaim him.

1 SCH. O, but I fear me nothing can reclaim him.   230

2 SCH. Yet let us try what we can do.   *[Exeunt.]*

---

1 *sic probo:* thus I prove.   2 *licentiate:* licensed to teach.
3 *corpus naturale:* natural body.   4 *mobile:* movable.
5 *place of execution:* dining room (where Faustus is eating and drinking).
6 *precisian:* Puritan. The rest of his speech is in the style of the Puritans.
7 *rector:* head of the University.

SCENE 3   *A grove.*

[Enter Faustus to conjure.]

FAUST. Now that the gloomy shadow[1] of the earth,
  Longing to view Orion's drizzling look,[2]
  Leaps from th' antartic world unto the sky,
  And dims the welkin[3] with her pitchy breath,   235
  Faustus, begin thine incantations,
  And try if devils will obey thy hest,[4]
  Seeing thou hast prayed and sacrificed to them.
  Within this circle is Jehovah's name,
  Forward and backward anagrammatized,   240
  The breviated names of holy saints,
  Figures of every adjunct to[5] the heavens,
  And characters of signs and erring[6] stars,
  By which the spirits are enforced to rise.
  Then fear not, Faustus, but be resolute,   245
  And try the uttermost magic can perform.
  Sint mihi Dei Acherontis propitii! Valeat numen triplex Jehovae!
  Ignei, aerii, aquatani spiritus, salvete! Orientis Princeps, Belzebub, in-
  ferni ardentis monarcha, et Demogorgon, propitiamus vos, ut appareat
  et surgat Mephistophilis. Quid tu moraris? Per Jehovam, Gehennam, et   250
  consecratam aquam quam nunc spargo, signumque crucis guod nunc
  facio, et per vota nostra, ipse nunc surgat nobis dicatus Mephis-
  tophilis![7]

[Enter Mephistophilis, a Devil.]

  I charge thee to return and change thy shape;
  Thou art too ugly to attend on me.   255
  Go, and return an old Franciscan friar;
  That holy shape becomes a devil best.

                        [Exit Devil.]

  I see there's virtue in my heavenly words.
  Who would not be proficient in this art?

1 *gloomy shadow:* dark night.
2 *Orion's drizzling look:* Orion appears at the beginning of winter.
3 *welkin:* sky.   4 *hest:* command.   5 *every adjunct to:* every star of.
6 *erring:* wandering.
7 *Sint . . . Mephistophilis:* May the gods of Acheron be propitious to me! Away with
the triple deity of Jehovah! Hail, spirits of fire, air, water! Prince of the East (Lucifer),
Beelzebub, monarch of burning hell, and Demogorgon, we beg you that Mephistophilis may appear and rise. Why do you delay? By Jehovah, Gehenna, and the holy
water which I now sprinkle, and the sign of the cross which I now make, and by our
vows, let Mephistophilis himself now rise, having been called upon by us.

How pliant is this Mephistophilis,   260
Full of obedience and humility!
Such is the force of magic and my spells.
No, Faustus, thou art conjuror laureate,
That canst command great Mephistophilis;
Quin regis, Mephistophilis, fratris imagine. [8]   265

[Enter Mephistophilis as a Franciscan friar.]

MEPH. Now, Faustus, what wouldst thou have me do?
FAUST. I charge thee wait upon me whilst I live,
    To do whatever Faustus shall command,
    Be it to make the moon drop from her sphere,
    Or the ocean to overwhelm the world.   270
MEPH. I am a servant to great Lucifer,
    And may not follow thee without his leave;
    No more than he commands must we perform.
FAUST. Did he not charge thee to appear to me?
MEPH. No, I came now hither of mine own accord.   275
FAUST. Did not my conjuring speeches raise thee? Speak!
MEPH. That was the cause, but yet per accident;
    For, when we hear one rack[9] the name of God,
    Abjure the Scriptures and his Savior Christ,
    We fly in hope to get his glorious soul;   280
    Nor will we come, unless he use such means
    Whereby he is in danger to be damned.
    Therefore the shortest cut for conjuring
    Is stoutly to abjure the Trinity,
    And pray devoutly to the Prince of Hell.   285
FAUST. So Faustus hath
    Already done, and holds this principle:
    There is no chief but only Belzebub,
    To whom Faustus doth dedicate himself.
    This word "damnation" terrifies not him,   290
    For he confounds hell in Elysium.[10]
    His ghost be with the old philosophers![11]
    But, leaving these vain trifles of men's souls,
    Tell me what is that Lucifer, thy lord?
MEPH. Arch-regent and commander of all spirits.   295
FAUST. Was not that Lucifer an angel once?
MEPH. Yes, Faustus, and most dearly loved of God.

8 *Quin . . . imagine:* Indeed, Mephistophilis, you rule in the likeness of a brother
(a friar).   9 *rack:* abuse.
10 *Confounds . . . Elysium:* makes no distinction between hell and paradise.
11 *old philosophers:* Plato, Aristotle, and other pagan philosophers who could not
enter heaven because they had never been baptized.

FAUST. How comes it then that he is prince of devils?
MEPH. O, by aspiring pride and insolence,
  For which God threw him from the face of heaven.   300
FAUST. And what are you that live with Lucifer?
MEPH. Unhappy spirits that fell with Lucifer,
  Conspired against our God with Lucifer,
  And are forever damned with Lucifer,
FAUST. Where are you damned?   305
MEPH. In hell.
FAUST. How comes it then that thou art out of hell?
MEPH. Why, this is hell, nor am I out of it.
  Think'st thou that I who saw the face of God,
  And tasted the eternal joys of heaven,   310
  Am not tormented with ten thousand hells,
  In being deprived of everlasting bliss?
  O Faustus, leave these frivolous demands,
  Which strike a terror to my fainting soul!
FAUST. What, is great Mephistophilis so passionate[12]   315
  For being deprived of the joys of heaven?
  Learn thou of Faustus manly fortitude,
  And scorn those joys thou never shalt possess.
  Go bear those tidings to great Lucifer:
  Seeing Faustus hath incurred eternal death   320
  By desp'rate thoughts against Jove's deity,
  Say he surrenders up to him his soul,
  So he will spare him four-and-twenty years,
  Letting him live in all voluptuousness,
  Having thee ever to attend on me,   325
  To give me whatsoever I shall ask,
  To tell me whatsoever I demand,
  To slay mine enemies, and aid my friends,
  And always be obedient to my will.·
  Go and return to mighty Lucifer,   330
  And meet me in my study at midnight,
  And then resolve[13] me of thy master's mind.
MEPH. I will, Faustus.   *[Exit.]*
FAUST. Had I as many souls as there be stars,
  I'd give them all for Mephistophilis.   335
  By him I'll be great emp'ror of the world,
  And make a bridge through the moving air,
  To pass the ocean with a band of men.
  I'll join the hills that bind the Afric shore,
  And make that land continent to[14] Spain,   340

12 *passionate:* emotional.   13 *resolve:* inform.
14 *continent to:* next to.

And both contributory[15] to my crown.
The emp'ror shall not live but by my leave,
Nor any potentate of Germany.
Now that I have obtained what I desire,
I'll live in speculation[16] of this art   345
Till Mephistophilis return again.   *[Exit.]*

SCENE 4   *A street.*

[Enter Wagner and the Clown.]

WAG. Sirrah boy, come hither.
CLO. How, "boy"? Swowns,[1] "boy"! I hope you have seen many
boys with such pickadevaunts[2] as I have. "Boy," quotha!
WAG. Tell me, sirrah, hast thou any comings-in?[3]   350
CLO. Ay, and goings-out too. You may see else.[4]
WAG. Alas, poor slave! See how poverty[5] jesteth in his nakedness!
The villain is bare and out of service, and so hungry that I know he
would give his soul to the devil for a shoulder of mutton, though it
were blood-raw.   355
CLO. How? My soul to the devil for a shoulder of mutton, though
'twere blood-raw! Not so, good friend. Burladie,[6] I had need have it
well roasted and good sauce to it, if I pay so dear.
WAG. Well, wilt thou serve me, and I'll make thee go like *"Qui
mihi discipulus?"*[7]   360
CLO. How, in verse?
WAG. No, sirrah; in beaten[8] silk and stavesacre.[9]
CLO. How, how, Knave's Acre![10] Ay, I thought that was all the
land his father left him. Do you hear? I would be sorry to rob you
of your living.   365
WAG. Sirrah, I say in stavesacre.

15 *contributory:* subservient.
16 *speculation:* contemplation.
1 *Swowns:* contraction of "God's wounds," used as an oath.
2 *pickadevaunts:* pointed beards.   3 *comings-in:* income
4 *else:* even more.   5 *poverty:* the poor clown.   6 *Burladie:* By Our Lady.
7 *Qui . . . discipulus?* one who is my pupil?
8 *beaten:* stamped and embroidered.
9 *stavesacre:* larkspur (plant used for killing lice).
10 *Knave's Acre:* name of a low street in London, where junk-dealers were established.

CLO. Oho! Oho! Stavesacre! Why, then, belike[11] if I were your man I should be full of vermin.

WAG. So thou shalt, whether thou beest with me or no. But, sirrah, leave your jesting, and bind yourself presently[12] unto me for seven years, or I'll turn all the lice about thee into familiars,[13] and they shall tear thee in pieces.   370

CLO. Do you hear, sir? You may save that labor; they are too familiar with me already. Swowns! They are as bold with my flesh as if they had paid for my meat and drink.   375

WAG. Well, do you hear, sirrah? Hold, take these guilders.[14]

[Gives money.]

CLO. Gridirons! What be they?

WAG. Why, French crowns.

CLO. Mass,[15] but for the name of French crowns, a man were as good have[16] as many English counters.[17] And what should I do with these?   380

WAG. Why, now, sirrah, thou art at an hour's warning, whensoever and wheresoever the devil shall fetch thee.

CLO. No, no. Here, take your gridirons again.

WAG. Truly, I'll none of them.   385

CLO. Truly, but you shall.

WAG. Bear witness I gave them him.

CLO. Bear witness I give them you again.

WAG. Well, I will cause two devils presently to fetch thee away— Baliol and Belcher.   390

CLO. Let your Balio and your Belcher come here, and I'll knock them, they were never so knocked since they were devils. Say I should kill one of them, what would folks say? "Do you see yonder tall fellow in the round slop?[18] He has killed the devil." So I should be called Kill-devil all the parish over.   395

[Enter two Devils; the Clown runs up and down crying.]

WAG. Baliol and Belcher! Spirits, away!   *[Exeunt Devils.]*

CLO. What, are they gone? A vengeance on them, they have vile long nails! There was a he-devil and a she-devil! I'll tell you how you

---

11 *belike:* it seems.   12 *presently:* at once.   13 *familiars:* attendant spirits.
14 *guilders:* Dutch coins.   15 *Mass:* by the Mass, a mild oath.
16 *were as good have:* might as well have.
17 *counters:* a contemptuous term for money, sometimes even for an imitation coin. Thus the Clown is saying that the French coins (which had become very numerous in England) were worth no more than English counters. The humor of the entire passage is based on the Clown's misunderstanding of words, that is *stavesacre* for *Knave's Acre*, *guilders* for *gridirons*, etc.   18 *round slop:* wide breeches.

shall know them: all he-devils has horns, and all she-devils has
clefts and cloven feet.   400

WAG. Well, sirrah, follow me.

CLO. But, do you hear—if I should serve you, would you teach
me to raise up Banios and Belcheos?

WAG. I will teach thee to turn thyself to anything—to a dog, or a
cat, or a mouse, or a rat, or anything.   405

CLO. How? A Christian fellow to a dog or a cat, a mouse or a rat?
No, no, sir. If you turn me into anything, let it be in the likeness of
a little pretty frisking flea, that I may be here and there and everywhere. O, I'll tickle the pretty wenches' plackets;[19] I'll be amongst
them, i' faith.   410

WAG. Well, sirrah, come.

CLO. But, do you hear, Wagner?

WAG. How!—Baliol and Belcher!

CLO. O Lord! I pray, sir, let Banio and Belcher go sleep.

WAG. Villain, call me Master Wagner, and let thy left eye be   415
diametarily[20] fixed upon my right heel, with *quasi vestigias nostras
insistere.*[21]   [*Exit.*]

CLO. God forgive me, he speaks Dutch fustian.[22] Well, I'll follow
him; I'll serve him; that's flat.   [*Exit.*]

SCENE 5

[Enter Faustus in his study.]

FAUST. Now, Faustus, must thou needs be damned,   420
     And canst thou not be saved.
     What boots it then to think of God or heaven?
     Away with such vain fancies, and despair.
     Despair in God, and trust in Belzebub.
     Now go not backward; no, Faustus, be resolute.   425
     Why waverest thou? O, something soundeth in mine ears:
     "Abjure this magic; turn to God again!"
     Ay, and Faustus will turn to God again.
     To God?—He loves thee not.
     The God thou servest is thine own appetite,   430
     Wherein is fixed the love of Belzebub.

19 *plackets:* slits in women's petticoats.   20 *diametarily:* directly.
21 *quasi . . . insistere:* as if to tread in our tracks.
22 *fustian:* nonsense.

To him I'll build an altar and a church,
And offer lukewarm blood of newborn babes.

[Enter Good Angel and Evil.]

GOOD A. Sweet Faustus, leave that execrable art!
FAUST. Contrition, prayer, repentance! What of them? 435
GOOD A. O, they are means to bring thee unto heaven.
EVIL A. Rather illusions, fruits of lunacy,
  That makes men foolish that do trust them most.
GOOD A. Sweet Faustus, think of heaven and heavenly things.
EVIL A. No, Faustus, think of honor and of wealth! 440

                                [Exeunt Angels.]

FAUST. Of wealth!
  Why, the signiory¹ of Emden² shall be mine.
  When Mephistophilis shall stand by me,
  What God can hurt thee, Faustus? Thou art safe;
  Cast no more doubts. Come, Mephistophilis, 445
  And bring glad tidings from great Lucifer.
  Is't not midnight? Come, Mephistophilis;
  *Veni,*³ *veni, Mephistophile!*

[Enter Mephistophilis.]

  Now tell me, what says Lucifer, thy lord?
MEPH. That I shall wait on Faustus whilst he lives, 450
  So he will buy my service with his soul.
FAUST. Already Faustus hath hazarded that for thee.
MEPH. But, Faustus, thou must bequeath it solemnly,
  And write a deed of gift with thine own blood,
  For that security craves great Lucifer. 455
  If thou deny it, I will back to hell.
FAUST. Stay, Mephistophilis, and tell me what good
  Will my soul do thy lord.
MEPH.   Enlarge his kingdom.
FAUST. Is that the reason he tempts us thus?
MEPH. *Solamen miseris socios habuisse doloris.*⁴ 460
FAUST. Have you any pain that tortures others?
MEPH. As great as have the human souls of men.
  But tell me, Faustus, shall I have thy soul?
  And I will be thy slave, and wait on thee,
  And give thee more than thou hast wit to ask. 465
FAUST. Ay, Mephistophilis, I give it thee.
MEPH. Then stab thine arm courageously,

---

1 *signiory:* dominion.   2 *Emden:* Seaport city in northern Germany.
3 *Veni:* come!
4 *Solamen . . . doloris:* 'Tis a solace to the miserable to have had company in sorrow.

And bind thy soul that at some certain day
Great Lucifer may claim it as his own;
And then be thou as great as Lucifer.   470
FAUST. *[Stabbing his arm.]* Lo, Mephistophilis, for love of thee
I cut mine arm, and with my proper⁵ blood
Assure my soul to be great Lucifer's,
Chief lord and regent of perpetual night!
View here the blood that trickles from mine arm,   475
And let it be propitious for my wish.
MEPH. But, Faustus, thou must
Write it in manner of a deed of gift.
FAUST. Ay, so I will. *[Writes.]* But, Mephistophilis,
My blood congeals, and I can write no more.   480
MEPH. I'll fetch thee fire to dissolve it straight.   *[Exit.]*
FAUST. What might the staying of my blood portend?
Is it unwilling I should write this bill?
Why streams it not that I may write afresh?
"Faustus gives to thee his soul." Ah, there it stayed.   485
Why shouldst thou not? Is not thy soul thine own?
Then write again, "Faustus gives to thee his soul."

[Enter Mephistophilis with a chafer⁶ of coals.]

MEPH. Here's fire. Come, Faustus, set it on.
FAUST. So now the blood begins to clear again;
Now will I make an end immediately.   *[Writes.]*   490
MEPH. *[Aside.]* O, what will not I do to obtain his soul?
FAUST. *Consummatum est:*⁷ this bill is ended,
And Faustus hath bequeathed his soul to Lucifer.
But what is this inscription on mine arm?
*"Homo, fuge!"*⁸ Whither should I fly?   495
If unto God, he'll throw me down to hell.
My senses are deceived; here's nothing writ.
I see it plain; here in this place is writ,
"Homo, fuge!" Yet shall not Faustus fly.
MEPH. I'll fetch him somewhat to delight his mind.   *[Exit.]* 500

*[Enter Mephistophilis with Devils, giving crowns and rich apparel
to Faustus, dance, and then depart.]*

FAUST. Speak, Mephistophilis, what means this show?
MEPH. Nothing, Faustus, but to delight thy mind withal,
And to show thee what magic can perform.

---

5 *proper:* own.   6 *chafer:* a portable grate.
7 *Consummatum est:* Faustus blasphemously parodies Christ's final words on the
cross, "It is consummated."   8 *Homo, fuge!* Man, fly!

FAUST. But may I raise up spirits when I please?
MEPH. Ay, Faustus, and do greater things than these.　　　505
FAUST. Then there's enough for a thousand souls.
　Here, Mephistophilis, receive this scroll,
　A deed of gift of body and of soul—
　But yet conditionally that thou perform
　All articles prescribed between us both.　　　510
MEPH. Faustus, I swear by hell and Lucifer
　To effect all promises between us made.
　　FAUST. Then hear me read them: "On these conditions following:
—First, that Faustus may be a spirit in form and substance; secondly,
that Mephistophilis shall be his servant, and at his command;　　　515
thirdly, that Mephistophilis shall do for him and bring him whatsoever;[9] fourthly, that he shall be in his chamber or house invisible;
lastly, that he shall appear to the said John Faustus, at all times, in
what form or shape soever he please—I, John Faustus, of Wertenberg, Doctor, by these presents do give both body and soul to　　　520
Lucifer, Prince of the East, and his minister, Mephistophilis; and
furthermore grant unto them that, twenty-four years being expired,
the articles above written inviolate, full power to fetch or carry the
said John Faustus, body and soul, flesh, blood, or goods, into their
habitation wheresoever. By me, John Faustus."　　　525
MEPH. Speak, Faustus, do you deliver this as your deed?
FAUST. Ay, take it, and the devil give thee good on't.[10]
MEPH. Now, Faustus, ask what thou wilt.
FAUST. First will I question with thee about hell.
　Tell me, where is the place that men call hell?　　　530
MEPH. Under the heavens.
FAUST.　　　　　　　　　　Ay, but whereabout?
MEPH. Within the bowels of these elements,
　Where we are tortured and remain forever.
　Hell hath no limits, nor is circumscribed
　In one self[11] place, for where we are is hell,　　　535
　And where hell is there must we ever be;
　And, to conclude, when all the world dissolves,
　And every creature shall be purified,
　All places shall be hell that is not heaven.
FAUST. Come, I think hell's a fable.　　　540
MEPH. Ay, think so still, till experience change thy mind.
FAUST. Why, think'st thou then that Faustus shall be damned?
MEPH. Ay, of necessity, for here's the scroll
　Wherein thou hast given thy soul to Lucifer.
FAUST. Ay, and body too; but what of that?　　　545

9 *whatsoever:* anything.　　10 *on't:* for it.　　11 *one self:* one

Think'st thou that Faustus is so fond[12] to imagine
That, after this life, there is any pain?
Tush, these are trifles, and mere old wives' tales.
MEPH. But, Faustus, I am an instance to prove the contrary,
For I am damnéd, and am now in hell.   550
FAUST. How? Now in hell? Nay, if this be hell, I'll willingly be
damned here. What? Walking, disputing, etc.? But, leaving off this,
let me have a wife, the fairest maid in Germany, for I am wanton
and lascivious, and cannot live without a wife.
MEPH. How? A wife? I prithee, Faustus, talk not of a wife.   555
FAUST. Nay, sweet Mephistophilis, fetch me one, for I will have
one.
MEPH. Well—thou wilt have one. Sit there till I come. I'll fetch
thee a wife in the devil's name.   *[Exit.]*

[Enter with a Devil dressed like a woman, with fireworks.]

MEPH. Tell, Faustus, how dost thou like thy wife?   560
FAUST. A plague on her for a hot whore!
MEPH.   Tut, Faustus,
   Marriage is but a ceremonial toy;
   If thou lovest me, think no more of it.
   I'll cull thee out the fairest courtesans,
   And bring them every morning to thy bed.   565
   She whom thine eye shall like, thy heart shall have,
   Be she as chaste as was Penelope[13]
   As wise as Saba,[14] or as beautiful
   As was bright Lucifer before his fall.
   Hold, take this book; peruse it thoroughly.   *[Gives him a book.]* 570
   The iterating[15] of these lines brings gold;
   The framing of this circle on the ground
   Brings whirlwinds, tempests, thunder, and lightning;
   Pronounce this thrice devoutly to thyself,
   And men in armor shall appear to thee,   575
   Ready to execute what thou desir'st.
FAUST. Thanks, Mephistophilis; yet fain would I have a book
wherein I might behold all spells and incantations, that I might raise
up spirits when I please.
MEPH. Here they are, in this book.   *[Turns to them.]*   580
FAUST. Now would I have a book where I might see all characters
and planets of the heavens, that I might know their motions and
dispositions.[16]

12 *fond:* foolish.
13 *Penelope:* beautiful and faithful wife of Ulysses.
14 *Saba:* Queen of Sheba.   15 *iterating:* repeating.
16 *dispositions:* relative positions.

MEPH. Here they are too.   *[Turns to them.]*

FAUST. Nay, let me have one book more—and then I have done   585
—wherein I might see all plants, herbs, and trees that grow upon
the earth.

MEPH. Here they be.

FAUST. O, thou art deceived.[17]

MEPH. Tut, I warrant[18] thee.   *[Turns to them.]*   590
                                         [Exeunt.]

SCENE 6   *The same.*

[Enter Faustus in his study and Mephistophilis.]

FAUST. When I behold the heavens, then I repent,
   And curse thee, wicked Mephistophilis,
   Because thou hast deprived me of those joys.

MEPH. Why, Faustus,
   Think'st thou heaven is such a glorious thing?   595
   I tell thee 'tis not half so fair as thou,
   Or any man that breathes on earth.

FAUST. How provest thou that?

MEPH. It was made for man; therefore is man more excellent.

FAUST. If it were made for man, 'twas made for me;   600
   I will renounce this magic and repent.

         [Enter Good Angel and Evil Angel.]

GOOD A. Faustus, repent; yet God will pity thee.

EVIL A. Thou art a spirit;[1] God cannot pity thee.

FAUST. Who buzzeth in mine ears I am a spirit?
   Be I a devil, yet God may pity me;   605
   Ay, God will pity me if I repent.

EVIL A. Ay, but Faustus never shall repent.   *[Exeunt Angels.]*

FAUST. My heart's so hardened I cannot repent.
   Scarce can I name salvation, faith, or heaven,
   But fearful echoes thunders in mine ears,   610
   "Faustus, thou art damned!" Then swords and knives,
   Poison, guns, halters, and envenomed steel
   Are laid before me to despatch myself,
   And long ere this I should have slain myself,

17 *deceived:* deceiving me.
18 *warrant:* guarantee.
1 *spirit:* evil spirit, devil (*spirit* generally has this meaning in Marlowe).

Had not sweet pleasure conquered deep despair, 615
Have not I made blind Homer sing to me
Of Alexander's love and Oenon's death?[2]
And hath not he that built the walls of Thebes
With ravishing sound of his melodious harp[3]
Made music with my Mephistophilis? 620
Why should I die then, or basely despair?
I am resolved: Faustus shall ne'er repent.
Come, Mephistophilis, let us dispute again,
And argue of divine astrology.
Tell me, are there many heavens above the moon? 625
Are all celestial bodies but one globe,[4]
As is the substance of this centric earth?[5]

MEPH. As are the elements, such are the spheres
Mutually folded in each other's orb,
And, Faustus, 630
All jointly move upon one axletree[6]
Whose terminine is termed[7] the world's wide pole;
Nor are the names of Saturn, Mars, or Jupiter
Feigned,[8] but are erring[9] stars.

FAUST. But tell me, have they all one motion, both *situ et tempore?*[10] 635

MEPH. All jointly move from east to west in four-and-twenty hours
upon the poles of the world, but differ in their motion upon the
poles of the zodiac.

FAUST. Tush, these slender trifles Wagner can decide.
Hath Mephistophilis no greater skill? 640
Who knows not the double motion of the planets?
The first is finished in a natural day; the second thus: as Saturn
in thirty years; Jupiter in twelve; Mars in four; the sun, Venus, and
Mercury in a year; the moon in eight-and-twenty days. Tush, these

---

2 Paris of Troy, also called Alexander, son of Priam, married Oenon, whom he
deserted. He went to Sparta where he carried off Helen, the wife of Menelaus. The
Trojan war followed when Menelaus attacked Troy.
3 Amphion, son of Zeus and Antiope, built a wall around Thebes, charming the
stones into place with a lyre.
4 Faustus asks whether all the apparently different celestial bodies form really one
globe, like the earth. Mephistophilis answers that like the elements, which are
separate but combined, the heavenly bodies are separate, though their spheres are
infolded, and they move on one axle.
5 *centric earth:* earth, which comprises the center of the universe.
6 *axletree:* fixed axle or pole upon which the earth and spheres supposedly turn.
7 *termine is termed:* end is called.   8 *Feigned:* fictitious.   9 *erring:* wandering.
10 *situ et tempore:* in position and time, that is, in the direction of their movements
and the time they take to move around the earth.

are freshmen's suppositions. But tell me, hath every sphere a   645
dominion or intelligentia? [11]

MEPH. Ay.

FAUST. How many heavens, or spheres, are there?

MEPH. Nine: the seven planets, the firmament, and the imperial
heaven.   650

FAUST. Well, resolve me in this question: Why have we not
conjunctions, oppositions, aspects, eclipses, all at one time, but in
some years we have more, in some less?

MEPH. *Per inaequalem motum respectu totius.* [12]

FAUST. Well, I am answered. Tell me who made the world.   655

MEPH. I will not.

FAUST. Sweet Mephistophilis, tell me.

MEPH. Move me not, for I will not tell thee.

FAUST. Villain, have I not bound thee to tell me anything?

MEPH. Ay, that is not against our kingdom; but this is.   660
   Think thou on hell, Faustus, for thou art damned.

FAUST. Think, Faustus, upon God that made the world.

MEPH. Remember this.   *[Exit.]*

FAUST. Ay, go, accurséd spirit, to ugly hell.
   'Tis thou hast damned distresséd Faustus' soul.   665
   Is't not too late?

               [Enter Good Angel and Evil Angel.]

EVIL A. Too late.

GOOD A. Never too late, if Faustus can repent.

EVIL A. If thou repent, devils shall tear thee in pieces.

GOOD A. Repent, and they shall never rase [13] thy skin.   670

                                    [Exeunt Angels.]

FAUST. Ah, Christ, my Savior,
   Seek to save distresséd Faustus' soul!

          [Enter Lucifer, Belzebub, and Mephistophilis.]

LUC. Christ cannot save thy soul, for he is just;
   There's none but I have int'rest in the same.

FAUST. O, who art thou that look'st so terrible?   675

LUC. I am Lucifer,
   And this is my companion prince in hell.

FAUST. O Faustus, they are come to fetch away thy soul!

LUC. We come to tell thee thou dost injure us.
   Thou talk'st of Christ, contrary to thy promise;   680
   Thou shouldst not think of God. Think of the devil,
   And of his dame, too.

---

11 *intelligentia:* intelligence; each planet was thought to have a ruling spirit or angel.
12 *Per . . . totius:* Because of their uneven motion with respect to the whole.
13 *rase:* scratch.

FAUST. Nor will I henceforth. Pardon me in this,
And Faustus vows never to look to heaven,
Never to name God, or to pray to him;   685
To burn his Scriptures, slay his ministers,
And make my spirits pull his churches down.
LUC. Do so, and we will highly gratify thee. Faustus, we are come
from hell to show thee some pastime. Sit down, and thou shalt see
all the Seven Deadly Sins appear in their proper shapes.   690
FAUST. That sight will be as pleasing unto me
As paradise was to Adam the first day
Of his creation.
LUC. Talk not of paradise nor creation, but mark this show. Talk
of the devil, and nothing else.—Come away!   695

[Enter the Seven Deadly Sins.]

Now, Faustus, examine them of their several names and dispositions.
FAUST. What art thou, the first?
PRIDE. I am Pride. I disdain to have any parents. I am like to
Ovid's flea:[14] I can creep into every corner of a wench. Sometimes,
like a periwig, I sit upon her brow; or, like a fan of feathers, I kiss   700
her lips; indeed I do—what do I not? But, fie, what a scent is here!
I'll not speak another word except the ground were perfumed, and
covered with cloth of arras.[15]
FAUST. What art thou, the second?
COVET. I am Covetousness, begotten of an old churl in an old   705
leathern bag; and, might I have my wish, I would desire that this
house and all the people in it were turned to gold, that I might lock
you up in my good chest. O, my sweet gold!
FAUST. What art thou, the third?
WRATH. I am Wrath. I had neither father nor mother. I leaped   710
out of a lion's mouth when I was scarce half an hour old and, ever
since, I have run up and down the world with this case of rapiers,
wounding myself when I had nobody to fight withal. I was born in
hell; and look to it, for some of you shall be my father.
FAUST. What art thou, the fourth?   715
ENVY. I am Envy, begotten of a chimney sweeper and an oyster
wife. I cannot read, and therefore wish all books were burnt. I am
lean with seeing others eat. O, that there would come a famine
through all the world, that all might die, and I live alone! Then thou
shouldst see how fat I would be. But must thou sit and I stand?   720
Come down with a vengeance!
FAUST. Away, envious rascal!—What art thou, the fifth?
GLUT. Who, I, sir? I am Gluttony. My parents are all dead, and
the devil a penny they have left me but a bare pension, and that is

---

14 A reference to the anonymous obscene Latin poem "Song about a Flea," which
during the Renaissance was falsely thought to be Ovid's.
15 *cloth of arras:* cloth woven in Arras, Flanders.

thirty meals a day and ten bevers[16]—a small trifle to suffice nature. 725
O, I come of a royal parentage! My grandfather was a Gammon of
Bacon, my grandmother a Hogshead of Claret Wine. My god-
fathers were these—Peter Pickleherring and Martin Martlemas-beef.
O, but my godmother she was a jolly gentlewoman, and well be-
loved in every good town and city. Her name was Mistress Margery 730
Marchbeer. Now, Faustus, thou hast heard all my progeny,[17] wilt
thou bid me to supper?

FAUST. No, I'll see thee hanged; thou wilt eat up all my victuals.

GLUT. Then the devil choke thee!

FAUST. Choke thyself, glutton!—What art thou, the sixth? 735

SLOTH. I am Sloth. I was begotten on a sunny bank, where I have
lain ever since; and you have done me great injury to bring me from
thence. Let me be carried thither again by Gluttony and Lechery. I'll
not speak another word for a king's ransom.

FAUST. What are you, Mistress Minx, the seventh and last? 740

LECH. Who, I, sir? I am one that loves an inch of raw mutton[18]
better than an ell[19] of fried stockfish; and the first letter of my name
begins with Lechery.

LUC. Away to hell, to hell!   *[Exeunt the Sins.]*

Now, Faustus, how dost thou like this? 745

FAUST. O, this feeds my soul!

LUC. Tut, Faustus, in hell is all manner of delight.

FAUST. O, might I see hell, and return again,
How happy were I then!

LUC. Thou shalt; I will send for thee at midnight. 750
In meantime take this book; peruse it throughly,
And thou shalt turn thyself into what shape thou wilt.

FAUST. Great thanks, mighty Lucifer!
This will I keep as chary as my life.

LUC. Farewell, Faustus, and think on the devil. 755

FAUST. Farewell, great Lucifer! Come, Mephistophilis.

                                        [Exeunt.]

CHORUS

[Enter Wagner alone.]

WAG. Learned Faustus,
To know the secrets of astronomy

---

16 *bevers:* between meal snacks.
17 *progeny:* ancestry.
18 *mutton:* in addition to the literal meaning, the term in Elizabethan slang meant
prostitute.
19 *ell:* a measurement of 45 inches.

Graven in the book of Jove's high firmament,
Did mount himself to scale Olympus' top,   760
Being seated in a chariot burning bright,
Drawn by the strength of yoky dragons' necks.
He now is gone to prove cosmography,[20]
And, as I guess, will first arrive at Rome,
To see the pope and manner of his court,   765
And take some part of holy Peter's feast,
That to this day is highly solemnized.   *[Exit Wagner.]*

SCENE 7   *The Pope's privy chamber.*

[Enter Faustus and Mephistophilis.]

FAUST. Having now, my good Mephistophilis,
  Passed with delight the stately town of Trier,[1]
  Environed round with airy mountain tops,   770
  With walls of flint, and deep entrenchéd lakes,[2]
  Not to be won by any conquering prince,
  From Paris next, coasting[3] the realm of France,
  We saw the river Maine fall into Rhine,
  Whose banks are set with groves of fruitful vines;   775
  Then up to Naples, rich Campania,
  Whose buildings fair and gorgeous to the eye,
  The streets straight forth, and paved with finest brick,
  Quarters the town in four equivalents.
  There saw we learned Maro's[4] golden tomb,   780
  The way he cut, an English mile in length,
  Thorough a rock of stone in one night's space;
  From thence to Venice, Padua, and the rest,
  In midst of which a sumptuous temple stands,
  That threats the stars with her aspiring top.   785
  Thus hitherto hath Faustus spent his time.
  But tell me, now, what resting place is this?
  Hast thou, as erst[5] I did command,
  Conducted me within the walls of Rome?

20 *cosmography:* science which describes and maps the main features of the heavens and the earth.
1 *Trier:* ancient German city on the Moselle River, now Treves.
2 *entrenchéd lakes:* moats.   3 *coasting:* skirting.
4 *Maro's:* Virgil's. In the Middle Ages Virgil was thought to have been a magician.
5 *erst:* first.

MEPH. Faustus, I have; and, because we will not be unprovided, I   790
have taken up his holiness' privy chamber for our use.
    FAUST. I hope his holiness will bid us welcome.
MEPH. Tut, 'tis no matter, man; we'll be bold with his good cheer.
    And now, my Faustus, that thou mayst perceive
    What Rome containeth to delight thee with,   795
    Know that this city stands upon seven hills
    That underprops the groundwork of the same.
    Just through the midst runs flowing Tiber's stream,
    With winding banks that cut it in two parts,
    Over the which four stately bridges lean,   800
    That makes safe passage to each part of Rome.
    Upon the bridge called Ponto Angelo,
    Erected is a castle passing strong,
    Within whose walls such store of ordonance are,
    And double cannons, framed of carvéd brass,   805
    As match the days within one complete year,
    Besides the gates and high pyramides,
    Which Julius Caesar brought from Africa.
FAUST. Now by the kingdoms of infernal rule,
    Of Styx, Acheron, and the fiery lake   810
    Of ever-burning Phlegeton,[6] I swear
    That I do long to see the monuments
    And situation of bright, splendent Rome.
    Come therefore; let's away.
MEPH. Nay, Faustus, stay; I know you'd fain see the pope,   815
    And take some part of holy Peter's feast,
    Where thou shalt see a troop of baldpate friars,
    Whose *summum bonum*[7] is in belly-cheer.
FAUST. Well, I am content to compass then some sport,
    And by their folly make us merriment.   820
    Then charm me, that I may be invisible, to do what I please,
    Unseen of any whilst I stay in Rome.
MEPH. *[Charming him.]* So, Faustus, now
    Do what thou wilt; thou shalt not be discerned.

*[Sound a sennet.[8] Enter the Pope and the Cardinal of Lorrain to the banquet,
with Friars attending.]*

POPE. My Lord of Lorrain, wilt please you draw near?   825
FAUST. Fall to, and the devil choke you, and you spare![9]
POPE. How now! Who's that which spake?—Friars, look about.
FRIAR. Here's nobody, if it like your holiness.

6 *Styx, Acheron, . . . Phlegeton:* mythological rivers of the underworld.
7 *summum bonum:* highest good.   8 *sennet:* fanfare of trumpets.
9 *and you spare:* if you leave.

POPE. My lord, here is a dainty dish was sent me from the Bishop
of Milan. 830

FAUST. I thank you, sir. *[Snatches it.]*

POPE. How now! Who's that which snatched the meat from me?
Will no man look? My lord, this dish was sent me from the Cardinal
of Florence.

FAUST. You say true; I'll ha't. *[Snatches it.]* 835

POPE. What, again? My lord, I'll drink to your grace.

FAUST. I'll pledge your graces. *[Snatches the cup.]*

LOR. My lord, it may be some ghost newly crept out of purgatory,
come to beg a pardon of your holiness.

POPE. It may be so. Friars, prepare a dirge to lay the fury of this 840
ghost. Once again, my lord, fall to. *[The Pope crosses himself.]*

FAUST. What, are you crossing of yourself?
Well, use that trick no more, I would advise you.

[Crosses again.]

Well, there's the second time. Aware[10] the third,
I give you fair warning. 845

[Crosses again, and Faustus hits him a box of the ear; and they all run away.]

FAUST. Come on, Mephistophilis, what shall we do?

MEPH. Nay, I know not. We shall be cursed with bell, book, and
candle.[11]

FAUST. How? Bell, book, and candle; candle, book, and bell—
Forward and backward to curse Faustus to hell! 850
Anon you shall hear a hog grunt, a calf bleat, and an ass bray, be-
cause it is Saint Peter's holiday.[12]

[Enter all the Friars to sing the dirge.]

[Friars sing.]

FRIAR. Come, brethren, let's about our business with good devotion.
Cursed be he that stole away his holiness' meat from the table!
Maledicat Dominus![13] 855
Cursed be he that struck his holiness a blow on the face! *Male-
dicat Dominus!*
Cursed be he that took Friar Sandelo a blow on the pate! *Male,
etc.*
Cursed be he that disturbeth our holy dirge! *Male., etc.* 860

---

10 *Aware:* beware.
11 *bell . . . candle:* at the close of the excommunication ceremony the bell was tolled,
the book closed, and the candle extinguished.
12 You shall hear a hog grunt (because of gluttony), a calf bleat (the calf was thought
of as a silly dolt), and an ass bray (the ass represented a type of stupidity). All of this
will be heard from the Pope and the three friars as he excommunicates them on his
holiday (February 14).
13 *Maledicat Dominus:* May the Lord curse him.

Cursed be he that took away his holiness' wine! *Maledicat Domi-nus! Et omnes sancti!*[14] *Amen.*

[Mephistophilis and Faustus beat the Friars, and fling fireworks among them, and so exeunt.]

[Enter Chorus.]

When Faustus had with pleasure ta'en the view
Of rarest things and royal courts of kings,
He stayed his course, and so returnéd home,   865
Where such as bear his absence but with grief—
I mean his friends and nearest companions—
Did gratulate[15] his safety with kind words,
And in their conference of what befell,
Touching his journey through the world and air,   870
They put forth questions of astrology,
Which Faustus answered with such learned skill,
As they admired and wondered at his wit.
Now is his fame spread forth in every land.
Amongst the rest the emperor is one,   875
Carolus the Fifth,[16] at whose palace now
Faustus is feasted 'mongst his noblemen.
What there he did in trial of his art,
I leave untold—your eyes shall see performed.   *[Exit.]*

SCENE 8   *An innyard.*

[Enter Robin the Ostler with a book in his hand.]

ROBIN. O, this is admirable! Here I ha' stolen one of Doctor   880
Faustus' conjuring books, and i' faith I mean to search some circles
for my own use. *[Draws circles on the ground.]* Now will I make all
the maidens in our parish dance at my pleasure, stark naked before
me; and so by that means I shall see more than e'er I felt or saw yet.

[Enter Rafe,[1] calling Robin.]

RAFE. Robin, prithee come away. There's a gentleman tarries to   885
have his horse, and he would have his things rubbed and made

14 *Et . . . sancti:* And all the saints.   15 *gratulate:* express joy at.
16 *Carolus the Fifth:* Charles V, Holy Roman emperor from 1519 to 1556, when he
retired to a monastery.
1 *Rafe:* Ralf.

clean. He keeps such a chafing[2] with my mistress about it, and she has sent me to look thee out. Prithee come away.

ROBIN. Keep out, keep out, or else you are blown up; you are dismembered, Rafe! Keep out, for I am about a roaring piece of work.   890

RAFE. Come, what doest thou with that same book thou canst not read?

ROBIN. Yes, my master and mistress shall find that I can read, he for his forehead,[3] she for her private study. She's born to bear with me, or else my art fails.   895

RAFE. Why, Robin, what book is that?

ROBIN. What book? Why, the most intolerable book for conjuring that e'er was invented by any brimstone devil.

RAFE. Canst thou conjure with it?

ROBIN. I can do all these things easily with it; first, I can make thee drunk with ippocras[4] at any tabern in Europe for nothing; that's one of my conjuring works.   900

RAFE. Our Master Parson says that's nothing.

ROBIN. True, Rafe. And more, Rafe, if thou has any mind to Nan Spit, our kitchenmaid, then turn her and wind her to thy own use as often as thou wilt, and at midnight.   905

RAFE. O brave Robin, shall I have Nan Spit, and to mine own use? On that condition I'll feed thy devil with horse bread as long as he lives, of free cost.

ROBIN. No more, sweet Rafe. Let's go and make clean our boots, which lie foul upon our hands, and then to our conjuring in the devil's name.   *[Exeunt.]*   910

SCENE 9   *The same.*

[Enter Robin and Rafe with a silver goblet.]

ROBIN. Come, Rafe, did not I tell thee we were forever made by this Doctor Faustus' book? *Ecce signum.*[1] Here's a simple purchase[2] for horse keepers; our horses shall eat no hay as long as this lasts.   915

[Enter the Vintner.[3]]

---

2 *chafing:* fussing.
3 *forehead:* allusion to horns which were supposed to grow on a husband whose wife was unfaithful.   4 *ippocras:* sweet, spiced wine.
1 *Ecce signum:* behold the sign.
2 *purchase:* prize.
3 *Vintner:* wine merchant.

RAFE. But, Robin, here comes the Vintner.

ROBIN. Hush! I'll gull[4] him supernaturally. Drawer,[5] I hope all is paid. God be with you! Come, Rafe.

VINT. Soft, sir; a word with you. I must yet have a goblet paid from you ere you go.   920

ROBIN. I a goblet? Rafe, I a goblet? I scorn you, and you are but a &c.[6] I a goblet? Search me!

VINT. I mean so, sir, with your favor.   *[Searches him.]*

ROBIN. How say you now?

VINT. I must say somewhat to your fellow. You, sir!   925

RAFE. Me, sir? Me, sir? Search your fill. *[Vintner searches him.]* Now, sir, you may be ashamed to burden honest men with a matter of truth.[7]

VINT. Well, t'one of you hath this goblet about you.

ROBIN. *[Aside.]* You lie, drawer, 'tis afore me.—Sirrah you, I'll   930
teach ye to impeach honest men! Stand by! I'll scour you for a goblet! Stand aside you had best, I charge you in the name of Belzebub.— *[Aside to Rafe.]* Look to the goblet, Rafe.

VINT. What mean you, sirrah?

ROBIN. I'll tell you what I mean. *[He reads.]* Sanctobulorum[8]   935
Periphrasticon!—Nay, I'll tickle you, Vintner.— *[Aside.]* Look to the goblet, Rafe.—*Polypragmos Belseborams framanto pacostiphos tostu, Mephistophilis, etc.*

[Enter Mephistophilis, sets squibs[9] at their backs and then exit. They run about.]

VINT. O, *nomine Domine!*[10] What mean'st thou, Robin, thou hast no goblet?   940

RAFE. *Peccatum peccatorum!*[11] Here's thy goblet, good Vintner.
                    [Gives goblet to Vintner. Exit Vintner.]

ROBIN. *Misericordia pro nobis!*[12] What shall I do? Good devil, forgive me now, and I'll never rob thy library more.

[Enter to them Mephistophilis.]

MEPH. Monarch of hell, under whose black survey
    Great potentates do kneel with awful fear,   945
    Upon whose altars thousand souls do lie,

---

4 *gull:* trick.

5 *Drawer:* one who draws liquor; a tapster in a tavern.

6 *&c:* At this point the lines are to be supplied by the actor.

7 *truth:* their honesty.

8 *Sanctobulorum . . . etc.:* meaningless Latin and Greek phrases used as incantation.

9 *squibs:* firecrackers.

10 *O . . . Domine:* garbled Latin for *In the name of the Lord.*

11 *Peccatum peccatorum:* sin of sins.   12 *Misericordia . . . nobis:* mercy on us.

How am I vexéd with these villains' charms!
From Constantinople am I hither come
Only for pleasure of these damnéd slaves.

ROBIN. How, from Constantinople? You have had a great journey.   950
Will you take sixpence in your purse to pay for your supper, and be
gone?

MEPH. Well, villains, for your presumption I transform thee into
an ape, and thee into a dog. And so be gone.   *[Exit.]*

ROBIN. How, into an ape? That's brave! I'll have fine sport with   955
the boys. I'll get nuts and apples enow.

RAFE. And I must be a dog.

ROBIN. I' faith, thy head will never be out of the pottage pot.

[Exeunt.]

SCENE 10   *The German Court.*

[Enter Emperor, Faustus, Mephistophilis, and a Knight, with Attendants.]

EMP. Master Doctor Faustus, I have heard strange report of thy
knowledge in the black art, how that none in my empire nor in the   960
whole world can compare with thee for the rare effects of magic.
They say thou has a familiar spirit, by whom thou canst accomplish
what thou list.[1] This, therefore, is my request, that thou let me
see some proof of thy skill, that mine eyes may be witnesses to
confirm what mine ears have heard reported; and here I swear to   965
thee by the honor of mine imperial crown that, whatever thou doest,
thou shalt be no ways prejudiced or endamaged.

KNIGHT. *[Aside.]* I' faith, he looks much like a conjuror.

FAUST. My gracious sovereign, though I must confess myself far
inferior to the report men have published, and nothing answerable[2]   970
to the honor of your imperial majesty, yet in that love and duty
binds me thereunto, I am content to do whatsoever your majesty
shall command me.

EMP. Then, Doctor Faustus, mark what I shall say.

As I was sometime solitary set   975
Within my closet, sundry thoughts arose
About the honor of mine ancestors,
How they had won by prowess such exploits,
Got such riches, subdued so many kingdoms,

---

1 *list:* wish.   2 *answerable:* corresponding.

As we that do succeed, or they that shall   980
Hereafter possess our throne, shall,
I fear me, never attain to that degree
Of high renown and great authority;
Amongest which kings is Alexander the Great,
Chief spectacle of the world's preeminence,   985
The bright shining of whose glorious acts
Lightens the world with his reflecting beams;
So, when I heard but motion³ made of him,
It grieves my soul I never saw the man.
If, therefore, thou by cunning of thine art   990
Canst raise this man from hollow vaults below,
Where lies entombed this famous conqueror,
And bring with him his beauteous paramour,
Both in their right shapes, gesture, and attire
They used to wear during their time of life,   995
Thou shalt both satisfy my just desire,
And give me cause to praise thee whilst I live.

FAUST. My gracious lord, I am ready to accomplish your request
so far forth as by art and power of my spirit I am able to perform.

KNIGHT. *[Aside.]* I' faith, that's just nothing at all.   1000

FAUST. But, if it like your grace, it is not in my ability to present
before your eyes the true substantial bodies of those two deceased
princes, which long since are consumed to dust.

KNIGHT.. *[Aside.]* Ay, marry, Master Doctor, now there's a sign
of grace in you, when you will confess the truth.   1005

FAUST. But such spirits as can lively⁴ resemble Alexander and his
paramour shall appear before your grace in that manner that they
best lived in, in their most flourishing estate, which I doubt not
shall sufficiently content your imperial majesty.

EMP. Go to, Master Doctor, let me see them presently.   1010

KNIGHT. Do you hear, Master Doctor? You bring Alexander and
his paramour before the emperor!

FAUST. How then, sir?

KNIGHT. I' faith, that's as true as Diana⁵ turned me to a stag!

FAUST. No, sir, but when Actaeon⁶ died, he left the horns⁷ for you. 1015
Mephistophilis, begone!   *[Exit Mephistophilis]*

KNIGHT. Nay, and you go to conjuring, I'll be gone.

[Exit Knight]

FAUST. I'll meet with you anon⁸ for interrupting me so. Here they
are, my gracious lord.

---

3 *motion:* mention.   4 *lively:* in a lifelike manner.
5 *Diana:* in Roman mythology the goddess of the moon, of hunting, and of virginity.
6 *Actaeon:* the hunter who made Diana angry by watching her bathe: she changed
him into a stag, and he was torn to pieces by his own dogs.
7 *horns:* the horns said to grow on the husband of an unfaithful wife.   8 *anon:* soon.

[Enter Mephistophilis with Alexander and his Paramour.]

EMP. Master Doctor, I heard this lady while she lived had a wart   1020
or mole in her neck. How shall I know whether it be so or no?
FAUST. Your highness may boldly go and see.
EMP. *[Examining her.]* Sure, these are no spirits, but the true
substantial bodies of those two deceased princes.

                    [Exit Alexander with his Paramour.]

FAUST. Will 't please your highness now to send for the knight   1025
that was so pleasant with me here of late?
EMP. One of you call him forth.   *[Attendant calls.]*

   [Enter the Knight with a pair of horns on his head.]

EMP. How now, Sir Knight! Why, I had thought thou hadst been
a bachelor, but now I see thou hast a wife, that not only gives thee
horns, but makes thee wear them. Feel on thy head!   1030
KNIGHT. Thou damnéd wretch and execrable dog,
   Bred in the concave⁹ of some monstrous rock,
   How dar'st thou thus abuse a gentleman?
   Villain, I say, undo what thou hast done!
FAUST. O, not so fast, sir; there's no haste. But, good,¹⁰ are you   1035
remembered how you crossed me in my conference with the emperor? I think I have met with you for it.
EMP. Good Master Doctor, at my entreaty release him; he hath
done penance sufficient.
FAUST. My gracious lord, not so much for the injury he offered   1040
me here in your presence, as to delight you with some mirth, hath
Faustus worthily requited this injurious knight, which being all I
desire, I am content to release him of his horns. And, Sir Knight,
hereafter speak well of scholars. Mephistophilis, transform him
straight. *[Mephistophilis removes the horns.]* Now, my good lord,   1045
having done my duty, I humbly take my leave.
EMP. Farewell, Master Doctor; yet, ere you go,
   Expect from me a bounteous reward.

                         [Exit Emperor with the others.]

SCENE 11   *A common.*

         [Enter Faustus and Mephistophilis.]

FAUST. Now, Mephistophilis, the restless course
   That Time doth run with calm and silent foot,   1050

---

9 *concave:* hollow.   10 *good:* good man.

Short'ning my days and thread of vital life,
Calls for the payment of my latest years;
Therefore, sweet Mephistophilis, let us
Make haste to Wertenberg.

MEPH. What, will you go on horseback or on foot?   1055

FAUST. Nay, till I am past this fair and pleasant green, I'll walk on
foot.

[*Enter a Horse-Corser.*[1]]

HORSE-C. I have been all this day seeking one Master Fustian.
Mass,[2] see where he is! God save you, Master Doctor!

FAUST. What, horse-corser! You are well met.   1060

HORSE-C. Do you hear, sir? I have brought you forty dollars for
your horse.

FAUST. I cannot sell him so. If thou lik'st him for fifty, take him.

HORSE-C. Alas, sir, I have no more.—I pray you speak for me.

MEPH. I pray you let him have him. He is an honest fellow, and   1065
he has a great charge,[3] neither wife nor child.

FAUST. Well, come, give me your money.

[*Horse-Corser gives Faustus the money.*]

My boy will deliver him to you. But I must tell you one thing before
you have him: ride him not into the water at any hand.[4]

HORSE-C. Why, sir, will he not drink of all waters?[5]   1070

FAUST. O, yes, he will drink of all waters, but ride him not into
the water. Ride him over hedge or ditch, or where thou wilt, but
not into the water.

HORSE-C. Well, sir.— [*Aside.*] Now am I made man[6] forever.
I'll not leave my horse for forty. If he had but the quality of hey-   1075
ding-ding, hey-ding-ding,[7] I'd make a brave living on him. He has
a buttock as slick as an eel.—Well, God buy,[8] sir. Your boy will
deliver him me. But hark ye, sir; if my horse be sick or ill at ease, if
I bring his water to you, you'll tell me what it is?

[*Exit Horse-Corser.*]

FAUST. Away, you villain! What, dost think I am a horse doctor?   1080
[*Retires into his study.*]

1 *Horse-Corser:* dealer in horses.
2 *Mass:* by the Mass, a mild oath.   3 *charge:* financial burden.
4 *at any hand:* in any case.
5 *drink of all waters:* to be ready for anything, to go anywhere.
6 *made man:* a made man.
7 *quality . . . ding:* ability to dance.
8 *God buy:* good-by (God be with you).

SCENE 12   *Faustus' study.*

FAUST. What art thou, Faustus, but a man condemned to die?
  Thy fatal time doth draw to final end;
  Despair doth drive distrust into my thoughts;
  Confound[1] these passions with a quiet sleep.
  Tush, Christ did call the thief upon the Cross;   1085
  Then rest thee, Faustus, quiet in conceit.[2]

                                    [Sleeps in his chair.]

              [Enter Horse-Corser, all wet, crying.]

HORSE-C. Alas, alas! Doctor Fustian, quotha?[3] Mass, Doctor
Lopus[4] was never such a doctor. Has[5] given me a purgation, has
purged me of forty dollars; I shall never see them more. But yet,
like an ass as I was, I would not be ruled by him, for he bade me   1090
I should ride him into no water. Now I, thinking my horse had
had some rare quality that he would not have had me known of,
I, like a vent'rous youth, rid him into the deep pond at the town's
end. I was no sooner in the middle of the pond, but my horse
vanished away, and I sat upon a bottle[6] of hay, never so near   1095
drowning in my life. But I'll seek out my doctor, and have my
forty dollars again, or I'll make it the dearest horse!—

                    [Enter Mephistophilis.]

O, yonder is his snipper-snapper.[7]—Do you hear? You hey-pass,[8]
where's your master?
  MEPH. Why, sir, what would you? You cannot speak with him.   1100
  HORSE-C. But I will speak with him.
  MEPH. Why, he's fast asleep. Come some other time.
  HORSE-C. I'll speak with him now, or I'll break his glass windows[9]
about his ears.
  MEPH. I tell thee he has not slept this eight nights.   1105
  HORSE-C. And he have not slept this eight weeks, I'll speak with
him.
  MEPH. See where he is, fast asleep.

---

1 *Confound:* overcome, undo.   2 *conceit:* mind.   3 *quotha:* indeed!
4 *Doctor Lopus:* Doctor Lopez, Queen Elizabeth's physician, who was hanged in 1594
for a supposed attempt to poison her.   5 *Has:* The one who has.
6 *bottle:* bundle.
7 *snipper-snapper:* impertinent fellow, whipper-snapper.
8 *hey-pass:* juggler, also the commands given by jugglers during an act.
9 *windows:* spectacles.

HORSE-C. Ay, this is he. God save ye, Master Doctor! Master
Doctor, Master Doctor Fustian!—Forty dollars, forty dollars for a   1110
bottle of hay!

MEPH. Why, thou seest he hears thee not.

HORSE-C. So ho, ho!—So ho, ho! *[Hallos in his ear.]* No, will you
not wake? I'll make you wake ere I go! *[Pulls him by the leg, and
pulls it away.]* Alas, I am undone! What shall I do?   1115

FAUST. O, my leg, my leg! Help, Mephistophilis! Call the officers.
My leg, my leg!

MEPH. Come, villain, to the constable.

HORSE-C. O Lord, sir, let me go, and I'll give you forty dollars
more.   1120

MEPH. Where be they?

HORSE-C. I have none about me. Come to my ostry[10] and I'll give
them you.

MEPH. Be gone quickly!   *[Horse-Corser runs away.]*

FAUST. What, is he gone? Farewell he! Faustus has his leg again,   1125
and the horse-corser, I take it, a bottle of hay for his labor. Well,
this trick shall cost him forty dollars more.

[Enter Wagner.]

How now, Wagner, what's the news with thee?

WAG. Sir, the Duke of Vanholt doth earnestly entreat your
company.   1130

FAUST. The Duke of Vanholt! An honorable gentleman, to whom
I must be no niggard of my cunning. Come, Mephistophilis, let's
away to him.   *[Exeunt.]*

SCENE 13   *The court of the Duke of Vanholt.*

[Enter the Duke of Vanholt, the Duchess, Faustus, and Mephistophilis.]

DUKE. Believe me, Master Doctor, this merriment hath much
pleased me.   1135

FAUST. My gracious lord, I am glad it contents you so well.—But
it may be, madam, you take no delight in this. I have heard that
great-bellied women do long for some dainties or other. What is
it, madam? Tell me, and you shall have it.

DUCH. Thanks, good Master Doctor; and, for I see your courteous   1140
intent to pleasure me, I will not hide from you the thing my heart
desires. And were it now summer, as it is January and the dead

10 *ostry:* inn.

time of the winter, I would desire no better meat than a dish of ripe grapes.

    FAUST. Alas, madam, that's nothing! Mephistophilis, begone.   1145

                    [Exit Mephistophilis.]

Were it a greater thing than this, so it would content you, you should have it.

      [Enter Mephistophilis with the grapes.]

Here they be, madam. Wilt please you taste on them?

    DUKE. Believe me, Master Doctor, this makes me wonder above the rest, that being in the dead time of winter, and in the month of   1150 January, how you should come by these grapes.

    FAUST. If it like your grace, the year is divided into two circles over the whole world, that, when it is here winter with us, in the contrary circle it is summer with them, as in India, Saba,[1] and farther countries in the East; and by means of a swift spirit that I   1155 have, I had them brought hither as ye see.—How do you like them, madam; be they good?

    DUCH. Believe me, Master Doctor, they be the best grapes that e'er I tasted in my life before.

    FAUST. I am glad they content you so, madam.   1160

    DUKE. Come, madam, let us in, where you must well reward this learned man for the great kindness he hath showed to you.

    DUCH. And so I will, my lord; and, whilst I live,
      Rest beholding[2] for this courtesy.

    FAUST. I humbly thank your grace.   1165

    DUKE. Come, Master Doctor, follow us and receive your reward.

                    [Exeunt.]

SCENE 14   *Faustus' study.*

      [Enter Wagner alone.]

    WAG. I think my master means to die shortly,
      For he hath given to me all his goods;
      And yet methinks, if that death were near,
      He would not banquet and carouse and swill   1170
      Amongst the students, as even now he doth,
      Who are at supper with such bellycheer
      As Wagner ne'er beheld in all his life.
      See where they come! Belike the feast is ended.

1 *Saba:* Arabia.   2 *beholding:* obliged.

[Enter Faustus, with two or three Scholars, and Mephistophilis.]

1 sch. Master Doctor Faustus, since our conference about fair   1175
ladies, which was the beautifull'st in all the world, we have determined with ourselves that Helen of Greece was the admirablest lady
that ever lived. Therefore, Master Doctor, if you will do us that
favor, as to let us see that peerless dame of Greece, whom all the
world admires for majesty, we should think ourselves much behold-   1180
ing unto you.

faust. Gentlemen,
     For that I know your friendship is unfeigned,
     And Faustus' custom is not to deny
     The just requests of those that wish him well,   1185
     You shall behold that peerless dame of Greece,
     No otherways for pomp and majesty
     Than when Sir Paris crossed the seas with her,
     And brought the spoils to rich Dardania.
     Be silent, then, for danger is in words.   1190

[Music sounds, and Helen passeth over the stage.]

2 sch. Too simple is my wit to tell her praise,
     Whom all the world admires for majesty.
3 sch. No marvel though the angry Greeks pursued
     With ten years' war the rape[1] of such a queen,
     Whose heavenly beauty passeth all compare.   1195
1 sch. Since we have seen the pride of Nature's works
     And only paragon of excellence,

[Enter an Old Man.]

     Let us depart; and for this glorious deed
     Happy and blessed be Faustus evermore.
faustus. Gentlemen, farewell—the same I wish to you.   1200
                                   [Exeunt Scholars.]
old man. Ah, Doctor Faustus, that I might prevail
     To guide thy steps unto the way of life,
     By which sweet path thou mayst attain the goal
     That shall conduct thee to celestial rest!
     Break heart, drop blood, and mingle it with tears,   1205
     Tears falling from repentant heaviness
     Of thy most vile and loathsome filthiness,
     The stench whereof corrupts the inward soul
     With such flagitious[2] crimes of heinous sins
     As no commiseration may expel,   1210
     But mercy, Faustus, of thy Savior sweet,
     Whose blood alone must wash away thy guilt.

1 *rape:* seizure.   2 *flagitious:* vicious.

FAUST. Where art thou, Faustus? Wretch, what hast thou done?
  Damned art thou, Faustus, damned; despair and die!
  Hell calls for right, and with a roaring voice   1215
  Says, "Faustus, come! Thine hour is come!"
  And Faustus will come to do thee right.
                    [*Mephistophilis gives him a dagger.*]
OLD MAN. Ah, stay, good Faustus, stay thy desperate steps!
  I see an angel hovers o'er thy head,
  And, with a vial full of precious grace,   1220
  Offers to pour the same into thy soul.
  Then call for mercy, and avoid despair.
FAUST. Ah, my sweet friend, I feel
  Thy words to comfort my distresséd soul.
  Leave me a while to ponder on my sins.   1225
OLD MAN. I go, sweet Faustus, but with heavy cheer,
  Fearing the ruin of thy hopeless soul.   [*Exit.*]
FAUST. Accurséd Faustus, where is mercy now?
  I do repent, and yet I do despair;
  Hell strives with grace for conquest in my breast.   1230
  What shall I do to shun the snares of death?
MEPH. Thou traitor Faustus, I arrest thy soul
  For disobedience to my sovereign lord;
  Revolt,³ or I'll in piecemeal tear thy flesh.
FAUST. Sweet Mephistophilis, entreat thy lord   1235
  To pardon my unjust presumption,
  And with my blood again I will confirm
  My former vow I made to Lucifer.
MEPH. Do it then quickly, with unfeignéd heart,
  Lest greater danger do attend thy drift.   1240

[*Faustus pricks his arm and signs a paper with his blood.*]

FAUST. Torment, sweet friend, that base and crooked age,⁴
  That durst dissuade me from thy Lucifer,
  With greatest torments that our hell affords.
MEPH. His faith is great; I cannot touch his soul
  But what I may afflict his body with   1245
  I will attempt, which is but little worth. ·
FAUST. One thing, good servant, let me crave of thee,
  To glut the longing of my heart's desire:
  That I might have unto my paramour
  That heavenly Helen, which I saw of late,   1250
  Whose sweet embraces may extinguish clean
  These thoughts that do dissuade me from my vow,
  And keep mine oath I made to Lucifer.

3 *Revolt:* turn back.
4 *age:* old man.

MEPH. Faustus, this or what else thou shalt desire
    Shall be performed in twinkling of an eye.   1255

[Enter Helen.]

FAUST. Was this the face that launched a thousand ships,
    And burnt the topless towers of Ilium?
    Sweet Helen, make me immortal with a kiss.   *[Kisses her.]*
    Her lips sucks forth my soul; see where it flies!—
    Come, Helen, come, give me my soul again.   1260
    Here will I dwell, for heaven be in these lips,
    And all is dross that is not Helena.

[Enter Old Man.]

    I will be Paris, and for love of thee,
    Instead of Troy, shall Wertenberg be sacked;
    And I will combat with weak Menelaus,[5]   1265
    And wear thy colors on my pluméd crest;
    Yea, I will wound Achilles[6] in the heel,
    And then return to Helen for a kiss.
    O, thou art fairer than the evening air
    Clad in the beauty of a thousand stars;   1270
    Brighter art thou than flaming Jupiter
    When he appeared to hapless Semele;[7]
    More lovely than the monarch of the sky
    In wanton Arethusa's[8] azured arms;
    And none but thou shalt be my paramour.   1275

[Exeunt all except Old Man.]

OLD MAN. Accurséd Faustus, miserable man,
    That from thy soul exclud'st the grace of heaven,
    And fliest the throne of his tribunal seat!

[Enter the Devils.]

    Satan begins to sift me with his pride.
    As in this furnace God shall try my faith,   1280
    My faith, vile hell, shall triumph over thee.
    Ambitious fiends, see how the heavens smiles
    At your repulse, and laughs your state to scorn!
    Hence, hell; for hence I fly unto my God!   *[Exeunt.]*

5 *Menelaus:* younger brother of Agamemnon and king of Sparta who was married to Helen. The seizure of Helen by Paris was the cause of the Trojan War.
6 *Achilles:* the hero of the *Iliad* and the greatest fighter of the Greeks in the Trojan War. He was killed by Paris whose arrow struck him in the heel, his only vulnerable spot.
7 *Semele:* In Greek mythology, Semele was the daughter of Cadmus and mother by Zeus (Jupiter) of Dionysus (the god of wine). When Semele desired to see Zeus as he appeared before the gods, she was killed by his lightning.
8 *Arethusa:* the nymph of the fountain of Arethusa on the island of Ortygia near Syracuse.

SCENE 15   *The same.*

[Enter Faustus with the Scholars.]

FAUST. Ah, gentlemen!   1285

1 SCH. What ails Faustus?

FAUST. Ah, my sweet chamber-fellow, had I lived with thee,
then had I lived still, but now I die eternally. Look, comes he not,
comes he not?

2 SCH. What means Faustus?   1290

3 SCH. Belike he is grown into some sickness by being over-
solitary.

1 SCH. If it be so, we'll have physicians to cure him. 'Tis but a
surfeit. Never fear, man.

FAUST. A surfeit of deadly sin that hath damned both body and   1295
soul.

2 SCH. Yet, Faustus, look up to heaven; remember God's mercies are infinite.

FAUST. But Faustus' offense can ne'er be pardoned. The serpent
that tempted Eve may be saved, but not Faustus. Ah, gentlemen,   1300
hear me with patience, and tremble not at my speeches! Though
my heart pants and quivers to remember that I have been a student here these thirty years, O, would I had never seen Wertenberg, never read book! And what wonders I have done, all
Germany can witness, yea, all the world; for which Faustus hath 1305
lost both Germany and the world, yea, heaven itself, heaven, the
seat of God, the throne of the blessed, the kingdom of joy, and
must remain in hell forever, hell, ah, hell, forever! Sweet friends,
what shall become of Faustus, being in hell forever?

3 SCH. Yet, Faustus, call on God.   1310

FAUST. On God, whom Faustus hath abjured! On God, whom
Faustus hath blasphemed! Ah, my God, I would weep, but the
devil draws in my tears. Gush forth blood instead of tears! Yea,
life and soul! O, he stays my tongue! I would lift up my hands,
but see, they hold them, they hold them!   1315

ALL. Who, Faustus?

FAUST. Lucifer and Mephistophilis. Ah, gentlemen, I gave them
my soul for my cunning!

ALL. God forbid!

FAUST. God forbade it indeed, but Faustus hath done it. For   1320
vain pleasure of four-and-twenty years hath Faustus lost eternal
joy and felicity. I writ them a bill with mine own blood. The date
is expired; the time will come, and he will fetch me.

1 SCH. Why did not Faustus tell us of this before, that divines
might have prayed for thee?   1325

FAUST. Oft have I thought to have done so; but the devil threat-
ened to tear me in pieces if I named God; to fetch both body and

soul if I once gave ear to divinity. And now 'tis too late. Gentlemen, away, lest you perish with me!

    2 SCH. O, what shall we do to save Faustus?   1330

    FAUST. Talk not of me, but save yourselves, and depart.

    3 SCH. God will strengthen me. I will stay with Faustus.

    1 SCH. Tempt not God, sweet friend; but let us into the next
room, and there pray for him.

    FAUST. Ay, pray for me, pray for me, and what noise soever   1335
ye hear, come not unto me, for nothing can rescue me.

    2 SCH. Pray thou, and we will pray that God may have mercy
upon thee.

    FAUST. Gentlemen, farewell! If I live till morning, I'll visit you.
If not—Faustus is gone to hell.   1340

    ALL. Faustus, farewell! *[Exeunt Scholars. The clock strikes eleven.]*

FAUST. Ah, Faustus,
    Now hast thou but one bare hour to live,
    And then thou must be damned perpetually!
    Stand still, you ever-moving spheres of heaven,   1345
    That time may cease, and midnight never come!
    Fair Nature's eye, rise, rise again and make
    Perpetual day; or let this hour be but
    A year, a month, a week, a natural day,
    That Faustus may repent and save his soul!   1350
    O lente, lente, currite, noctis equi![1]
    The stars move still, time runs, the clock will strike,
    The devil will come, and Faustus must be damned.
    O, I'll leap up to my God! Who pulls me down?
    See, see where Christ's blood streams in the firmament!   1355
    One drop would save my soul—half a drop. Ah, my Christ!
    Ah, rend not my heart for naming of my Christ!
    Yet will I call on him! O, spare me, Lucifer!—
    Where is it now? 'Tis gone; and see where God
    Stretcheth out his arm, and bends his ireful brows!   1360
    Mountains and hills, come, come and fall on me,
    And hide me from the heavy wrath of God!
    No! No!
    Then will I headlong run into the earth.
    Earth gape! O, no, it will not harbor me!   1365
    You stars that reigned at my nativity,
    Whose influence hath allotted death and hell,
    Now draw up Faustus like a foggy mist
    Into the entrails of yon lab'ring clouds,
    That, when you vomit forth into the air,   1370
    My limbs may issue from your smoky mouths,
    So that my soul may but ascend to heaven.

1 *O . . . equi:* O horses of night, run slowly, slowly.

[The clock strikes the half hour.]

Ah, half the hour is past!
'Twill all be past anon!
O God!   1375
If thou wilt not have mercy on my soul,
Yet, for Christ's sake whose blood hath ransomed me,
Impose some end to my incessant pain.
Let Faustus live in hell a thousand years
A hundred thousand, and at last be saved!   1380
O, no end is limited to damnéd souls!
Why wert thou not a creature wanting soul?
Or why is this immortal that thou hast?
Ah, Pythagoras' metempsychosis!² Were that true,
This soul should fly from me, and I be changed   1385
Unto some brutish beast! All beasts are happy,
For, when they die,
Their souls are soon dissolved in elements.
But mine must live, still to be plagued in hell.
Cursed be the parents that engendered me!   1390
No, Faustus, curse thyself; curse Lucifer
That hath deprived thee of the joys of heaven.
                              [The clock strikes twelve.]
O, it strikes, it strikes! Now, body, turn to air,
Or Lucifer will bear thee quick³ to hell.   *[Thunder and lightning.]*
O soul, be changed into little waterdrops,   1395
And fall into the ocean—ne'er be found.
My God, my God, look not so fierce on me!

     . *[Enter Devils.]*

Adders and serpents, let me breathe awhile!
Ugly hell, gape not! Come not, Lucifer!
I'll burn my books!—Ah, Mephistophilis!   *[Exeunt with him.]*   1400
          [Enter Chorus.]

Cut is the branch that might have grown full straight,
And burnéd is Apollo's laurel bough
That sometime⁴ grew within this learned man.
Faustus is gone; regard his hellish fall
Whose fiendful fortune may exhort the wise   1405
Only to wonder at unlawful things,
Whose deepness doth entice such forward wits
To practice more than heavenly power permits.   *[Exit.]*

     TERMINAT HORA DIEM; TERMINAT AUTHOR OPUS.⁵

---

2 *Pythagoras' metempsychosis:* Pythagoras' doctrine that the soul passes into
another body after death.   3 *quick:* alive.   4 *sometime:* once.
5 *Terminat . . . Opus:* The hour ends the day; the author ends his work.

Hamlet

Introduction

More has been written about William Shakespeare's *Hamlet* than there is in the entire national literature of many Continental European countries. Interpretations of Hamlet have been unduly plentiful and varied: he has been interpreted as the conventional hero, as too philosophical, as too Christian, as charming but weak, as cowardly, as a man having an Oedipus complex, as hysterical and neurotic, as sad and depressed, as a case study in mental disorder, as mad, as the sanest of geniuses, and in some studies as the most normal of Shakespeare's heroes. The truth may lie in one or other of the many interpretations, but it very likely lies in a combination of several of them; because, as Aristotle might agree, a tragic action tending toward catastrophe may well require various kinds of defective attitudes or miscalculations on the part of the hero.

Some of the questions which have been raised about the play are obviously more important than others. Most of them arise because of the psychological complexity of the character of Hamlet; a few of the more recent questions have come up because of ignorance of Elizabethan theology or the psychological and moral beliefs of Shakespeare's day. Gertrude's marriage with Claudius, after the death of Hamlet's father, for example, was clearly considered incestuous. When Gertrude married Hamlet's father, she contracted a relationship with his brother Claudius which made her later marriage to Claudius invalid. On this question few critical controversies have grown up. This is not the case with other aspects of the play.

For example, was Hamlet merely pretending madness in order to achieve his end—revenge upon Claudius? What is the role of the ghost of Hamlet's father? Was the ghost actually that of the dead king, or was it a disguise assumed by the devil to tempt Hamlet to murder? These questions are central to any interpretation of the play. Certainly in *Hamlet* Shakespeare has provided many more questions than he has answers. Since it is not possible to present here all of the many conflicting interpretations of this intriguing play, we will briefly consider only one of them.

First, the play is in the revenge tradition. The subject matter is the revenge of a son for his father, a revenge directed by the ghost of the murdered father. Furthermore, as the play opens, Hamlet is deeply saddened by his father's recent death and horrified by his mother's overhasty marriage to his uncle. In his eyes and according to the ethical and theological standards of sixteenth-century England, which here (as in all his plays) Shakespeare is following, the marriage was incestuous. This was the law and the official teaching of the English church. When Gertrude married Hamlet's father, she contracted a relationship with Claudius which made her later marriage to him invalid.

Hamlet also is confused. He finds the world "an unweeded garden," but he does not wish to bear the burden of setting things straight:

> The time is out of joint. O cursèd spite
> That ever I was born to set it right!

As the son of the dead Hamlet, he was the rightful heir to the throne and
the true king. Therefore, he had not only the rights of the king but also all
the corresponding duties. As rightful king he was duty bound to restore
order to the kingdom by removing Claudius from the throne.

Adding to his confusion is his uncertainty, until after the play before the
king, as to where the ghost came from. The ghostly figure may have come
to tell him the truth about his father's murder, or it

> May be the devil, and the devil hath power
> T'assume a pleasing shape, yea, and perhaps
> Out of my weakness and my melancholy,
> As he is very potent with such spirits,
> Abuses me to damn me.

It is damnation, not death, he fears. For he tells us very straightforwardly
that death is a "consummation devoutly to be wished," and he only wishes

> . . . that the Everlasting had not fixed
> His canon 'gainst self-slaughter.

In a word he would gladly commit suicide if he were not afraid of going to
hell for all eternity.

Through all of this Hamlet knows that due process, the correct course of
legal proceedings, has not been followed in Claudius' assumption of the
throne in his place. He resents the fact that Claudius

> . . . hath killed my king, and whored my mother,
> Popped in between th' election and my hopes.

Shakespeare was writing according to the Christian beliefs as held by the
age in which he lived. He combines his play in the revenge tradition with
the Christian beliefs held by his contemporaries. Hamlet, as a son, and
according to the revenge code, was bound *personally* to avenge his
father's death. As the prince, and according to the Christian ethics of the
sixteenth century, he must act officially because he is an agent of God's justice. In avenging his father's death he acts on the personal impulses of a
son rather than as a public agent, and, in consequence, must make satisfaction for his action by his own death.*

Before his death, however, Hamlet clearly faces the problem of evil—evil
in the world around him and in his own little world (himself). He attains a
sense of resignation, and he comes to the realization (as have men in every

---

*Fredson Bowers, "Hamlet as Minister and Scourge," *Publications of the Modern
Language Association*, LXX (September, 1955), 740–749.

Christian age) that God is the ultimate judge and at the core of all events:

There is a special providence in the fall of a sparrow.

This is not stoic acceptance; this is the theological acceptance that Hamlet and all men subscribing to essentially the same religious beliefs must come to. Hamlet has finally come to a sense of resignation to the justice of God; and, as Horatio states at the end of the play, flights of angels sing him to his rest. Like Faustus, he pays for his mistakes with his death, but, stated very simply, he goes to heaven while Faustus goes to hell.

The Tragedy of Hamlet
Prince of Denmark

WILLIAM SHAKESPEARE

Names of the Actors

CLAUDIUS *King of Denmark*

HAMLET *son to the late, and nephew to the present, King*

POLONIUS *Lord Chamberlain*

HORATIO *friend to Hamlet*

LAERTES *son to Polonius*

VOLTEMAND
CORNELIUS
ROSENCRANTZ
GUILDENSTERN *courtiers*
OSRIC
A GENTLEMAN

A PRIEST

MARCELLUS
BERNARDO *officers*

FRANCISCO *a soldier*

REYNALDO *servant to Polonius*

PLAYERS

TWO CLOWNS *gravediggers*

FORTINBRAS *Prince of Norway*

A NORWEGIAN CAPTAIN

ENGLISH AMBASSADORS

GERTRUDE *Queen of Denmark and mother of Hamlet*

OPHELIA *daughter to Polonius*

GHOST *of Hamlet's father*

[Lords, Ladies, Officers, Soldiers, Sailors, Messengers, Attendants]

ACT I

SCENE 1 ELSINORE. *A platform before the castle.*

[Enter Bernardo and Francisco, two sentinels.]

BERNARDO. Who's there?

FRANCISCO. Nay, answer me! Stand and unfold yourself.

BERNARDO. Long live the king!

FRANCISCO. Bernardo?

BERNARDO. He.   5

FRANCISCO. You come most carefully upon your hour.[1]

BERNARDO. 'Tis now struck twelve. Get thee to bed, Francisco.

FRANCISCO. For this relief much thanks. 'Tis bitter cold,
  And I am sick at heart.

BERNARDO. Have you had quiet guard?

FRANCISCO.   Not a mouse stirring.   10

BERNARDO. Well, good night.
  If you do meet Horatio and Marcellus,
  The rivals[2] of my watch, bid them make haste.

FRANCISCO. I think I hear them. Stand, ho! Who is there?

[Enter Horatio and Marcellus.]

HORATIO. Friends to this ground.

MARCELLUS.   And liegemen to the Dane.[3]   15

FRANCISCO. Give you[4] good night.

MARCELLUS.   O, farewell, honest soldier.
  Who hath relieved you?

FRANCISCO.   Bernardo has my place.
  Give you good night.   *[Exit Francisco.]*

MARCELLUS.   Holla, Bernardo!

BERNARDO.   Say—
  What, is Horatio there?

HORATIO.   A piece of him.

BERNARDO. Welcome, Horatio. Welcome, good Marcellus.   20

HORATIO. What, has this thing appeared again to-night?

BERNARDO. I have seen nothing.

MARCELLUS. Horatio says 'tis but our fantasy,
  And will not let belief take hold of him
  Touching this dreaded sight twice seen of us.   25
  Therefore I have entreated him along
  With us to watch the minutes of this night,
  That, if again this apparition come,
  He may approve[5] our eyes and speak to it.

---

1. *carefully . . . hour:* right on time. 2. *rivals:* partners.
3. *Dane:* king of Denmark. 4. *Give you:* God give you. 5. *approve:* confirm.

HORATIO. Tush, tush, 'twill not appear.

BERNARDO.   Sit down awhile,   30
  And let us once again assail your ears,
  That are so fortified against our story,
  What we two nights have seen.

HORATIO.   Well, sit we down,
  And let us hear Bernardo speak of this.

BERNARDO. Last night of all,   35
  When yond same star that's westward from the pole
  Had made his course t' illume that part of heaven
  Where now it burns, Marcellus and myself,
  The bell then beating one—

[Enter the Ghost.]

MARCELLUS. Peace, break thee off. Look where it comes again.   40
BERNARDO. In the same figure like the king that's dead.
MARCELLUS. Thou art a scholar; speak to it, Horatio.
BERNARDO. Looks it not like the king? Mark it, Horatio.
HORATIO. Most like. It harrows me with fear and wonder.
BERNARDO. It would be spoke to.
MARCELLUS.   Question it, Horatio.[6]   45
HORATIO. What art thou that usurp'st this time of night
  Together with that fair and warlike form
  In which the majesty of buried Denmark[7]
  Did sometimes march? By heaven I charge thee, speak.
MARCELLUS. It is offended.
BERNARDO.   See, it stalks away.   50
HORATIO. Stay. Speak, speak. I charge thee, speak.
                                   [Exit the Ghost.]
MARCELLUS. 'Tis gone and will not answer.
BERNARDO. How now, Horatio? You tremble and look pale.
  Is not this something more than fantasy?
  What think you on't?   55
HORATIO. Before my God, I might not this believe
  Without the sensible and true avouch
  Of mine own eyes.
MARCELLUS.   Is it not like the king?
HORATIO. As thou art to thyself.
  Such was the very armor he had on   60
  When he th' ambitious Norway combated.
  So frowned he once when, in an angry parle,[8]
  He smote the sledded Polacks on the ice.
  'Tis strange.

6. Ghosts could not speak until spoken to.
7. *buried Denmark:* the dead king of Denmark.   8. *parle:* parley, conference.

MARCELLUS. Thus twice before, and just at this dead hour,   65
  With martial stalk hath he gone by our watch.
HORATIO. In what particular thought to work I know not;
  But, in the gross and scope[9] of my opinion,
  This bodes some strange eruption to our state.
MARCELLUS. Good now, sit down, and tell me he that knows,   70
  Why this same strict and most observant watch
  So nightly toils the subject of the land,
  And why such daily cast of brazen cannon[10]
  And foreign mart[11] for implements of war,
  Why such impress[12] of shipwrights, whose sore task   75
  Does not divide the Sunday from the week.
  What might be toward that this sweaty haste
  Doth make the night joint-laborer with the day?
  Who is't that can inform me?
HORATIO.   That can I.
  At least the whisper goes so. Our last king,   80
  Whose image even but now appeared to us,
  Was as you know by Fortinbras of Norway,
  Thereto pricked on by a most emulate[14] pride,
  Dared to the combat; in which our valiant Hamlet[15]
  (For so this side of our known world esteemed him)   85
  Did slay this Fortinbras; who, by a sealed compact
  Well ratified by law and heraldry,[16]
  Did forfeit, with his life, all those his lands
  Which he stood seized on[17] to the conqueror;
  Against the which a moiety competent[18]   90
  Was gagèd[19] by our king, which had[20] returned
  To the inheritance of Fortinbras
  Had he been vanquisher, as, by the same comart[21]
  And carriage[22] of the article[23] designed,
  His fell to Hamlet. Now, sir, young Fortinbras,   95
  Of unimproved mettle hot and full,
  Hath in the skirts of Norway here and there
  Sharked up a list of lawless resolutes[24]
  For food and diet to some enterprise
  That hath a stomach[25] in't; which is no other,   100
  As it doth well appear unto our state,

9. *gross and scope:* general view, main drift.
10. *cast of brazen cannon:* casting of brass cannon.   11. *mart:* trading.
12. *impress:* forced service, conscription.   13. *toward:* impending, in preparation.
14. *emulate:* envious, ambitious.   15. *Hamlet:* the dead Danish king.
16. *heraldry:* laws regulating combat.   17. *seized on:* possessed of.
18. *moiety competent:* equal share.   19. *gagèd:* pledged.
20. *which had:* which would have.   21. *comart:* agreement.
22. *carriage:* general sense.   23. *article:* treaty.   24. *resolutes:* desperadoes.
25. *stomach:* challenge (of adventure).

But to recover of us by strong hand
And terms compulsatory those foresaid lands
So by his father lost; and this, I take it,
Is the main motive of our preparations,   105
The source of this our watch, and the chief head
Of this posthaste and romage²⁶ in the land.
BERNARDO. I think it be no other but e'en so.
    Well may it sort²⁷ that this portentous figure
Comes armèd through our watch so like the king   110
That was and is the question of these wars.
HORATIO. A mote²⁸ it is to trouble the mind's eye.
In the most high and palmy²⁹ state of Rome,
A little ere the mightiest Julius fell,
The graves stood tenantless and the sheeted dead   115
Did squeak and gibber in the Roman streets;
As stars with trains of fire and dews of blood,
Disasters³⁰ in the sun; and the moist star³¹
Upon whose influence Neptune's empire³² stands
Was sick almost to doomsday³³ with eclipse.   120
And even the like precurse³⁴ of feared events,
As harbingers³⁵ preceding still³⁶ the fates
And prologue to the omen coming on,
Have heaven and earth together demonstrated
Unto our climatures³⁷ and countrymen.   125

[Re-enter Ghost.]

But soft, behold, lo where it comes again!
I'll cross it, though it blast me.—Stay, illusion.

                         [He spreads his arms.]

If thou hast any sound or use of voice,
Speak to me.
If there be any good thing to be done   130
That may to thee do ease and grace to me,
Speak to me.
If thou art privy to thy country's fate,
Which happily³⁸ foreknowing may avoid,
O, speak!   135
Or if thou hast uphoarded in thy life
Extorted³⁹ treasure in the womb of earth,

---

26. *romage:* bustle, uproar or turmoil.
27. *sort:* be fitting.   28. *mote:* speck of dust.   29. *palmy:* victorious.
30. *Disasters:* unfavorable aspects.   31. *moist star:* moon.
32. *Neptune's empire:* the seas.
33. *almost to doomsday:* an allusion to the prophecy that at Christ's second coming "the moon shall not give her light"; *Matt.* 24:29.   34. *precurse:* precursor, sign.
35. *harbingers:* forerunners.   36. *still:* always.   37. *climatures:* regions.
38. *happily:* perhaps, perchance.   39. *Extorted:* ill won.

For which, they say, you spirits oft walk in death,

                 [The cock crows.]

  Speak of it. Stay and speak. Stop it, Marcellus.

MARCELLUS. Shall I strike at it with my partisan?[40]   140

HORATIO. Do, if it will not stand.

BERNARDO.   'Tis here.

HORATIO.   'Tis here.

MARCELLUS. 'Tis gone.   *[Exit Ghost.]*

  We do it wrong, being so majestical,

  To offer it the show of violence,

  For it is as the air invulnerable,   145

  And our vain blows malicious mockery.

BERNARDO. It was about to speak when the cock crew.

HORATIO. And then it started, like a guilty thing

  Upon a fearful summons. I have heard

  The cock, that is the trumpet to the morn,   150

  Doth with his lofty and shrill-sounding throat

  Awake the god of day, and at his warning,

  Whether in sea or fire, in earth or air,

  Th' extravagant[41] and erring spirit hies

  To his confine; and of the truth herein   155

  This present object made probation.[42]

MARCELLUS. It faded on the crowing of the cock.

  Some say that ever 'gainst[43] that season comes

  Wherein our Saviour's birth is celebrated,

  This bird of dawning singeth all night long,   160

  And then, they say, no spirit dare stir abroad,

  The nights are wholesome,[44] then no planets strike,[45]

  No fairy takes,[46] nor witch hath power to charm.

  So hallowed and so gracious is that time.

HORATIO. So have I heard and do in part believe it.   165

  But look, the morn in russet mantle clad

  Walks o'er the dew of yon high eastward hill.

  Break we our watch up, and by my advice

  Let us impart what we have seen to-night

  Unto young Hamlet, for upon my life   170

  This spirit, dumb to us, will speak to him.

  Do you consent we shall acquaint him with it,

  As needful in our loves, fitting our duty?

MARCELLUS. Let's do't, I pray, and I this morning know

  Where we shall find him most conveniently.   *[Exeunt.]*   175

---

40. *partisan:* long-handled spear.
41. *extravagant:* vagrant, wandering beyond bounds.
42. *made probation:* gave proof.   43. *ever 'gainst:* whenever.
44. *wholesome:* healthy (night air was commonly believed to be a source of contagion).   45. *strike:* work evil by influence.   46. *takes:* bewitches.

SCENE 2   *A room of state in the castle.*

[Enter Claudius the King of Denmark, Gertrude the Queen, Hamlet,
Polonius, Laertes, Voltemand, Cornelius, Lords and Attendants.]

KING. Though yet of Hamlet our dear brother's death
    The memory be green, and that it us befitted
    To bear our hearts in grief, and our whole kingdom
    To be contracted in one brow of woe,
    Yet so far hath discretion fought with nature   5
    That we with wisest sorrow think on him
    Together with remembrance of ourselves.
    Therefore our sometime[1] sister, now our queen,
    Th' imperial jointress[2] to this warlike state,
    Have we, as 'twere with a defeated[3] joy,   10
    With an auspicious[4] and a dropping[5] eye,
    With mirth in funeral and with dirge in marriage,
    In equal scale weighing delight and dole,
    Taken to wife. Nor have we herein barred
    Your better wisdoms, which have freely gone   15
    With this affair along. For all, our thanks.
    Now follows, that[6] you know, young Fortinbras,
    Holding a weak supposal[7] of our worth,
    Or thinking by our late dear brother's death
    Our state to be disjoint and out of frame,   20
    Colleaguèd[8] with this dream of his advantage,
    He hath not failed to pester us with message
    Importing the surrender of those lands
    Lost by his father, with all bands of law,
    To our most valiant brother. So much for him.   25
    Now for ourself and for this time of meeting.
    Thus much the business is: we have here writ
    To Norway, uncle of young Fortinbras—
    Who, impotent and bedrid, scarcely hears
    Of this his nephew's purpose—to suppress   30
    His further gait[9] herein, in that the levies,[10]
    The lists, and full proportions[11] are all made
    Out of his subjects; and we here dispatch
    You, good Cornelius, and you, Voltemand,
    For bearers of this greeting to old Norway,   35
    Giving to you no further personal power
    To business with the king, more than the scope

1. *sometime:* former.   2. *jointress:* joint ruler.   3. *defeated:* ruined, impaired.
4. *auspicious:* cheerful.   5. *dropping:* tearful.   6. *that:* that which.
7. *weak supposal:* low esteem.   8. *Colleaguèd:* united.   9. *gait:* progress.
10. *levies:* conscripted forces.   11. *proportions:* amounts of supplies and forces.

Of these delated[12] articles allow.
Farewell, and let your haste commend[13] your duty.

CORNELIUS. ⎱
VOLTEMAND. ⎰ In that, and all things, will we show our duty.   40

KING. We doubt it nothing. Heartily farewell.

                    [Exeunt Voltemand and Cornelius.]

And now, Laertes, what's the news with you?
You told us of some suit. What is't, Laertes?
You cannot speak of reason to the Dane[14]
And lose your voice.[15] What wouldst thou beg, Laertes,   45
That shall not be my offer, not thy asking?
The head is not more native[16] to the heart,
The hand more instrumental to the mouth,
Than is the throne of Denmark to thy father.
What wouldst thou have, Laertes?

LAERTES.   My dread lord,   50
Your leave and favor to return to France,
From whence though willingly I came to Denmark
To show my duty in your coronation,
Yet now I must confess, that duty done,
My thoughts and wishes bend again toward France   55
And bow them to your gracious leave and pardon.[17]

KING. Have you your father's leave? What says Polonius?

POLONIUS. He hath, my lord, wrung from me my slow leave
By laborsome petition, and at last
Upon his will I sealed my hard consent.   60
I do beseech you give him leave to go.

KING. Take thy fair hour, Laertes. Time be thine,
And thy best graces spend it at thy will.
But now, my cousin[18] Hamlet, and my son—

HAMLET. *[aside]* A little more than kin,[19] and less than kind![20]   65

KING. How is it that the clouds still hang on you?

HAMLET. Not so, my lord. I am too much in the sun.[21]

QUEEN. Good Hamlet, cast thy nighted color off,
And let thine eye look like a friend on Denmark.
Do not for ever with thy vailèd[22] lids   70
Seek for thy noble father in the dust.
Thou know'st 'tis common. All that lives must die,
Passing through nature to eternity.

---

12. *delated:* expressly stated.   13. *commend:* express.
14. *Dane:* King of Denmark.   15. *lose your voice:* waste your words.
16. *native:* closely connected, related.   17. *pardon:* permission to leave.
18. *cousin:* kinsman, used of any kinsman. In Shakespeare it is used most often in the uncle-nephew relationship.   19. *kin:* kinsman.   20. *kind:* natural.
21. *sun:* the Elizabethan figure of speech, or image, that represented the king.
22. *vailèd:* downcast.

HAMLET. Ay, madam, it is common.

QUEEN.   If it be,
Why seems it so particular with thee?   75

HAMLET. Seems, madam? Nay, it is. I know not 'seems.'
'Tis not alone my inky cloak, good mother,
Nor customary suits of solemn black,
Nor windy suspiration[23] of forced breath,
No, nor the fruitful[24] river in the eye,   80
Nor the dejected havior of the visage,
Together with all forms, moods, shapes of grief,
That can denote me truly. These indeed seem,
For they are actions that a man might play,
But I have that within which passeth show—   85
These but the trappings and the suits of woe.

KING. 'Tis sweet and commendable in your nature, Hamlet,
To give these mourning duties to your father,
But you must know your father lost a father,
That father lost, lost his, and the survivor bound   90
In filial obligation for some term
To do obsequious[25] sorrow. But to persever
In obstinate condolement is a course
Of impious stubbornness. 'Tis unmanly grief.
It shows a will most incorrect to heaven,   95
A heart unfortified, a mind impatient,
An understanding simple and unschooled.
For what we know must be and is as common
As any the most vulgar[26] thing to sense,
Why should we in our peevish opposition   100
Take it to heart? Fie, 'tis a fault to heaven,
A fault against the dead, a fault to nature,
To reason most absurd, whose common theme
Is death of fathers, and who still hath cried,
From the first corse[27] till he that died to-day,   105
'This must be so.' We pray you throw to earth
This unprevailing[28] woe, and think of us
As of a father, for let the world take note
You are the most immediate to our throne,
And with no less nobility of love   110
Than that which dearest father bears his son
Do I impart toward you. For your intent
In going back to school in Wittenberg,
It is most retrograde[29] to our desire,

23. *suspiration:* sigh.   24. *fruitful:* teeming.
25. *obsequious:* proper to obsequies, or funerals.   26. *vulgar:* common, ordinary.
27. *corse:* corpse.   28. *unprevailing:* unavailing.   29. *retrograde:* contrary.

And we beseech you, bend you to remain　　　　　115
Here in the cheer and comfort of our eye,
Our chiefest courtier, cousin, and our son.
QUEEN. Let not thy mother lose her prayers, Hamlet.
I pray thee stay with us, go not to Wittenberg.
HAMLET. I shall in all my best obey you, madam.　　　　　120
KING. Why, 'tis a loving and a fair reply.
Be as ourself in Denmark. Madam, come.
This gentle and unforced accord of Hamlet
Sits smiling to my heart, in grace whereof
No jocund health that Denmark drinks to-day　　　　　125
But the great cannon to the clouds shall tell,
And the king's rouse[30] the heaven shall bruit[31] again,
Respeaking earthly thunder. Come away.

　　　　　　[Flourish. Exeunt all but Hamlet.]

HAMLET. O that this too too solid flesh would melt,
Thaw, and resolve itself into a dew,　　　　　130
Or that the Everlasting had not fixed
His canon[32] 'gainst self-slaughter. O God, God,
How weary, stale, flat, and unprofitable
Seem to me all the uses[33] of this world!
Fie on't, ah, fie, 'tis an unweeded garden　　　　　135
That grows to seed. Things rank and gross in nature
Possess it merely.[34] That it should come to this,
But two months dead, nay, not so much, not two,
So excellent a king, that was to this
Hyperion to a satyr,[35] so loving to my mother　　　　　140
That he might not beteem[36] the winds of heaven
Visit her face too roughly. Heaven and earth,
Must I remember? Why, she would hang on him
As if increase of appetite had grown
By what it fed on, and yet within a month—　　　　　145
Let me not think on't; frailty, thy name is woman—
A little month, or ere those shoes were old
With which she followed my poor father's body
Like Niobe,[37] all tears, why she, even she—
O God, a beast that wants discourse[38] of reason　　　　　150
Would have mourned longer—married with my uncle,
My father's brother, but no more like my father

---

30. *rouse:* drink, carouse.　　31. *bruit:* report, echo.　　32. *canon:* law, decree.
33. *uses:* customs.　　34. *merely:* completely, entirely.
35. *Hyperion . . . satyr:* Hamlet compares his father to Apollo, the sun god, and
Claudius to a satyr, a man given to lechery.　　36. *beteem:* allow.
37. *Niobe:* Greek goddess whose children were slain by Artemus and Apollo. She
was later turned into a rock that constantly dripped water (tears).
38. *discourse:* power.

Than I to Hercules. Within a month,
Ere yet the salt of most unrighteous tears
Had left the flushing[39] in her gallèd[40] eyes,   155
She married. O, most wicked speed, to post
With such dexterity to incestuous[41] sheets!
It is not, nor it cannot come to good.
But break my heart, for I must hold my tongue.

[Enter Horatio, Marcellus, and Bernardo.]

HORATIO. Hail to your lordship!
HAMLET.   I am glad to see you well.   160
  Horatio!—or I do forget myself.
HORATIO. The same, my lord, and your poor servant ever.
HAMLET. Sir, my good friend, I'll change[42] that name with you.
  And what make you from Wittenberg, Horatio?
  Marcellus?   165
MARCELLUS. My good lord!
HAMLET. I am very glad to see you. *[To Bernardo.]* Good even, sir.
  But what, in faith, make you from Wittenberg?
HORATIO. A truant disposition, good my lord.
HAMLET. I would not have your enemy say so,   170
  Nor shall you do my ear that violence
  To make it truster[43] of your own report
  Against yourself. I know you are no truant.
  But what is your affair in Elsinore?
  We'll teach you to drink deep ere you depart.   175
HORATIO. My lord, I came to see your father's funeral.
HAMLET. I prithee do not mock me, fellow student.
  I think it was to see my mother's wedding.
HORATIO. Indeed, my lord, it followed hard upon.[44]
HAMLET. Thrift, thrift,[45] Horatio. The funeral baked meats   180
  Did coldly furnish forth the marriage tables.
  Would I had met my dearest[46] foe in heaven
  Or ever[47] I had seen that day, Horatio!
  My father—methinks I see my father.
HORATIO. Where, my lord?
HAMLET.   In my mind's eye, Horatio.   185
HORATIO. I saw him once. He was a goodly king.
HAMLET. He was a man, take him for all in all,
  I shall not look upon his like again.
HORATIO. My lord, I think I saw him yesternight.

---

39. *flushing:* reddening.   40. *gallèd:* sore with weeping.
41. *incestuous:* the marriage of a woman to her dead husband's brother was
considered incestuous and invalid.   42. *change:* exchange.   43. *truster:* believer.
44. *hard upon:* closely afterward.   45. *Thrift, thrift:* economy.
46. *dearest:* most costly; hence his most dangerous or worst.   47. *Or ever:* before.

HAMLET. Saw? who?   190
HORATIO. My lord, the king your father.
HAMLET.   The king my father?
HORATIO. Season your admiration[48] for a while
  With an attent ear till I may deliver
  Upon the witness of these gentlemen
  This marvel to you.
HAMLET.   For God's love let me hear!   195
HORATIO. Two nights together had these gentlemen,
  Marcellus and Bernardo, on their watch
  In the dead waste and middle of the night
  Been thus encountered. A figure like your father,
  Armed at point exactly,[49] cap-a-pe,[50]   200
  Appears before them and with solemn march
  Goes slow and stately by them. Thrice he walked
  By their oppressed[51] and fear-surprisèd eyes
  Within his truncheon's[52] length, whilst they, distilled
  Almost to jelly with the act of fear,   205
  Stand dumb and speak not to him. This to me
  In dreadful[53] secrecy impart they did,
  And I with them the third night kept the watch,
  Where, as they had delivered, both in time,
  Form of the thing, each word made true and good,   210
  The apparition comes. I knew your father.
  These hands are not more like.
HAMLET.   But where was this?
MARCELLUS. My lord, upon the platform where we watched.
HAMLET. Did you not speak to it?
HORATIO.   My lord, I did,
  But answer made it none. Yet once methought   215
  It lifted up its head and did address
  Itself to motion like as it would speak.
  But even then the morning cock crew loud;
  And at the sound it shrunk in haste away
  And vanished from our sight.
HAMLET.   'Tis very strange.   220
HORATIO. As I do live, my honored lord, 'tis true,
  And we did think it writ down in our duty
  To let you know of it.
HAMLET. Indeed, indeed, sirs; but this troubles me.
  Hold you the watch to-night?
MARCELLUS. ⎤
                              We do, my lord.
BERNARDO. ⎦   225

48. *admiration:* astonishment.   49. *at point exactly:* completely.
50. *cap-a-pe:* from head to foot.   51. *oppressed:* distressed.
52. *truncheon's:* baton's or staff's.   53. *dreadful:* solemn.

HAMLET. Armed, say you?

MARCELLUS. ⎱ Armed, my lord.
BERNARDO. ⎰

HAMLET. From top to toe?

MARCELLUS. ⎱   My lord, from head to foot.
BERNARDO. ⎰

HAMLET. Then saw you not his face?

HORATIO. O, yes, my lord; he wore his beaver⁵⁴ up.   230

HAMLET. What, looked he frowningly?

HORATIO. A countenance more in sorrow than in anger.

HAMLET. Pale or red?

HORATIO. Nay, very pale.

HAMLET.   And fixed his eyes upon you?

HORATIO. Most constantly.

HAMLET.   I would I had been there.   235

HORATIO. It would have much amazed you.

HAMLET. Very like, very like. Stayed it long?

HORATIO. While one with moderate haste might tell⁵⁵ a hundred.

MARCELLUS. ⎱ Longer, longer.
BERNARDO. ⎰

HORATIO. Not when I saw't.

HAMLET.   His beard was grizzly? No?   240

HORATIO. It was as I have seen it in his life,
  A sable silvered.⁵⁶

HAMLET.   I will watch to-night.
  Perchance 'twill walk again.

HORATIO.   I warrant you it will.

HAMLET. If it assume my noble father's person,
  I'll speak to it though hell itself should gape   245
  And bid me hold my peace. I pray you all,
  If you have hitherto concealed this sight,
  Let it be tenable⁵⁷ in your silence still;
  And whatsoever else shall hap to-night,
  Give it an understanding but no tongue.   250
  I will requite your loves. So fare you well.
  Upon the platform, 'twixt eleven and twelve,
  I'll visit you.

ALL.   Our duty to your honor.

HAMLET. Your love, as mine to you. Farewell.

                              [Exeunt all but Hamlet.]
  My father's spirit in arms? All is not well.   255
  I doubt some foul play. Would the night were come!
  Till then sit still, my soul. Foul deeds will rise,
  Though all the earth o'erwhelm them, to men's eyes.   *[Exit.]*

---

54. *beaver:* visor on a helmet.   55. *tell:* count.
56. *sable silvered:* dark brown or black mingled with white.   57. *tenable:* held.

SCENE 3   *A room in Polonius' house.*

[Enter Laertes and Ophelia.]

LAERTES. My necessaries are embarked. Farewell.
  And, sister, as¹ the winds give benefit
  And convoy is assistant,² do not sleep,
  But let me hear from you.
OPHELIA.   Do you doubt that?
LAERTES. For Hamlet, and the trifling of his favors,   5
  Hold it a fashion and a toy in blood,³
  A violet in the youth of primy⁴ nature,
  Forward,⁵ not permanent, sweet, not lasting,
  The perfume and suppliance⁶ of a minute,
  No more.
OPHELIA.   No more but so?
LAERTES.   Think it no more.   10
  For nature crescent⁷ does not grow alone
  In thews⁸ and bulk, but as this temple⁹ waxes
  The inward service of the mind and soul
  Grows wide withal.¹⁰ Perhaps he loves you now,
  And now no soil¹¹ nor cautel¹² doth besmirch   15
  The virtue of his will,¹³ but you must fear,
  His greatness weighed,¹⁴ his will is not his own.
  For he himself is subject to his birth.
  He may not, as unvalued persons do,
  Carve for himself; for on his choice depends   20
  The safety and health of this whole state,
  And therefore must his choice be circumscribed
  Unto the voice and yielding¹⁵ of that body
  Whereof he is the head. Then if he says he loves you,
  It fits your wisdom so far to believe it   25
  As he in his particular act and place
  May give his saying deed, which is no further
  Than the main¹⁶ voice of Denmark goes withal.
  Then weigh what loss your honor may sustain
  If with too credent ear you list his songs,   30
  Or lose your heart, or your chaste treasure open

1. *as:* whenever.   2. *convoy is assistant:* means of conveyance are at hand.
3. *a fashion . . . blood:* a fad and passing amorous fancy.   4. *primy:* springlike.
5. *Forward:* undeveloped, early.   6. *suppliance:* pastime.   7. *crescent:* growing.
8. *thews:* bodily strength.   9. *temple:* body.   10. *withal:* also, at the same time.
11. *soil:* blemish.   12. *cautel:* deceit.   13. *will:* desire.
14. *His greatness weighed:* If his noble birth is considered.
15. *voice and yielding:* support, approval.   16. *main:* mighty.

To his unmastered importunity.[17]
Fear it, Ophelia, fear it, my dear sister,
And keep within the rear of your affection,
Out of the shot and danger of desire. 35
The chariest[18] maid is prodigal[19] enough
If she unmask her beauty to the moon.
Virtue itself scapes not calumnious strokes.
The canker galls the infants of the spring[20]
Too oft before their buttons be disclosed,[21] 40
And in the morn and liquid dew[22] of youth
Contagious blastments[23] are most imminent.
Be wary then; best safety lies in fear.
Youth to itself rebels, though none else near.
OPHELIA. I shall the effect of this good lesson keep 45
As watchman to my heart; but, good my brother,
Do not as some ungracious pastors do,
Show me the steep and thorny way to heaven,
Whiles like a puffed and reckless libertine
Himself the primrose path of dalliance treads 50
And recks[24] not his own rede.[25]
LAERTES.　　　　　　　　　　　O, fear me not.

[Enter Polonius.]

I stay too long. But here my father comes.
A double blessing is a double grace;[26]
Occasion[27] smiles upon a second leave.
POLONIUS. Yet here, Laertes? Aboard, aboard, for shame! 55
The wind sits in the shoulder of your sail,
And you are stayed for. There—my blessing with you,
And these few precepts in thy memory
See thou character.[28] Give thy thoughts no tongue,
Nor any unproportioned[29] thought his act. 60
Be thou familiar, but by no means vulgar.
The friends thou hast, and their adoption tried,
Grapple them to thy soul with hoops of steel,
But do not dull thy palm[30] with entertainment
Of each new-hatched, unfledged comrade. Beware 65
Of entrance to a quarrel; but being in,

---

17. *importunity:* insistence.　18. *chariest:* most reserved.　19. *prodigal:* reckless.
20. *canker . . . spring:* the canker worms destroy the young buds of spring.
21. *buttons be disclosed:* buds have opened.　22. *liquid dew:* time when dew is fresh.
23. *blastments:* blights.　24. *recks:* heeds.　25. *rede:* advice.
26. Laertes has already said goodby to his father once.　27. *Occasion:* opportunity.
28. *character:* inscribe.　29. *unproportioned:* unsuitable.
30. *dull thy palm:* make yourself less sensitive to true friends by shaking hands with everybody.

Bear't that th' opposèd may beware of thee.
Give every man thine ear, but few thy voice;
Take each man's censure,[31] but reserve thy judgment.
Costly thy habit as thy purse can buy,　　　　　　　70
But not expressed in fancy; rich, not gaudy,
For the apparel oft proclaims the man,
And they in France of the best rank and station
Are of a most select and generous chief in that.
Neither a borrower nor a lender be,　　　　　　　75
For loan oft loses both itself and friend,
And borrowing dulls the edge of husbandry.[32]
This above all, to thine own self be true,
And it must follow as the night the day
Thou canst not then be false to any man.　　　　　　80
Farewell! My blessing season[33] this in thee!
LAERTES. Most humbly do I take my leave, my lord.
POLONIUS. The time invites you. Go, your servants tend.
LAERTES. Farewell, Ophelia, and remember well
　What I have said to you.
OPHELIA.　　　　　　　'Tis in my memory locked,　　85
　And you yourself shall keep the key of it.
LAERTES. Farewell.　　　　　　　　*[Exit Laertes.]*
POLONIUS. What is't, Ophelia, he hath said to you?
OPHELIA. So please you, something touching the Lord Hamlet.
POLONIUS. Marry, well bethought.　　　　　　　90
　'Tis told me he hath very oft of late
　Given private time to you, and you yourself
　Have of your audience been most free and bounteous.
　If it be so—as so 'tis put on me,
　And that in way of caution—I must tell you　　　95
　You do not understand yourself so clearly
　As it behooves my daughter and your honor.
　What is between you? Give me up the truth.
OPHELIA. He hath, my lord, of late made many tenders[34]
　Of his affection to me.　　　　　　　100
POLONIUS. Affection? Pooh! You speak like a green girl,
　Unsifted[35] in such perilous circumstance.
　Do you believe his tenders, as you call them?
OPHELIA. I do not know, my lord, what I should think.
POLONIUS. Marry, I'll teach you. Think yourself a baby　105
　That you have ta'en these tenders for true pay
　Which are not sterling. Tender[36] yourself more dearly,
　Or—not to crack the wind[37] of the poor phrase,

---

31. *censure:* opinion.　32. *husbandry:* thrift.　33. *season:* mature.
34. *tenders:* offers.　35. *Unsifted:* untried.　36. *Tender:* hold.
37. *crack the wind:* make wheeze like a horse driven too hard.

Running it thus—you'll tender me a fool.[38]
OPHELIA. My lord, he hath importuned[39] me with love   110
    In honorable fashion.
POLONIUS. Ay, fashion you may call it. Go to, go to.[40]
OPHELIA. And hath given countenance to his speech, my lord,
    With almost all the holy vows of heaven.
POLONIUS. Ay, springes[41] to catch woodcocks.[42] I do know,   115
    When the blood burns, how prodigal the soul
    Gives the tongue vows. These blazes, daughter,
    Giving more light than heat, extinct in both,
    Even in their promise, as it is a-making,
    You must not take for fire. From this time, daughter,   120
    Be something scanter of your maiden presence.
    Set your entreatments[43] at a higher rate
    Than a command to parley.[44] For Lord Hamlet,
    Believe so much in him, that he is young,
    And with a larger tether may he walk   125
    Than may be given you. In few,[45] Ophelia,
    Do not believe his vows; for they are brokers,[46]
    Not of that dye[47] which their investments[48] show,
    But mere implorators[49] of unholy suits,
    Breathing like sanctified and pious bawds,   130
    The better to beguile. This is for all:
    I would not, in plain terms, from this time forth,
    Have you so slander[50] any moment leisure
    As to give words or talk with the Lord Hamlet.
    Look to't, I charge you. Come your ways.   135
OPHELIA. I shall obey, my lord.   *[Exeunt.]*

SCENE 4   *The platform.*

[Enter Hamlet, Horatio, and Marcellus.]

HAMLET. The air bites shrewdly;[1] it is very cold!
HORATIO. It is a nipping and an eager air.
HAMLET. What hour now?
HORATIO.   I think it lacks of twelve.

---

38. *tender me a fool:* make me out a fool.   39. *importuned:* persistently courted.
40. *Go to, go to:* exclamation showing impatience.   41. *springes:* snares.
42. *woodcocks:* birds easily caught, birds thought to be foolish.
43. *entreatments:* negotiations for surrender or simply a conversation.
44. *parley:* confer, as with a besieger.   45. *in few:* in a word.
46. *brokers:* go-betweens, procurers.   47. *dye:* color or sort.
48. *investments:* clothes.   49. *implorators:* solicitors.   50. *slander:* misuse.

1. *shrewdly:* sharply.

MARCELLUS. No, it is struck.

HORATIO. Indeed? I heard it not. Then it draws near the season   5
Wherein the spirit held his wont to walk.

[A flourish of trumpets, and two pieces go off within.]

What does this mean, my lord?

HAMLET. The king doth wake[2] to-night and takes his rouse,[3]
Keeps wassail,[4] and the swaggering upspring reels,[5]
And as he drains his draughts of Rhenish down   10
The kettledrum and trumpet thus bray out
The triumph of his pledge.[6]

HORATIO.   Is it a custom?

HAMLET. Ay, marry, is't,
But to my mind, though I am native here
And to the manner born, it is a custom   15
More honored in the breach[7] than the observance.
This heavy-headed revel east and west
Makes us traduced and taxed of[8] other nations.
They clepe[9] us drunkards and with swinish phrase
Soil our addition;[10] and indeed it takes   20
From our achievements, though performed at height,
The pith and marrow of our attribute.[11]
So oft it chances in particular men
That for some vicious mole[12] of nature in them,
As in their birth—werein they are not guilty,   25
Since nature cannot choose his origin—
By the o'ergrowth of some complexion,[13]
Oft breaking down the pales[14] and forts of reason,
Or by some habit that too much o'erleavens[15]
The form of plausive[16] manners, that these men—   30
Carrying, I say, the stamp of one defect,
Being nature's livery,[17] or fortune's star,
Their virtues else—be they as pure as grace,
As infinite as man may undergo—
Shall in the general censure take corruption   35
From that particular fault. The dram[18] of evil
Doth all the noble substance often dout,[19]
To his own scandal.

---

2. *wake:* hold revel.   3. *rouse:* carouse.
4. *wassail:* feasting, drinking bout.   5. *upspring reels:* riotous dances.
6. *pledge:* toast of friendship in which cup is completely drained.
7. *breach:* breaking.   8. *traduced and taxed of:* disgraced and censured by.
9. *clepe:* call.   10. *addition:* honor.   11. *attribute:* reputation.
12. *mole:* defect.
13. *o'ergrowth . . . complexion:* overdevelopment of some natural tendency.
14. *pales:* fences or palisades.   15. *too much o'erleavens:* too much changes.
16. *plausive:* pleasing.
17. *nature's livery:* endowment from nature, nature's uniform.
18. *dram:* a small amount.   19. *dout:* doubt, corrupt.

[Enter Ghost.]

HORATIO.   Look, my lord, it comes.

HAMLET. Angels and ministers of grace defend us!
Be thou a spirit of health or goblin[20] damned,   40
Bring with thee airs from heaven or blasts from hell,
Be thy intents wicked or charitable,
Thou com'st in such a questionable shape
That I will speak to thee. I'll call thee Hamlet,
King, father, royal Dane. O, O, answer me!   45
Let me not burst in ignorance, but tell
Why thy canonized[21] bones, hearsèd[22] in death,
Have burst their cerements,[23] why the sepulchre
Wherein we saw thee quietly interred
Hath oped his ponderous and marble jaws   50
To cast thee up again. What may this mean
That thou, dead corse, again in complete steel,
Revisits thus the glimpses of the moon,[24]
Making night hideous, and we fools of nature
So horridly to shake our disposition   55
With thoughts beyond the reaches of our souls?
Say, why is this? wherefore? what should we do?

[Ghost beckons Hamlet.]

HORATIO. It beckons you to go away with it,
As if it some impartment[25] did desire
To you alone.

MARCELLUS.   Look with what courteous action   60
It waves you to a more removèd ground.
But do not go with it.

HORATIO.   No, by no means.

HAMLET. It will not speak; then will I follow it.

HORATIO. Do not, my lord.

HAMLET.   Why, what should be the fear?
I do not set my life at a pin's fee,[26]   65
And for my soul, what can it do to that,
Being a thing immortal as itself?
It waves me forth again. I'll follow it.

HORATIO. What if it tempt you toward the flood, my lord,
Or to the dreadful summit of the cliff   70
That beetles o'er[27] his base into the sea,
And there assume some other horrible form,
Which might deprive your sovereignty of reason
And draw you into madness? Think of it.
The very place puts toys of desperation,[28]   75

---

20. *goblin:* evil spirit.
21. *canonized:* buried according to the canon of the church.   22. *hearsèd:* coffined.
23. *cerements:* waxed grave clothes.   24. *glimpses of the moon:* the earth by night.
25. *impartment:* communication.   26. *fee:* value.   27. *beetles o'er:* hangs over.
28. *toys of desperation:* freakish thoughts of suicide.

Without more motive, into every brain
That looks so many fathoms to the sea
And hears it roar beneath.

HAMLET.   It waves me still.
Go on. I'll follow thee.

MARCELLUS. You shall not go, my lord.

HAMLET.   Hold off your hand.   80

HORATIO. Be ruled. You shall not go.

HAMLET.   My fate cries out
And makes each petty artery in this body
As hardy as the Nemean lion's²⁹ nerve.³⁰
Still am I called! Unhand me, gentlemen.
By heaven, I'll make a ghost of him that lets³¹ me!   85
I say, away! Go on. I'll follow thee.

                              [Exeunt Ghost and Hamlet.]

HORATIO. He waxes desperate with imagination.

MARCELLUS. Let's follow. 'Tis not fit thus to obey him.

HORATIO. Have after. To what issue³² will this come?

MARCELLUS. Something is rotten in the state of Denmark.   90

HORATIO. Heaven will direct it.

MARCELLUS.   Nay, let's follow him.   *[Exeunt.]*

SCENE 5   *Another part of the platform.*

[Enter Ghost and Hamlet.]

HAMLET. Whither wilt thou lead me? Speak. I'll go no further.

GHOST. Mark me.

HAMLET.   I will.

GHOST.   My hour is almost come,
When I to sulphurous and tormenting flames¹
Must render up myself.

HAMLET.   Alas, poor ghost!

GHOST. Pity me not, but lend thy serious hearing   5
To what I shall unfold.

HAMLET.   Speak. I am bound to hear.

GHOST. So art thou to revenge, when thou shalt hear.

HAMLET. What?

GHOST. I am thy father's spirit,
Doomed for a certain term to walk the night;   10

---

29. *Nemean lion's:* one of the mythical monsters slain by Hercules.
30. *nerve:* muscle, sinew.   31. *lets:* hinders.   32. *issue:* outcome.

1. *flames:* purgatory.

And for the day confined to fast in fires,
Till the foul crimes done in my days of nature
Are burnt and purged away. But that I am forbid
To tell the secrets of my prison house,
I could a tale unfold whose lightest word 15
Would harrow up thy soul, freeze thy young blood,
Make thy two eyes, like stars, start from their spheres,
Thy knotty and combinèd locks to part,
And each particular hair to stand on end
Like quills upon the fretful porpentine.[2] 20
But this eternal blazon[3] must not be
To ears of flesh and blood. List, Hamlet, O, list!
If thou didst ever thy dear father love—
HAMLET. O God!
GHOST. Revenge his foul and most unnatural murther. 25
HAMLET. Murther?
GHOST. Murther most foul, as in the best it is,
But this most foul, strange, and unnatural.
HAMLET. Haste me to know't, that I, with wings as swift
As meditation or the thoughts of love, 30
May sweep to my revenge.
GHOST.   I find thee apt,
And duller shouldst thou be than the fat weed
That rots itself in ease on Lethe wharf,[4]
Wouldst thou not stir in this. Now, Hamlet, hear.
'Tis given out that, sleeping in my orchard, 35
A serpent stung me. So the whole ear of Denmark
Is by a forgèd process of my death
Rankly abused. But know, thou noble youth,
The serpent that did sting thy father's life
Now wears his crown.
HAMLET.   O my prophetic soul! 40
My uncle?
GHOST. Ay, that incestuous, that adulterate beast,
With witchcraft of his wit, with traitorous gifts—
O wicked wit and gifts, that have the power
So to seduce!—won to his shameful lust 45
The will of my most seeming-virtuous queen.
O Hamlet, what a falling-off was there,
From me, whose love was of that dignity
That it went hand in hand even with the vow
I made to her in marriage, and to decline[5] 50
Upon a wretch whose natural gifts were poor

2. *porpentine:* porcupine.
3. *eternal blazon:* revelation of the hereafter.
4. *Lethe wharf:* bank of the river of forgetfulness in Hades.
5. *decline:* fall back.

To those of mine!
But virtue, as it never will be moved,
Though lewdness court it in a shape of heaven,
So lust, though to a radiant angel linked,   55
Will sate itself in a celestial bed
And prey on garbage.
But soft, methinks I scent the morning air.
Brief let me be. Sleeping within mine orchard,
My custom always in the afternoon,   60
Upon my secure hour thy uncle stole
With juice of cursed hebenon[6] in a vial,
And in the porches of my ears did pour
The leperous distilment, whose effect
Holds such an enmity with blood of man   65
That swift as quicksilver it courses through
The natural gates and alleys of the body,
And with a sudden vigor it doth posset[7]
And curd, like eager[8] droppings into milk,
The thin and wholesome blood. So did it mine,   70
And a most instant tetter[9] barked about[10]
Most lazar-like[11] with vile and loathsome crust
All my smooth body.
Thus was I, sleeping, by a brother's hand
Of life, of crown, of queen at once dispatched,   75
Cut off even in the blossoms of my sin,
Unhouseled,[12] disappointed,[13] unaneled,[14]
No reckoning made, but sent to my account
With all my imperfections on my head.
O, horrible! O, horrible! most horrible!   80
If thou hast nature in thee, bear it not.
Let not the royal bed of Denmark be
A couch for luxury[15] and damnèd incest.
But howsoever thou pursuest this act,
Taint not thy mind,[16] nor let thy soul contrive   85
Against thy mother aught. Leave her to heaven
And to those thorns that in her bosom lodge
To prick and sting her. Fare thee well at once.
The glowworm shows the matin[17] to be near
And gins to pale his uneffectual fire.   90
Adieu, adieu, adieu. Remember me.   *[Exit.]*

6. *hebenon:* a poisonous herb.   7. *posset:* coagulate.   8. *eager:* sour, acid.
9. *tetter:* eruption, as eczema.   10. *barked about:* covered as with bark.
11. *lazar-like:* like a leper.   12. *Unhouseled:* without the sacrament of Communion.
13. *disappointed:* unable to go to Confession.
14. *unaneled:* without Extreme Unction (the sacrament in which a dying person is
anointed with oil).   15. *luxury:* lust.
16. *Taint . . . mind:* deprave not your character.   17. *matin:* morning.

HAMLET. O all you host of heaven! O earth! What else?
And shall I couple[18] hell? O fie! Hold, hold, my heart,
And you, my sinews, grow not instant old,
But bear me stiffly up. Remember thee?   95
Ay, thou poor ghost, while memory holds a seat
In this distracted globe.[19] Remember thee?
Yea, from the table[20] of my memory
I'll wipe away all trivial fond[21] records,
All saws[22] of books, all forms, all pressures[23] past   100
That youth and observation copied there,
And thy commandment all alone shall live
Within the book and volume of my brain,
Unmixed with baser matter. Yes, yes, by heaven!
O most pernicious woman!   105
O villain, villain, smiling, damnèd villain!
My tables,[24]—meet[25] it is I set it down
That one may smile, and smile, and be a villain.
At least I am sure it may be so in Denmark.   *[Writes.]*
So, uncle, there you are. Now to my word: 110
It is "Adieu, adieu, remember me."
I have sworn't.
HORATIO. My lord, my lord! *[Within.]*
MARCELLUS.   Lord Hamlet! *[Within.]*
HORATIO. *[Within.]*   Heaven secure him!
HAMLET. So be it!   115
MARCELLUS. Illo, ho, ho,[26] my lord! *[Within.]*

[Enter Horatio and Marcellus.]

MARCELLUS. How is't, my noble lord?
HORATIO.   What news, my lord?
HAMLET. O, wonderful!
HORATIO. Good my lord, tell it.
HAMLET.   No, you'll reveal it.
HORATIO. Not I, my lord, by heaven.
MARCELLUS.   Nor I, my lord.   120
HAMLET. How say you then? Would heart of man once think it?
But you'll be secret?
BOTH.   Ay, by heaven, my lord.
HAMLET. There's never a villain dwelling in all Denmark
But he's an arrant[27] knave.
HORATIO. There needs no ghost, my lord, come from the grave   125
To tell us this.

18. *couple:* add.   19. *distracted globe:* confused head.   20. *table:* tablet.
21. *fond:* foolish.   22. *saws:* wise sayings.   23. *pressures:* impressions.
24. *tables:* writing tablets.   25. *meet:* proper.
26. *Illo, ho, ho:* the cry of the falconer to summon his hawk.
27. *arrant:* thoroughgoing.

HAMLET. Why, right, you are i'th' right,
And so, without more circumstance[28] at all,
I hold it fit that we shake hands and part:
You, as your business and desires shall point you,
For every man has business and desire 130
Such as it is; and for my own poor part,
Look you, I'll go pray.
HORATIO. These are but wild and whirling words, my lord.
HAMLET. I am sorry they offend you, heartily;
Yes, faith, heartily.
HORATIO. There's no offense, my lord. 135
HAMLET. Yes, by Saint Patrick, but there is, Horatio,
And much offense too. Touching this vision here,
It is an honest ghost, that let me tell you.
For your desire to know what is between us,
O'ermaster't as you may. And now, good friends, 140
As you are friends, scholars, and soldiers,
Give me one poor request.
HORATIO. What is't, my lord? We will.
HAMLET. Never make known what you have seen to-night.
BOTH. My lord, we will not.
HAMLET. Nay, but swear't.
HORATIO. In faith, 145
My lord, not I.
MARCELLUS. Nor I, my lord—in faith.
HAMLET. Upon my sword.
MARCELLUS. We have sworn, my lord, already.
HAMLET. Indeed, upon my sword, indeed.

[Ghost cries under the stage.]

GHOST. Swear.
HAMLET. Ha, ha, boy, say'st thou so? Art thou there, truepenny?[29] 150
Come on. You hear this fellow in the cellarage.[30]
Consent to swear.
HORATIO. Propose the oath, my lord.
HAMLET. Never to speak of this that you have seen,
Swear by my sword.
GHOST. *[Beneath.]* Swear. 155
HAMLET. *Hic et ubique?*[31] Then we'll shift our ground.
Come hither, gentlemen,
And lay your hands again upon my sword.
Never to speak of this that you have heard.
Swear by my sword. 160

28. *circumstance:* ceremony.
29. *truepenny:* slang for honest old boy.
30. *cellarage:* underground rooms or vaults.
31. *Hic et ubique:* Here and everywhere.

GHOST. *[Beneath.]* Swear.

HAMLET. Well said, old mole! Canst work i' th' ground so fast?
A worthy pioner!³² Once more remove, good friends.

HORATIO. O day and night, but this is wondrous strange!

HAMLET. And therefore as a stranger give it welcome.   165
There are more things in heaven and earth, Horatio,
Than are dreamt of in our philosophy.
But come:
Here as before, never, so help you mercy,
How strange or odd soe'er I bear myself   170
(As I perchance hereafter shall think meet
To put an antic disposition³³ on),
That you, at such times seeing me, never shall,
With arms encumb'red³⁴ thus, or this head-shake,
Or by pronouncing of some doubtful phrase,   175
As "Well, well, we know," or "We could, an if³⁵ we would,"
Or "If we list to speak," or "There be, an if they might,"
Or such ambiguous giving out, to note
That you know aught of me—this not to do,
So grace and mercy at your most need help you,   180
Swear.

GHOST. *[Beneath.]* Swear.   *[They swear.]*

HAMLET. Rest, rest, perturbèd spirit! So, gentlemen,
With all my love I do commend me to you,
And what so poor a man as Hamlet is   185
May do t' express his love and friending to you,
God willing, shall not lack. Let us go in together,
And still your fingers on your lips, I pray.
The time is out of joint. O cursèd spite
That ever I was born to set it right!   190
Nay, come, let's go together.   *[Exeunt.]*

ACT II

SCENE 1   *A room in Polonius' house.*

[Enter Polonius and Reynaldo.]

POLONIUS. Give him this money and these notes, Reynaldo.

REYNALDO. I will, my lord.

32. *pioner:* foot soldiers who dug trenches.
33. *antic disposition:* mad or fantastic behavior.   34. *encumb'red:* folded.
35. *an if:* if.

POLONIUS. You shall do marvellous wisely, good Reynaldo,
  Before you visit him, to make inquiry
  Of his behavior.
REYNALDO.   My lord, I did intend it.   5
POLONIUS. Marry, well said, very well said. Look you, sir,
  Enquire me[1] first what Danskers[2] are in Paris,
  And how, and who, what means, and where they keep,[3]
  What company, at what expense; and finding
  By this encompassment and drift of question[4]   10
  That they do know my son, come you more nearer
  Than your particular demands will touch it.
  Take you as 'twere some distant knowledge of him,
  As thus, "I know his father and his friends,
  And in part him." Do you mark this, Reynaldo?   15
REYNALDO. Ay, very well, my lord.
POLONIUS. "And in part him, but," you may say, "not well,
  But if't be he I mean, he's very wild
  Addicted so and so." And there put on him
  What forgeries[5] you please; marry, none so rank   20
  As may dishonor him—take heed of that;
  But, sir, such wanton, wild, and usual slips
  As are companions noted and most known
  To youth and liberty.
REYNALDO.   As gaming, my lord.
POLONIUS. Ay, or drinking, fencing, swearing, quarrelling,   25
  Drabbing.[6] You may go so far.
REYNALDO. My lord, that would dishonor him.
POLONIUS. Faith, no, as you may season[7] it in the charge.
  You must not put another scandal on him,
  That he is open to incontinency.[8]   30
  That's not my meaning. But breathe his faults so quaintly[9]
  That they may seem the taints of liberty,[10]
  The flash and outbreak of a fiery mind,
  A savageness in unreclaimèd[11] blood,
  Of general assault.[12]
REYNALDO.   But, my good lord—   35
POLONIUS. Wherefore should you do this?
REYNALDO.   Ay, my lord,
  I would know that.
POLONIUS.   Marry, sir, here's my drift,
  And I believe it is a fetch of warrant.[13]

1. *me:* for me.   2. *Danskers:* Danes.   3. *keep:* lodge.
4. *encompassment . . . question:* roundabout talk.   5. *forgeries:* invented tales.
6. *Drabbing:* associating with harlots.   7. *season:* qualify.
8. *incontinency:* extreme lewdness.   9. *quaintly:* cleverly, artfully.
10. *taints of liberty:* weaknesses or blemishes due to freedom.
11. *unreclaimèd:* untamed.   12. *Of general assault:* tendency common to all youth.
13. *fetch of warrant:* justifiable trick.

You laying these slight sullies on my son
As 'twere a thing a little soiled i' th' working,[14]   40
Mark you,
Your party in converse, him you would sound,[15]
Having ever seen[16] in the prenominate[17] crimes
The youth you breathe of[18] guilty, be assured
He closes[19] with you in this consequence:[20]   45
"Good sir," or so, or "friend," or "gentleman"—
According to the phrase or the addition[21]
Of man and country.
REYNALDO.   Very good, my lord.
POLONIUS. And then, sir, does he this—he does—
What was I about to say? By the mass, I was about to say   50
something! Where did I leave?
REYNALDO. At "closes in the consequence," at "friend or so,"
and "gentleman."
POLONIUS. At "closes in the consequence"—Ay, marry!
He closes thus: "I know the gentleman;   55
I saw him yesterday, or t'other day,
Or then, or then, with such and such, and, as you say,
There was he gaming, there o'ertook in's rouse,[22]
There falling out[23] at tennis"; or perchance,
"I saw him enter such a house of sale,"   60
Videlicet,[24] a brothel, or so forth.
See you now;
Your bait of falsehood takes this carp[25] of truth,
And thus do we of wisdom and of reach,[26]
With windlasses[27] and with assays of bias,[28]   65
By indirections find directions[29] out.
So, by my former lecture and advice,
Shall you my son. You have me,[30] have you not?
REYNALDO. My lord, I have.
POLONIUS.   God bye you, fare you well.
REYNALDO. Good my lord.   70
POLONIUS. Observe his inclination in yourself.[31]
REYNALDO. I shall, my lord.
POLONIUS. And let him ply his music.

14. *soiled i' th' working*: soiled by the usual experiences of growing up.
15. *sound*: sound out.   16. *Having ever seen*: If he has ever seen.
17. *prenominate*: above mentioned.   18. *breathe of*: call, or speak of.
19. *closes*: agrees.   20. *in this consequence*: in the following way.
21. *addition*: title.   22. *o'ertook in's rouse*: overcome by drink.
23. *falling out*: quarreling.   24. *Videlicet*: namely.
25. *carp*: Polonius carries out his figure of a fish being caught.   26. *reach*: capacity.
27. *windlasses*: roundabout ways.
28. *assays of bias*: indirect attempts, a bowling term.
29. *directions*: straight courses (the truth).   30. *have me*: understand me.
31. *in yourself*: by personal observation.

REYNALDO.   Well, my lord.
POLONIUS. Farewell.   *[Exit Reynaldo.]*

                    [Enter Ophelia.]

                How now, Ophelia, what's the matter?
OPHELIA. Alas my lord, I have been so affrighted!   75
POLONIUS. With what, in the name of God?
OPHELIA. My lord, as I was sewing in my chamber,
  Lord Hamlet, with his doublet[32] all unbraced,[33]
  No hat upon his head, his stockings fouled,
  Ungartered, and down-gyvèd[34] to his ankle,   80
  Pale as his shirt, his knees knocking each other,
  And with a look so piteous in purport[35]
  As if he had been loosèd out of hell
  To speak of horrors—he comes before me.
POLONIUS. Mad for thy love?
OPHELIA.   My lord, I do not know,   85
  But truly I do fear it.
POLONIUS.   What said he?
OPHELIA. He took me by the wrist and held me hard.
  Then goes he to the length of all his arm,
  And with his other hand thus o'er his brow
  He falls to such perusal of my face   90
  As[36] he would draw it. Long stayed he so.
  At last, a little shaking of mine arm
  And thrice his head thus waving up and down,
  He raised a sigh so piteous and profound
  As it did seem to shatter all his bulk   95
  And end his being. That done, he lets me go,
  And with his head over his shoulder turned
  He seemed to find his way without his eyes,
  For out o' doors he went without their help,
  And to the last bended their light on me.   100
POLONIUS. Come, go with me. I will go seek the king.
  This is the very ecstasy[37] of love,
  Whose violent property[38] fordoes[39] itself
  And leads the will to desperate undertakings
  As oft as any passion under heaven   105
  That does afflict our natures. I am sorry.
  What, have you given him any hard words of late?
OPHELIA. No, my good lord; but as you did command
  I did repel his letters and denied
  His access to me.

---

32. *doublet:* close-fitting coat.
33. *unbraced:* unfastened.   34. *down-gyvèd:* hanging down.
35. *purport:* expression.   36. *As:* as if.   37. *ecstasy:* madness.
38. *property:* nature.   39. *fordoes:* destroys.

POLONIUS. That hath made him mad. 110
I am sorry that with better heed and judgment
I had not quoted[40] him. I feared he did but trifle
And meant to wrack thee; but beshrew my jealousy.[41]
It seems it is as proper to our age
To cast beyond[42] ourselves in our opinions 115
As it is common for the younger sort
To lack discretion. Come, go we to the king.
This must be known, which, being kept close,[43] might move[44]
More grief to hide than hate to utter love.[45]
Come. *[Exeunt.]* 120

SCENE 2 *A room in the castle.*

[Flourish. Enter King and Queen, Rosencrantz and Guildenstern,
with others.]

KING. Welcome, dear Rosencrantz and Guildenstern.
Moreover[1] that we much did long to see you,
The need we have to use you did provoke
Our hasty sending. Something have you heard,
Of Hamlet's transformation—so I call it, 5
Since not th' exterior nor the inward man
Resembles that it was. What it should be,
More than his father's death, that thus hath put him
So much from th' understanding of himself,
I cannot dream of. I entreat you both 10
That, being of so young days brought up with him,
And since so neighbored[2] to his youth and humour,
That you vouchsafe your rest[3] here in our court
Some little time, so by your companies
To draw him on to pleasures, and to gather 15
So much as from occasion[4] you may glean,
Whether aught to us unknown afflicts him thus,
That opened[5] lies within our remedy.
QUEEN. Good gentlemen, he hath much talked of you,
And sure I am two men there are not living 20
To whom he more adheres. If it will please you

40. *quoted:* observed.
41. *beshrew my jealousy:* curse my suspicion. 42. *cast beyond:* overreach, mis-
calculate. 43. *close:* secret. 44. *move:* cause.
45. *hate to utter love:* aversion to admitting love (although Polonious has a high
office, he feels the king would object to Hamlet's marrying below his station).
1. *Moreover:* besides the fact. 2. *neighbored:* near.
3. *vouchsafe your rest:* agree to stay. 4. *occasion:* chance.
5. *opened:* made known.

To show us so much gentry[6] and good will
As to expend your time with us awhile
For the supply and profit[7] of our hope,
Your visitation shall receive such thanks   25
As fits a king's remembrance.
ROSENCRANTZ.   Both your majesties
  Might, by the sovereign power you have of us,
  Put your dread pleasures more into command
  Than to entreaty.
GUILDENSTERN.   We both obey,
  And here give up ourselves in the full bent[8]   30
  To lay our services freely at your feet,
  To be commanded.
KING. Thanks, Rosencrantz and gentle Guildenstern.
QUEEN. Thanks, Guildenstern and gentle Rosencrantz.
  And I beseech you instantly to visit   35
  My too much changèd son. Go, some of you,
  And bring the gentlemen where Hamlet is.
GUILDENSTERN. Heavens make our presence and our practices
  Pleasant and helpful to him!
QUEEN.   Amen!
      [Exeunt Rosencrantz and Guildenstern with some Attendants.]

                    [Enter Polonius.]

POLONIUS. Th' ambassadors from Norway, my good lord,   40
  Are joyfully returned.
KING. Thou still[9] hast been the father of good news.
POLONIUS. Have I, my lord? Assure you, my good liege,
  I hold my duty as I hold my soul,
  Both to my God and to my gracious king   45
  And I do think, or else this brain of mine
  Hunts not the trail of policy so sure
  As I have used to do, that I have found
  The very cause of Hamlet's lunacy.
KING. O, speak of that! That do I long to hear.   50
POLONIUS. Give first admittance to th' ambassadors.
  My news shall be the fruit[10] to that great feast.
KING. Thyself do grace[11] to them and bring them in.
                                        [Exit Polonius.]
He tells me, my sweet queen, that he hath found   55
The head and source of all your son's distemper.[12]
QUEEN. I doubt it is no other but the main,[13]
  His father's death and our o'erhasty marriage.

6. *gentry:* courtesy.
7. *supply and profit:* aid and successful outcome.
8. *in . . . bent:* to the highest degree of our ability.   9. *still:* always.
10. *fruit:* dessert.   11. *grace:* honor.   12. *distemper:* mental disorder.
13. *main:* main concern of his thought.

KING. Well, we shall sift him.

[Enter Polonius, Voltemand, and Cornelius.]

                          Welcome, good friends.
Say, Voltemand, what from our brother Norway?
VOLTEMAND. Most fair return of greetings and desires.   60
  Upon our first,[14] he sent out to suppress
  His nephew's levies, which to him appeared
  To be a preparation 'gainst the Polack,[15]
  But better looked into, he truly found
  It was against your highness, whereat grieved,   65
  That so his sickness, age, and impotence
  Was falsely borne in hand,[16] sends out arrests[17]
  On Fortinbras; which he in brief obeys,
  Receives rebuke from Norway, and in fine[18]
  Makes vow before his uncle never more   70
  To give th' assay[19] of arms against your majesty.
  Whereon old Norway, overcome with joy,
  Gives him three thousand crowns in annual fee
  And his commission to employ those soldiers,
  So levied as before, against the Polack,   75
  With an entreaty, herein further shown,   *[Gives a paper.]*
  That it might please you to give quiet pass
  Through your dominions for this enterprise,
  On such regards of safety and allowance[20]
  As therein are set down.
KING.   It likes us well;   80
  And at our more considered[21] time we'll read,
  Answer, and think upon this business.
  Meantime we thank you for your well-took labor.
  Go to your rest; at night we'll feast together.
  Most welcome home!   *[Exeunt Ambassadors.]*
POLONIUS.   This business is well ended.   85
  My liege and madam, to expostulate[22]
  What majesty should be, what duty is,
  Why day is day, night night, and time is time,
  Were nothing but to waste night, day, and time.
  Therefore, since brevity is the soul of wit,[23]   90
  And tediousness the limbs and outward flourishes,[24]
  I will be brief. Your noble son is mad.

---

14. *first:* initial meeting with the king of Norway.   15. *Polack:* Polish nation.
16. *borne in hand:* taken advantage of.   17. *arrests:* orders to stop.
18. *in fine:* finally.   19. *assay:* trial, test.
20. *On . . . allowance:* On such assurances as those of safety to the country
(Denmark) and of permission to pass through.   21. *considered:* suitable.
22. *expostulate:* discuss.   23. *wit:* wisdom.
24. *flourishes:* ornaments, embellishments.

Mad call I it, for, to define true madness,
What is't but to be nothing else but mad?
But let that go.
QUEEN.   More matter, with less art.   95
POLONIUS. Madam, I swear I use no art at all.
That he is mad, 'tis true: 'tis true 'tis pity,
And pity it is true—a foolish figure!²⁵
But farewell it, for I will use no art.
Mad let us grant him then, and now remains   100
That we find out the cause of this effect
Or rather say, the cause of this defect,
For this effect defective comes by cause.
Thus it remains, and the remainder thus.
Perpend.²⁶   105
I have a daughter (have while she is mine),
Who in her duty and obedience, mark,
Hath given me this. Now gather, and surmise.
*[Reads the letter.] To the celestial, and my soul's idol, the most
beautified Ophelia,—*   110
That's an ill phrase, a vile phrase; "beautified"²⁷ is a vile phrase.
But you shall hear. Thus:
[Reads.] In her excellent white bosom, these, &c.
QUEEN. Came this from Hamlet to her?
POLONIUS. Good madam, stay awhile. I will be faithful.   115

         [Reads.]
         Doubt thou the stars are fire;
           Doubt that the sun doth move;
         Doubt truth to be a liar;
           But never doubt I love.

O dear Ophelia, I am ill at these numbers.²⁸ I have not art²⁹ to   120
*reckon my groans, but that I love thee best, O most best, believe it.
Adieu.*
         Thine evermore, most dear lady,
       whilst this machine³⁰ is to³¹ him, HAMLET.

This in obedience hath my daughter shown me,   125
And more above³² hath his solicitings,
As they fell out³³ by time, by means,³⁴ and place,
All given to mine ear.
KING.   But how hath she
Received his love?

---

25. *figure:* figure of speech.
26. *Perpend:* consider my words.
27. *beautified:* beautiful. (Polonius evidently takes the word to mean "beautified by
artificial means.")   28. *numbers:* verse writing.   29. *art:* skill.
30. *machine:* body.   31. *to:* attached to.   32. *more above:* moreover.
33. *fell out:* occurred.   34. *means:* opportunities.

POLONIUS.   What do you think of me?
KING. As of a man faithful and honorable.   130
POLONIUS. I would fain prove so. But what might you think,
  When I had seen this hot love on the wing
  (As I perceived it, I must tell you that,
  Before my daughter told me), what might you,
  Or my dear majesty your queen here, think,   135
  If I had played the desk or table book,[35]
  Or given my heart a winking,[36] mute and dumb,
  Or looked upon this love with idle sight?
  What might you think? No, I went round[37] to work
  And my young mistress thus I did bespeak: 140
  "Lord Hamlet is a prince, out of thy star.[38]
  This must not be." And then I prescripts[39] gave her,
  That she should lock herself from his resort,
  Admit no messengers, receive no tokens.
  Which done, she took the fruits of my advice,   145
  And he, repulsed, a short tale to make,
  Fell into a sadness, then into a fast,
  Thence to a watch,[40] thence into a weakness,
  Thence to a lightness, and, by this declension,[41]
  Into the madness whereon now he raves,   150
  And all we mourn for.
KING.   Do you think 'tis this?
QUEEN. It may be, very likely.
POLONIUS. Hath there been such a time—I'd fain[42] know that—
  That I have positively said "'Tis so,"
  When it proved otherwise?
KING.   Not that I know.   155
POLONIUS. *[Pointing to his head and shoulder.]* Take this from this,
    if this be otherwise.
  If circumstances lead me, I will find
  Where truth is hid, though it were hid indeed
  Within the center.[43]
KING.   How may we try it further?   160
POLONIUS. You know sometimes he walks four hours together
  Here in the lobby.
QUEEN.   So he does indeed.
POLONIUS. At such a time I'll loose my daughter to him.
  Be you and I behind an arras[44] then.

35. *If . . . book:* if I had remained shut up like a desk or an unopened book
on a table.   36. Or given my heart a signal to keep silent.
37. *round:* straight.   38. *star:* sphere or social position.
39. *prescripts:* definite orders.   40. *watch:* sleeplessness.   41. *declension:* decline.
42. *fain:* gladly.   43. *center:* center of the earth.
44. *arras:* hanging tapestry, for which the town of Arras was famous.

Mark the encounter. If he love her not,   165
And be not from his reason fallen thereon,[45]
Let me be no assistant for a state
But keep a farm and carters.
KING.   We will try it.

[Enter Hamlet reading on a book.]

QUEEN. But look where sadly the poor wretch comes reading.
POLONIUS. Away, I do beseech you both, away.   170
I'll board[46] him presently.   *[Exeunt King and Queen.]*
          O, give me leave.
How does my good Lord Hamlet?
    HAMLET. Well, God-a-mercy.[47]
    POLONIUS. Do you know me, my lord?
    HAMLET. Excellent well. Y'are a fishmonger.[48]   175
    POLONIUS. Not I, my lord.
    HAMLET. Then I would you were so honest a man.[49]
    POLONIUS. Honest, my lord?
    HAMLET. Ay, sir. To be honest, as this world goes, is to be one man
picked out of two thousand.   180
    POLONIUS. That's very true, my lord.
    HAMLET. For if the sun breed maggots in a dead dog, being a good
kissing carrion[50]—Have you a daughter?
    POLONIUS. I have, my lord.
    HAMLET. Let her not walk i' th' sun.[51] Conception[52] is a blessing,   185
but not as your daughter may conceive, friend, look to't.
    POLONIUS. *[Aside.]* How[53] say you by[54] that? Still harping on my
daughter. Yet he knew me not at first. He said I was a fishmonger.
He is far gone, far gone. And truly in my youth I suffered much
extremity for love, very near this. I'll speak to him again.—What   190
do you read, my lord?
    HAMLET. Words, words, words.
    POLONIUS. What is the matter, my lord?
    HAMLET. Between who?
    POLONIUS. I mean the matter that you read, my lord.   195
    HAMLET. Slanders, sir, for the satirical rogue says here that old
men have grey beards, that their faces are wrinkled, their eyes
purging[55] thick amber and plum-tree gum, and that they have a

---

45. *thereon:* on that account.   46. *board:* accost.
47. *God-a-mercy:* God have mercy.   48. *fishmonger:* fish seller.
49. *Then . . . man:* Then I wish you were that honest.
50. *good kissing carrion:* carrion (dead body) fit for kissing or warming by the sun.
51. *Let . . . sun:* Hamlet refers to the belief widespread among primitive people
that a person could become impregnated by the sun. Hamlet may be
warning Polonius against the King (the sun), who he believes is quite
capable of seducing Ophelia.   52. *Conception:* understanding *or* pregnancy.
53. *How:* what.   54. *by:* about.   55. *purging:* discharging.

plentiful lack of wit, together with weak hams.[56] All which, sir,
though I most powerfully and potently believe, yet I hold it not   200
honesty[57] to have it thus set down, for you yourself, sir, should be
old as I am if, like a crab, you could go backward.[58]

POLONIUS. *[Aside.]* Though this be madness, yet there is method[59]
in't.—Will you walk out of the air, my lord?

HAMLET. Into my grave?   205

POLONIUS. Indeed, that is out o' th' air. *[Aside.]* How pregnant
sometimes his replies are! a happiness that often madness hits on,
which reason and sanity could not so prosperously[60] be delivered
of. I will leave him and suddenly contrive the means of meeting
between him and my daughter.—My honorable lord, I will most   210
humbly take my leave of you.

HAMLET. You cannot, sir, take from me anything that I will more
willingly part withal[61]—except my life, my life.

POLONIUS. Fare you well, my lord.

HAMLET. These tedious old fools!   215

[Enter Guildenstern and Rosencrantz.]

POLONIUS. You go to seek the Lord Hamlet. There he is.

ROSENCRANTZ. *[To Polonius.]* God save you, sir!   *[Exit Polonius.]*

GUILDENSTERN. My honored lord!

ROSENCRANTZ. My most dear lord!

HAMLET. My excellent good friends! How dost thou, Guildenstern?   220
Ah, Rosencrantz! Good lads, how do ye both?

ROSENCRANTZ. As the indifferent[62] children of the earth.

GUILDENSTERN. Happy[63] in that we are not over-happy. On Fortune's cap we are not the very button.

HAMLET. Nor the soles of her shoe?   225

ROSENCRANTZ. Neither, my lord.

HAMLET. Then you live about her waist, or in the middle of her
favors?

GUILDENSTERN. Faith, her privates we.

HAMLET. In the secret parts of Fortune? O, most true! she is a   230
strumpet. What's the news?

ROSENCRANTZ. None, my lord, but that the world's grown honest.

HAMLET. Then is doomsday[64] near. But your news is not true.
Let me question more in particular. What have you, my good friends,
deserved at the hands of Fortune that she sends you to prison hither?   235

GUILDENSTERN. Prison, my lord?

HAMLET. Denmark's a prison.

---

56. *hams:* thigh muscles.   57. *honesty:* good manners, decency.
58. *if . . . backward:* if you could go from age to youth.   59. *method:* sense.
60. *prosperously:* successfully.   61. *withal:* with.   62. *indifferent:* average.
63. *Happy:* fortunate (a common belief of the time was that too much happiness
was usually followed by disaster).   64. *doomsday:* the day of the final judgement.

ROSENCRANTZ. Then is the world one.

HAMLET A goodly one; in which there are many confines, wards, and dungeons, Denmark being one o' th' worst. 240

ROSENCRANTZ. We think not so, my lord.

HAMLET. Why, then 'tis none to you, for there is nothing either good or bad but thinking makes it so. To me it is a prison.

ROSENCRANTZ. Why, then your ambition makes it one. 'Tis too narrow for your mind. 245

HAMLET. O God, I could be bounded in a nutshell and count myself a king of infinite space, were it not that I have bad dreams.

GUILDENSTERN. Which dreams indeed are ambition, for the very substance of the ambitious is merely the shadow of a dream.

HAMLET. A dream itself is but a shadow. 250

ROSENCRANTZ. Truly, and I hold ambition of so airy and light a quality[65] that it is but a shadow's shadow.

HAMLET. Then are our beggars bodies,[66] and our monarchs and outstretched[67] heroes the beggars' shadows. Shall we to th' court, for, by my fay, I cannot reason. 255

BOTH. We'll wait upon you.

HAMLET. No such matter. I will not sort[68] you with the rest of my servants, for, to speak to you like an honest man, I am most dreadfully attended. But in the beaten[69] way of friendship, what make you at Elsinore? 260

ROSENCRANTZ. To visit you, my lord; no other occasion.

HAMLET. Beggar that I am, I am even poor in thanks, but I thank you; and sure, dear friends, my thanks are too dear[70] a halfpenny. Were you not sent for? Is it your own inclining? Is it a free visitation? Come, deal justly with me. Come, come. Nay, speak. 265

GUILDENSTERN. What should we say, my lord?

HAMLET. Why, anything. But to th' purpose: you were sent for, and there is a kind of confession in your looks, which your modesties[71] have not craft enough to color. I know the good king and queen have sent for you. 270

ROSENCRANTZ. To what end, my lord?

HAMLET. That you must teach me. But let me conjure[72] you by the rights of our fellowship, by the consonancy of our youth,[73] by the obligation of our ever-preserved love, and by what more dear[74] a better proposer[75] could charge you withal, be even and direct with 275 me whether you were sent for or no.

ROSENCRANTZ. *[Aside to Guildenstern.]* What say you?

HAMLET. *[Aside.]* Nay then, I have an eye on you.—If you love me, hold not off.

---

65. *quality:* nature.   66. *bodies:* solid or real substances.
67. *outstretched:* strutting.   68. *sort:* class.   69. *beaten:* well worn, familiar.
70. *too dear:* not worth.   71. *modesties:* sense of shame.   72. *conjure:* entreat.
73. *by the consonancy of our youth:* by the friendship of our youth.
74. *dear:* precious reason.   75. *proposer:* talker, debater.

GUILDENSTERN. My lord, we were sent for.   280

HAMLET. I will tell you why. So shall my anticipation prevent
your discovery,[76] and your secrecy to the king and queen moult no
feather.[77] I have of late—but wherefore I know not—lost all my
mirth, forgone all custom of exercises; and indeed, it goes so heavily
with my disposition that this goodly frame the earth seems to me a   285
sterile promontory; this most excellent canopy, the air, look you,
this brave o'erhanging firmament, this majestical roof fretted[78] with
golden fire—why, it appears no other thing to me than a foul and
pestilent congregation of vapors. What a piece of work is a man!
How noble in reason, how infinite in faculties, in form and moving   290
how express[79] and admirable, in action how like an angel, in apprehension[80] how like a god: the beauty of the world, the paragon of
animals! And yet to me what is this quintessence[81] of dust? Man
delights not me; no, nor woman neither, though by your smiling
you seem to say so.   295

ROSENCRANTZ. My lord, there was no such stuff in my thoughts.

HAMLET. Why did you laugh then when I said "Man delights
not me"?

ROSENCRANTZ. To think, my lord, if you delight not in man, what
lenten[82] entertainment the players shall receive from you. We coted[83] 300
them on the way, and hither are they coming to offer you service.

HAMLET. He that plays the king shall be welcome; his majesty
shall have tribute of me; the adventurous knight shall use his foil
and target;[84] the lover shall not sigh gratis; the humorous man[85]
shall end his part in peace;[86] the clown shall make those laugh   305
whose lungs are tickled a' th' sere;[87] and the lady shall say her mind
freely, or the blank verse shall halt[88] for't. What players are they?

ROSENCRANTZ. Even those you were wont to take delight in, the
tragedians of the city.

HAMLET. How chances it they travel? Their residence,[89] both in   310
reputation and profit, was better both ways.

ROSENCRANTZ. I think their inhibition[90] comes by the means of
the late innovation.[91]

HAMLET. Do they hold the same estimation they did when I was
in the city? Are they so followed?   315

ROSENCRANTZ. No indeed, are they not.

---

76. *discovery:* disclosure.   77. *moult no feather:* be left intact or unimpaired.
78. *fretted:* adorned.   79. *express:* well framed, precisely suited to its function.
80. *apprehension:* understanding.   81. *quintessence:* highest or finest extract.
82. *lenten:* scanty.   83. *coted:* passed.   84. *foil and target:* sword and shield.
85. *humorous man:* actor who portrays a particular humor. These were
stereotypes in the Elizabethan Theater.
86. *end . . . peace:* shall not be interrupted.
87. *tickled a' th' sere:* easily triggered to laughter.   88. *halt:* go lame, limp.
89. *residence:* remaining in one place.   90. *inhibition:* difficulties.
91. *late innovation:* the private companies of boy actors (children's acting companies).

HAMLET. How comes it? Do they grow rusty?

ROSENCRANTZ. Nay, their endeavor keeps in the wonted[92] pace, but there is, sir, an eyrie[93] of children, little eyases,[94] that cry out on the top of question[95] and are most tyrannically[96] clapped for't. These are now the fashion, and so berattle[97] the common stages[98] (so they call them) that many wearing rapiers are afraid of goosequills[99] and dare scarce come thither.

HAMLET. What, are they children? Who maintains 'em? How are they escoted?[100] Will they pursue the quality[101] no longer than they can sing?[102] Will they not say afterwards, if they should grow themselves to common players (as it is like most, if their means are no better), their writers do them wrong to make them exclaim against their own succession?[103]

ROSENCRANTZ. Faith, there has been much to do on both sides, and the nation holds it no sin to tarre[104] them to controversy. There was, for a while, no money bid for argument[105] unless the poet and the player went to cuffs[106] in the question.

HAMLET. Is't possible?

GUILDENSTERN. O, there has been much throwing about of brains.

HAMLET. Do the boys carry it away?

ROSENCRANTZ. Ay, that they do, my lord—Hercules and his load too.[107]

HAMLET. It is not strange, for my uncle is King of Denmark, and those that would make mows[108] at him while my father lived give twenty, forty, a hundred ducats apiece for his picture in little.[109] 'Sblood,[110] there is something in this more than natural, if philosophy could find it out.　　　　　　　*[Flourish for the Players.]*

GUILDENSTERN. There are the players.

HAMLET. Gentlemen, you are welcome to Elsinore. Your hands, come. Th' appurtenance[111] of welcome is fashion and ceremony. Let me comply[112] with you in this garb,[113] lest my extent[114] to the

320

325

330

335

340

345

---

92. *wonted:* customary.　　93. *eyrie:* nest.　　94. *eyases:* nestling hawks.
95. *cry . . . question:* cry out on the burning questions of the day.
96. *tyrannically:* outrageously.　　97. *berattle:* cry down, satirize.
98. *common stages:* public theaters of adult players.
99. *goosequills:* attacks by satirists.　　100. *escoted:* maintained.
101. *quality:* profession of acting.　　102. *can sing:* that is, as boy sopranos.
103. *succession:* future careers.　　104. *tarre:* incite.
105. *bid for argument:* paid for the story or subject matter of a play.
106. *went to cuffs:* came to blows.
107. *Hercules . . . too:* an allusion to Hercules bearing the world for Atlas. This was the sign of the Globe Theater, which had suffered competition from the boy actors.
108. *mows:* grimaces. Hamlet recalls the fickleness of the public as demonstrated by the citizens of Denmark.　　109. *little:* miniature.　　110. *'Sblood:* God's blood.
111. *appurtenance:* proper accompaniment.
112. *comply:* observe the formalities of courtesy.　　113. *garb:* fashion, manner.
114. *extent:* showing of welcome.

players (which, I tell you, must show fairly outwards) should more
appear like entertainment than yours.[115] You are welcome. But my
uncle-father and aunt-mother are deceived.   350

GUILDENSTERN. In what, my dear lord?

HAMLET. I am but mad north-north-west.[116] When the wind is
southerly I know a hawk from a handsaw.

[Enter Polonius.]

POLONIUS. Well be with you, gentlemen.

HAMLET. Hark you, Guildenstern—and you too—at each ear a   355
hearer. That great baby you see there is not yet out of his swaddling
clouts.

ROSENCRANTZ. Happily[117] he's the second time come to them,
for they say an old man is twice a child.

HAMLET. I will prophesy he comes to tell me of the players. Mark   360
it.—You say right, sir; for a Monday morning, 'twas so indeed.[118]

POLONIUS. My lord, I have news to tell you.

HAMLET. My lord, I have news to tell you. When Roscius[119] was
an actor in Rome—

POLONIUS. The actors are come hither, my lord.   365

HAMLET. Buzz, buzz.[120]

POLONIUS. Upon my honor—

HAMLET. Then came each actor on his ass—

POLONIUS. The best actors in the world, either for tragedy,
comedy, history, pastoral, pastoral-comical, historical-pastoral,   370
tragical-historical, tragical-comical-historical-pastoral; scene individable,[121] or poem unlimited. Seneca[122] cannot be too heavy, nor
Plautus[123] too light. For the law of writ and the liberty,[124] these are
the only men.

HAMLET. O Jephthah,[125] judge of Israel, what a treasure hadst thou!   375

POLONIUS. What treasure had he, my lord?

HAMLET. Why,

> *One fair daughter, and no more,*
> *The which he lovèd passing well.*

115. *should . . . yours:* should seem to be greater welcome than that given to you.
116. *I . . . west:* I am mad only when the wind is blowing in one direction.
117. *Happily:* perhaps.
118. *You . . . indeed:* Hamlet is pretending to be deep in conversation with
Rozencrantz.   119. *Roscius:* a very famous Roman actor.
120. *Buzz, buzz:* chatter. (Hamlet is saying he is bringing stale news.)
121. *scene individable:* play observing the classical unities of time, place, and
matter as contrasted with "poem unlimited" which disregards the established
rules of composition.   122. *Seneca:* Roman author of tragedies.
123. *Plautus:* Roman author of comedies.
124. *law . . . liberty:* plays which abide by the classical rules of drama
strictly and those which ignore them.
125. *Jephthah:* a man who sacrificed a dearly beloved daughter (*Judges* 11).
This and the verse lines that follow are from a popular ballad of the day,
Jephtha's Daughter, extant in several forms.

POLONIUS. *[Aside.]* Still on my daughter.   380

HAMLET. Am I not i' th' right, old Jephthah?

POLONIUS. If you call me Jephthah, my lord, I have a daughter
that I love passing well.

HAMLET. Nay, that follows not.

POLONIUS. What follows then, my lord?   385

HAMLET. Why,

           As by lot, God wot,[126]

and then, you know,

           It came to pass, as most like it was.

The first row of the pious chanson[127] will show you more, for look   390
where my abridgments[128] come.

[Enter four or five Players.]

Y'are welcome, masters, welcome, all.—I am glad to see thee well.
Welcome, good friends. O, my old friend, why, thy face is valanced[129]
since I saw thee last. Com'st thou to beard me in Denmark? What,
What, my young lady[130] and mistress? By'r lady, your ladyship is   395
nearer to heaven[131] than when I saw you last by the altitude of a
chopine.[132] Pray God your voice, like a piece of uncurrent[133] gold, be
not cracked within the ring. Masters, you are all welcome. We'll
e'en to't like French falconers, fly at anything we see. We'll have a
speech straight. Come, give us a taste of your quality. Come, a   400
passionate speech.

FIRST PLAYER. What speech, my good lord?

HAMLET. I heard thee speak me a speech once, but it was never
acted, or if it was, not above once, for the play, I remember, pleased
not the million; 'twas caviare to the general,[134] but it was (as I re-   405
ceived it, and others, whose judgment in such matters cried in the
top of mine)[135] an excellent play, well digested in the scenes, set
down with as much modesty as cunning.[136] I remember one said
there were no sallets[137] in the lines to make the matter savory, nor
no matter in the phrase that might indict the author of affectation,   410
but called it an honest method. One speech in't I chiefly loved.
'Twas Aeneas' tale to Dido,[138] and thereabout of it especially where

126. *As . . . wot:* as by chance, God knows.   127. *chanson:* song.
128. *abridgments:* that which cuts short my speech—the players.
129. *valanced:* fringed (with a beard).
130. *lady:* the young boy who played the female roles.
131. *is . . . heaven:* grown up and older.   132. *chopine:* a thick-soled shoe.
133. *uncurrent:* not passable as lawful coinage.
134. *caviare to the general:* too choice for the public.
135. *cried . . . mine:* had more authority than mine.
136. *modesty as cunning:* moderation as skill.
137. *sallets:* salads or spicy, highly seasoned passages.
138. *Aeneas' tale to Dido:* In Book II of the *Aeneid* Aeneas tells Dido the story
of the fall of Troy and of Priam's death. Priam was the king of Troy and
husband of Hecuba.

he speaks of Priam's slaughter. If it live in your memory, begin at
this line—let me see, let me see:

"The rugged Pyrrhus,[139] like th' Hyrcanian beast—"[140]   415

Is it not so; it begins with Pyrrhus:

"The rugged Pyrrhus, he whose sable[141] arms,
Black as his purpose, did the night resemble
When he lay couched in the ominous horse,[142]
Hath now this dread and black complexion smeared   420
With heraldry[143] more dismal. Head to foot
Now is he total gules,[144] horridly tricked[145]
With blood of fathers, mothers, daughters, sons,
Baked and impasted with the parching streets,[146]
That lend a tyrannous and a damned light   425
To their vile murthers. Roasted in wrath and fire,
And thus o'ersized[147] with coagulate gore,[148]
With eyes like carbuncles, the hellish Pyrrhus
Old grandsire Priam seeks."

POLONIUS. Fore God, my lord, well spoken, with good accent and   430
good discretion.

FIRST PLAYER.   "Anon he finds him,
Striking too short at Greeks. His antique sword,
Rebellious to his arm, lies where it falls,
Repugnant to command. Unequal matched,   435
Pyrrhus at Priam drives, in rage strikes wide,
But with the whiff and wind of his fell[149] sword
Th' unnervèd father falls. Then senseless Ilium,[150]
Seeming to feel this blow, with flaming top
Stoops to his base,[151] and with a hideous crash   440
Takes prisoner Pyrrhus' ear. For lo! his sword,
Which was declining on the milky head
Of reverend Priam, seemed i' th' air to stick.
So as a painted tyrant Pyrrhus stood,
And like a neutral to his will and matter[152]   445
Did nothing.
But as we often see, against[153] some storm,
A silence in the heavens, the rack[154] stand still,
The bold winds speechless, and the orb below

---

139. *Pyrrhus:* A Greek hero in the Trojan War.
140. *Hyrcanian beast:* tiger.   141. *sable:* black.
142. *horse:* the Trojan horse, the device by which the Greeks gained entrance into
Troy.   143. *heraldry:* painted symbol.   144. *total gules:* all red.
145. *tricked:* painted, as in heraldry.
146. *Baked . . . streets:* hardened and incrusted by fires raging in the streets.
147. *o'ersized:* covered over with size (glue).
148. *coagulate gore:* hardened blood.   149. *fell:* cruel.
150. *Ilium:* the palace in Troy.   151. *Stoops . . . base:* collapses.
152. *And . . . matter:* and as if indifferent to his own will and the matter at hand.
153. *against:* before.   154. *rack:* a mass of clouds.

As hush as death, anon the dreadful thunder   450
Doth rend the region, so after Pyrrhus' pause,
Arousèd vengeance sets him new awork,
And never did the Cyclops' hammers[155] fall
On Mars's[156] armor, forged for proof eterne,[157]
With less remorse than Pyrrhus' bleeding sword   455
Now falls on Priam.
Out, out, thou strumpet Fortune! All you gods,
In general synod take away her power,
Break all the spokes and fellies[158] from her wheel,[159]
And bowl the round nave[160] down the hill of heaven,   460
As low as to the fiends."
POLONIUS. This is too long.
HAMLET. It shall to the barber's, with your beard.—Prithee say on. He's for a jig or a tale of bawdry,[161] or he sleeps. Say on; come to Hecuba.[162]   465
FIRST PLAYER. "But who, O, who had seen the mobled[163] queen—"
HAMLET. "The mobled queen"?
POLONIUS. That's good. "Mobled queen" is good.
FIRST PLAYER. "Run barefoot up and down, threat'ning the flames
With bisson rheum;[164] a clout[165] upon that head   470
Where late the diadem stood, and for a robe,
About her lank and all o'erteemèd[166] loins,
A blanket in the alarm of fear caught up—
Who this had seen, with tongue in venom steeped
'Gainst Fortune's state[167] would treason have pronounced!   475
But if the gods themselves did see her then,
When she saw Pyrrhus make malicious sport
In mincing with his sword her husband's limbs,
The instant burst of clamor that she made
(Unless things mortal move them not at all)   480
Would have made milch[168] the burning eyes of heaven
And passion in the gods."
POLONIUS. Look, whet'r he has not turned his color, and has tears in's eyes. Prithee no more.
HAMLET. 'Tis well. I'll have thee speak out the rest soon. Good   485

155. *Cyclop's hammers:* a race of one-eyed giants said to have worked as smithies and with their hammers produced armor for the gods.
156. *Mars:* God of war.   157. *proof eterne:* everlasting protection.
158. *fellies:* rims.
159. *wheel:* Fortune's wheel was a favorite Medieval and Renaissance emblem. In Shakespeare's time Fortune sat and turned a wheel which rode people to the pinnacle of success before it brought them down again.   160. *nave:* hub.
161. *bawdry:* indecency.   162. *Hecuba:* Queen of Troy.   163. *mobled:* muffled.
164. *bisson rheum:* blinding tears.   165. *clout:* piece of cloth.
166. *o'erteemèd:* worn out with bearing children.   167. *state:* government or rule.
168. *milch:* moist (tearful).

my lord, will you see the players well bestowed? Do you hear? Let them be well used, for they are the abstracts[169] and brief chronicles of the time. After your death you were better have a bad epitaph than their ill report while you live.

POLONIUS. My lord, I will use them according to their desert.   490

HAMLET. God's bodykins,[170] man, much better! Use every man after his desert, and who should scape whipping? Use them after your own honor and dignity. The less they deserve, the more merit is in your bounty. Take them in.

POLONIUS. Come, sirs.   495

[Exit Polonius with all the Players but the First.]

HAMLET. Follow him, friends. We'll hear a play to-morrow. *[Aside to First Player.]* Dost thou hear me, old friend? Can you play *The Murther of Gonzago?*

FIRST PLAYER. Ay, my lord.

HAMLET. We'll ha't to-morrow night. You could, for a need,[171]   500
study a speech of some dozen or sixteen lines which I would set down and insert in't, could you not?

FIRST PLAYER. Ay, my lord.

HAMLET. Very well. Follow that lord, and look you mock him not.[172]

[Exit First Player.]

My good friends, I'll leave you till night. You are welcome to Elsinore.   505

ROSENCRANTZ. Good my lord.

[Exeunt Rosencrantz and Guildenstern.]

HAMLET. Ay, so, God bye 'ye. Now I am alone.
O, what a rogue and peasant slave am I!
Is it not monstrous that this player here,
But in a fiction, in a dream of passion,
Could force his soul so to his own conceit[173]   510
That from her working all his visage warm'd,
Tears in his eyes, distraction in's aspect,
A broken voice, and his whole function suiting
With forms to his conceit?[174] And all for nothing!   515
For Hecuba!
What's Hecuba to him, or he to Hecuba,
That he should weep for her? What would he do
Had he the motive and the cue for passion
That I have? He would drown the stage with tears   520
And cleave the general[175] ear with horrid speech,
Make mad the guilty and appal the free,[176]

169. *abstracts:* summaries.
170. *God's bodykins:* God's little bodies (the sacramental bread).
171. *for a need:* in case of necessity.
172. *mock him not:* do not you mock him. It is all right for Hamlet to mock Polonius because he is pretending to be mad.   173. *conceit:* imagination.
174. *whole . . . conceit:* his entire being responded with forms to suit his thought.
175. *general:* public.   176. *free:* innocent.

Confound the ignorant, and amaze indeed
The very faculties of eyes and ears.
Yet I,   525
A dull and muddy-mettled[177] rascal, peak
Like John-a-dreams,[178] unpregnant of[179] my cause,
And can say nothing. No, not for a king,
Upon whose property and most dear life
A damned defeat was made. Am I a coward?   530
Who calls me villain? breaks my pate across?
Plucks off my beard and blows it in my face?
Tweaks me by th' nose? gives me the lie i' th' throat
As deep as to the lungs?[180] Who does me this?
Ha, 'swounds, I should take it, for it cannot be   535
But I am pigeon-livered and lack gall[181]
To make oppression bitter, or ere this
I should have fatted all the region kites[182]
With this slave's offal.[183] Bloody, a bawdy villain,
Remorseless, treacherous, lecherous, kindless villain!   540
O, vengeance!
Why, what an ass am I! This is most brave,
That I, the son of a dear father murdered,
Prompted to my revenge by heaven and hell,
Must like a whore unpack my heart with words   545
And fall a-cursing like a very drab,[184]
A scullion![185] Fie upon't, foh! About,[186] my brains.
I have heard that guilty creatures sitting at a play
Have by the very cunning of the scene
Been struck so to the soul that presently   550
They have proclaimed their malefactions.[187]
For murther, though it have no tongue, will speak
With most miraculous organ. I'll have these players
Play something like the murder of my father
Before mine uncle. I'll observe his looks.   555
I'll tent[188] him to the quick. If he but blench,[189]
I know my course. The spirit that I have seen
May be a devil, and the devil hath power
T' assume a pleasing shape, yea, and perhaps
Out of my weakness and my melancholy,   560
As he is very potent with such spirits,[190]

177. *muddy-mettled:* poor-spirited.
178. *peak . . . John-a-dreams:* mope like one in a dream.
179. *unpregnant of:* unstirred by.
180. *gives . . . lungs:* calls me the worst kind of liar.   181. *gall:* spirit.
182. *kites:* scavenger birds.   183. *offal:* guts.   184. *drab:* whore.
185. *scullion:* a kitchen wench.   186. *About:* bestir yourself.
187. *proclaimed their malefactions:* shouted out their crimes.   188. *tent:* probe.
189. *blench:* wince.   190. *spirits:* moods, humours.

Abuses[191] me to damn me. I'll have grounds
More relative[192] than this. The play's the thing
Wherein I'll catch the conscience of the king.   *[Exit.]*

ACT III

SCENE 1   *A room in the castle.*

[Enter King, Queen, Polonius, Ophelia, Rosencrantz, Guildenstern,
and Lords.]

KING. And can you by no drift of circumstance[1]
  Get from him why he puts on this confusion,
  Grating[2] so harshly all his days of quiet
  With turbulent and dangerous lunacy?
ROSENCRANTZ. He does confess he feels himself distracted,   5
  But from what causes he will by no means speak.
GUILDENSTERN. Nor do we find him forward[3] to be sounded,
  But with a crafty madness keeps aloof
  When we would bring him on to some confession
  Of his true state.
QUEEN.   Did he receive you well?   10
ROSENCRANTZ. Most like a gentleman.
GUILDENSTERN. But with much forcing of his disposition.
ROSENCRANTZ. Niggard of question,[4] but of our demands
  Most free in his reply.
QUEEN.   Did you assay[5] him
  To any pastime?   15
ROSENCRANTZ. Madam, it so fell out that certain players
  We o'erraught[6] on the way. Of these we told him,
  And there did seem in him a kind of joy
  To hear of it. They are here about the court,
  And, as I think, they have already order   20
  This night to play before him.
POLONIUS.   'Tis most true,
  And he beseeched me to entreat your majesties
  To hear and see the matter.

191. *Abuses:* deludes.   192. *relative:* conclusive.

1. *circumstance:* conversation.   2. *Grating:* disturbing, irritating.
3. *forward:* eager.   4. *Niggard of question:* reluctant to ask questions.
5. *assay:* try to win.   6. *o'erraught:* overtook.

KING. With all my heart, and it doth much content me
  To hear him so inclined. 25
  Good gentlemen, give him a further edge,[7]
  And drive his purpose on to these delights.
ROSENCRANTZ. We shall, my lord.
                    [Exeunt Rosencrantz and Guildenstern.]
KING.   Sweet Gertrude, leave us too,
  For we have closely[8] sent for Hamlet hither,
  That he, as 'twere by accident, may here 30
  Affront[9] Ophelia.
  Her father and myself (lawful espials[10])
  Will so bestow ourselves that, seeing unseen,
  We may of their encounter frankly judge
  And gather by him, as he is behaved, 35
  If't be th' affliction of his love or no
  That thus he suffers for.
QUEEN.   I shall obey you;
  And for your part, Ophelia, I do wish
  That your good beauties be the happy cause
  Of Hamlet's wildness. So shall I hope your virtues 40
  Will bring him to his wonted[11] way again,
  To both your honors.
OPHELIA.   Madam, I wish it may.   *[Exit Queen.]*
POLONIUS. Ophelia, walk you here. *[To Claudius.]* Gracious, so
    please you,
  We will bestow ourselves. *[To Ophelia.]* Read on this book,[12] 45
  That show of such an exercise may color[13]
  Your loneliness.[14] We are oft to blame in this,
  'Tis too much proved, that with devotion's visage[15]
  And pious action we do sugar o'er
  The devil himself.
KING.   *[Aside.]* O, 'tis too true. 50
  How smart a lash that speech doth give my conscience!
  The harlot's cheek, beautied with plast'ring art,
  Is not more ugly to[16] the thing that helps it
  Than is my deed to my most painted[17] word.
  O heavy burthen! 55
POLONIUS. I hear him coming. Let's withdraw, my lord.
                    [Exeunt King and Polonius.]

---

7. *edge:* encouragement.
8. *closely:* secretly.   9. *Affront:* confront, meet face to face with.
10. *espials:* spies, observers.   11. *wonted:* usual.   12. *book:* book of devotions.
13. *color:* excuse, explain.   14. *loneliness:* your being alone.
15. *devotion's visage:* an outward show of devotion.
16. *ugly to:* ugly compared with.   17. *painted:* false.

[Enter Hamlet.]

HAMLET. To be, or not to be; that is the question.
Whether 'tis nobler in the mind to suffer
The slings and arrows of outrageous[18] fortune
Or to take arms against a sea of troubles   60
And by opposing end them. To die, to sleep—[19]
No more—and by a sleep to say we end
The heartache, and the thousand natural shocks
That flesh is heir to. 'Tis a consummation
Devoutly to be wished. To die; to sleep—   65
To sleep—perchance to dream; ay, there's the rub;[20]
For in that sleep of death what dreams may come
When we have shuffled off this mortal coil,
Must give us pause. There's the respect[21]
That makes calamity of so long life.[22]   70
For who would bear the whips and scorns of time,
Th' oppressor's wrong, the proud man's contumely,[23]
The pangs of disprized[24] love, the law's delay,
The insolence of office,[25] and the spurns
That patient merit of the unworthy takes,[26]   75
When he himself might his quietus[27] make
With a bare bodkin?[28] Who would fardels[29] bear,
To grunt and sweat under a weary life,
But that the dread of something after death,
The undiscovered country, from whose bourn[30]   80
No traveller returns, puzzles the will,
And makes us rather bear those ills we have
Than fly to others that we know not of?
Thus conscience[31] does make cowards of us all,
And thus the native[32] hue of resolution   85
Is sicklied o'er[33] with the pale cast[34] of thought,
And enterprises of great pitch and moment[35]
With this regard their currents turn away
And lose the name of action. Soft you now,
The fair Ophelia! Nymph, in thy orisons[36]   90
Be all my sins remembered.

---

18. *outrageous:* cruel.
19. *Sleep* commonly represented death from classical time on.   20. *rub:* obstacle.
21. *respect:* consideration.   22. *of . . . life:* of living so long.   23. *contumely:* scorn.
24. *disprized:* undervalued.   25. *office:* government officials.
26. *spurns . . . takes:* the ignoble treatment that the patient person takes from
evil men in authority.   27. *quietus:* final settlement or discharge of debt (death).
28. *bodkin:* dagger.   29. *fardels:* burdens.   30. *bourn:* boundary.
31. *conscience:* reflection.   32. *native:* natural, healthy.
33. *sicklied o'er:* takes on a sickly color.   34. *cast:* shade.
35. *pitch and moment:* height and importance.   36. *orisons:* prayers.

OPHELIA.   Good my lord,
How does your honor for this many a day?
HAMLET. I humbly thank you; well, well, well.
OPHELIA. My lord, I have remembrances[37] of yours
That I have longèd long to re-deliver.   95
I pray you, now receive them.
HAMLET.   No, no.
I never gave you aught.
OPHELIA. My honored lord, I know right well you did,
And with them words of so sweet breath composed
As made the things more rich. Their perfume lost,   100
Take these again, for to the noble mind
Rich gifts wax poor when givers prove unkind.
There, my lord.
HAMLET. Ha, ha! Are you honest?[38]
OPHELIA. My lord?   105
HAMLET. Are you fair?[39]
OPHELIA. What means your lordship?
HAMLET. That if you be honest and fair, your honesty should admit no discourse to your beauty.[40]
OPHELIA. Could beauty, my lord, have better commerce[41] than   110
with honesty?
HAMLET. Ay, truly; for the power of beauty will sooner transform
honesty from what it is to a bawd than the force of honesty can
translate beauty into his likeness. This was sometime a paradox, but
now the time[42] gives it proof. I did love you once.   115
OPHELIA. Indeed, my lord, you made me believe so.
HAMLET. You should not have believed me, for virtue cannot so
inoculate[43] our old stock[44] but we shall relish of it. I loved you not.
OPHELIA. I was the more deceived.
HAMLET. Get thee to a nunnery. Why wouldst thou be a breeder   120
of sinners? I am myself indifferent[45] honest, but yet I could accuse
me of such things that it were better my mother had not borne me:
I am very proud, revengeful, ambitious, with more offenses at my
beck[46] than I have thoughts to put them in, imagination to give them
shape, or time to act them in. What should such fellows as I do   125

37. *remembrances:* gifts.
38. *honest:* chaste, or truthful. It is probable that Hamlet at this point becomes
aware that someone is behind the arras. If he had heard a rustle or even seen
them, the rest of his conversation is for their benefit. This would account
for the bitterness with which he addresses her.
39. *fair:* a double meaning—beautiful or just.
40. *honesty . . . beauty:* your honesty (here *integrity*) should keep you from
using your beauty for dishonest purposes (as a lure to entrap me).
41. *commerce:* association.   42. *the time:* the present.
43. *inoculate:* change by grafting.   44. *old stock:* sinful nature.
45. *indifferent:* moderately.   46. *beck:* command.

crawling between heaven and earth? We are arrant knaves all; believe none of us. Go thy ways to a nunnery. Where's your father?

OPHELIA. At home, my lord.

HAMLET. Let the doors be shut upon him, that he may play the fool nowhere but in's own house. Farewell.   130

OPHELIA. O, help him, you sweet heavens!

HAMLET. If thou dost marry, I'll give thee this plague for thy dowry: be thou as chaste as ice, as pure as snow, thou shalt not escape calumny. Get thee to a nunnery. Go, farewell. Or if thou wilt needs marry, marry a fool, for wise men know well enough   135 what monsters[47] you make of them. To a nunnery, go, and quickly too. Farewell.

OPHELIA. O heavenly powers, restore him!

HAMLET. I have heard of your paintings[48] too, well enough. God hath given you one face, and you make yourselves another. You jig,   140 you amble, and you lisp, and nickname God's creatures and make your wantonness[49] your ignorance. Go to, I'll no more on't; it hath made me mad. I say we will have no more marriage. Those that are married already—all but one—shall live. The rest shall keep as they are. To a nunnery, go.   *[Exit Hamlet.]*   145

OPHELIA. O, what a noble mind is here o'erthrown!
The courtier's, soldier's, scholar's, eye, tongue, sword,
Th' expectancy and rose of the fair state,
The glass[50] of fashion and the mould of form,
Th' observed of all observers, quite, quite down!   150
And I, of ladies most deject and wretched,
That sucked the honey of his music vows,
Now see that noble and most sovereign reason
Like sweet bells jangled, out of time and harsh,
That unmatched form and feature of blown[51] youth   155
Blasted with ecstasy.[52] O, woe is me
T' have seen what I have seen, see what I see!

[Enter King and Polonius.]

KING. Love? his affections do not that way tend,
Nor what he spake, though it lacked form a little,
Was not like madness. There's something in his soul   160
O'er which his melancholy sits on brood,[53]
And I do doubt[54] the hatch and the disclose
Will be some danger; which for to prevent,
I have in quick determination

---

47. *monsters:* cuckolds. (Horns were supposed to grow on the head of a man whose wife was unfaithful—a widely used Elizabethan joke.)
48. *paintings:* make-up of the face.   49. *make your wantonness:* call your indecency.
50. *glass:* mirror.   51. *blown:* blooming.   52. *ecstasy:* madness.
53. *on brood:* hatching.   54. *doubt:* fear.

Thus set it down: he shall with speed to England   165
For the demand of our neglected tribute,
Haply[55] the seas, and countries different,
With variable objects, shall expel
This something-settled[56] matter in his heart,
Whereon his brains still beating puts him thus   170
From fashion of himself.[57] What think you on't?
POLONIUS. It shall do well. But yet do I believe
The origin and commencement of this grief
Sprung from neglected love. How now, Ophelia?
You need not tell us what Lord Hamlet said.   175
We heard it all. My lord, do as you please,
But if you hold it fit, after the play
Let his queen mother all alone entreat him
To show his griefs. Let her be round[58] with him,
And I'll be placed, so please you, in the ear   180
Of all their conference. If she find him not,
To England send him, or confine him where
Your wisdom best shall think.
KING.   It shall be so.
Madness in great ones must not unwatched go.   *[Exeunt.]*

SCENE 2   *A hall in the castle.*

[Enter Hamlet, and two or three of the Players.]

HAMLET. Speak the speech, I pray you, as I pronounced it to you,
trippingly on the tongue. But if you mouth it,[1] as many of our players
do, I had as lief the town crier spoke my lines. Nor do not saw the
air too much with your hand, thus, but use all gently, for in the
very torrent, tempest, and (as I may say) whirlwind of passion, you   5
must acquire and beget a temperance that may give it smoothness.
O, it offends me to the soul to hear a robustious periwig-pated[2] fellow
tear a passion to tatters, to very rags, to split the ears of the groundlings,[3] who, for the most part, are capable of nothing but inexpli-
cable dumb shows and noise. I could have such a fellow whipped   10

---

55. *Haply:* perhaps.
56. *something-settled:* somewhat settled.
57. *From . . . himself:* from his normal self.   58. *round:* outspoken, direct.

1. *mouth it:* use a pompous or affected style, "ham" it.   2. *periwig-pated:* bewigged.
3. *groundlings:* those who paid the cheapest admission price (a penny) and
stood in the pit (or "yard") of the theater.

for o'erdoing Termagant.[4] It out-herods Herod.[5] Pray you avoid it.

PLAYER. I warrant[6] your honor.

HAMLET. Be not too tame neither, but let your own discretion be your tutor. Suit the action to the word, the word to the action, with this special observance, that you o'erstep not the modesty[7] of nature. For anything so overdone is from the purpose of playing, whose end, both at the first and now, was and is, to hold, as 'twere, the mirror up to nature, to show virtue her own feature, scorn her own image, and the very age[8] and body[9] of the time his form and pressure.[10] Now this overdone, or come tardy off, though it make the unskillful laugh, cannot but make the judicious grieve, the censure of the which one must in your allowance o'erweigh a whole theatre of others. O, there be players that I have seen play, and heard others praise, and that highly (not to speak it profanely),[11] that neither having the accent of Christians, nor the gait of Christian, pagan, nor man, have so strutted and bellowed that I have thought some of Nature's journeymen had made men, and not made them well, they imitated humanity so abominably.

PLAYER. I hope we have reformed that indifferently[12] with us, sir.

HAMLET. O, reform it altogether! And let those that play your clowns speak no more than is set down for them, for there be of them that will themselves laugh, to set on some quantity of barren[13] spectators to laugh too, though in the mean time some necessary question of the play be then to be considered. That's villainous and shows a most pitiful ambition in the fool that uses it. Go make you ready.   *[Exeunt Players.]*

[Enter Polonius, Guildenstern, and Rosencrantz.]

How now, my lord? Will the king hear this piece of work?

POLONIUS. And the queen too, and that presently.

HAMLET. Bid the players make haste.

[Exit Polonius.]

Will you two help to hasten them?

ROSENCRANTZ. ⎫
GUILDENSTERN. ⎭ We will, my lord.

[Exeunt.]

HAMLET. What, ho, Horatio!

---

4. *Termagant:* an imaginary Mohammedan deity popular in Saint Nicholas plays and in medieval romances wherein he howls loudly when he finds some of his goods stolen.
5. *out-herods Herod:* the tradition for Herod in the mystery plays required that he rant and rave.   6. *warrant:* guarantee.   7. *modesty:* moderation.
8. *very age:* actual generation.   9. *body:* appearance.   10. *pressure:* character.
11. *not . . . profanely:* he apologizes for his apparent sneering in comparing the Creation with work of a master craftsman and his journeyman (an unskillful workman).   12. *indifferently:* moderately well.   13. *barren:* foolish, dull.

[*Enter Horatio.*]

HORATIO. Here, sweet lord, at your service.
HAMLET. Horatio, thou art e'en as just a man
  As e'er my conversation coped[14] withal.   45
HORATIO. O, my dear lord—
HAMLET.   Nay, do not think I flatter.
  For what advancement may I hope from thee,
  That no revenue hast but thy good spirits
  To feed and clothe thee? Why should the poor be flattered?
  No, let the candied[15] tongue lick absurd pomp,   50
  And crook the pregnant[16] hinges of the knee
  Where thrift[17] may follow fawning. Dost thou hear?
  Since my dear soul was mistress of my choice
  And could of men distinguish, her election
  Hath sealed thee for herself, for thou hast been   55
  As one in suffering all that suffers nothing,
  A man that Fortune's buffets and rewards
  Hath ta'en with equal thanks; and blest are those
  Whose blood[18] and judgment are so well commingled[19]
  That they are not a pipe[20] for Fortune's finger   60
  To sound what stop she please. Give me that man
  That is not passion's slave, and I will wear him
  In my heart's core, ay, in my heart of heart,
  As I do thee. Something too much of this—
  There is a play to-night before the king.   65
  One scene of it comes near the circumstance
  Which I have told thee, of my father's death.
  I prithee, when thou seest that act afoot,
  Even with the very comment of thy soul[21]
  Observe mine uncle. If his occulted[22] guilt   70
  Do not itself unkennel[23] in one speech,
  It is a damnèd ghost that we have seen,
  And my imaginations are as foul
  As Vulcan's stithy.[24] Give him heedful note,
  For I mine eyes will rivet to his face,   75
  And after we will both our judgments join
  In censure[25] of his seeming.
HORATIO.   Well, my lord.
  If he steal aught the whilst this play is playing,

---

14. *coped:* encountered.   15. *candied:* flattering.   16. *pregnant:* supple.
17. *thrift:* worldly gain.   18. *blood:* passions.   19. *commingled:* balanced.
20. *pipe:* wind instrument.   21. *the . . . soul:* your deepest sagacity.
22. *occulted:* hidden, concealed.
23. *unkennel:* come to light, that is, like a dog or fox from his den.
24. *stithy:* forge (of Vulcan, who was blacksmith of the gods).
25. *censure:* judgment.

And 'scape detecting, I will pay the theft.

HAMLET. They are coming to the play. I must be idle.²⁶   80
Get you a place.

*[Enter King, Queen, Polonius, Ophelia, Rosencrantz, Guildenstern,
and other Lords attendant, with the King's guard carrying torches.
Danish march. Sound a flourish.]*

KING. How fares our cousin Hamlet?

HAMLET. Excellent, i' faith, of the chameleon's dish. I eat the air,
promise-crammed. You cannot feed capons so.

KING. I have nothing with²⁷ this answer, Hamlet. These words   85
are not mine.

HAMLET. No, nor mine now. *[To Polonius.]* My lord, you played
once i' th' university, you say?

POLONIUS. That did I, my lord, and was accounted a good actor.

HAMLET. And what did you enact?   90

POLONIUS. I did enact Julius Caesar. I was killed i' th' Capitol;
Brutus killed me.

HAMLET. It was a brute part of him to kill so capital a calf there.
Be the players ready?

ROSENCRANTZ. Ay, my lord. They stay upon your patience.   95

QUEEN. Come hither, my good Hamlet, sit by me.

HAMLET. No, good mother. Here's metal more attractive.

POLONIUS. *[To the King.]* O ho! do you mark that?

HAMLET. Lady, shall I lie in your lap?   *[He lies at Ophelia's feet.]*

OPHELIA. No, my lord.   100

HAMLET. I mean, my head upon your lap?

OPHELIA. Ay, my lord.

HAMLET. Do you think I meant country²⁸ matters?

OPHELIA. I think nothing, my lord.

HAMLET. That's a fair thought to lie between maids' legs.   105

OPHELIA. What is, my lord?

HAMLET. Nothing.

OPHELIA. You are merry, my lord.

HAMLET. Who, I?

OPHELIA. Ay, my lord.   110

HAMLET. O God, your only²⁹ jig-maker! What should a man do
but be merry? For look you how cheerfully my mother looks, and
my father died within's two hours.

OPHELIA. Nay, 'tis twice two months, my lord.

HAMLET. So long? Nay then, let the devil wear black, for I'll have   115
a suit of sables.³⁰ O heavens! die two months ago, and not forgotten
yet? Then there's hope a great man's memory may outlive his life

---

26. *be idle:* be foolish, act the madman.
27. *have nothing with:* make nothing out of.   28. *country:* indecent.
29. *only:* best.   30. *sables:* expensive furs.

half a year. But, by'r Lady, he must build churches then, or else shall he suffer not thinking on,[31] with the hobby-horse,[32] whose epitaph is "For O, for O, the hobby-horse is forgot!"   120

[Hautboys[33] play. The dumb-show[34] enters.]

[Enter a King and Queen very lovingly, the Queen embracing him. She kneels, and makes show of protestation unto him. He takes her up, and declines his head upon her neck: lays him down upon a bank of flowers. She, seeing him asleep, leaves him. Anon comes in a fellow, takes off his crown, kisses it, and pours poison in the King's ears, and exits. The Queen returns; finds the King dead, and makes passionate action.[35] The Poisoner, with some two or three Mutes, comes in again, seeming to lament with her. The dead body is carried away. The Poisoner woos the Queen with gifts: she seems loath and unwilling awhile, but in the end accepts his love. Exeunt.]

OPHELIA. What means this, my lord?

HAMLET. Marry, this is miching mallecho;[36] it means mischief.

OPHELIA. Belike[37] this show imports the argument of the play.

[Enter Prologue.]

HAMLET. We shall know by this fellow. The players cannot keep counsel;[38] they'll tell all.   125

OPHELIA. Will 'a tell us what this show meant?

HAMLET. Ay, or any show that you'll show him. Be not you ashamed to show, he'll not shame to tell you what it means.

OPHELIA. You are naught,[39] you are naught. I'll mark[40] the play.

PROLOGUE. *For us and for our tragedy,*   130
       Here stooping to your clemency,
       We beg your hearing patiently.   *[Exit.]*

HAMLET. Is this a prologue, or the posy of a ring?[41]

OPHELIA. 'Tis brief, my lord.

HAMLET. As woman's love.   135

---

31. *build . . . on:* he must build churches to his own memory or people will quickly forget all about him.

32. *hobby-horse:* In the traditional dances of the May-day games a figure who wore a pasteboard horse that was attached to his waist—his legs covered by cloth hanging down from the horse. The term had become synonymous with someone who did foolish things.

33. *Hautboys:* A wooden wind instrument with a high pitch resembling the modern oboe.   34. *dumb-show:* pantomime.

35. *makes passionate action:* acts with extremely sorrowful action.

36. *miching mallecho:* sneaking crime or mischief.   37. *Belike:* probably.

38. *keep counsel:* keep secrets.   39. *naught:* indecent.   40. *mark:* pay attention to.

41. *posy of a ring:* brief motto in rhyme engraved in a ring.

[Enter two Players as King and Queen.]

PLAYER KING. Full thirty times hath Phoebus' cart[42] gone round
    Neptune's salt wash[43] and Tellus'[44] orbèd ground,
    And thirty dozen moons with borrowed sheen
    About the world have times twelve thirties been,
    Since love our hearts, and Hymen[45] did our hands,   140
    Unite commutual[46] in most sacred bands.
PLAYER QUEEN. So many journeys may the sun and moon
    Make us again count o'er ere love be done!
    But woe is me, you are so sick of late,
    So far from cheer and from your former state,   145
    That I distrust you.[47] Yet, though I distrust,
    Discomfort you, my lord, it nothing must.
    For women fear too much, even as they love,
    And women's fear and love hold quantity,[48]
    In neither aught, or in extremity.[49]   150
    Now what my love is, proof hath made you know,
    And as my love is sized, my fear is so.
    Where love is great, the littlest doubts are fear;
    Where little fears grow great, great love grows there.
PLAYER KING. Faith, I must leave thee, love, and shortly too;   155
    My operant[50] powers their functions leave to do.[51]
    And thou shalt live in this fair world behind,
    Honored, beloved, and haply[52] one as kind
    For husband shalt thou—
PLAYER QUEEN.   O, confound the rest!
    Such love must needs be treason in my breast.   160
    In second husband let me be accurst!
    None wed the second but who killed the first.
HAMLET. *[Aside.]* Wormwood,[53] wormwood!
PLAYER QUEEN. The instances[54] that second marriage move
    Are base respects of thrift,[55] but none of love.   165
    A second time I kill my husband dead
    When second husband kisses me in bed.
PLAYER KING. I do believe you think what now you speak,
    But what we do determine oft we break.
    Purpose is but the slave to memory,[56]   170

42. *Phoebus' cart:* the sun.   43. *Neptune's salt wash:* the sea.
44. *Tellus':* goddess of the earth.   45. *Hymen:* god of marriage.
46. *commutual:* intensely mutual.   47. *distrust you:* worry about you.
48. *hold quantity:* occur in equal proportions.
49. *In . . . extremity:* either in nothing or in the highest degree.   50. *operant:* vital.
51. *leave to do:* cease to operate.   52. *haply:* perhaps.
53. *Wormwood:* a bitter herb.   54. *instances:* motives.
55. *respects of thrift:* considerations of material profit.
56. *Purpose . . . memory:* the execution of a resolution is dependent on memory.

Of violent birth, but poor validity,[57]
Which now like fruit unripe sticks on the tree,
But fall unshaken when they mellow be.
Most necessary 'tis that we forget
To pay ourselves what to ourselves is debt.   175
What to ourselves in passion we propose,
The passion ending, doth the purpose lose.
The violence of either grief or joy
Their own enactures[58] with themselves destroy.
Where joy most revels, grief doth most lament;   180
Grief joys, joy grieves, on slender accident.
This world is not for aye,[59] nor 'tis not strange
That even our loves should with our fortunes change,
For 'tis a question left us yet to prove,[60]
Whether love lead fortune, or else fortune love.   185
The great man down, you mark his favorite flies,
The poor advanced makes friends of enemies;
And hitherto doth love on fortune tend,
For who not needs shall never lack a friend,
And who in want a hollow friend doth try,[61]   190
Directly seasons[62] him his enemy.
But, orderly to end where I begun,
Our wills and fates do so contrary run
That our devices[63] still[64] are overthrown;
Our thoughts are ours, their ends none of our own.   195
So think thou wilt no second husband wed,
But die thy thoughts when thy first lord is dead.
PLAYER QUEEN. Nor earth to me give food, nor heaven light,
   Sport[65] and repose lock from me day and night!
   To desperation turn my trust and hope,   200
   An anchor's[66] cheer in prison be my scope!
   Each opposite that blanks[67] the face of joy
   Meet what I would have well and it destroy!
   Both here and hence pursue me lasting strife,
   If, once a widow, ever I be wife!   205
HAMLET. If she should break it now!
PLAYER KING. 'Tis deeply sworn. Sweet, leave me here awhile.
   My spirits grow dull, and fain I would beguile
   The tedious day with sleep.
PLAYER QUEEN.   Sleep rock thy brain,   *[Sleeps.]*
   And never come mischance between us twain!   *[Exit.]*   210
HAMLET. Madam, how like you this play?

---

57. *validity:* strength.   58. *enactures:* actual performances.   59. *aye:* ever.
60. *prove:* test.   61. *doth try:* does test.   62. *seasons:* makes, ripens.
63. *devices:* plans.   64. *still:* always.   65. *Sport:* amorous pleasure.
66. *anchor's:* hermit's.   67. *blanks:* blanches, makes pale.

QUEEN. The lady doth protest too much, methinks.

HAMLET. O, but she'll keep her word.

KING. Have you heard the argument?[68] Is there no offense in't?

 HAMLET. No, no, they do but jest, poison in jest; no offense i' th' 215
world.

 KING. What do you call the play?

 HAMLET. 'The Mousetrap.'[69] Marry,[70] how? Tropically.[71] This play
is the image of a murder done in Vienna. Gonzago is the duke's
name; his wife, Baptista. You shall see anon. 'Tis a knavish piece of 220
work, but what o' that? Your majesty, and we that have free[72] souls,
it touches us not. Let the galled jade winch;[73] our withers are unwrung.[74]

[Enter Lucianus.]

This is one Lucianus, nephew to the king.

 OPHELIA. You are a good chorus, my lord. 225

 HAMLET. I could interpret between you and your love,[75] if I could
see the puppets dallying.[76]

 OPHELIA. You are keen, my lord, you are keen.

 HAMLET. It would cost you a groaning[77] to take off my edge.[78]

 OPHELIA. Still better, and worse.[79] 230

 HAMLET. So you mistake[80] husbands.—Begin, murtherer. Leave
thy damnable faces and begin.[81] Come, the croaking raven[82] doth
bellow for revenge.

LUCIANUS. Thoughts black, hands apt, drugs fit, and time agreeing,
 Confederate[83] season, else no[84] creature seeing, 235
 Thou mixture rank, of midnight weeds collected,
 With Hecate's[85] ban[86] thrice blasted, thrice infected,
 Thy natural magic and dire property[87]

68. *argument:* plot.

69. *Mousetrap:* The phrase was used to describe a device that would entice a
person to his own destruction.   70. *Marry:* indeed.

71. *Tropically:* The name of the play was actually *The Murder of Gonzago,* but
Hamlet says he is using a trope (a symbolic name).   72. *free:* innocent.

73. *galled jade winch:* chafed horse wince.

74. *our . . . unwrung:* our shoulders are not chafed or sensitive.

75. *love:* lover.

76. *puppets dallying:* puppets acting a scene of love. Hamlet uses *puppets* to
mean Ophelia and her imagined lover.   77. *groaning:* cry or groan of pain.

78. *edge:* desire.

79. *better, and worse:* keener as to wit, but more obscene as to meaning.

80. *mistake:* a punning reference (mis-take) to the marriage ceremony in which
the partners take each other "for better or for worse."

81. *leave . . . begin:* Hamlet is impatient for them to cease the conventional
gestures which the actor playing the murderer was supposed to go through
before committing the crime.

82. *croaking raven:* a croaking raven was supposed to prophesy a coming death.

83. *Confederate:* favorable.   84. *else no:* no other.

85. *Hecate's:* goddess of black magic and witchcraft.   86. *ban:* curse.

87. *dire property:* the poison's fatal effect.

On wholesome life usurps immediately.

[Pours the poison in the sleeper's ears.]

HAMLET. He poisons him i' th' garden for his estate. His name's   240
Gonzago. The story is extant, and written in very choice Italian.
You shall see anon how the murtherer gets the love of Gonzago's
wife.

OPHELIA. The king rises.

HAMLET. What, frighted with false fire?[88]   245

QUEEN. How fares my lord?

POLONIUS. Give o'er the play.

KING. Give me some light. Away!

ALL. Lights, lights, lights!

[Exeunt all but Hamlet and Horatio.]

HAMLET.   *Why, let the strucken deer go weep,*   250
         The hart ungalled play.
         For some must watch, while some must sleep;
         Thus runs the world away.

Would not this,[89] sir, and a forest of feathers[90]—if the rest of my
fortunes turn Turk[91] with me—with two Provincial roses[92] on my   255
razed shoes,[93] get me a fellowship[94] in a cry[95] of players, sir?

HORATIO. Half a share.

HAMLET. A whole one, I.
         For thou dost know, O Damon[96] dear,
         This realm dismantled was   260
         Of Jove[97] himself; and now reigns here
         A very, very peacock.

HORATIO. You might have rhymed.

HAMLET. O good Horatio, I'll take the ghost's word for a thousand
pound. Didst perceive?   265

HORATIO. Very well, my lord.

HAMLET. Upon the talk of the poisoning?

HORATIO. I did very well note him.

[Enter Rosencrantz and Guildenstern.]

HAMLET. Oh, ha! Come, some music! Come, the recorders![98]
         For if the king like not the comedy,   270
         Why then, belike he likes it not, perdy.[99]

Come, some music!

---

88. *false fire:* blank shot.

89. *this:* the play.   90. *feathers:* plumes worn by actors.

91. *turn Turk with:* go back on.   92. *roses:* rosettes.

93. *razed shoes:* slashed shoes—that is, shoes cut in designs common with
Elizabethan actors of that time.   94. *fellowship:* share partnership.

95. *cry:* pack, troupe.

96. *Damon:* character from Roman legend who barely escaped the death penalty
on behalf of his friend Pythias; regarded as model of perfect friendship.

97. *Jove:* Hamlet's father.   98. *recorders:* wooden flutes.

99. *perdy:* a corruption of the French *par Dieu* (by God).

GUILDENSTERN. Good my lord, vouchsafe me a word with you.

HAMLET. Sir, a whole history.

GUILDENSTERN. The king, sir—   275

HAMLET. Ay, sir, what of him?

GUILDENSTERN. Is in his retirement marvellous distempered.

HAMLET. With drink, sir?

GUILDENSTERN. No, my lord, rather with choler.[100]

HAMLET. Your wisdom should show itself more richer to signify   280
this to his doctor, for for me to put him to his purgation would perhaps plunge him into far more choler.

GUILDENSTERN. Good my lord, put your discourse into some frame,[101]
and start not so wildly from my affair.[102]

HAMLET. I am tame, sir; pronounce.   285

GUILDENSTERN. The queen, your mother, in most great affliction
of spirit hath sent me to you.

HAMLET. You are welcome.

GUILDENSTERN. Nay, good my lord, this courtesy is not of the
right breed. If it shall please you to make me a wholesome answer,   290
I will do your mother's commandment. If not, your pardon and
my return shall be the end of my business.

HAMLET. Sir, I cannot.

ROSENCRANTZ. What, my lord?

HAMLET. Make you a wholesome answer; my wit's diseased. But,   295
sir, such answers as I can make, you shall command, or rather,
you say, my mother. Therefore no more, but to the matter. My
mother, you say—

ROSENCRANTZ. Then thus she says: your behavior hath struck her
into amazement and admiration.[103]   300

HAMLET. O wonderful son, that can so astonish a mother! But is
there no sequel at the heels of this mother's admiration?

ROSENCRANTZ. She desires to speak with you in her closet ere you
go to bed.

HAMLET. We shall obey, were she ten times our mother. Have you   305
any further trade with us?

ROSENCRANTZ. My lord, you once did love me.

HAMLET. And do still, by these pickers and stealers.[104]

ROSENCRANTZ. Good my lord, what is your cause of distemper?
You do surely bar the door of your own liberty, if you deny your   310
griefs to your friend.

HAMLET. Sir, I lack advancement.[105]

ROSENCRANTZ. How can that be, when you have the voice of the
king himself for your succession in Denmark?

100. *choler:* anger.
101. *frame:* logical order.
102. *start . . . affair:* wander not so far from the point I am trying to make.
103. *admiration:* wonder.
104. *pickers and stealers:* hands (according to the Catechism a person was to keep
his hands from picking and stealing).   105. *advancement:* promotion.

HAMLET. Ay, sir, but "while the grass grows"[106]—the proverb is something musty.   315

[Enter Player with a recorder.]

O, the recorder. Let me see. To withdraw[107] with you—why do you go about to recover the wind[108] of me, as if you would drive me into a toil?[109]

GUILDENSTERN. O my lord, if my duty be too bold, my love is too unmannerly.[110]   320

HAMLET. I do not well understand that. Will you play upon this pipe?

GUILDENSTERN. My lord, I cannot.

HAMLET. I pray you.   325

GUILDENSTERN. Believe me, I cannot.

HAMLET. I do beseech you.

GUILDENSTERN. I know no touch of it, my lord.

HAMLET. 'Tis as easy as lying. Govern these ventages[111] with your finger and thumb, give it breath with your mouth, and it will discourse most eloquent music. Look you, these are the stops.   330

GUILDENSTERN. But these cannot I command to any utterance of harmony. I have not the skill.

HAMLET. Why, look you now, how unworthy a thing you make of me! You would play upon me, you would seem to know my stops,   335 you would pluck out the heart of my mystery, you would sound me from my lowest note to the top of my compass;[112] and there is much music, excellent voice, in this little organ, yet cannot you make it speak. 'Sblood,[113] do you think I am easier to be played on than a pipe? Call me what instrument you will, though you can fret[114] me,   340 you cannot play upon me.

[Enter Polonius.]

God bless you, sir!

POLONIUS. My lord, the queen would speak with you, and presently.

HAMLET. Do you see that cloud that's almost in shape like a camel?   345

POLONIUS. By th' mass and it's like a camel indeed.

HAMLET. Methinks it is like a weasel.

POLONIUS. It is backed like a weasel.

HAMLET. Or like a whale.

POLONIUS. Very like a whale.   350

106. *"while the grass grows"*: The rest of the proverb is "the silly horse starves."
107. *withdraw:* speak privately.
108. *recover the wind:* a hunting term, meaning to get on to the windward side.
109. *toil:* snare.
110. *if . . . unmannerly:* if my duty makes me too bold, my love also makes me too unmannerly.   111. *ventages:* holes, vents.   112. *compass:* musical range.
113. *'Sblood:* God's blood.
114. *fret:* irritate (with a pun on the fret-fingering of certain stringed instruments).

HAMLET. Then I will come to my mother by and by. *[Aside.]* They
fool me to the top of my bent.[115]—I will come by and by.

POLONIUS. I will say so.   *[Exit.]*

HAMLET. "By and by" is easily said. Leave me, friends.
                                        [Exeunt all but Hamlet.]
'Tis now the very witching time[116] of night,   355
When churchyards yawn, and hell itself breathes out
Contagion to this world. Now could I drink hot blood
And do such bitter business as the day
Would quake to look on. Soft, now to my mother!
O heart, lose not thy nature, let not ever   360
The soul of Nero[117] enter this firm bosom!
Let me be cruel, not unnatural;
I will speak daggers to her, but use none.
My tongue and soul in this be hypocrites:
How in my words somever she be shent,[118]   365
To give them seals[119] never, my soul, consent!   *[Exit.]*

SCENE 3   *A room in the castle.*

[Enter King, Rosencrantz, and Guildenstern.]

KING. I like him not, nor stands it safe with us
    To let his madness range. Therefore prepare you.
    I your commission will forthwith dispatch,
    And he to England shall along with you.
    The terms of our estate[1] may not endure   5
    Hazard so dangerous as doth hourly grow
    Out of his lunacies.

GUILDENSTERN.   We will ourselves provide.
    Most holy and religious fear[2] it is
    To keep those many many bodies safe
    That live and feed upon your majesty.   10

ROSENCRANTZ. The single and peculiar[3] life is bound
    With all the strength and armor of the mind
    To keep itself from noyance,[4] but much more
    That spirit upon whose weal[5] depends and rests
    The lives of many. The cease of majesty[6]   15

115. *top . . . bent:* limit of tension (as of a bow). Further strain will cause the bow
to break.   116. *witching time:* the time for witches to perform.
117. *Nero:* Roman emperor who murdered his mother.
118. *shent:* reproved, rebuked.   119. *give them seals:* confirm with deeds.
1. *our estate:* my rule.   2. *fear:* caution.   3. *peculiar:* individual.
4. *noyance:* harm.   5. *weal:* welfare, well-being.
6. *cease of majesty:* death of a king.

Dies not alone, but like a gulf[7] doth draw
What's near it with it. It is a massy[8] wheel
Fixed on the summit of the highest mount,
To whose huge spokes ten thousand lesser things
Are mortised and adjoined, which when it falls,   20
Each small annexment, petty consequence,
Attends the boist'rous ruin. Never alone
Did the king sigh, but with a general groan.

KING. Arm[9] you, I pray you, to this speedy voyage,
For we will fetters put upon this fear,   25
Which now goes too free-footed.

ROSENCRANTZ.   We will haste us.

[Exeunt Gentlemen.]

[Enter Polonius.]

POLONIUS. My lord, he's going to his mother's closet.
Behind the arras I'll convey myself
To hear the process. I'll warrant she'll tax him home,[10]
And, as you said, and wisely was it said,   30
'Tis meet that some more audience than a mother,
Since nature makes them partial, should o'erhear
The speech, of vantage.[11] Fare you well, my liege.
I'll call upon you ere you go to bed
And tell you what I know.

KING.   Thanks, dear my lord.   35

[Exit Polonius.]

O, my offense is rank, it smells to heaven;
It hath the primal eldest curse[12] upon't,
A brother's murther. Pray can I not,
Though inclination be as sharp as will.
My stronger guilt defeats my strong intent,   40
And like a man to double business bound
I stand in pause where I shall first begin,
And both neglect. What if this cursèd hand
Were thicker than itself with brother's blood,
Is there not rain enough in the sweet heavens   45
To wash it white as snow? Whereto[13] serves mercy
But to confront[14] the visage of offense?[15]
And what's in prayer but this twofold force,
To be forestallèd ere we come to fall,
Or pardoned being down? Then I'll look up.   50
My fault is past. But, O, what form of prayer

---

7. *gulf:* whirlpool.   8. *massy:* massive.
9. *Arm:* prepare.   10. *tax him home:* take him to task thoroughly.
11. *of vantage:* from some point of advantage.
12. *primal eldest curse:* the curse on Cain (who killed his brother Abel).
13. *Whereto:* what purpose.   14. *confront:* oppose directly.   15. *offense:* sin.

Can serve my turn? "Forgive me my foul murther"?
That cannot be, since I am still possessed
Of those effects for which I did the murther,
My crown, mine own ambition, and my queen.   55
May one be pardoned and retain th' offense?
In the corrupted currents of this world
Offense's gilded[16] hand may shove by justice,
And oft 'tis seen the wicked prize itself
Buys out the law. But 'tis not so above.   60
There is no shuffling;[17] there the action lies
In his true nature, and we ourselves compelled,
Even to the teeth and forehead of our faults,
To give in evidence. What then? What rests?[18]
Try what repentance can. What can it not?   65
Yet what can it when one cannot repent?
O wretched state! O bosom black as death!
O limèd[19] soul, that struggling to be free
Art more engaged! Help, angels! Make assay.
Bow, stubborn knees, and, heart with strings of steel,   70
Be soft as sinews of the new-born babe.
All may be well.   *[He kneels.]*

                    [Enter Hamlet.]

HAMLET. Now might I do it pat, now he is a-praying,
    And now I'll do't. And so he goes to heaven,
    And so am I revenged. That would be scanned.[20]   75
    A villain kills my father, and for that
    I, his sole son, do this same villain send
    To heaven.
    O, this is hire and salary, not revenge.
    He took my father grossly,[21] full of bread,   80
    With all his crimes[22] broad blown, as flush[23] as May;
    And how his audit stands, who knows save heaven?
    But in our circumstance and course of thought,
    'Tis heavy with him;[24] and am I then revenged,
    To take him in the purging of his soul,[25]   85
    When he is fit and seasoned for his passage?[26]
    No.
    Up, sword, and know thou a more horrid hent.[27]

16. *gilded:* golden.   17. *shuffling:* double-dealing.
18. *What rests?* What remains?   19. *limèd:* caught, as in bird-lime.
20. *scanned:* considered, looked at.
21. *grossly:* when he (my father) was unprepared.   22. *crimes:* sins.
23. *flush:* lusty.   24. *'Tis . . . him:* he is weighted down with sin.
25. *in . . . soul:* at the time he is praying.
26. *seasoned . . . passage:* ready to go to the hereafter.
27. *horrid hent:* horrible opportunity.

When he is drunk asleep, or in his rage,
Or in th' incestuous pleasure of his bed,   90
At gaming, swearing, or about some act
That has no relish of salvation in't—
Then trip him, that his heels may kick at heaven,
And that his soul may be as damned and black
As hell, whereto it goes. My mother stays.[28]   95
This physic[29] but prolongs thy sickly days.   *[Exit.]*
KING. My words fly up, my thoughts remain below.
Words without thoughts never to heaven go.   *[Exit.]*

SCENE 4   *The Queen's Closet.*

[Enter Queen and Polonius.]

POLONIUS. He will come straight. Look you lay[1] home to him.
Tell him his pranks have been too broad to bear with,
And that your grace hath screened and stood between
Much heat and him. I'll silence me even here.
Pray you be round[2] with him.   5
HAMLET. *[Within.]* Mother, mother, mother!
QUEEN. I'll warrant[3] you; fear me not. Withdraw; I hear him
coming.   *[Polonius hides behind the arras.]*

[Enter Hamlet.]

HAMLET. Now, mother, what's the matter?
QUEEN. Hamlet, thou hast thy father much offended.   10
HAMLET. Mother, you have my father much offended.
QUEEN. Come, come, you answer with an idle[4] tongue.
HAMLET. Go, go, you question with a wicked tongue.
QUEEN. Why, how now, Hamlet?
HAMLET.   What's the matter now?
QUEEN. Have you forgot me?
HAMLET.   No, by the rood,[5] not so!   15
You are the queen, your husband's brother's wife,
And (would it were not so) you are my mother.
QUEEN. Nay, then I'll set those to you that can speak.[6]
HAMLET. Come, come, and sit you down. You shall not budge.
You go not till I set you up a glass[7]   20
Where you may see the inmost part of you.

---

28. *stays:* awaits.
29. *physic:* medicine (that is, the delay).
1. *lay:* thrust.   2. *round:* straightforward.   3. *warrant:* guarantee.
4. *idle:* foolish.   5. *rood:* cross.   6. *that can speak:* that is, with more authority.
7. *glass:* mirror.

QUEEN. What wilt thou do? Thou wilt not murther me?
   Help, help, hoa!
POLONIUS. *[Behind.]* What, hoa! help! help!
HAMLET. *[Draws.]* How now? a rat? Dead for a ducat, dead!   25
            [Makes a pass through the arras and kills Polonius.]
POLONIUS. *[Behind.]* O, I am slain!
QUEEN.   O me, what hast thou done?
HAMLET. Nay, I know not. Is it the king?
QUEEN. O, what a rash and bloody deed is this!
HAMLET. A bloody deed—almost as bad good mother,
   As kill a king, and marry with his brother.   30
QUEEN. As kill a king?
HAMLET.   Ay, lady, it was my word.
                 [Lifts up the arras and sees Polonius.]
   Thou wretched, rash, intruding fool, farewell!
   I took thee for thy better.[8] Take thy fortune.
   Thou find'st to be too busy is some danger.—
   Leave wringing of your hands; peace, sit you down   35
   And let me wring your heart, for so I shall
   If it be made of penetrable stuff,
   If damnèd custom have not brazed[9] it so
   That it is proof and bulwark against sense.
QUEEN. What have I done that thou dar'st wag thy tongue   40
   In noise so rude against me?
HAMLET.   Such an act
   That blurs the grace and blush of modesty,
   Calls virtue hypocrite, takes off the rose
   From the fair forehead of an innocent love,
   And makes a blister[10] there, makes marriage vows   45
   As false as dicers' oaths. O, such a deed
   As from the body of contraction[11] plucks
   The very soul, and sweet religion[12] makes
   A rhapsody of words![13] Heaven's face[14] does glow,
   Yea, this solidity and compound mass,[15]   50
   With heated visage,[16] as against[17] the doom,
   Is thought-sick at the act.
QUEEN.   Ay me, what act,
   That roars so loud and thunders in the index?[18]
HAMLET. Look here upon this picture, and on this,
   The counterfeit presentment[19] of two brothers.   55

---

8. *I . . . better:* I thought you were the king.   9. *brazed:* hardened.
10. *blister:* women convicted of prostitution were branded on the forehead.
11. *contraction:* the marriage contract.   12. *religion:* sacred marriage vows.
13. *rhapsody of words:* meaningless words.   14. *Heaven's face:* the sun.
15. *solidity . . . mass:* the earth.   16. *heated visage:* burning face.
17. *against:* in expectation of.   18. *index:* table of contents, prologue.
19. *counterfeit presentment:* protrayed representation.

See what a grace was seated on this brow:
Hyperion's²⁰ curls, the front²¹ of Jove himself,
An eye like Mars, to threaten or command,
A station²² like the herald Mercury
New lighted on a heaven-kissing hill,   60
A combination and a form indeed
Where every god did seem to set his seal
To give the world assurance of a man.
This was your husband. Look you now what follows.
Here is your husband, like a mildewed ear²³   65
Blasting his wholesome brother. Have you eyes?
Could you on this fair mountain leave to feed,
And batten²⁴ on this moor? Ha! have you eyes?
You cannot call it love, for at your age
The heyday²⁵ in the blood is tame, it's humble,   70
And waits upon the judgment, and what judgment
Would step from this to this? Sense²⁶ sure you have,
Else could you not have motion,²⁷ but sure that sense
Is apoplexed,²⁸ for madness would not err,
Nor sense to ecstasy was ne'er so thralled²⁹   75
But it reserved some quantity of choice
To serve in such a difference. What devil was't
That thus hath cozened³⁰ you at hoodman-blind?³¹
Eyes without feeling, feeling without sight,
Ears without hands or eyes, smelling sans³² all,   80
Or but a sickly part of one true sense
Could not so mope.³³
O shame! where is thy blush? Rebellious hell,
If thou canst mutine³⁴ in a matron's bones,
To flaming youth let virtue be as wax   85
And melt in her own fire. Proclaim no shame
When the compulsive ardor gives the charge,³⁵
Since frost itself as actively doth burn,
And reason panders³⁶ will.
QUEEN.   O Hamlet, speak no more.
Thou turn'st mine eyes into my very soul,   90
And there I see such black and grainèd spots
As will not leave their tinct.³⁷

---

20. *Hyperion's:* the sun god's.   21. *front:* forehead.   22. *station:* standing figure.
23. *ear:* of wheat.   24. *batten:* feed greedily, gorge yourself.
25. *heyday:* excitement of passion, youthful passion.   26. *sense:* feeling.
27. *motion:* emotion, desire.   28. *apoplexed:* paralyzed.   29. *thralled:* enslaved.
30. *cozened:* tricked, cheated.   31. *hoodman-blind:* blindman's buff.
32. *sans:* without.   33. *Could . . . mope:* could not be so stupid.
34. *mutine:* rebel, mutiny.   35. *gives the charge:* attacks.
36. *panders:* becomes subject to.
37. *Will . . . tinct:* will not lose their color.

HAMLET.   Nay, but to live
In the rank sweat of an enseamèd[38] bed,
Stewed[39] in corruption, honeying and making love
Over the nasty sty—[40]
QUEEN.   O, speak to me no more.   95
These words like daggers enter in mine ears.
No more, sweet Hamlet.
HAMLET.   A murtherer and a villain,
A slave that is not twentieth part the tithe[41]
Of your precedent lord, a vice[42] of kings,
A cutpurse[43] of the empire and the rule,   100
That from a shelf the precious diadem stole
And put it in his pocket—
QUEEN.   No more.

[Enter Ghost.]

HAMLET. A king of shreds and patches—
Save me and hover o'er me with your wings,
You heavenly guards![44] What would your gracious figure?   105
QUEEN. Alas, he's mad.
HAMLET. Do you not come your tardy son to chide,
That, lapsed in time and passion,[45] lets go by
Th' important acting of your dread command?
O, say!   110
GHOST. Do not forget. This visitation
Is but to whet thy almost blunted purpose.
But look, amazement on thy mother sits.
O, step between her and her fighting soul!
Conceit[46] in weakest bodies strongest works.   115
Speak to her, Hamlet.
HAMLET.   How is it with you, lady?
QUEEN. Alas, how is't with you,
That you do bend your eye on vacancy,
And with th' incorporal[47] air do hold discourse?
Forth at your eyes your spirits wildly peep,   120
And as the sleeping soldiers in th' alarm
Your bedded[48] hair like life in excrements[49]
Start up and stand on end. O gentle son,
Upon the heat and flame of thy distemper

38. *enseamèd:* greasy.   39. *stewed:* bathed.   40. *sty:* pigsty, low or vicious place.
41. *tithe:* tenth sort.
42. *vice:* a character in the old morality plays, the buffoon.
43. *cutpurse:* pickpocket.   44. *heavenly guards:* guardian angels.
45. *laps'd . . . passion:* having delayed and allowed the emotions to cool.
46. *Conceit:* imagination.   47. *incorporal:* bodiless.   48. *bedded:* evenly laid.
49. *excrements:* anything that grows out of the body, such as fingernails, etc.

Sprinkle cool patience. Whereon do you look?   125
HAMLET. On him, on him! Look you, how pale he glares!
His form and cause conjoined,[50] preaching to stones,
Would make them capable.[51]—Do not look upon me,
Lest with this piteous action you convert
My stern effects.[52] Then what I have to do   130
Will want true color[53]; tears perchance for blood.
QUEEN. To whom do you speak this?
HAMLET.   Do you see nothing there?
QUEEN. Nothing at all; yet all that is I see.
HAMLET. Nor did you nothing hear?
QUEEN.   No, nothing but ourselves.
HAMLET. Why, look you there! Look how it steals away!   135
My father, in his habit[54] as he lived!
Look where he goes even now out at the portal!   *[Exit Ghost.]*
QUEEN. This is the very coinage of your brain.
This bodiless creation ecstasy[55]
Is very cunning in.
HAMLET.   Ecstasy?   140
My pulse as yours doth temperately keep time
And makes as healthful music. It is not madness
That I have uttered. Bring me to the test,
And I the matter will reword,[56] which madness
Would gambol[57] from. Mother, for love of grace,   145
Lay not a flattering unction[58] to your soul,
That not your trespass but my madness speaks.
It will but skin and film the ulcerous place
Whilst rank corruption, mining all within,
Infects unseen. Confess yourself to heaven,   150
Repent what's past, avoid what is to come,
And do not spread the compost[59] on the weeds
To make them rank. Forgive me this my virtue.[60]
For in the fatness[61] of these pursy[62] times
Virtue itself of vice must pardon beg,   155
Yea, curb[63] and woo for leave to do him good.
QUEEN. O Hamlet, thou hast cleft my heart in twain.
HAMLET. O, throw away the worser part of it,
And live the purer with the other half.

---

50. *His . . . conjoined:* his appearance and reason for appearing joined.
51. *capable:* possessed of feeling.
52. *effects:* deeds, that is, you will make me change my purpose.
53. *want true color:* will not be what it should be.   54. *habit:* clothes.
55. *ecstasy:* madness.   56. *Bring . . . reword:* try me and see if I can't talk rationally.
57. *gambol:* wander away.   58. *flattering unction:* soothing ointment.
59. *compost:* manure.   60. *Forgive . . . virtue:* Forgive me for talking so strongly.
61. *fatness:* grossness.   62. *pursy:* corpulent, obese.   63. *curb:* bow to.

Good night, but go not to my uncle's bed.   160
Assume a virtue, if you have it not.
That monster custom, who all sense doth eat,
Of habits evil,⁶⁴ is angel yet in this,
That to the use of actions fair and good
He likewise gives a frock or livery   165
That aptly is put on. Refrain to-night,
And that shall lend a kind of easiness
To the next abstinence; the next more easy;
For use almost can change the stamp of nature,
And either curb the devil, or throw him out   170
With wondrous potency. Once more, good night,
And when you are desirous to be blest,
I'll blessing beg of you.⁶⁵—For this same lord,⁶⁶
I do repent; but heaven hath pleased it so,
To punish me with this, and this with me,⁶⁷   175
That I must be their scourge and minister.
I will bestow him⁶⁸ and will answer well
The death I gave him. So again, good night.
I must be cruel only to be kind.
Thus bad begins, and worse remains behind.⁶⁹   180
One word more, good lady.
QUEEN.   What shall I do?
HAMLET. Not this, by no means, that I bid you do:
Let the bloat king tempt you again to bed,
Pinch wanton on your cheek, call you his mouse,
And let him, for a pair of reechy⁷⁰ kisses,   185
Or paddling in your neck with his damned fingers,
Make you to ravel all this matter out,⁷¹
That I essentially am not in madness,
But mad in craft. 'Twere good you let him know,
For who that's but a queen, fair, sober, wise,   190
Would from a paddock,⁷² from a bat, a gib,⁷³
Such dear concernings hide? Who would do so?
No, in despite of sense and secrecy,
Unpeg⁷⁴ the basket on the house's top,
Let the birds fly, and like the famous ape,⁷⁵   195

64. *of habits evil:* made up of evil habits.
65. *And . . . you:* And when you have repented, I'll beg a blessing of you (as a good son should).   66. *this same lord:* Polonius.
67. *and this with me:* and this (death of Polonius) by me.
68. *bestow him:* stow him away.   69. *worse remains behind:* worse is yet to come.
70. *reechy:* foul.   71. *ravel . . . out:* tell him of all that has happened here.
72. *paddock:* toad.   73. *gib:* tomcat.   74. *unpeg:* open.
75. In a fable the ape tried to fly like the birds and broke his neck.

To try conclusions, in the basket creep
And break your own neck down.
QUEEN. Be thou assured, if words be made of breath,
  And breath of life, I have no life to breathe
  What thou hast said to me.   200
HAMLET. I must to England; you know that?
QUEEN.   Alack,
  I had forgot. 'Tis so concluded on.
HAMLET. There's letters sealed, and my two schoolfellows,
  Whom I will trust as I will adders fanged,
  They bear the mandate; they must sweep my way[76]   205
  And marshal me to knavery.[77] Let it work.
  For 'tis the sport to have the enginer[78]
  Hoist with his own petar,[79] and 't shall go hard
  But I will delve one yard below their mines
  And blow them at the moon. O, 'tis most sweet   210
  When in one line two crafts directly meet.
  This man shall set me packing.
  I'll lug the guts into the neighbor room.
  Mother, good night. Indeed, this counsellor
  Is now most still, most secret, and most grave,   215
  Who was in life a foolish prating knave.
  Come, sir, to draw toward an end with you.
  Good night, mother.
          [Exit the Queen. Then exit Hamlet, tugging in Polonius.]

ACT IV

SCENE 1   *A room in the castle.*

[Enter King and Queen.]

KING. There's matter in these sighs. These profound heaves
  You must translate; 'tis fit we understand them.
  Where is your son?
QUEEN. Ah, my good lord, what have I seen to-night!

76. *sweep my way:* clear my path.
77. *marshal . . . knavery:* lead me to trickery or crafty dealing.
78. *enginer:* designer of machines of war and fortifications.
79. *Hoist with his own petar:* blown up with his own bomb.

KING. What, Gertrude? How does Hamlet?   5
QUEEN. Mad as the seas and wind when both contend
    Which is the mightier. In his lawless fit,
    Behind the arras hearing something stir,
    Whips out his rapier, cries, "A rat, a rat!"
    And in his brainish apprehension[1] kills   10
    The unseen good old man.
KING.   O heavy deed!
    It had been so with us, had we been there.
    His liberty is full of threats to all,
    To you yourself, to us, to every one.
    Alas, how shall this bloody deed be answered?[2]   15
    It will be laid to us, whose providence[3]
    Should have kept short, restrained, and out of haunt[4]
    This mad young man. But so much was our love
    We would not understand what was most fit,
    But, like the owner of a foul disease,   20
    To keep it from divulging, lets it feed
    Even on the pith of life. Where is he gone?
QUEEN. To draw apart the body he hath killed;
    O'er whom his very madness, like some ore
    Among a mineral[5] of metals base,   25
    Shows itself pure. He weeps for what is done.
KING. O Gertrude, come away!
    The sun no sooner shall the mountains touch
    But we will ship him hence, and this vile deed
    We must with all our majesty and skill   30
    Both countenance[6] and excuse. Ho, Guildenstern!

[Enter Rosencrantz and Guildenstern.]

    Friends both, go join you with some further aid.
    Hamlet in madness hath Polonius slain,
    And from his mother's closet hath he dragged him.
    Go seek him out; speak fair, and bring the body   35
    Into the chapel. I pray you haste in this.

[Exeunt Rosencrantz and Guildenstern.]

    Come, Gertrude, we'll call up our wisest friends
    To let them know both what we mean to do
    And what's untimely done. O, come away!
    My soul is full of discord and dismay.   40

[Exeunt.]

---

1. *brainish apprehension:* insane imagination.   2. *answered:* accounted for.
3. *providence:* foresight.   4. *haunt:* company.   5. *mineral:* mine.
6. *countenance:* defend, condone.

SCENE 2   *Another room in the castle.*

[Enter Hamlet.]

HAMLET. Safely stowed.

GENTLEMEN. *[Within.]* Hamlet! Lord Hamlet!

HAMLET. Who calls on Hamlet? O, here they come.

[Enter Rosencrantz, Guildenstern, and others.]

ROSENCRANTZ. What have you done, my lord, with the dead body?

HAMLET. Compounded[1] it with dust, whereto 'tis kin.   5

ROSENCRANTZ. Tell us where 'tis, that we may take it thence
   And bear it to the chapel.

HAMLET. Do not believe it.

ROSENCRANTZ. Believe what?

HAMLET. That I can keep your counsel and not mine own.[2] Besides,   10
to be demanded of[3] a sponge, what replication[4] should be made by
the son of a king?

ROSENCRANTZ. Take you me for a sponge, my lord?

HAMLET. Ay, sir, that soaks up the king's countenance, his rewards,
his authorities. But such officers do the king best service in the end.   15
He keeps them, like an ape, in the corner of his jaw, first mouthed,
to be last swallowed. When he needs what you have gleaned, it is
but squeezing you and, sponge, you shall be dry again.

ROSENCRANTZ. I understand you not, my lord.

HAMLET. I am glad of it. A knavish speech sleeps in a foolish ear.   20

ROSENCRANTZ. My lord, you must tell us where the body is and go
with us to the king.

HAMLET. The body is with the king, but the king is not with the
body.[5] The king is a thing—

GUILDENSTERN. A thing, my lord?   25

HAMLET. Of nothing. Bring me to him. Hide fox, and all after.[6]

                       [Exeunt.]

SCENE 3   *Another room in the castle.*

[Enter King and two or three.]

KING. I have sent to seek him and to find the body.
   How dangerous is it that this man goes loose!

---

1. *compounded:* mixed.
2. *keep . . . own:* keep your secret about spying from the king and not keep
my own secret (the location of the body).   3. *demanded of:* questioned by.
4. *replication:* reply.
5. *body:* Hamlet refers to the king's physical body as well as the political
body which, according to Hamlet, the present king does not lawfully hold.
6. *Hide fox, and all after:* name of a game such as hide and seek.

Yet must not we put the strong law on him;
He's loved of the distracted[1] multitude,
Who like[2] not in their judgment, but their eyes,   5
And where 'tis so, th' offender's scourge[3] is weighed,
But never the offense. To bear all smooth and even,
This sudden sending him away must seem
Deliberate pause.[4] Diseases desperate grown
By desperate appliance are relieved,   10
Or not at all.

[Enter Rosencrantz.]

How now? What hath befallen?
ROSENCRANTZ. Where the dead body is bestowed, my lord,
We cannot get from him.
KING.   But where is he?
ROSENCRANTZ. Without, my lord; guarded, to know your pleasure.
KING. Bring him before us.
ROSENCRANTZ.   Ho, Guildenstern! Bring in the lord.   15

[Enter Hamlet and Guildenstern.]

KING. Now, Hamlet, where's Polonius?
HAMLET. At supper.
KING. At supper? Where?
HAMLET. Not where he eats, but where he is eaten. A certain
convocation of worms are e'en at him. Your worm is your only em-   20
peror for diet. We fat all creatures else[5] to fat us, and we fat ourselves
for maggots. Your fat king and your lean beggar is but variable
service[6]—two dishes, but to one table. That's the end.
KING. Alas, alas!
HAMLET. A man may fish with the worm that hath eat of a king,   25
and eat of the fish that hath fed of that worm.
KING. What dost thou mean by this?
HAMLET. Nothing but to show you how a king may go a progress[7]
through the guts of a beggar.
KING. Where is Polonius?   30
HAMLET. In heaven. Send thither to see. If your messenger find
him not there, seek him i' th' other place yourself. But if indeed you
find him not within this month, you shall nose[8] him as you go up
the stairs into the lobby.
KING. *[To Attendants.]* Go seek him there.   35
HAMLET. He will stay till ye come.   *[Exeunt Attendants.]*
KING. Hamlet, this deed, for thine especial safety,

1. *distracted:* turbulent and foolish.   2. *like:* admire.   3. *scourge:* punishment.
4. *pause:* planning.   5. *else:* other than ourselves.
6. *variable service:* different servings of but one food.
7. *go a progress:* go on a ceremonial journey.   8. *nose:* smell.

Which we do tender[9] as we dearly grieve
For that which thou hast done, must send thee hence
With fiery quickness. Therefore prepare thyself. 40
The bark is ready and the wind at help,[10]
Th' associates tend, and everything is bent[11]
For England.
HAMLET. For England?
KING. Ay, Hamlet.
HAMLET. Good.
KING. So is it, if thou knew'st our purposes.

  HAMLET. I see a cherub[12] that sees them. But come, for England! 45
Farewell, dear mother.

  KING. Thy loving father, Hamlet.

  HAMLET. My mother—father and mother is man and wife, man
and wife is one flesh, and so, my mother. Come, for England!
[Exit.]

  KING. Follow him at foot;[13] tempt him with speed aboard. 50
Delay it not; I'll have him hence to-night.
Away! for everything is sealed and done
That else leans on[14] th' affair. Pray you make haste.
[Exeunt all but the King.]
And, England,[15] if my love thou hold'st at aught—
As my great power thereof may give thee sense, 55
Since yet thy cicatrice[16] looks raw and red
After the Danish sword, and thy free awe[17]
Pays homage to us—thou mayst not coldly set[18]
Our sovereign process,[19] which imports at full
By letters congruing[20] to that effect 60
The present death of Hamlet. Do it, England,
For like the hectic[21] in my blood he rages,
And thou must cure me. Till I know 'tis done,
Howe'er my haps,[22] my joys were ne'er begun. *[Exit.]*

SCENE 4 *A plain in Denmark.*

[Enter Fortinbras with a Captain and an army.]
FORTINBRAS. Go, captain, from me greet the Danish king.
  Tell him that by his license Fortinbras

---

9. *tender:* value highly. 10. *at help:* favorable. 11. *bent:* set in readiness.
12. *cherub:* an angel, which, of course, knows everything.
13. *at foot:* at his heels, close behind. 14. *leans on:* pertains to.
15. *England:* King of England. 16. *cicatrice:* scar.
17. *free awe:* voluntary submission. 18. *coldly set:* lightly regard.
19. *process:* formal command. 20. *congruing:* agreeing. 21. *hectic:* fever.
22. *haps:* fortunes.

Claims the conveyance[1] of a promised march
Over his kingdom. You know the rendezvous.
If that[2] his majesty would aught with us,[3]   5
We shall express our duty in his eye;[4]
And let him know so.
CAPTAIN.   I will do't, my lord.
FORTINBRAS. Go safely on.   *[Exeunt all but the Captain.]*

[Enter Hamlet, Rosencrantz, Guildenstern, and others.]

HAMLET. Good sir, whose powers are these?
CAPTAIN. They are of Norway, sir.   10
HAMLET. How purposed, sir, I pray you?
CAPTAIN. Against some part of Poland.
HAMLET. Who commands them, sir?
CAPTAIN. The nephew to old Norway, Fortinbras.
HAMLET. Goes it against the main[5] of Poland, sir,   15
Or for some frontier?
CAPTAIN. Truly to speak, and with no addition,
We go to gain a little patch of ground
That hath in it no profit but the name.
To pay[6] five ducats, five, I would not farm it,   20
Nor will it yield to Norway or the Pole
A ranker[7] rate, should it be sold in fee.[8]
HAMLET. Why, then the Polack never will defend it.
CAPTAIN. Yes, it is already garrisoned.
HAMLET. Two thousand souls and twenty thousand ducats   25
Will not debate the question of this straw.[9]
This is th' imposthume[10] of much wealth and peace,
That inward breaks, and shows no cause without
Why the man dies. I humbly thank you, sir.
CAPTAIN. God bye you, sir.   *[Exit.]*
ROSENCRANTZ.   Will't please you go, my lord?   30
HAMLET. I'll be with you straight. Go a little before.

[Exeunt all but Hamlet.]

How all occasions do inform against[11] me
And spur my dull[12] revenge! What is a man,
If his chief good and market[13] of his time
Be but to sleep and feed? A beast, no more.   35
Sure he that made us with such large discourse,[14]
Looking before and after,[15] gave us not

---

1. *conveyance:* escort.   2. *If that:* if.   3. *would . . . us:* wishes anything of us.
4. *eye:* presence.   5. *main:* main part.   6. *To pay:* for the rental of.
7. *ranker:* higher.   8. *in fee:* outright.
9. *debate . . . straw:* settle this minor argument.   10. *imposthume:* ulcer.
11. *inform against:* denounce, accuse.   12. *dull:* slow.   13. *market:* profit.
14. *discourse:* powers of reasoning.
15. *Looking . . . after:* able to relate cause to effect.

That capability and godlike reason
To fust¹⁶ in us unused. Now, whether it be
Bestial oblivion, or some craven scruple   40
Of thinking too precisely on th' event—¹⁷
A thought which, quartered, hath but one part wisdom
And ever three parts coward—I do not know
Why yet I live to say, "This thing's to do,"
Sith¹⁸ I have cause, and will, and strength, and means   45
To do't. Examples gross as earth exhort me.
Witness this army of such mass and charge,¹⁹
Led by a delicate and tender prince,
Whose spirit, with divine ambition puffed,
Makes mouths²⁰ at the invisible event,²¹   50
Exposing what is mortal and unsure
To all that fortune, death, and danger dare,
Even for an eggshell. Rightly²² to be great
Is not to stir without great argument,²³
But greatly to find quarrel in a straw   55
When honor's at the stake. How stand I then,
That have a father killed, a mother stained,
Excitements of my reason and my blood,
And let all sleep, while to my shame I see
The imminent death of twenty thousand men   60
That for a fantasy and trick²⁴ of fame
Go to their graves like beds, fight for a plot
Whereon the numbers cannot try the cause,²⁵
Which is not tomb enough and continent²⁶
To hide the slain? O, from this time forth,   65
My thoughts be bloody, or be nothing worth!   *[Exit.]*

SCENE 5   *A room in the castle.*

[Enter Queen and Horatio.]

QUEEN. I will not speak with her.
HORATIO. She is importunate,¹ indeed distract.
  Her mood will needs be pitied.
QUEEN.   What would she have?
HORATIO. She speaks much of her father, says she hears
  There's tricks² i' th' world, and hems, and beats her heart,   5

16. *fust:* become moldy.
17. *event:* outcome.   18. *Sith:* since.   19. *charge:* cost.
20. *makes mouths:* mocks or scorns.   21. *invisible event:* unknown outcome.
22. *Rightly:* truly.   23. *argument:* motive.   24. *trick:* toy, trifle.
25. *Whereon . . . cause:* which cannot even hold the number of men who fight for it.
26. *continent:* container.
  1. *importunate:* urgent in her demands.   2. *tricks:* plots, trickery.

Spurns enviously at straws,[3] speaks things in doubt
That carry but half sense. Her speech is nothing,
Yet the unshaped use of it doth move
The hearers to collection;[4] they aim at it,
And botch the words up fit to their own thoughts,   10
Which, as her winks and nods and gestures yield them,
Indeed would make one think there might be thought,
Though nothing sure, yet much unhappily.
QUEEN. 'Twere good she were spoken with, for she may strew
Dangerous conjectures in ill breeding minds.   15
Let her come in.   *[Exit Horatio.]*
To my sick soul (as sin's true nature is)
Each toy[5] seems prologue to some great amiss.[6]
So full of artless jealousy[7] is guilt
It spills itself in fearing to be spilt.   20

        [Enter Horatio with Ophelia, distracted.]

OPHELIA. Where is the beauteous majesty of Denmark?
QUEEN. How now, Ophelia?
OPHELIA. *[Sings.]*

        How should I your true-love know
          From another one?
        By his cockle hat and staff[8]   25
        And his sandal shoon.[9]

QUEEN. Alas, sweet lady, what imports[10] this song?
OPHELIA. Say you? Nay, pray you mark.[11]

        [She sings.]
        He is dead and gone, lady,
          He is dead and gone;   30
        At his head a grass-green turf,
          At his heels a stone.

QUEEN. Nay, but Ophelia—
OPHELIA. Pray you mark.

        [Sings.]
        White his shroud as the mountain snow—   35

        [Enter King.]

QUEEN. Alas, look here, my lord.
OPHELIA. *[Sings.]*

        Larded[12] *all with sweet flowers;*
        Which bewept to the grave did not go
        With true-love showers.

---

3. *Spurns . . . straws:* takes offense at trifles.
4. *collection:* conjecture, attempt to collect meaning.
5. *toy:* trifle.   6. *amiss:* misfortune, calamity.
7. *artless jealousy:* foolish or unreasonable suspicion.
8. *cockle hat and staff:* hat adorned with shells and staff (signs of a pilgrim).
9. *shoon:* shoes.   10. *imports:* means.
11. *Say . . . mark:* What did you say? No, please listen.   12. *larded:* garnished.

KING. How do you, pretty lady? 40

OPHELIA. Well, God dild[13] you! They say the owl was a baker's daughter.[14] Lord, we know what we are, but know not what we may be. God be at your table!

KING. Conceit[15] upon her father.

OPHELIA. Pray let's have no words of this, but when they ask you 45
what it means, say you this:
> [Sings.]
> *To-morrow is Saint Valentine's day.*
> *All in the morning betime,*
> *And I a maid at your window,*
> *To be your Valentine.* 50

> *Then up he rose and donned his clothes*
> *And dupped[16] the chamber door,*
> *Let in the maid, that out a maid*
> *Never departed more.*

KING. Pretty Ophelia! 55

OPHELIA. Indeed, la! without an oath, I'll make an end on't:
> [She sings.]
> *By Gis[17] and by Saint Charity,*
> *Alack, and fie for shame!*
> *Young men will do't if they come to't.*
> *By Cock,[18] they are to blame.[19]* 60

> *Quoth she, "Before you tumbled me,*
> *You promised me to wed."*
> *"So would I 'a'[20] done, by yonder sun,*
> *An thou hadst not come to my bed."*

KING. How long hath she been thus? 65

OPHELIA. I hope all will be well. We must be patient, but I cannot choose but weep to think they should lay him i' th' cold ground. My brother shall know of it; and so I thank you for your good counsel. Come, my coach! Good night, ladies, good night. Sweet ladies, good night, good night. *[Exit.]* 70

KING. Follow her close; give her good watch, I pray you.
[Exit Horatio.]

O, this is the poison of deep grief; it springs
All from her father's death. O Gertrude, Gertrude,
When sorrows come, they come not single spies,[21]
But in battalions: first, her father slain; 75

---

13. *dild:* yield, repay.
14. *baker's daughter:* according to a folktale, a baker's daughter was turned into an owl because of her lack of generosity when Christ came into her shop.
15. *Conceit:* brooding.   16. *dupped:* opened.   17. *Gis:* Jesus.
18. *By Cock:* A vulgar substitute for "By God."   19. *blame:* blame for pregnancy.
20. *'a':* have.   21. *spies:* soldiers.

Next, your son gone, and he most violent author
Of his own just remove;²² the people muddied,²³
Thick and unwholesome in their thoughts and whispers
For good Polonius' death, and we have done but greenly²⁴
In hugger ·mugger²⁵ to inter him; poor Ophelia   80
Divided from herself and her fair judgment,
Without the which we are pictures or mere beasts;
Last, and as much containing²⁶ as all these,
Her brother is in secret come from France,
Feeds on his wonder, keeps himself in clouds,²⁷   85
And wants²⁸ not buzzers²⁹ to infect his ear
With pestilent speeches of his father's death,
Wherein necessity, of matter beggared,³⁰
Will nothing stick³¹ our person to arraign³²
In ear and ear.³³ O my dear Gertrude, this,   90
Like to a murd'ring piece,³⁴ in many places
Gives me superfluous death.   *[A noise within.]*
QUEEN.   Alack, what noise is this?
KING. Where are my Switzers?³⁵ Let them guard the door.

[Enter a Messenger.]

What is the matter?
MESSENGER.   Save yourself, my lord.
The ocean, overpeering of his list,³⁶   95
Eats not the flats with more impiteous haste
Then young Laertes, in a riotous head,³⁷
O'erbears³⁸ your officers. The rabble call him lord.
And, as the world were now but to begin,³⁹
Antiquity forgot, custom not known,   100
The ratifiers⁴⁰ and props of every word,⁴¹
They cry, "Choose we! Laertes shall be king!"
Caps, hands, and tongues applaud it to the clouds,
"Laertes shall be king! Laertes king!"
QUEEN. How cheerfully on the false trail they cry!   105
O, this is counter,⁴² you false Danish dogs!

---

22. *remove:* exile.   23. *muddied:* agitated.
24. *greenly:* foolishly.   25. *hugger-mugger:* secret haste.
26. *much containing:* important.   27. *in clouds:* invisible.   28. *wants:* lacks.
29. *buzzers:* gossipers.   30. *of matter beggared:* without the true facts.
31. *will nothing stick:* will not hesitate at anything.   32. *arraign:* accuse.
33. *in ear and ear:* in the hearing of others.
34. *murd'ring piece:* a type of cannon loaded with shot that scattered in many
different directions.   35. *Switzers:* hired Swiss guards.
36. *overpeering of his list:* overflowing the highwater mark.
37. *riotous head:* rebellious armed band.   38. *O'erbears:* overwhelms.
39. *as . . . begin:* as if we were at the beginning of time.   40. *ratifiers:* supporters.
41. *word:* title.
42. *counter:* backwards; a hunting term for a dog who follows the scent backwards
to its start.

[Noise within. Enter Laertes with others.]

KING. The doors are broke.

LAERTES. Where is the king?—Sirs, stand you all without.

ALL. No, let's come in.

LAERTES.   I pray you give me leave.

ALL. We will, we will.   110

LAERTES. I thank you. Keep[43] the door.

            [Exeunt his Followers.]

    O thou vile king,

    Give me my father.

QUEEN.   Calmly, good Laertes.

LAERTES. That drop of blood that's calm proclaims me bastard,

    Cries cuckold[44] to my father, brands the harlot   115

    Even here[45] between the chaste unsmirchèd brows

    Of my true mother.

KING.   What is the cause, Laertes,

    That thy rebellion looks so giant-like?

    Let him go, Gertrude. Do not fear[46] our person.

    There's such divinity doth hedge[47] a king   120

    That treason can but peep[48] to what it would,[49]

    Acts little of his[50] will. Tell me, Laertes,

    Why thou art thus incensed. Let him go, Gertrude.

    Speak, man.

LAERTES. Where is my father?

KING.   Dead.

QUEEN.   But not by him.   125

KING. Let him demand his fill.

LAERTES. How came he dead? I'll not be juggled with.

    To hell allegiance, vows to the blackest devil,

    Conscience and grace to the profoundest pit!

    I dare damnation. To this point I stand,   130

    That both the worlds[51] I give to negligence,

    Let come what comes, only I'll be revenged

    Most throughly for my father!

KING.   Who shall stay[52] you?

LAERTES. My will, not all the world.

    And for[53] my means, I'll husband[54] them so well   135

    They shall go far with little.

KING.   Good Laertes,

    If you desire to know the certainty

    Of your dear father's death, is't writ in your revenge

---

43. *Keep:* guard.   44. *cuckold:* one whose wife has been unfaithful.
45. *here:* the forehead, where harlots were branded.   46. *fear:* fear for.
47. *hedge:* surround, guard.   48. *peep:* peep through the hedge of divinity.
49. *would:* desires.   50. *his:* its.
51. *both the worlds:* this world and the hereafter.   52. *stay:* stop.
53. *for:* as for.   54. *husband:* manage.

That swoopstake[55] you will draw both friend and foe,
Winner and loser?   140
LAERTES. None but his enemies.
KING.   Will you know them then?
LAERTES. To his good friends thus wide I'll ope my arms
    And like the kind life-rend'ring pelican[56]
    Repast[57] them with my blood.
KING.   Why, now you speak
    Like a good child and a true gentleman.   145
    That I am guiltless of your father's death,
    And am most sensibly in grief for it,
    It shall as level[58] to your judgment pierce
    As day does to your eye.
            [A noise and voices within: "Let her come in."]
LAERTES. How now? What noise is that?   150

                    [Enter Ophelia.]

    O heat, dry up my brains; tears seven times salt
    Burn out the sense and virtue[59] of mine eye!
    By heaven, thy madness shall be paid by weight
    Till our scale turns the beam.[60] O rose of May,
    Dear maid, kind sister, sweet Ophelia!   155
    O heavens, is't possible a young maid's wits
    Should be as mortal as an old man's life?
    Nature is fine[61] in love, and where 'tis fine,
    It sends some precious instance[62] of itself
    After the thing it loves.   160
OPHELIA. *[Sings.]*
            They bore him barefaced on the bier;
                Hey non nony, nony, hey nony;
                And in his grave rains many a tear—
    Fare you well, my dove!
LAERTES. Hadst thou thy wits, and didst persuade revenge,   165
    It could not move thus.[63]
OPHELIA. You must sing "A-down a-down, and you call him a ·down-
    a." O, how the wheel[64] becomes it![65] It is[66] the false steward, that
    stole his master's daughter.
LAERTES. This nothing's more than matter.[67]   170

---

55. *swoopstake:* without making any distinctions.
56. *pelican:* the mythical pelican was supposed to feed its children with its own
blood.   57. *Repast:* feed.   58. *level:* plain.   59. *virtue:* power, faculty.
60. *beam:* arm of a scale.   61. *fine:* delicate.
62. *instance:* token (that is, Ophelia's mind or sanity).   63. *thus:* as this does.
64. *wheel:* the spinning wheel, at which women frequently sang ballads.
65. *becomes it:* suits the ballad.   66. *It is:* It (the ballad) tells about.
67. *This . . . matter:* This nothingness is more expressive of her grief than any
true statement (matter).

OPHELIA. There's rosemary,[68] that's for remembrance. Pray love, remember. And there is pansies, that's for thoughts.

LAERTES. A document[69] in madness, thoughts and remembrance fitted.[70]

OPHELIA. There's fennel for you, and columbines.[71] There's rue[72] for   175
you, and here's some for me. We may call it herb of grace o'
Sundays. O, you must wear your rue with a difference.[73] There's
a daisy.[74] I would give you some violets,[75] but they withered all
when my father died. They say he made a good end.
>   [Sings.]
>   *For bonny sweet Robin is all my joy.*   180

LAERTES. Thought[76] and affliction, passion,[77] hell itself,
She turns to favor[78] and to prettiness.

OPHELIA. *[Sings.]*

> *And will he not come again?*
> *And will he not come again?*
>   *No, no, he is dead;*   185
>   *Go to thy deathbed;*
> *He never will come again.*

> *His beard as white as snow,*
> *All flaxen was his poll.*[79]
>   *He is gone, he is gone,*   190
>   *And we cast away moan.*[80]
> *God 'a' mercy on his soul!*

And of all Christian souls, I pray God. God bye you.
>   *[Exit Ophelia.]*

LAERTES. Do you see this, you gods?

KING. Laertes, I must commune with[81] your grief,   195
Or you deny me right.[82] Go but apart,
Make choice of whom your wisest friends you will,
And they shall hear and judge 'twixt you and me.
If by direct or by collateral[83] hand
They find us touched,[84] we will our kingdom give,   200
Our crown, our life, and all that we call ours,
To you in satisfaction; but if not,

---

68. *rosemary:* it symbolized remembrance.
69. *document:* lesson.   70. *fitted:* related.
71. *fennel . . . columbines:* emblems of flattery and cuckolding (for Claudius).
72. *rue:* emblem of sorrow or repentance (for the Queen and Ophelia).
73. *difference:* the Queen's sorrow or repentance would be different than Ophelia's.
74. *daisy:* symbol for dissembling or infidelity (for Queen).
75. *violets:* symbol of loyalty, faithfulness.
76. *Thought:* melancholy, distress of mind.   77. *passion:* suffering.
78. *favor:* charm.   79. *poll:* head.   80. *cast away moan:* moan in vain.
81. *commune with:* sympathize with, share.   82. *right:* just treatment.
83. *collateral:* indirect.   84. *touched:* implicated, involved.

Be you content to lend your patience to us,
And we shall jointly labor with your soul
To give it due content.

LAERTES.   Let this be so.   205
His means of death, his obscure burial—
No trophy,[85] sword, nor hatchment[86] o'er his bones,
No noble rite nor formal ostentation—
Cry to be heard, as 'twere from heaven to earth,
That I must call't in question.

NG.   So you shall;   210
And where th' offense is, let the great axe fall.
I pray you go with me.   *[Exeunt.]*

SCENE 6   *Another room in the castle.*

[Enter Horatio with an Attendant.]

HORATIO. What are they that would speak with me?
GENTLEMAN. Sailors, sir. They say they have letters for you.
HORATIO. Let them come in.   *[Exit Attendant.]*
I do not know from what part of the world
I should be greeted, if not from Lord Hamlet.   5

[Enter Sailors.]

SAILOR. God bless you, sir.
HORATIO. Let him bless thee too.
SAILOR. He shall, sir, and't please him. There's a letter for you,
sir—it comes from th' ambassador that was bound for England—if
your name be Horatio, as I am let to know it is.   10
HORATIO. *[Reads the letter.]* Horatio, when thou shalt have overlooked[1] this, give these fellows some means[2] to the king. They have
letters for him. Ere we were two days old at sea, a pirate of very warlike appointment[3] gave us chase. Finding ourselves too slow of sail,
we put on a compelled valor, and in the grapple I boarded them. On   15
the instant they got clear of our ship; so I alone became their prisoner.
They have dealt with me like thieves of mercy, but they knew what
they did: I am to do a good turn for them. Let the king have the letters
I have sent, and repair[4] thou to me with as much speed as thou wouldest fly death. I have words to speak in thine ear will make thee dumb;   20
yet are they much too light for the bore[5] of the matter. These good
fellows will bring thee where I am. Rosencrantz and Guildenstern hold
their course for England. Of them I have much to tell thee. Farewell.
                          He that thou knowest thine, HAMLET.

---

85. *trophy:* memorial.   86. *hatchment:* a tablet bearing a coat of arms.
1. *overlooked:* looked over, read.   2. *means:* access.
3. *appointment:* equipment.   4. *repair:* report, return,
5. *bore:* size, importance.

Come, I will give you way⁶ for these your letters,　　　　25
And do't the speedier that you may direct me
To him from whom you brought them.　　　　*[Exeunt.]*

SCENE 7　*Another room in the castle.*

[Enter King and Laertes.]

KING. Now must your conscience my acquittance seal,
And you must put me in your heart for friend,
Sith you have heard, and with a knowing ear,
That he which hath your noble father slain
Pursued my life.

LAERTES.　　　　　　It well appears. But tell me　　　5
Why you proceeded not against these feats¹
So crimeful and so capital in nature,
As by your safety, wisdom, all things else,
You mainly were stirred up.²

KING.　　　　　　　　O, for two special reasons,
Which may to you perhaps seem much unsinewed,³　　　10
And yet to me they're strong. The queen his mother
Lives almost by his looks, and for myself—
My virtue or my plague, be it either which—
She is so conjunctive⁴ to my life and soul
That, as the star moves not but in his sphere,　　　15
I could not but by her.⁵ The other motive
Why to a public count⁶ I might not go
Is the great love the general gender⁷ bear him,
Who, dipping all his faults in their affection,
Would, like the spring that turneth wood to stone,⁸　　　20
Convert his gyves⁹ to graces; so that my arrows,
Too slightly timbered¹⁰ for so loud¹¹ a wind,
Would have reverted to my bow again,
And not where I had aimed them.

LAERTES. And so have I a noble father lost,　　　25
A sister driven into desperate terms,
Whose worth, if praises may go back again,
Stood challenger on mount of all the age
For her perfections.¹² But my revenge will come.

---

6. *way:* passage.
1. *feats:* deeds.　2. *You . . . up:* you were strongly moved (to action).
3. *unsinewed:* weak.　4. *conjunctive:* inseparably joined.
5. *but by her:* except by her approval.　6. *count:* trial.
7. *general gender:* common people.
8. *like . . . stone:* like a spring so full of lime that it turns wood into stone.
9. *gyves:* fetters.　10. *slightly timbered:* light.　11. *loud:* strong.
12. *Stood . . . perfections:* challenged from above the whole world to rival her perfections.

KING. Break not your sleeps for that. You must not think   30
    That we are made of stuff so flat and dull
    That we can let our beard be shook with danger,
    And think it pastime. You shortly shall hear more.
    I loved your father, and we love ourself,
    And that, I hope, will teach you to imagine—   35

[Enter a Messenger with letters.]

    How now? What news?
MESSENGER.   Letters, my lord, from Hamlet:
    These to your majesty, this to the queen.
KING. From Hamlet? Who brought them?
MESSENGER. Sailors, my lord, they say; I saw them not.
    They were given me by Claudio; he received them   40
    Of him that brought them.
KING.   Laertes, you shall hear them.
    Leave us.   *[Exit Messenger.]*
    [Reads.] High and mighty, you shall know I am set naked[13] *on your*
kingdom. To-morrow shall I beg leave to see your kingly eyes; when I
shall (first asking your pardon thereunto) recount the occasions of my
sudden and more strange return.   *HAMLET*   45
    What should this mean? Are all the rest come back?
    Or is it some abuse?[14] Or no such thing?
LAERTES. Know you the hand?
KING.   'Tis Hamlet's character.[15] "Naked"
    And in a postscript here, he says "alone."
    Can you advise me?   50
LAERTES. I am lost in it, my lord. But let him come.
    It warms the very sickness in my heart
    That I shall live and tell him to his teeth,
    "Thus diddest thou."
KING.   If it be so, Laertes
    (As how should it be so? how otherwise?)   55
    Will you be ruled by me?
LAERTES. If so you will not o'errule[16] me to a peace.
KING. To thine own peace. If he be now returned,
    As checking at[17] his voyage, and that he means
    No more to undertake it, I will work him   60
    To an exploit now ripe in my device,[18]
    Under the which he shall not choose but fall;
    And for his death no wind of blame shall breathe,
    But even his mother shall uncharge the practice[19]
    And call it accident.

13. *naked:* destitute.   14. *abuse:* deception.
15. *character:* handwriting.   16. *o'errule:* command.
17. *As checking at:* thus turning aside from.   18. *device:* plan.
19. *uncharge the practice:* fail to see the plot.

LAERTES.   My lord, I will be ruled;   65
   The rather if you could devise it so
   That I might be the organ.[20]
KING.   It falls right.
   You have been talked of since your travel much,
   And that in Hamlet's hearing, for a quality
   Wherein they say you shine. Your sum of parts[21]   70
   Did not together pluck such envy from him
   As did that one, and that, in my regard,
   Of the unworthiest siege.[22]
LAERTES.   What part is that, my lord?
KING. A very riband[23] in the cap of youth,
   Yet needful too, for youth no less becomes[24]   75
   The light and careless livery[25] that it wears
   Than settled age his sables and his weeds,[26]
   Importing[27] health and graveness. Some two months since
   Here was a gentleman of Normandy.
   I've seen myself, and served against, the French,   80
   And they ran well on horseback, but this gallant
   Had witchcraft in't. He grew unto his seat,
   And to such wondrous doing brought his horse
   As had he been incorpsed[28] and demi-natured[29]
   With the brave beast. So far he topped my thought[30]   85
   That I, in forgery of shapes and tricks,[31]
   Come short of what he did.
LAERTES.   A Norman was't?
KING. A Norman.
LAERTES. Upon my life, Lamound.
KING.   The very same.
LAERTES. I know him well. He is the brooch[32] indeed   90
   And gem of all the nation.
KING. He made confession of you,
   And gave you such a masterly report
   For art and exercise in your defense,[33]
   And for your rapier most especial,   95
   That he cried out 'twould be a sight indeed
   If one could match you, sir. The scrimers[34] of their nation
   He swore had neither motion, guard, nor eye,
   If you opposed them. Sir, this report of his

20. *organ:* instrument, agent.
21. *sum of parts:* accomplishments as a whole.
22. *unworthiest siege:* least important.   23. *riband:* decoration.
24. *becomes:* is the appropriate age for.   25. *livery:* clothes.
26. *weeds:* clothing.   27. *importing:* signifying.   28. *incorpsed:* one body.
29. *demi-natured:* united.   30. *topped my thought:* surpassed my imagination.
31. *in forgery . . . tricks:* in imagining skills and methods of horsemanship.
32. *brooch:* ornament.   33. *defense:* fencing.   34. *scrimers:* fencers.

Did Hamlet so envenom[35] with his envy   100
That he could nothing do but wish and beg
Your sudden coming o'er to play with him.
Now, out of this—
LAERTES.   What out of this, my lord?
KING. Laertes, was your father dear to you?
Or are you like the painting of a sorrow,   105
A face without a heart?
LAERTES.   Why ask you this?
KING. Not that I think you did not love your father,
But that I know love is begun by time,
And that I see, in passages of proof,[36]
Time qualifies[37] the spark and fire of it.   110
There lives within the very flame of love
A kind of wick or snuff[38] that will abate it,
And nothing is at a like goodness still,[39]
For goodness, growing to a plurisy,[40]
Dies in his own too-much. That[41] we would[42] do   115
We should do when we would, for this 'would' changes,
And hath abatements[43] and delays as many
As there are tongues, are hands, are accidents,
And then this 'should' is like a spendthrift[44] sigh,
That hurts by easing. But to the quick o' th' ulcer[45]—   120
Hamlet comes back; what would you undertake
To show yourself your father's son in deed
More than in words?
LAERTES.   To cut his throat i' th' church!
KING. No place indeed should murder sanctuarize;[46]
Revenge should have no bounds.[47] But, good Laertes,   125
Will you do this? Keep close within your chamber.
Hamlet returned shall know you are come home.
We'll put on those[48] shall praise your excellence
And set a double varnish on the fame
The Frenchman gave you, bring you in fine[49] together   130
And wager on your heads. He, being remiss,[50]
Most generous, and free from all contriving,

---

35. *envenom:* poison.   36. *passages of proof:* experiences that prove it.
37. *qualifies:* limits, weakens.
38. *snuff:* the partly consumed portion of a wick that causes it to smoulder.
39. *still:* always.   40. *plurisy:* excess.   41. *That:* that which.
42. *would:* desire (to).   43. *abatements:* reductions in intensity.
44. *spendthrift:* harmful (a sigh was thought to draw blood from the heart).
45. *to . . . ulcer:* to get to the heart of the trouble.
46. *sanctuarize:* protect from punishment.
47. *Revenge . . . bounds:* your just revenge should have no limitations.
48. *put on those:* arrange for those who.   49. *in fine:* finally.
50. *remiss:* careless.

Will not peruse[51] the foils, so that with ease,
Or with a little shuffling, you may choose
A sword unbated,[52] and, in a pass of practice,[53]   135
Requite him for your father.
LAERTES.   I will do't,
And for that purpose I'll anoint my sword.
I bought an unction of a mountebank,[54]
So mortal that, but dip a knife in it,
Where it draws blood no cataplasm[55] so rare,   140
Collected from all simples[56] that have virtue
Under the moon, can save the thing from death
That is but scratched withal. I'll touch my point
With this contagion, that, if I gall him slightly,
It may be death.
KING.   Let's further think of this,   145
Weigh what convenience both of time and means
May fit us to our shape. If this should fail,
And that our drift[57] look through[58] our bad performance,
'Twere better not assayed.[59] Therefore this project
Should have a back[60] or second, that might hold   150
If this did blast in proof.[61] Soft, let me see.
We'll make a solemn wager on your cunnings—
I ha't!
When in your motion you are hot and dry—
As make your bouts more violent to that end—   155
And that he calls for drink, I'll have prepared him
A chalice for the nonce,[62] whereon but sipping,
If he by chance escape your venomed stuck,
Our purpose may hold there.

[Enter Queen.]

                              How now, sweet queen!
QUEEN. One woe doth tread upon another's heel,   160
So fast they follow. Your sister's drowned, Laertes.
LAERTES. Drowned! O, where?
QUEEN. There is a willow grows aslant the brook,
That shows his hoar[63] leaves in the glassy stream.
Therewith fantastic garlands did she make   165

51. *peruse:* look closely at.
52. *unbated:* not blunted (as swords for practice usually were).
53. *pass of practice:* a treacherous thrust.
54. *mountebank:* seller of quack medicines.   55. *cataplasm:* plaster.
56. *simples:* healing herbs.   57. *drift:* design, plan.
58. *look through:* become apparent through.   59. *assayed:* attempted.
60. *back:* back-up plan, an alternative plan.   61. *blast in proof:* fail in the test.
62. *nonce:* particular occasion.
63. *hoar:* grey (as willow leaves are on the underside).

Of crowflowers, nettles, daisies, and long purples,
That liberal[64] shepherds give a grosser name,
But our cold[65] maids do dead men's fingers call them.
There on the pendent boughs her crownet weeds[66]
Clamb'ring to hang, an envious sliver broke,   170
When down her weedy trophies and herself
Fell in the weeping brook. Her clothes spread wide,
And mermaid-like awhile they bore her up,
Which time she chanted snatches of old tunes,
As one incapable of[67] her own distress,   175
Or like a creature native and indued[68]
Unto that element. But long it could not be
Till that her garments, heavy with their drink,
Pulled the poor wretch from her melodious lay
To muddy death.
LAERTES.   Alas, then she is drowned?   180
QUEEN. Drowned, drowned.
LAERTES. Too much of water hast thou, poor Ophelia,
And therefore I forbid my tears; but yet
It is our trick;[69] nature her custom holds,
Let shame say what it will. When these[70] are gone,   185
The woman will be out.[71] Adieu, my lord.
I have a speech of fire, that fain would blaze
But that this folly drowns it.   *[Exit.]*
KING.   Let's follow, Gertrude.
How much I had to do to calm his rage!
Now fear I this will give it start again;   190
Therefore let's follow.   *[Exeunt.]*

ACT V

SCENE 1   *A churchyard.*

[Enter Two Clowns.]

CLOWN. Is she to be buried in Christian burial that willfully seeks
her own salvation?[1]

OTHER. I tell thee she is. Therefore make her grave straight.[2] The

---

64. *liberal:* vulgar-tongued.   65. *cold:* chaste.
66. *crownet weeds:* crowns of wildflowers.   67. *incapable of:* not realizing.
68. *indued:* adapted.   69. *trick:* habit.   70. *these:* his tears.
71. *The woman . . . out:* the woman in me will be gone.
  1. *willfully seeks her own salvation:* commits suicide.   2. *straight:* at once.

crowner[3] hath sate[4] on her and finds it Christian burial.

CLOWN. How can that be, unless she drowned herself in her own 5
defense?

OTHER. Why, 'tis found so.

CLOWN. It must be *se offendendo;*[5] it cannot be else. For here lies
the point: if I drown myself wittingly, it argues an act, and an act
hath three branches—it is to act, to do, and to perform. Argal,[6] she 10
drowned herself wittingly.

OTHER. Nay, but hear you, Goodman Delver.[7]

CLOWN. Give me leave. Here lies the water—good. Here stands
the man—good. If the man go to this water and drown himself, it
is, will he nill he, he goes, mark you that. But if the water come to 15
him and drown him, he drowns not himself. Argal, he that is not
guilty of his own death shortens not his own life.

OTHER. But is this law?

CLOWN. Ay marry, is't—crowner's quest[8] law.

OTHER. Will you ha' the truth on't? If this had not been a gentle- 20
woman, she should have been buried out of Christian burial.

CLOWN. Why, there thou say'st. And the more pity that great folk
should have countenance[9] in this world to drown or hang themselves more than their even-Christen.[10] Come, my spade. There is
no ancient gentlemen but gardeners, ditchers, and grave-makers. 25
They hold up[11] Adam's profession.[12]

OTHER. Was he a gentleman?

CLOWN. He was the first that ever bore arms.[13]

OTHER. Why, he had none.

CLOWN. What, art a heathen? How dost thou understand the 30
Scripture? The Scripture says Adam digged. Could he dig without
arms? I'll put another question to thee. If thou answerest me not
to the purpose,[14] confess thyself—

OTHER. Go to.

CLOWN. What is he that builds stronger than either the mason, 35
the shipwright, or the carpenter?

OTHER. The gallows-maker, for that frame outlives a thousand
tenants.

CLOWN. I like thy wit well, in good faith. The gallows does well.
But how does it well? It does well to those that do ill. Now thou dost 40
ill to say the gallows is built stronger than the church. Argal, the
gallows may do well to thee. To't again, come.

OTHER. Who builds stronger than a mason, a shipwright, or a
carpenter?

3. *crowner:* coroner.   4. *sate:* judged.
5. *se offendendo:* self-offense, which is a blunder for *self-defence.*
6. *Argal:* the Clown's blunder for *ergo,* therefore.   7. *Delver:* digger.
8. *quest:* inquest.   9. *countenance:* sanction.
10. *even-Christen:* fellow Christian.   11. *hold up:* carry on.
12. *Adam's profession:* Adam was traditionally pictured with a spade in his hand.
13. *bore arms:* bore a coat of arms.   14. *to the purpose:* correctly.

CLOWN. Ay, tell me that, and unyoke.[15]   45
OTHER. Marry, now I can tell.
CLOWN. To't.
OTHER. Mass,[16] I cannot tell.

[Enter Hamlet and Horatio afar off.]

CLOWN. Cudgel thy brains no more about it, for your dull ass
will not mend his pace with beating. And when you are asked this   50
question next, say "a grave-maker." The houses he makes last
till doomsday. Go, get thee in, and fetch me a stoup[17] of liquor.

        [Exit Other Clown as First Clown digs and sings.[18]]
        In youth when I did love, did love,
        Methought it was very sweet;
        To contract[19] O the time for my behoove,[20]   55
        O methought there was nothing sweet.

HAMLET. Has this fellow no feeling of his business, that he sings
at grave-making?
HORATIO. Custom hath made it in him a property of easiness.
HAMLET. 'Tis e'en so. The hand of little employment hath the   60
daintier sense.[21]

CLOWN. *[Sings.] But Age with his stealing steps*
        Hath caught me in his clutch:
        And hath shipped me intil[22] the land[23]
        As if I had never been such. [Throws up a skull.]   65

HAMLET. That skull had a tongue in it, and could sing once. How
the knave jowls[24] it to th' ground, as if it were Cain's jawbone,[25] that
did the first murther! It might be the pate of a politician, which this
ass now o'erreaches[26]; one that would circumvent God, might it not?
HORATIO. It might, my lord.   70
HAMLET. Or of a courtier, which could say "Good morrow, sweet
lord! How dost thou, sweet lord?" This might be my Lord Such-
a-one, that praised my Lord Such-a-one's horse when he meant to
beg it,[27] might it not?
HORATIO. Ay, my lord.   75
HAMLET. Why, e'en so, and now my Lady Worm's, chapless,[28] and
knocked about the mazzard[29] with a sexton's spade. Here's fine
revolution,[30] if we had the trick[31] to see't. Did these bones cost no

15. *unyoke:* get it over with, and then you can relax.
16. *Mass:* by the Mass (a mild oath).   17. *stoup:* a large mug or tankard.
18. The song is an inaccurate version of a song that appeared in an early
anthology published in 1557.   19. *contract:* shorten.   20. *behoove:* benefit.
21. *The hand . . . sense:* the hand that is not used to manual labor is more sensitive.
22. *intil:* into.   23. *land:* grave.   24. *jowls:* dashes.
25. *Cain's jawbone:* Cain slew his brother Abel with the jawbone of an ass.
26. *o'erreaches:* outwits.   27. *beg it:* ask a favor.
28. *chapless:* without the lower jaw.   29. *mazzard:* head, pate.
30. *revolution:* turn of events (probably with an allusion to a turn of the Wheel of
Fortune).   31. *trick:* faculty, skill.

more the breeding but to play at loggets[32] with 'em? Mine ache to
think on't.   80

    CLOWN. *[Sings.]*

> *A pickaxe and a spade, a spade,*
> *For and[33] a shrouding sheet;*
> *O, a pit of clay[34] for to be made*
> *For such a guest is meet.[35]*

                      [Throws up another skull.]

    HAMLET. There's another. Why may not that be the skull of a   85
lawyer? Where be his quiddities[36] now, his quillets,[37] his cases, his
tenures,[38] and his tricks? Why does he suffer this rude knave now to
knock him about the sconce[39] with a dirty shovel, and will not tell
him of his action of battery? Hum! This fellow might be in's time a
great buyer of land, with his statutes, his recognizances, his fines,   90
his double vouchers, his recoveries.[40] Is this the fine of his fines,[41]
and the recovery of his recoveries,[42] to have his fine pate full of fine
dirt? Will his vouchers vouch him no more of his purchases, and
double ones too, than the length and breadth of a pair of indentures?[43] The very conveyances[44] of his lands will scarcely lie in this   95
box, and must the inheritor[45] himself have no more, ha?

    HORATIO. Not a jot more, my lord.

    HAMLET. Is not parchment made of sheepskins?

    HORATIO. Ay, my lord, and of calveskins too.

    HAMLET. They are sheep and calves which seek out assurance in   100
that.[46] I will speak to this fellow. Whose grave's this, sirrah?

    CLOWN. Mine, sir.

    [Sings.]

> *O, a pit of clay for to be made*
> *For such a guest is meet.*

    HAMLET. I think it be thine indeed, for thou liest in't.   105

    CLOWN. You lie out on't,[47] sir, and therefore it is not yours. For
my part, I do not lie in't, yet it is mine.

    HAMLET. Thou dost lie in't, to be in't and say it is thine. 'Tis for
the dead, not for the quick;[48] therefore thou liest.

---

32. *loggets:* a game in which small pieces of bone (or wood) were thrown at a
stake.   33. *For and:* and.   34. *pit of clay:* a grave.   35. *meet:* fitting.
36. *quiddities:* subtle definitions or distinctions, quibbles.
37. *quillets:* subtle distinctions. A wry comment on the redundancy of legal terms.
38. *tenures:* holdings of property.   39. *sconce:* head.
40. *statutes . . . recoveries:* legal terms connected with the transfer of land.
41. *Is . . . fines:* Is this (death) the end of his contracts?
42. *recovery of his recoveries:* Hamlet puns on the legal term and the recovery
of health.
43. *Will . . . indentures:* Will his guaranteeors vouch him only as much ground
as a couple of his legal papers will cover, that is, his grave?
44. *conveyances:* contracts, deeds.   45. *inheritor:* owner, possessor.
46. *seek . . . that:* seek safety in legal documents.   47. *on't:* of it.
48. *quick:* living.

CLOWN. 'Tis a quick lie, sir; 'twill away again from me to you.   110
HAMLET. What man dost thou dig it for?
CLOWN. For no man, sir.
HAMLET. What woman then?
CLOWN. For none neither.
HAMLET. Who is to be buried in't?   115
CLOWN. One that was a woman, sir; but, rest her soul, she's dead.
HAMLET. How absolute[49] the knave is! We must speak by the
card,[50] or equivocation[51] will undo us. By the Lord, Horatio, this three
years I have taken note of it, the age is grown so picked[52] that the
toe of the peasant comes so near the heels of the courtier he galls   120
his kibe.[53]—How long hast thou been a grave-maker?
CLOWN. Of all the days i' th' year, I came to't that day that our
last king Hamlet overcame Fortinbras.
HAMLET. How long is that since?
CLOWN. Cannot you tell that? Every fool can tell that. It was the   125
very day that young Hamlet was born—he that was mad, and sent
into England.
HAMLET. Ay, marry, why was he sent into England?
CLOWN. Why, because he was mad. He shall recover his wits there;
or, if he do not, 'tis no great matter there.   130
HAMLET. Why?
CLOWN. 'Twill not be seen in him there. There the men are as
mad as he.
HAMLET. How came he mad?
CLOWN. Very strangely, they say.   135
HAMLET. How strangely?
CLOWN. Faith, e'en with losing his wits.
HAMLET. Upon what ground?
CLOWN. Why, here in Denmark. I have been sexton here, man
and boy, thirty years.   140
HAMLET. How long will a man lie i' th' earth ere he rot?
CLOWN. Faith, if he be not rotten before he die (as we have many
pocky corses[54] now-a-days that will scarce hold the laying in),[55] he
will last you some eight year or nine year. A tanner will last you
nine year.   145
HAMLET. Why he more than another?
CLOWN. Why, sir, his hide is so tanned with his trade that he will
keep out water a great while, and your water is a sore decayer of
your whoreson dead body. Here's a skull now. This skull has lain
in the earth three and twenty years.   150
HAMLET. Whose was it?

---

49. *absolute:* precise.   50. *card:* chart, that is, with exactness.
51. *equivocation:* double talk.   52. *picked:* refined.
53. *kibe:* chilblain (painfull swelling on the heel caused by exposure to cold).
54. *pocky corses:* disease-ridden corpses.   55. Hold together till they are buried.

CLOWN. A whoreson mad fellow's it was. Whose do you think it was?

HAMLET. Nay, I know not.

CLOWN. A pestilence on him for a mad rogue! 'A poured a flagon   155
of Rhenish on my head once. This same skull, sir, was Yorick's
skull, the king's jester.

HAMLET This?

CLOWN. E'en that.

HAMLET. Let me see. *[Takes the skull.]* Alas, poor Yorick! I knew   160
him, Horatio, a fellow of infinite jest, of most excellent fancy. He
hath borne me on his back a thousand times. And now how abhorred in
my imagination it is! My gorge rises[56] at it. Here hung those lips
that I have kissed I know not how oft. Where be your gibes now?
Your gambols, your songs, your flashes of merriment that were   165
wont to set the table on a roar? Not one now to mock your own
grinning? Quite chapfall'n?[57] Now get you to my lady's chamber,
and tell her, let her paint an inch thick, to this favor[58] she must come.
Make her laugh at that. Prithee, Horatio, tell me one thing.

HORATIO. What's that, my lord?   170

HAMLET. Dost thou think Alexander looked o' this fashion i' th'
earth?

HORATIO. E'en so.

HAMLET. And smelt so? Pah!   *[Puts down the skull.]*

HORATIO. E'en so, my lord.   175

HAMLET. To what base uses we may return, Horatio! Why may
not imagination trace the noble dust of Alexander till he find it
stopping a bunghole?[59]

HORATIO. 'Twere to consider too curiously,[60] to consider so.

HAMLET. No, faith, not a jot, but to follow him thither with mod-   180
esty enough, and likelihood to lead it; as thus: Alexander died,
Alexander was buried, Alexander returneth to dust; the dust is earth;
of earth we make loam;[62] and why of that loam whereto he was
converted might they not stop a beer barrel?

Imperial Caesar, dead and turned to clay,   185
Might stop a hole to keep the wind away.
O, that that earth which kept the world in awe
Should patch a wall t' expel the winter's flaw![63]
But soft, but soft aside! Here comes the king—

*[Enter King, Queen, Laertes, and a coffin, with Lords, Attendants,
and a Priest.]*

The queen, the courtiers. Who is that they follow?   190

56. *My gorge rises:* I feel sick.
57. *chapfall'n:* downcast.   58. *favor:* appearance.
59. *bunghole:* mouth of a cask.   60. *curiously:* minutely.
61. *modesty:* reasonableness.
62. *loam:* mixture of earth and clay used in masonry.   63. *flaw:* gust of wind.

And with such maimèd[64] rites? This doth betoken
The corse they follow did with desperate hand
Fordo it[65] own life. 'Twas of some estate.
Couch we awhile, and mark.　　　　*[Retires with Horatio.]*

LAERTES. What ceremony else?[66]

HAMLET.　　　　　　　　　That is Laertes.　　　　　　195
A very noble youth. Mark.

LAERTES. What ceremony else?

PRIEST. Her obsequies have been as far enlarged
As we have warranty. Her death was doubtful,
And, but[67] that great command o'ersways the order,　　　200
She should in ground unsanctified have lodged
Till the last trumpet. For[68] charitable prayers,
Shards,[69] flints, and pebbles should be thrown on her.
Yet here she is allowed her virgin rites,
Her maiden strewments,[70] and the bringing home[71]　　　205
Of bell and burial.[72]

LAERTES. Must there no more be done?

PRIEST. No more be done.
We should profane the service of the dead
To sing a requiem and such rest to her　　　　　　210
As to peace-parted[73] souls.

LAERTES.　　　　　　　Lay her i' th' earth,
And from her fair and unpolluted flesh
May violets spring! I tell thee, churlish priest,
A minist'ring angel shall my sister be
When thou liest howling.

HAMLET.　　　　　　　What, the fair Ophelia?　　　215

QUEEN. Sweets to the sweet! Farewell.　　　*[Scatters flowers.]*
I hoped thou shouldst have been my Hamlet's wife.
I thought thy bride-bed to have decked, sweet maid,
And not t'have strewed thy grave.

LAERTES.　　　　　　　　　O, treble woe
Fall ten times treble on that cursèd head　　　　　　220
Whose wicked deed thy most ingenious sense[74]
Deprived thee of! Hold off the earth awhile,
Till I have caught her once more in mine arms.
　　　　　　　　　　　　　　　[Leaps in the grave.]
Now pile your dust upon the quick and dead
Till of this flat a mountain you have made　　　　　225

---

64. *maimèd:* incomplete.　　65. *Fordo it:* take its.　　66. *else:* other than this.
67. *but:* except.　　68. *For:* instead of.　　69. *Shards:* broken pieces of pottery.
70. *strewments:* flowers scattered on the grave.　　71. *bringing home:* laying to rest.
72. *Of bell and burial:* with the tolling of the church bell and proper burial.
73. *peace-parted:* fortified with the rites of the church.
74. *thy most ingenious sense:* thy mind which was so quick and alert.

T' o'ertop old Pelion[75] or the skyish head
Of blue Olympus.

HAMLET.   *[Coming forward.]* What is he whose grief
  Bears such an emphasis? whose phrase of sorrow
  Conjures[76] the wand'ring stars, and makes them stand
  Like wonder-wounded hearers? This is I,   230
  Hamlet the Dane.   *[Leaps in after Laertes.]*
LAERTES.   The devil take thy soul!   *[Grapples with him.]*
HAMLET. Thou pray'st not well.
  I prithee take thy fingers from my throat;
  Sir, though I am not splenitive[77] and rash,
  Yet have I in me something dangerous,   235
  Which let thy wiseness fear. Away thy hand.
KING. Pluck them asunder.
QUEEN.   Hamlet, Hamlet!
ALL. Gentlemen!
HORATIO.   Good my lord, be quiet.
  [Attendants part them, and they come out of the grave.]
HAMLET. Why, I will fight with him upon this theme
  Until my eyelids will no longer wag.[78]   240
QUEEN. O my son, what theme?
HAMLET. I loved Ophelia. Forty thousand brothers
  Could not with all their quantity of love
  Make up my sum. What wilt thou do for her?
KING. O, he is mad, Laertes.   245
QUEEN. For love of God, forbear him.
HAMLET. 'Swounds, show me what thou'lt do.
  Woo't[79] weep? woo't fight? woo't tear thyself?
  Woo't drink up esill?[80] eat a crocodile?
  I'll do't. Dost thou come here to whine?   250
  To outface[81] me with leaping in her grave?
  Be buried quick with her, and so will I.
  And if thou prate of mountains, let them throw
  Millions of acres on us, till our ground,
  Singeing his pate against the burning zone,   255
  Make Ossa[82] like a wart! Nay, and thou'lt mouth,
  I'll rant as well as thou.
QUEEN.   This is mere madness;
  And thus a while the fit will work on him.
  Anon, as patient as the female dove
  When that her golden couplets are disclosed,[83]   260
  His silence will sit drooping.

---

75. *Pelion:* like Olympus, a mountain in Greece.   76 *Conjures:* puts a spell upon.
77. *splenitive:* hot-tempered.   78. *wag:* move.
79. *Woo't:* contraction of *wouldst thou.*   80. *esill:* vinegar.   81. *outface:* outdo.
82. *Ossa:* mountain in Greece.
83. *couplets are disclosed:* pair of young doves are hatched.

HAMLET.   Hear you, sir.
What is the reason that you use me thus?
I loved you ever. But it is no matter.
Let Hercules himself do what he may,
The cat will mew, and dog will have his day.[84]   265
KING. I pray thee, good Horatio, wait upon him.
                              [Exeunt Hamlet and Horatio.]
[To Laertes.] Strengthen your patience in[85] our last night's speech.
We'll put the matter to the present push.—
Good Gertrude set some watch over your son.
This grave shall have a living monument.   270
An hour of quiet shortly shall we see;
Till then in patience our proceeding be.   *[Exeunt.]*

SCENE 2   *A hall in the castle.*

[Enter Hamlet and Horatio.]

HAMLET. So much for this,[1] sir; now shall you see the other.[2]
You do remember all the circumstance?
HORATIO. Remember it, my lord!
HAMLET. Sir, in my heart there was a kind of fighting
That would not let me sleep. Methought I lay   5
Worse than the mutines in the bilboes.[3] Rashly,
And praise be rashness for it—let us know,
Our indiscretion sometime serves us well
When our deep plots do pall,[4] and that should teach us
There's a divinity that shapes our ends,   10
Rough-hew them how we will—
HORATIO.   That is most certain.
HAMLET. Up from my cabin,
My sea-gown scarfed about me, in the dark
Groped I to find out them, had my desire,
Fingered[5] their packet, and in fine[6] withdrew   15
To mine own room again, making so bold,
My fears forgetting manners, to unseal
Their grand commission; where I found, Horatio—
Oh, royal knavery!—an exact command,
Larded[7] with many several sorts of reasons,   20
Importing Denmark's health, and England's too,
With, ho! such bugs and goblins in my life,[8]

84. *The cat . . . day:* life will go on in its usual manner.   85. *in:* by thinking of.
1. *this:* the fate of Ophelia.   2. *the other:* Hamlet's adventures.
3. *mutines in the bilboes:* mutineers in iron fetters.
4. *pall:* lose their effectiveness.   5. *Fingered:* stole.   6. *in fine:* finally.
7. *Larded:* enriched, greased.
8. *such . . . life:* such imaginary dangers to be encountered if I should live.

That on the supervise,[9] no leisure bated,[10]
No, not to stay the grinding of the axe,[11]
My head should be struck off.
HORATIO.   Is't possible?   25
HAMLET. Here's the commission; read it at more leisure.
But wilt thou hear me how I did proceed?
HORATIO. I beseech you.
HAMLET. Being thus benetted round with villainies,
Ere I could make a prologue to my brains,   30
They had begun the play. I sat me down,
Devised a new commission, wrote it fair.[12]
I once did hold it, as our statists[13] do,
A baseness to write fair, and labored much
How to forget that learning, but, sir, now   35
It did me yeoman's service.[14] Wilt thou know
Th' effect[15] of what I wrote?
HORATIO.   Ay, good my lord.
HAMLET. An earnest conjuration from the king,
As England was his faithful tributary,
As love between them like the palm should flourish,   40
As peace should still her wheaten garland[16] wear
And stand a comma[17] 'tween their amities,[18]
And many such-like "as"-es of great charge,[19]
That on the view and knowing of these contents,
Without debatement[20] further, more or less,   45
He should the bearers put to sudden death,
Not shriving time allowed.[21]
HORATIO.   How was this sealed?
HAMLET. Why, even in that was heaven ordinant.[22]
I had my father's signet in my purse,
Which was the model of that Danish seal,   50
Folded the writ up in the form of th' other,
Subscribed[23] it, gave't th' impression, placed it safely,
The changeling[24] never known. Now, the next day
Was our sea-fight, and what to this was sequent[25]
Thou know'st already.   55

9. *supervise:* reading of the instructions.
10. *no leisure bated:* no time being wasted.
11. *No . . . axe:* no, not to stop long enough to sharpen the axe.
12. *fair:* in a clear hand.   13. *statists:* statesmen.
14. *yeoman's service:* excellent service.   15. *effect:* substance.
16. *wheaten garland:* symbol of peace.   17. *comma:* link.
18. *amities:* friendship.   19. *charge:* burden or importance.
20. *debatement:* argument.
21. *Not shriving time allowed:* no time allowed for them to go to confession.
22. *ordinant:* directing.   23. *Subscribed:* signed.
24. *changeling:* exchange.   25. *sequent:* subsequent.

HORATIO. So Guildenstern and Rosencrantz go to't.

HAMLET. Why, man, they did make love to this employment;
　　They are not near my conscience; their defeat[26]
　　Does by their own insinuation[27] grow.
　　'Tis dangerous when the baser nature comes　　　　　　　60
　　Between the pass[28] and fell incensèd points[29]
　　Of mighty opposites.

HORATIO.　　　　　　　　Why, what a king is this!

HAMLET. Does it not, think thee, stand me now upon—[30]
　　He that hath killed my king, and whored my mother,
　　Popped in between th' election and my hopes,　　　　　　65
　　Thrown out his angle[31] for my proper[32] life,
　　And with such cozenage[33]—is't not perfect conscience
　　To quit him[34] with this arm? And is't not to be damned
　　To let this canker of our nature come
　　In further evil?　　　　　　　　　　　　　　　　　　70

HORATIO. It must be shortly known to him from England
　　What is the issue of the business there.

HAMLET. It will be short; the interim is mine,
　　And a man's life's no more than to say 'one.'
　　But I am very sorry, good Horatio,　　　　　　　　　　75
　　That to Laertes I forgot myself,
　　For by the image of my cause I see
　　The portraiture of his. I'll court his favors.
　　But sure the bravery[35] of his grief did put me
　　Into a tow'ring passion.

HORATIO.　　　　　　　　Peace, who comes here?　　　　80

[Enter young Osric.]

OSRIC. Your lordship is right welcome back to Denmark.

HAMLET. I humbly thank you, sir. *[Aside to Horatio.]* Dost know
this waterfly?

HORATIO. *[Aside to Hamlet.]* No, my good lord.

HAMLET. *[Aside to Horatio.]* Thy state is the more gracious, for　　85
'tis a vice to know him. He hath much land, and fertile. Let a beast
be lord of beasts, and his crib shall stand at the king's mess.[36]
'Tis a chough,[37] but, as I say, spacious[38] in the possession of dirt.

OSRIC. Sweet lord, if your lordship were at leisure, I should impart a thing to you from his majesty.　　　　　　　　　　90

---

26. *defeat:* destruction.　　27. *insinuation:* meddling.　　28. *pass:* thrust.
29. *fell incensèd points:* fierce angered swordpoints.
30. *stand me now upon:* become my duty.　　31. *angle:* fishhook.
32. *proper:* very.　　33. *cozenage:* cheating.　　34. *quit him:* pay him back.
35. *bravery:* ostentatious display.
36. *Let . . . mess:* In a kingdom where a beast is a lord of other beasts, his feeding
place shall be next to that of the king.　　37. *chough:* a chattering bird.
38. *spacious:* wealthy.

HAMLET. I will receive it with all diligence of spirit. Put your bonnet[39] to his right use. 'Tis for the head.

OSRIC. I thank your lordship, it is very hot.

HAMLET. No, believe me, 'tis very cold; the wind is northerly.

OSRIC. It is indifferent[40] cold, my lord, indeed.   95

HAMLET. But yet methinks it is very sultry and hot for my complexion.

OSRIC. Exceedingly, my lord; it is very sultry, as 'twere—I cannot tell how. But, my lord, his majesty bade me signify to you that he has laid a great wager on your head. Sir, this is the matter—   100

HAMLET. I beseech you remember.

[Hamlet moves him to put on his hat.]

OSRIC. Nay, in good faith; for mine ease, in good faith. Sir, here is newly come to court Laertes—believe me, an absolute gentleman, full of most excellent differences,[41] of very soft society[42] and great showing. Indeed, to speak feelingly of him, he is the card   105
or calendar[43] of gentry; for you shall find in him the continent[44] of what part a gentleman would see.[45]

HAMLET. Sir, his definement[46] suffers no perdition[47] in you, though, I know, to divide him inventorially[48] would dozy[49] th' arithmetic of memory, and yet but yaw neither in respect of his   110
quick sail.[50] But, in the verity of extolment, I take him to be a soul of great article, and his infusion[51] of such dearth and rareness as, to make true diction of him, his semblable is his mirror,[52] and who else would trace[53] him, his umbrage,[54] nothing more.

OSRIC. Your lordship speaks most infallibly of him.   115

HAMLET. The concernancy,[55] sir? Why do we wrap the gentleman[56] in our more rawer breath?[57]

OSRIC. Sir?

HORATIO. Is't not possible to understand in another tongue?[58] You will to't,[59] sir, really.   120

HAMLET. What imports the nomination[60] of this gentleman?

---

39. *bonnet:* Osric has removed his large hat.
40. *indifferent:* somewhat.   41. *excellent differences:* special qualities.
42. *soft society:* pleasing manners.   43. *card or calendar:* map or guide.
44. *continent:* embodiment, personification.
45. *part a gentleman would see:* quality a gentleman would wish to see.
46. *definement:* definition.   47. *perdition:* loss.
48. *divide him inventorially:* to make an inventory of his fine qualities.
49. *dozy:* stagger.
50. *and yet . . . sail:* and yet but falter in comparison with his lively sail.
51. *infusion:* essence.
52. *his . . . mirror:* his true likeness can be found only in his mirror.
53. *trace:* follow.   54. *umbrage:* shadow.   55. *concernancy:* meaning.
56. *gentleman:* Osric.   57. *rawer breath:* crude speech.
58. *another tongue:* a foreign language or jargon.
59. *You . . . to't:* you (Hamlet) will come to it.
60. *What . . . nomination:* what is the purpose of the naming.

OSRIC. Of Laertes?

HORATIO. *[Aside to Hamlet.]* His purse is empty already. All's golden words are spent.

HAMLET. Of him, sir.   125

OSRIC. I know you are not ignorant—

HAMLET. I would you did, sir; yet, in faith, if you did, it would not much approve me. Well, sir?

OSRIC. You are not ignorant of what excellence Laertes is—

HAMLET. I dare not confess that, lest I should compare[61] with him   130
in excellence; but to know a man well were to know himself.

OSRIC. I mean, sir, for his weapon; but in the imputation[62] laid on him by them, in his meed[63] he's unfellowed.[64]

HAMLET. What's his weapon?

OSRIC. Rapier and dagger.   135

HAMLET. That's two of his weapons—but well.

OSRIC. The king, sir, hath wag'd with him six Barbary horses, against the which he has imponed,[65] as I take it, six French rapiers and poniards, with their assigns,[66] as girdle, hangers, and so. Three of the carriages,[67] in faith, are very dear to fancy, very responsive[68]   140
to the hilts, most delicate carriages, and of very liberal conceit.[69]

HAMLET. What call you the carriages?

HORATIO. *[Aside to Hamlet.]* I knew you must be edified by the margent[70] ere you had done.

OSRIC. The carriages, sir, are the hangers.   145

HAMLET. The phrase would be more germane[71] to the matter if we could carry a cannon by our sides. I would it might be hangers till then. But on! Six Barbary horses against six French swords, their assigns, and three liberal-conceited carriages—that's the French bet against the Danish. Why is this "imponed," as you call it?   150

OSRIC. The king, sir, hath laid, sir, that in a dozen passes between you and him he shall not exceed you three hits; he hath laid on twelve for nine, and it would come to immediate trial if your lordship would vouchsafe the answer.

HAMLET. How if I answer no?   155

OSRIC. I mean, my lord, the opposition of your person in trial.

HAMLET. Sir, I will walk here in the hall. If it please his majesty, 'tis the breathing time[72] of day with me. Let the foils be brought, the gentleman willing, and the king hold his purpose; I will win for him an[73] I can; if not, I'll gain nothing but my shame and the odd hits.   160

OSRIC. Shall I redeliver you e'en so?

---

61. *compare:* compete.   62. *imputation:* reputation.   63. *meed:* worth.
64. *unfellowed:* unequalled.   65. *imponed:* wagered.   66. *assigns:* appendages.
67. *carriages:* ornamented straps by which rapiers were hung from the belt.
68. *responsive:* harmonious in design.   69. *liberal conceit:* elegant conception.
70. *margent:* margin (that is, the explanatory notes there printed).
71. *germane:* pertinent.   72. *breathing time:* exercise hour.   73. *an:* if.

HAMLET. To this effect, sir, after what flourish your nature will.

OSRIC. I commend my duty to your lordship.

HAMLET. Yours, yours. *[Exit Osric.]* He does well to commend it himself; there are no tongues else for's turn.

HORATIO. This lapwing runs away with the shell on his head.[74]

HAMLET. He did comply,[75] sir, with his dug[76] before he sucked it. Thus has he, and many more of the same bevy that I know the drossy[77] age dotes on, only got the tune of the time and, out of an habit of encounter,[78] a kind of yeasty[79] collection, which carries them through and through the most fanned and winnowed opinions;[80] and do but blow them to their trial; the bubbles are out.[81]

[Enter a Lord.]

LORD. My lord, his majesty commended him to you by young Osric, who brings back to him that you attend him in the hall. He sends to know if your pleasure hold to play with Laertes, or that you will take longer time.

HAMLET. I am constant to my purposes; they follow the king's pleasure. If his fitness speaks, mine is ready; now or whensoever, provided I be so able as now.

LORD. The king and queen and all are coming down.

HAMLET. In happy time.

LORD. The queen desires you to use some gentle entertainment[82] to Laertes before you fall to play.

HAMLET. She well instructs me.   *[Exit Lord.]*

HORATIO. You will lose this wager, my lord.

HAMLET. I do not think so. Since he went into France I have been in continual practice. I shall win at the odds. But thou wouldst not think how ill all's here about my heart. But it is no matter.

HORATIO. Nay, good my lord—

HAMLET. It is but foolery, but it is such a kind of gaingiving[83] as would perhaps trouble a woman.

HORATIO. If your mind dislike anything, obey it. I will forestall their repair hither and say you are not fit.

HAMLET. Not a whit, we defy augury.[84] There is special providence in the fall of a sparrow. If it be now, 'tis not to come; if it be not to come, it will be now; if it be not now, yet it will come. The readiness[85] is all. Since no man has aught of what he leaves, what is't to leave betimes?[86] Let be.

---

74. *shell on his head:* that is, before he is completely hatched.

75. *did comply:* observed formal courtesies.   76. *dug:* mother's breast.

77. *drossy:* frivolous.   78. *habit of encounter:* customary style of polite greeting.

79. *yeasty:* frothy.   80. *fanned and winnowed:* threshed, that is, sifted and refined.

81. *and do . . . out:* but test them and their bubbles burst.

82. *gentle entertainment:* pleasant words of greeting.   83. *gaingiving:* misgiving.

84. *augury:* omen.   85. *readiness:* state of preparation.   86. *betimes:* early.

*[Enter King, Queen, Laertes, Lords, and other Attendants with foils
and gauntlets, a table, and flagons of wine on it.]*

KING. Come, Hamlet, come, and take this hand from me.

[The King puts Laertes' hand into Hamlet's.]

HAMLET. Give me your pardon, sir. I have done you wrong,   200
But pardon't, as you are a gentleman.
This presence[87] knows, and you must needs have heard,
How I am punished with a sore distraction.
What I have done
That might your nature, honor, and exception[88]   205
Roughly awake, I here proclaim was madness.
Was't Hamlet wronged Laertes? Never Hamlet.
If Hamlet from himself be ta'en away,
And when he's not himself does wrong Laertes,
Then Hamlet does it not, Hamlet denies it.   210
Who does it then? His madness. If't be so,
Hamlet is of the faction that is wronged;
His madness is poor Hamlet's enemy.
Sir, in this audience,
Let my disclaiming from a purposed evil   215
Free me so far in your most generous thoughts
That I have shot my arrow o'er the house
And hurt my brother.
LAERTES.   I am satisfied in nature,[89]
Whose motive in this case should stir me most
To my revenge. But in my terms of honor   220
I stand aloof, and will no reconcilement
Till by some elder masters of known honor
I have a voice and precedent of peace[90]
To keep my name ungored.[91] But till that time
I do receive your offered love like love,   225
And will not wrong it.
HAMLET.   I embrace it freely,
And will this brother's wager[92] frankly[93] play.
Give us the foils. Come on.
LAERTES.   Come, one for me.
HAMLET. I'll be your foil,[94] Laertes. In mine ignorance
Your skill shall, like a star i' th' darkest night,   230
Stick fiery off[95] indeed.

87. *presence:* assembly.   88. *exception:* disapproval.
89. *in nature:* in so far as my natural feelings are concerned.
90. *I . . . peace:* I have agreement on and precedent for reconciliation.
91. *ungored:* uninjured.   92. *brother's wager:* a bet as if between two good friends.
93. *frankly:* freely, without rancor.
94. *foil:* contrasting background; that is, I'll enhance your performance by contrast.
95. *Stick fiery off:* stand out brilliantly.

LAERTES.   You mock me, sir.
HAMLET. No, by this hand.
KING. Give them the foils, young Osric. Cousin Hamlet,
   You know the wager?
HAMLET.   Very well, my lord.
   Your grace has laid the odds a' th' weaker side.   235
KING. I do not fear it, I have seen you both;
   But since he is bettered,⁹⁶ we have therefore odds.
LAERTES. This is too heavy; let me see another.
HAMLET. This likes me well. These foils have all a length?⁹⁷
                              [Prepare to play.]
OSRIC. Ay, my good lord.   240
KING. Set me the stoups of wine upon that table.
   If Hamlet give the first or second hit,
   Or quit⁹⁸ in answer of the third exchange,
   Let all the battlements their ordnance fire.
   The king shall drink to Hamlet's better breath,   245
   And in the cup an union⁹⁹ shall he throw
   Richer than that which four successive kings
   In Denmark's crown have worn. Give me the cups,
   And let the kettle to the trumpet speak,
   The trumpet to the cannoneer without,   250
   The cannons to the heavens, the heaven to earth,
   "Now the king drinks to Hamlet." Come, begin.
                              [Trumpets the while.]
   And you, the judges, bear a wary eye.
HAMLET. Come on, sir.
LAERTES.   Come on, sir.   *[They fence.]*
HAMLET.   One.
LAERTES.   No.
HAMLET.   Judgment?
OSRIC. A hit, a very palpable hit.
LAERTES.   Well, again.   255
KING. Stay, give me drink. Hamlet, this pearl is thine.
   Here's to thy health. Give him the cup.
                    [Trumpets sound, and shot goes off.]
HAMLET. I'll play this bout first; set it by awhile.
   Come. *[They fence.]* Another hit. What say you?
LAERTES. A touch, a touch; I do confess.   260
KING. Our son shall win.
QUEEN.   He's fat, and scant of breath.¹⁰⁰
   Here, Hamlet, take my napkin, rub thy brows.
   The queen carouses¹⁰¹ to thy fortune, Hamlet.

96. *is bettered:* has the better reputation.
97. *have . . . length:* are all the same length.   98. *quit:* repay by a hit.
99. *union:* pearl.   100. *fat . . . breath:* overweight and out of training.
101. *carouses:* drinks.

HAMLET. Good madam!
KING.   Gertrude, do not drink.
QUEEN. I will, my lord; I pray you pardon me.   *[Drinks.]*   265
KING. *[Aside]* It is the poisoned cup; it is too late.
HAMLET. I dare not drink yet, madam—by and by.
QUEEN. Come, let me wipe thy face.
LAERTES. My lord, I'll hit him now.
KING.   I do not think't.
LAERTES. *[Aside]* And yet 'tis almost against my conscience.   270
HAMLET. Come for the third, Laertes. You but dally.
  I pray you pass with your best violence;
  I am afeard you make a wanton of me.[102]
LAERTES. Say you so? Come on.   *[They fence.]*
OSRIC. Nothing neither way.[103]   275
LAERTES. Have at you now!

  *[In scuffling they change rapiers, and both are wounded with the
                                          poisoned weapon.]*

KING.   Part them. They are incensed.
HAMLET. Nay, come—again!   *[The Queen falls.]*
OSRIC.   Look to the queen there, ho!
HORATIO. They bleed on both sides. How is it, my lord?
OSRIC. How is't, Laertes?
LAERTES. Why, as a woodcock[104] to mine own springe,[105] Osric.   280
  I am justly killed with mine own treachery.
HAMLET. How does the queen?
KING.   She swounds[106] to see them bleed.
QUEEN. No, no, the drink, the drink! O my dear Hamlet!
  The drink, the drink! I am poisoned.   *[Dies.]*
HAMLET. O villainy! Ho! let the door be locked.   285
  Treachery! Seek it out.

                                          [Laertes falls.]

LAERTES. It is here, Hamlet. Hamlet, thou art slain;
  No medicine in the world can do thee good.
  In thee there is not half an hour's life.
  The treacherous instrument is in thy hand,   290
  Unbated[107] and envenomed. The foul practice
  Hath turned itself on me. Lo, here I lie,
  Never to rise again. Thy mother's poisoned.
  I can no more. The king, the king's to blame.
HAMLET. The point envenomed too?   295
  Then, venom, to thy work.   *[Wounds the King.]*
ALL. Treason! treason!
KING. O, yet defend me, friends. I am but hurt.

102. *make . . . me:* treat me like a child.
103. *Nothing neither way:* no hit on either side.
104. *woodcock:* a bird reputed to be stupid.   105. *springe:* snare.
106. *swounds:* swoons.   107. *Unbated:* unblunted.

HAMLET. Here, thou incestuous, murd'rous, damnèd Dane,
  Drink off this potion. Is thy union[108] here?   300
  Follow my mother.   *[King dies.]*
LAERTES.   He is justly served.
  It is a poison tempered[109] by himself.
  Exchange forgiveness with me, noble Hamlet.
  Mine and my father's death come not upon thee,[110]
  Nor thine on me!   *[Dies.]* 305
HAMLET. Heaven make thee free of it! I follow thee.
  I am dead, Horatio. Wretched queen, adieu!
  You that look pale and tremble at this chance,[111]
  That are but mutes[112] or audience to this act,
  Had I but time (as this fell sergeant,[113] Death,   310
  Is strict in his arrest), O, I could tell you.
  But let it be. Horatio, I am dead;
  Thou livest; report me and my cause aright
  To the unsatisfied.
HORATIO.   Never believe it.
  I am more an antique Roman[114] than a Dane.   315
  Here's yet some liquor left.
HAMLET.   As th' art a man,
  Give me the cup. Let go. By heaven, I'll have't!
  O good Horatio, what a wounded name;
  Things standing thus unknown, shall live behind me!
  If thou didst ever hold me in thy heart,   320
  Absent thee from felicity awhile,
  And in this harsh world draw thy breath in pain,
  To tell my story.   *[A march afar off, and shot within.]*
        What warlike noise is this?
OSRIC. Young Fortinbras, with conquest come from Poland,
  To th' ambassadors of England gives   325
  This warlike volley.
HAMLET.   O, I die, Horatio!
  The potent poison quite o'ercrows[115] my spirit.
  I cannot live to hear the news from England,
  But I do prophesy th' election[116] lights
  On Fortinbras. He has my dying voice.[117]   330
  So tell him, with the occurrents, more and less,[118]
  Which have solicited[119]—the rest is silence.   *[Dies.]*

---

108. *union:* both the pearl and the union with death.
109. *tempered:* prepared, mixed.   110. *come not upon thee:* are not upon your head.
111. *chance:* mishap.   112. *mutes:* actors without speaking parts.
113. *sergeant:* sheriff's officer.
114. *antique Roman:* for whom suicide was considered honorable.
115. *o'ercrows:* overcomes.   116. *election:* choice.
117. *He . . . voice:* He has my vote.
118. *occurrents, more and less:* events, large and small.
119. *solicited:* prompted my action.

HORATIO. Now cracks a noble heart. Good night, sweet prince,
   And flights of angels sing thee to thy rest!   *[March within.]*
   Why does the drum come hither?   335

[Enter Fortinbras and English Ambassador, with drum, colors, and Attendants.]

FORTINBRAS. Where is this sight?
HORATIO.   What is it ye would see?
   If aught of woe or wonder, cease your search.
FORTINBRAS. This quarry[120] cries on havoc. O proud Death,
   What feast is toward[121] in thine eternal cell
   That thou so many princes at a shot   340
   So bloodily hast struck?
AMBASSADOR.   The sight is dismal;
   And our affairs from England come too late.
   The ears are senseless that should give us hearing
   To tell him his commandment is fulfilled,
   That Rosencrantz and Guildenstern are dead.   345
   Where should we have our thanks?
HORATIO.   Not from his mouth,
   Had it th' ability of life to thank you.
   He never gave commandment for their death.
   But since, so jump[122] upon this bloody question,
   You from the Polack wars, and you from England,   350
   Are here arrived, give order that these bodies
   High on a stage be plac`ed to the view,
   And let me speak to th' yet unknowing world
   How these things came about. So shall you hear
   Of carnal, bloody, and unnatural acts,   355
   Of accidental judgments,[123] casual[124] slaughters,
   Of deaths put on by cunning and forced cause,
   And, in this upshot, purposes mistook
   Fall'n on the inventors' heads. All this can I
   Truly deliver.
FORTINBRAS.   Let us haste to hear it,   360
   And call the noblest to the audience.
   For me, with sorrow I embrace my fortune.
   I have some rights of memory[125] in this kingdom,
   Which now to claim my vantage[126] doth invite me.
HORATIO. Of that I shall have also cause to speak,   365
   And from his mouth whose voice will draw on more.[127]
   But let this same be presently performed,

120. *quarry:* pile of dead bodies.
121. *toward:* imminent.   122. *jump:* opportunely, precisely.
123. *judgments:* retributions.   124. *casual:* accidental.
125. *rights of memory:* remembered rights.   126. *vantage:* advantageous position.
127. *more:* more voices of support.

Even while men's minds are wild, lest more mischance
On plots and errors happen.
FORTINBRAS.   Let four captains
Bear Hamlet like a soldier to the stage,   370
For he was likely, had he been put on,[128]
To have proved most royally; and for his passage[129]
The soldiers' music and the rites of war
Speak loudly for him.
Take up the bodies. Such a sight as this   375
Becomes the field, but here shows much amiss.
Go, bid the soldiers shoot.
    [Exeunt marching; after which a peal of ordinance is shot off.]

---

128. *been put on:* been tried as a king.
129. *passage:* death.

Ghosts

Introduction

Ghosts caused the biggest disturbance among the critics of all of Henrik Ibsen's plays. Published in 1881, it caused such a commotion that no Scandanavian theater would produce it. According to the best records we have, its first public performance was in Chicago in 1882. Even as late as 1891 the official British censors refused to license a production of the play, which they felt was immoral.

Although the furor over the morality or immorality of *Ghosts* has long since subsided, there have been a variety of theories regarding the basic meaning of the play. The question regarding what the author was saying to his ultra-prudish, Victorian audience has come up repeatedly. One interpretation is that *Ghosts* is nothing more than an answer to the criticism of one of Ibsen's earlier plays, *The Doll's House*. The critics had objected to the morality of the wife in *The Doll's House* because she left a marriage which she felt was destroying her. This interpretation holds that in *Ghosts* Ibsen tried to show what could happen if the wife in a destructive marriage stayed with her husband.

A second interpretation is that Oswald and Mrs. Alving are victimized by laws of heredity in an absurdly illogical world. Still a third interpretation is that hereditary disease is the symbol of all deterministic forces—that men have little or no control over their own destinies.

Whatever interpretation we give to *Ghosts,* we must recognize the importance of heredity in its theme: the "ghosts" of men who have lived in the past haunt us in our present lives. Heredity, in this scheme of things, takes the place of the ancient Greek idea of fate. The play, however, is far more than a study of the effects of heredity; it is an attack upon the society for which it was written and the standards of that society. It questions man's most cherished views of himself and brings into question his moral codes.

Mrs. Alving had married Captain Alving because her mother and her aunts wished her to. When she realized that she was married to a drunken and sexually immoral man, she fled. She sought out Pastor Manders, who was not only her pastor but her friend. Had Manders not used the weight of his influence to back up conventional morality, or had Helen Alving had the courage to defy the pressures of society and leave her husband, Oswald would not have been brought into the world cursed with syphilis. Ironically, like Oedipus, Mrs. Alving discovers these truths too late.

Unlike *Oedipus,* however, *Ghosts* states its theme through the lives of everyday people. By dealing with everyday society and by examining the basic ills inherent in that society, Ibsen makes the common man the subject of tragedy. Pity and fear are not produced in the audience or the reader by observing a man of high rank destroyed. These emotions are aroused through identification with a common man who is brought down through surrender to the injustice, bigotry, and falseness which Ibsen saw in his society.

Ghosts
A Family Drama in Three Acts

HENRIK IBSEN

Characters

MRS. HELEN ALVING   *widow of Captain Alving, late Chamberlain to the King*

OSWALD ALVING   *her son, a painter*

PASTOR MANDERS

JACOB ENGSTRAND   *a carpenter*

REGINA ENGSTRAND   *Mrs. Alving's maid*

Ghosts

Act 1

*A spacious garden-room, with one door to the left, and two doors to the
right. In the middle of the room a round table, with chairs about it. On
the table lie books, periodicals, and newspapers. In the foreground to the
left a window, and by it a small sofa, with a work-table in front of it. In
the background, the room is continued into a somewhat narrower
conservatory, the walls of which are formed by large panes of glass. In
the right-hand wall of the conservatory is a door leading down into the
garden. Through the glass wall a gloomy fjord-landscape is faintly visible,
veiled by steady rain.*

*[Engstrand, the carpenter, stands by the garden door. His left leg is somewhat
bent; he has a clump of wood under the sole of his boot. Regina, with an empty
garden syringe in her hand, hinders him from advancing.]*

REGINA. *[In a low voice.]* What do you want? Stop where you are.
You're positively dripping.

ENGSTRAND. It's the Lord's own rain, my girl.

REGINA. It's the devil's rain, *I* say.

ENGSTRAND. Lord, how you talk, Regina. *[Limps a step or two forward into the room.]* It's just this as I wanted to say——

REGINA. Don't clatter so with that foot of yours, I tell you! The
young master's asleep upstairs.

ENGSTRAND. Asleep? In the middle of the day?

REGINA. It's no business of yours.

ENGSTRAND. I was out on the loose last night——

REGINA. I can quite believe that.

ENGSTRAND. Yes, we're weak vessels, we poor mortals, my girl——

REGINA. So it seems.

ENGSTRAND. ——and temptations are manifold in this world, you
see. But all the same, I was hard at work, God knows, at half-past
five this morning.

REGINA. Very well; only be off now. I won't stop here and have
rendezvous's with you.

ENGSTRAND. What do you say you won't have?

REGINA. I won't have any one find you here; so just you go about
your business.

ENGSTRAND. *[Advances a step or two.]* Blest if I go before I've had a talk with you. This afternoon I shall have finished my work at the school-house, and then I shall take to-night's boat and be off home to the town.

REGINA. *[Mutters.]* Pleasant journey to you!

ENGSTRAND. Thank you, my child. To-morrow the Orphanage is to be opened, and then there'll be fine doings, no doubt, and plenty of intoxicating drink going, you know. And nobody shall say of Jacob Engstrand that he can't keep out of temptation's way.

REGINA. Oh!

ENGSTRAND. You see, there's to be heaps of grand folks here to-morrow. Pastor Manders is expected from town, too.

REGINA. He's coming to-day.

ENGSTRAND. There, you see! And I should be cursedly sorry if he found out anything against me, don't you understand?

REGINA. Oho! is that your game?

ENGSTRAND. Is what my game?

REGINA. *[Looking hard at him.]* What are you going to fool Pastor Manders into doing, this time?

ENGSTRAND. Sh! sh! Are you crazy? Do *I* want to fool Pastor Manders? Oh no! Pastor Manders has been far too good a friend to me for that. But I just wanted to say, you know—that I mean to be off home again to-night.

REGINA. The sooner the better, say I.

ENGSTRAND. Yes, but I want you with me, Regina.

REGINA. *[Open-mouthed.]* You want me——? What are you talking about?

ENGSTRAND. I want you to come home with me, I say.

REGINA. *[Scornfully.]* Never in this world shall you get me home with you.

ENGSTRAND. Oh, we'll see about that.

REGINA. Yes, you may be sure we'll see about it! Me, that have been brought up by a lady like Mrs Alving! Me, that am treated almost as a daughter here! Is it me you want to go home with you?—to a house like yours? For shame!

ENGSTRAND. What the devil do you mean? Do you set yourself up against your father, you hussy?

REGINA. *[Mutters without looking at him.]* You've said often enough I was no concern of yours.

ENGSTRAND. Pooh! Why should you bother about that——

REGINA. Haven't you many a time sworn at me and called me a——? *Fi donc!*

ENGSTRAND. Curse me, now, if ever I used such an ugly word.

REGINA. Oh, I remember very well what word you used.

ENGSTRAND. Well, but that was only when I was a bit on, don't you know? Temptations are manifold in this world, Regina.

REGINA. Ugh!

ENGSTRAND. And besides, it was when your mother was that aggravating—I had to find something to twit her with, my child. She was always setting up for a fine lady. *[Mimics.]* "Let me go, Engstrand; let me be. Remember I was three years in Chamberlain Alving's family at Rosenvold." *[Laughs.]* Mercy on us! She could never forget that the Captain was made a Chamberlain[1] while she was in service here.

REGINA. Poor mother! you very soon tormented her into her grave.

ENGSTRAND. *[With a twist of his shoulders.]* Oh, of course! I'm to have the blame for everything.

REGINA. *[Turns away; half aloud.]* Ugh——! And that leg too!

ENGSTRAND. What do you say, my child?

REGINA. *Pied de mouton.*[2]

ENGSTRAND. Is that English, eh?

REGINA. Yes.

ENGSTRAND. Ay, ay; you've picked up some learning out here; and that may come in useful now, Regina.

REGINA. *[After a short silence.]* What do you want with me in town?

ENGSTRAND. Can you ask what a father wants with his only child? A'n't I a lonely, forlorn widower?

REGINA. Oh, don't try on any nonsense like that with me! Why do you want me?

ENGSTRAND. Well, let me tell you, I've been thinking of setting up in a new line of business.

REGINA. *[Contemptuously.]* You've tried that often enough, and much good you've done with it.

ENGSTRAND. Yes, but this time you shall see, Regina! Devil take me——

REGINA. *[Stamps.]* Stop your swearing!

ENGSTRAND. Hush, hush; you're right enough there, my girl. What I wanted to say was just this—I've laid by a very tidy pile from this Orphanage job.

REGINA. Have you? That's a good thing for you.

ENGSTRAND. What can a man spend his ha'pence on here in this country hole?

REGINA. Well, what then?

ENGSTRAND. Why, you see, I thought of putting the money into some paying speculation. I thought of a sort of a sailor's tavern——

REGINA. Pah!

ENGSTRAND. A regular high-class affair, of course; not any sort of pig-sty for common sailors. No! damn it! it would be for captains and mates, and—and—regular swells, you know.

---

1 *Chamberlain:* the only honorary title in Norway. It is awarded by the King to men of position.   2 *Pied . . . mouton:* insulting term.

REGINA. And I was to——?

ENGSTRAND. You were to help, to be sure. Only for the look of the thing, you understand. Devil a bit of hard work shall you have, my girl. You shall do exactly what you like.

REGINA. Oh, indeed!

ENGSTRAND. But there must be a petticoat in the house; that's as clear as daylight. For I want to have it a bit lively-like in the evenings, with singing and dancing, and so on. You must remember they're weary wanderers on the ocean of life. *[Nearer.]* Now don't be a fool and stand in your own light, Regina. What's to become of you out here? Your mistress has given you a lot of learning; but what good is that to you? You're to look after the children at the new Orphanage, I hear. Is that the sort of thing for you, eh? Are you so dead set on wearing your life out for a pack of dirty brats?

REGINA. No; if things go as I want them to—— Well there's no saying—there's no saying.

ENGSTRAND. What do you mean by "there's no saying"?

REGINA. Never you mind.—How much money have you saved?

ENGSTRAND. What with one thing and another, a matter of seven or eight hundred crowns.

REGINA. That's not so bad.

ENGSTRAND. It's enough to make a start with, my girl.

REGINA. Aren't you thinking of giving me any?

ENGSTRAND. No, I'm blest if I am!

REGINA. Not even of sending me a scrap of stuff for a new dress?

ENGSTRAND. Come to town with me, my lass, and you'll soon get dresses enough.

REGINA. Pooh! I can do that on my own account, if I want to.

ENGSTRAND. No, a father's guiding hand is what you want, Regina. Now, I've got my eye on a capital house in Little Harbour Street. They don't want much ready-money; and it could be a sort of a Sailors' Home, you know.

REGINA. But I will not live with you! I have nothing whatever to do with you. Be off!

ENGSTRAND. You wouldn't stop long with me, my girl. No such luck! If you knew how to play your cards, such a fine figure of a girl as you've grown in the last year or two——

REGINA. Well?

ENGSTRAND. You'd soon get hold of some mate—or maybe even a captain——

REGINA. I won't marry any one of that sort. Sailors have no *savoir vivre.*

ENGSTRAND. What's that they haven't got?

REGINA. I know what sailors are, I tell you. They're not the sort of people to marry.

ENGSTRAND. Then never mind about marrying them. You can make it pay all the same. *[More confidentially.]* He—the English-

man—the man with the yacht—he came down with three hundred
dollars, he did; and she wasn't a bit handsomer than you.

REGINA. *[Making for him.]* Out you go!

ENGSTRAND. *[Falling back.]* Come, come! You're not going to hit
me, I hope.

REGINA. Yes, if you begin talking about mother I shall hit you.
Get away with you, I say! *[Drives him back towards the garden door.]*
And don't slam the doors. Young Mr. Alving——

ENGSTRAND. He's asleep; I know. You're mightily taken up about
young Mr. Alving—— *[More softly.]* Oho! you don't mean to say
it's him as——?

REGINA. Be off this minute! You're crazy, I tell you! No, not that
way. There comes Pastor Manders. Down the kitchen stairs with
you.

ENGSTRAND. *[Towards the right.]* Yes, yes, I'm going. But just
you talk to him as is coming there. He's the man to tell you what a
child owes its father. For I am your father all the same, you know. I
can prove it from the church register.

*[He goes out through the second door to the right, which Regina has opened,
and closes again after him. Regina glances hastily at herself in the mirror, dusts
herself with her pocket handkerchief, and settles her necktie; then she busies
herself with the flowers.*

*Pastor Manders, wearing an overcoat, carrying an umbrella, and with a
small travelling-bag on a strap over his shoulder, comes through the garden
door into the conservatory.]*

MANDERS. Good-morning, Miss Engstrand.

REGINA. *[Turning round, surprised and pleased.]* No, really! Good-
morning, Pastor Manders. Is the steamer in already?

MANDERS. It is just in. *[Enters the sitting-room.]* Terrible weather
we have been having lately.

REGINA. *[Follows him.]* It's such blessëd weather for the country,
sir.

MANDERS. No doubt; you are quite right. We townspeople give
too little thought to that.

[He begins to take off his overcoat.]

REGINA. Oh, mayn't I help you?—There! Why, how wet it is!
I'll just hang it up in the hall. And your umbrella, too—I'll open it
and let it dry.

*[She goes out with the things through the second door on the right. Pastor
Manders takes off his travelling-bag and lays it and his hat on a chair. Meanwhile Regina comes in again.]*

MANDERS. Ah, it's a comfort to get safe under cover. I hope everything is going on well here?

REGINA. Yes, thank you, sir.

MANDERS. You have your hands full, I suppose, in preparation for to-morrow?

REGINA. Yes, there's plenty to do, of course.

MANDERS. And Mrs. Alving is at home, I trust?

REGINA. Oh dear, yes. She's just upstairs, looking after the young master's chocolate.

MANDERS. Yes, by-the-bye—I heard down at the pier that Oswald had arrived.

REGINA. Yes, he came the day before yesterday. We didn't expect him before to-day.

MANDERS. Quite strong and well, I hope?

REGINA. Yes, thank you, quite; but dreadfully tired with the journey. He has made one rush right through from Paris—the whole way in one train, I believe. He's sleeping a little now, I think; so perhaps we'd better talk a little quietly.

MANDERS. Sh!—as quietly as you please.

REGINA. *[Arranging an arm-chair beside the table.]* Now, do sit down, Pastor Manders, and make yourself comfortable. *[He sits down; she places a footstool under his feet.]* There! Are you comfortable now, sir?

MANDERS. Thanks, thanks, extremely so. *[Looks at her.]* Do you know, Miss Engstrand, I positively believe you have grown since I last saw you.

REGINA. Do you think so, sir? Mrs. Alving says I've filled out too.

MANDERS. Filled out? Well, perhaps a little; just enough.

[Short pause.]

REGINA. Shall I tell Mrs. Alving you are here?

MANDERS. Thanks, thanks, there is no hurry, my dear child. —By-the-bye, Regina, my good girl, tell me: how is your father getting on out here?

REGINA. Oh, thank you, sir, he's getting on well enough.

MANDERS. He called upon me last time he was in town.

REGINA. Did he, indeed? He's always so glad of a chance of talking to you, sir.

MANDERS. And you often look in upon him at his work, I daresay?

REGINA. I? Oh, of course, when I have time, I——

MANDERS. Your father is not a man of strong character, Miss Engstrand. He stands terribly in need of a guiding hand.

REGINA. Oh, yes; I daresay he does.

MANDERS. He requires some one near him whom he cares for, and whose judgment he respects. He frankly admitted as much when he last came to see me.

REGINA. Yes, he mentioned something of the sort to me. But I don't know whether Mrs. Alving can spare me; especially now that we've got the new Orphanage to attend to. And then I should be so sorry to leave Mrs. Alving; she has always been so kind to me.

MANDERS. But a daughter's duty, my good girl—— Of course, we should first have to get your mistress's consent.

REGINA. But I don't know whether it would be quite proper for me, at my age, to keep house for a single man.

MANDERS. What! My dear Miss Engstrand! When the man is your own father!

REGINA. Yes, that may be; but all the same—— Now, if it were in a thoroughly nice house, and with a real gentleman——

MANDERS. Why, my dear Regina——

REGINA. ——one I could love and respect, and be a daughter to——

MANDERS. Yes, but my dear, good child——

REGINA. Then I should be glad to go to town. It's very lonely out here; you know yourself, sir, what it is to be alone in the world. And I can assure you I'm both quick and willing. Don't you know of any such place for me, sir?

MANDERS. I? No, certainly not.

REGINA. But, dear, dear sir, do remember me if——

MANDERS. *[Rising.]* Yes, yes, certainly, Miss Engstrand.

REGINA. For if I——

MANDERS. Will you be so good as to tell your mistress I am here?

REGINA. I will, at once, sir.   *[She goes out to the left.]*

[Pastor Manders paces the room two or three times, stands a moment in the background with his hands behind his back, and looks out over the garden. Then he returns to the table, takes up a book, and looks at the title-page; starts, and looks at several books.]

MANDERS. Ha—indeed!

[Mrs. Alving enters by the door on the left; she is followed by Regina, who immediately goes out by the first door on the right.]

MRS. ALVING. *[Holds out her hand.]* Welcome, my dear Pastor.

MANDERS. How do you do, Mrs. Alving? Here I am as I promised.

MRS. ALVING. Always punctual to the minute. ˙

MANDERS. You may believe it was not so easy for me to get away. With all the Boards and Committees I belong to——

MRS. ALVING. That makes it all the kinder of you to come so early. Now we can get through our business before dinner. But where is your portmanteau?

MANDERS. *[Quickly.]* I left it down at the inn. I shall sleep there to-night.

MRS. ALVING. *[Suppressing a smile.]* Are you really not to be persuaded, even now, to pass the night under my roof?

MANDERS. No, no, Mrs. Alving; many thanks. I shall stay at the inn, as usual. It is so conveniently near the landing-stage.

MRS. ALVING. Well, you must have your own way. But I really should have thought we two old people——

MANDERS. Now you are making fun of me. Ah, you're naturally in great spirits to-day—what with to-morrow's festival and Oswald's return.

MRS. ALVING. Yes; you can think what a delight it is to me! It's more than two years since he was home last. And now he has promised to stay with me all the winter.

MANDERS. Has he really? That is very nice and dutiful of him. For I can well believe that life in Rome and Paris has very different attractions from any we can offer here.

MRS. ALVING. Ah, but here he has his mother, you see. My own darling boy—he hasn't forgotten his old mother!

MANDERS. It would be grievous indeed, if absence and absorption in art and that sort of thing were to blunt his natural feelings.

MRS. ALVING. Yes, you may well say so. But there's nothing of that sort to fear with him. I'm quite curious to see whether you know him again. He'll be down presently; he's upstairs just now, resting a little on the sofa. But do sit down, my dear Pastor.

MANDERS. Thank you. Are you quite at liberty——?

MRS. ALVING. Certainly.   *[She sits by the table.]*

MANDERS. Very well. Then let me show you——

[He goes to the chair where his travelling-bag lies, takes out a packet of papers, sits down on the opposite side of the table, and tries to find a clear space for the papers.]

Now, to begin with, here is—— *[Breaking off.]* Tell me, Mrs. Alving, how do these books come to be here?

MRS. ALVING. These books? They are books I am reading.

MANDERS. Do you read this sort of literature?

MRS. ALVING. Certainly I do.

MANDERS. Do you feel better or happier for such reading?

MRS. ALVING. I feel, so to speak, more secure.

MANDERS. That is strange. How do you mean?

MRS. ALVING. Well, I seem to find explanation and confirmation of all sorts of things I myself have been thinking. For that is the wonderful part of it, Pastor Manders—there is really nothing new in these books, nothing but what most people think and believe. Only most people either don't formulate it to themselves, or else keep quiet about it.

MANDERS. Great heavens! Do you really believe that most people——?

MRS. ALVING. I do, indeed.

MANDERS. But surely not in this country? Not here among us?

MRS. ALVING. Yes, certainly; here as elsewhere.

MANDERS. Well, I really must say——!

MRS. ALVING. For the rest, what do you object to in these books?

MANDERS. Object to in them? You surely do not suppose that I have nothing better to do than to study such publications as these?

MRS. ALVING. That is to say, you know nothing of what you are condemning?

MANDERS. I have read enough about these writings to disapprove of them.

MRS. ALVING. Yes; but your own judgment——

MANDERS. My dear Mrs. Alving, there are many occasions in life when one must rely upon others. Things are so ordered in this world; and it is well that they are. Otherwise, what would become of society?

MRS. ALVING. Well, well, I daresay you're right there.

MANDERS. Besides, I of course do not deny that there may be much that is attractive in such books. Nor can I blame you for wishing to keep up with the intellectual movements that are said to be going on in the great world—where you have let your son pass so much of his life. But——

MRS. ALVING. But?

MANDERS. [Lowering his voice.] But one should not talk about it, Mrs. Alving. One is certainly not bound to account to everybody for what one reads and thinks within one's own four walls.

MRS. ALVING. Of course not; I quite agree with you.

MANDERS. Only think, now, how you are bound to consider the interests of this Orphanage, which you decided on founding at a time when—if I understand you rightly—you thought very differently on spiritual matters.

MRS. ALVING. Oh, yes; I quite admit that. But it was about the Orphanage——

MANDERS. It was about the Orphanage we were to speak; yes. All I say is: prudence, my dear lady! And now let us get to business. [Opens the packet, and takes out a number of papers.] Do you see these?

MRS. ALVING. The documents?

MANDERS. All—and in perfect order. I can tell you it was hard work to get them in time. I had to put on strong pressure. The authorities are almost morbidly scrupulous when there is any decisive step to be taken. But here they are at last. [Looks through the bundle.] See! here is the formal deed of gift of the parcel of ground known as Solvik in the Manor of Rosenvold, with all the newly constructed buildings, schoolrooms, master's house, and chapel. And here is the legal fiat for the endowment and for the Bye-laws of the Institution. Will you look at them? [Reads.] "Bye-laws for the Children's Home to be known as 'Captain Alving's Foundation.'"

MRS. ALVING. [Looks long at the paper.] So there it is.

MANDERS. I have chosen the designation "Captain" rather than "Chamberlain." "Captain" looks less pretentious.

MRS. ALVING. Oh, yes; just as you think best.

MANDERS. And here you have the Bank Account of the capital lying at interest to cover the current expenses of the Orphanage.

MRS. ALVING. Thank you; but please keep it—it will be more convenient.

MANDERS. With pleasure. I think we will leave the money in the Bank for the present. The interest is certainly not what we could wish—four per cent, and six months' notice of withdrawal. If a good mortgage could be found later on—of course it must be a first mortgage and an unimpeachable security—then we could consider the matter.

MRS. ALVING. Certainly, my dear Pastor Manders. You are the best judge in these things.

MANDERS. I will keep my eyes open at any rate.—But now there is one thing more which I have several times been intending to ask you.

MRS. ALVING. And what is that?

MANDERS. Shall the Orphanage buildings be insured or not?

MRS. ALVING. Of course they must be insured.

MANDERS. Well, wait a moment, Mrs. Alving. Let us look into the matter a little more closely.

MRS. ALVING. I have everything insured; buildings and movables and stock and crops.

MANDERS. Of course you have—on your own estate. And so have I—of course. But here, you see, it is quite another matter. The Orphanage is to be consecrated, as it were, to a higher purpose.

MRS. ALVING. Yes, but that's no reason——

MANDERS. For my own part, I should certainly not see the smallest impropriety in guarding against all contingencies——

MRS. ALVING. No, I should think not.

MANDERS. But what is the general feeling in the neighbourhood? You, of course, know better than I.

MRS. ALVING. Well—the general feeling——

MANDERS. Is there any considerable number of people—really responsible people—who might be scandalised?

MRS. ALVING. What do you mean by "really responsible people"?

MANDERS. Well, I mean people in such independent and influential positions that one cannot help attaching some weight to their opinions.

MRS. ALVING. There are several people of that sort here, who would very likely be shocked if——

MANDERS. There, you see! In town we have many such people. Think of all my colleague's adherents! People would be only too ready to interpret our action as a sign that neither you nor I had the right faith in a Higher Providence.

MRS. ALVING. But for your own part, my dear Pastor, you can at least tell yourself that——

MANDERS. Yes, I know—I know; my conscience would be quite easy, that is true enough. But nevertheless we should not escape grave misinterpretation; and that might very likely react unfavourably upon the Orphanage.

MRS. ALVING. Well, in that case——

MANDERS. Nor can I entirely lose sight of the difficult—I may even say painful—position in which *I* might perhaps be placed. In the leading circles of the town, people take a lively interest in this Orphanage. It is, of course, founded partly for the benefit of the town, as well; and it is to be hoped it will, to a considerable extent, result in lightening our Poor Rates. Now, as I have been your adviser, and have had the business arrangements in my hands, I cannot but fear that I may have to bear the brunt of fanaticism——

MRS. ALVING. Oh, you mustn't run the risk of that.

MANDERS. To say nothing of the attacks that would assuredly be made upon me in certain papers and periodicals, which——

MRS. ALVING. Enough, my dear Pastor Manders. That consideration is quite decisive.

MANDERS. Then you do not wish the Orphanage to be insured?

MRS. ALVING. No. We will let it alone.

MANDERS. *[Leaning back in his chair.]* But if, now, a disaster were to happen? One can never tell—— Should you be able to make good the damage?

MRS. ALVING. No; I tell you plainly I should do nothing of the kind.

MANDERS. Then I must tell you, Mrs. Alving—we are taking no small responsibility upon ourselves.

MRS. ALVING. Do you think we can do otherwise?

MANDERS. No, that is just the point; we really cannot do otherwise. We ought not to expose ourselves to misinterpretation; and we have no right whatever to give offence to the weaker brethren.

MRS. ALVING. You, as a clergyman, certainly should not.

MANDERS. I really think, too, we may trust that such an institution has fortune on its side; in fact, that it stands under a special providence.

MRS. ALVING. Let us hope so, Pastor Manders.

MANDERS. Then we will let it take its chance?

MRS. ALVING. Yes, certainly.

MANDERS. Very well. So be it. *[Makes a note.]* Then—no insurance.

MRS. ALVING. It's odd that you should just happen to mention the matter to-day——

MANDERS. I have often thought of asking you about it——

MRS. ALVING. ——for we very nearly had a fire down there yesterday.

MANDERS. You don't say so!

MRS. ALVING. Oh, it was a trifling matter. A heap of shavings had caught fire in the carpenter's workshop.

MANDERS. Where Engstrand works?

MRS. ALVING. Yes. They say he's often very careless with matches.

MANDERS. He has so much on his mind, that man—so many things to fight against. Thank God, he is now striving to lead a decent life, I hear.

MRS. ALVING. Indeed! Who says so?

MANDERS. He himself assures me of it. And he is certainly a capital workman.

MRS. ALVING. Oh, yes; so long as he's sober——

MANDERS. Ah, that melancholy weakness! But he is often driven to it by his injured leg, he says. Last time he was in town I was really touched by him. He came and thanked me so warmly for having got him work here, so that he might be near Regina.

MRS. ALVING. He doesn't see much of her.

MANDERS. Oh, yes; he has a talk with her every day. He told me so himself.

MRS. ALVING. Well, it may be so.

MANDERS. He feels so acutely that he needs some one to keep a firm hold on him when temptation comes. That is what I cannot help liking about Jacob Engstrand: he comes to you so helplessly, accusing himself and confessing his own weakness. The last time he was talking to me—— Believe me, Mrs. Alving, supposing it were a real necessity for him to have Regina home again——

MRS. ALVING. [Rising hastily.] Regina!

MANDERS. ——you must not set yourself against it.

MRS. ALVING. Indeed I shall set myself against it. And besides —Regina is to have a position in the Orphanage.

MANDERS. But, after all, remember he is her father——

MRS. ALVING. Oh, I know very well what sort of a father he has been to her. No! She shall never *go* to him with my goodwill.

MANDERS. [Rising.] My dear lady, don't take the matter so warmly. You sadly misjudge poor Engstrand. You seem to be quite terrified——

MRS. ALVING. [More quietly.] It makes no difference. I have taken Regina into my house, and there she shall stay. [Listens.] Hush, my dear Mr. Manders; say no more about it. [Her face lights up with gladness.] Listen! there is Oswald coming downstairs. Now we'll think of no one but him.

[Oswald Alving, in a light overcoat, hat in hand, and smoking a large meerschaum, enters by the door on the left; he stops in the doorway.]

OSWALD. Oh, I beg your pardon; I thought you were in the study. [Comes forward.] Good-morning, Pastor Manders.

MANDERS. [Staring.] Ah——! How strange——!

MRS. ALVING. Well now, what do you think of him, Mr. Manders?

MANDERS. I—I—can it really be——?

OSWALD. Yes, it's really the Prodigal Son, sir.

MANDERS. [Protesting.] My dear young friend——

OSWALD. Well, then, the Lost Sheep Found.

MRS. ALVING. Oswald is thinking of the time when you were so much opposed to his becoming a painter.

MANDERS. To our human eyes many a step seems dubious, which afterwards proves—— [Wrings his hand.] But first of all, welcome,

welcome home! Do not think, my dear Oswald—I suppose I may call you by your Christian name?

OSWALD. What else should you call me?

MANDERS. Very good. What I wanted to say was this, my dear Oswald—you must not think that I utterly condemn the artist's calling. I have no doubt there are many who can keep their inner self unharmed in that profession, as in any other.

OSWALD. Let us hope so.

MRS. ALVING. [Beaming with delight.] I know one who has kept both his inner and his outer self unharmed. Just look at him, Mr. Manders.

OSWALD. [Moves restlessly about the room.] Yes, yes, my dear mother; let's say no more about it.

MANDERS. Why, certainly—that is undeniable. And you have begun to make a name for yourself already. The newspapers have often spoken of you, most favourably. Just lately, by-the-bye, I fancy I haven't seen your name quite so often.

OSWALD. [Up in the conservatory.] I haven't been able to paint so much lately.

MRS. ALVING. Even a painter needs a little rest now and then.

MANDERS. No doubt, no doubt. And meanwhile he can be preparing himself and mustering his forces for some great work.

OSWALD. Yes.—Mother, will dinner soon by ready?

MRS. ALVING. In less than half an hour. He has a capital appetite, thank God.

MANDERS. And a taste for tobacco, too.

OSWALD. I found my father's pipe in my room——

MANDERS. Aha—then that accounts for it!

MRS. ALVING. For what?

MANDERS. When Oswald appeared there, in the doorway, with the pipe in his mouth, I could have sworn I saw his father, large as life.

OSWALD. No, really?

MRS. ALVING. Oh, how can you say so? Oswald takes after me.

MANDERS. Yes, but there is an expression about the corners of the mouth—something about the lips—that reminds one exactly of Alving; at any rate, now that he is smoking.

MRS. ALVING. Not in the least. Oswald has rather a clerical curve about his mouth, I think.

MANDERS. Yes, yes; some of my colleagues have much the same expression.

MRS. ALVING. But put your pipe away, my dear boy; I won't have smoking in here.

OSWALD. [Does so.] By all means. I only wanted to try it; for I once smoked it when I was a child.

MRS. ALVING. You?

OSWALD. Yes. I was quite small at the time. I recollect I came up to father's room one evening when he was in great spirits.

MRS. ALVING. Oh, you can't recollect anything of those times.

OSWALD. Yes, I recollect it distinctly. He took me on his knee, and gave me the pipe. "Smoke, boy," he said; "smoke away, boy!" And I smoked as hard as I could, until I felt I was growing quite pale, and the perspiration stood in great drops on my forehead. Then he burst out laughing heartily——

MANDERS. That was most extraordinary.

MRS. ALVING. My dear friend, it's only something Oswald has dreamt.

OSWALD. No, mother, I assure you I didn't dream it. For—don't you remember this?—you came and carried me out into the nursery. Then I was sick, and I saw that you were crying.—Did father often play such practical jokes?

MANDERS. In his youth he overflowed with the joy of life——

OSWALD. And yet he managed to do so much in the world; so much that was good and useful; although he died so early.

MANDERS. Yes, you have inherited the name of an energetic and admirable man, my dear Oswald Alving. No doubt it will be an incentive to you——

OSWALD. It ought to, indeed.

MANDERS. It was good of you to come home for the ceremony in his honour.

OSWALD. I could do no less for my father.

MRS. ALVING. And I am to keep him so long! That is the best of all.

MANDERS. You are going to pass the winter at home, I hear.

OSWALD. My stay is indefinite, sir.—But, ah! it is good to be at home!

MRS. ALVING. [Beaming.] Yes, isn't it, dear?

MANDERS. [Looking sympathetically at him.] You went out into the world early, my dear Oswald.

OSWALD. I did. I sometimes wonder whether it wasn't too early.

MRS. ALVING. Oh, not at all. A healthy lad is all the better for it; especially when he's an only child. He oughtn't to hang on at home with his mother and father, and get spoilt.

MANDERS. That is a very disputable point, Mrs. Alving. A child's proper place is, and must be, the home of his fathers.

OSWALD. There I quite agree with you, Pastor Manders.

MANDERS. Only look at your own son—there is no reason why we should not say it in his presence—what has the consequence been for him? He is six or seven and twenty, and has never had the opportunity of learning what a well-ordered home really is.

OSWALD. I beg your pardon, Pastor; there you're quite mistaken.

MANDERS. Indeed? I thought you had lived almost exclusively in artistic circles.

OSWALD. So I have.

MANDERS. And chiefly among the younger artists?

OSWALD. Yes, certainly.

MANDERS. But I thought few of those young fellows could afford to set up house and support a family.

OSWALD. There are many who cannot afford to marry, sir.

MANDERS. Yes, that is just what I say.

OSWALD. But they may have a home for all that. And several of them have, as a matter of fact; and very pleasant, well-ordered homes they are, too.

[Mrs. Alving follows with breathless interest; nods, but says nothing.]

MANDERS. But I'm not talking of bachelors' quarters. By a "home" I understand the home of a family, where a man lives with his wife and children.

OSWALD. Yes; or with his children and his children's mother.

MANDERS. *[Starts; clasps his hands.]* But, good heavens——

OSWALD. Well?

MANDERS. Lives with—his children's mother!

OSWALD. Yes. Would you have him turn his children's mother out of doors?

MANDERS. Then it is illicit relations you are talking of! Irregular marriages, as people call them!

OSWALD. I have never noticed anything particularly irregular about the life these people lead.

MANDERS. But how is it possible that a—a young man or young woman with any decency of feeling can endure to live in that way? —in the eyes of all the world!

OSWALD. What are they to do? A poor young artist—a poor girl— marriage costs a great deal. What are they to do?

MANDERS. What are they to do? Let me tell you, Mr. Alving, what they ought to do. They ought to exercise self-restraint from the first; that is what they ought to do.

OSWALD. That doctrine will scarcely go down with warmblooded young people who love each other.

MRS. ALVING. No, scarcely!

MANDERS. *[Continuing.]* How can the authorities tolerate such things! Allow them to go on in the light of day! *[Confronting Mrs. Alving.]* Had I not cause to be deeply concerned about your son? In circles where open immorality prevails, and has even a sort of recognised position——!

OSWALD.. Let me tell you, sir, that I have been in the habit of spending nearly all my Sundays in one or two such irregular homes——

MANDERS. Sunday of all days!

OSWALD. Isn't that the day to enjoy one's self? Well, never have I heard an offensive word, and still less have I witnessed anything that could be called immoral. No; do you know when and where I have come across immorality in artistic circles?

MANDERS. No, thank heaven, I don't!

OSWALD. Well, then, allow me to inform you. I have met with it when one or other of our pattern husbands and fathers has come to Paris to have a look round on his own account, and has done the artists the honour of visiting their humble haunts. They knew what was what. These gentlemen could tell us all about places and things we had never dreamt of.

MANDERS. What! Do you mean to say that respectable men from here would——?

OSWALD. Have you never heard these respectable men, when they got home again, talking about the way in which immorality runs rampant abroad?

MANDERS. Yes, no doubt——

MRS. ALVING. I have too.

OSWALD. Well, you may take their word for it. They know what they are talking about! [*Presses his hands to his head.*] Oh! that that great, free, glorious life out there should be defiled in such a way!

MRS. ALVING. You mustn't get excited, Oswald. It's not good for you.

OSWALD. Yes; you're quite right, mother. It's bad for me, I know. You see, I'm wretchedly worn out. I shall go for a little turn before dinner. Excuse me, Pastor: I know you can't take my point of view; but I couldn't help speaking out.

[*He goes out by the second door to the right.*]

MRS. ALVING. My poor boy!

MANDERS. You may well say so. Then this is what he has come to! [*Mrs. Alving looks at him silently.*]

MANDERS. [*Walking up and down.*] He called himself the Prodigal Son. Alas! alas! [*Mrs. Alving continues looking at him.*]

MANDERS. And what do you say to all this?

MRS. ALVING. I say that Oswald was right in every word.

MANDERS. [*Stands still.*] Right? Right! In such principles?

MRS. ALVING. Here, in my loneliness, I have come to the same way of thinking, Pastor Manders. But I have never dared to say anything. Well! now my boy shall speak for me.

MANDERS. You are greatly to be pitied, Mrs. Alving. But now I must speak seriously to you. And now it is no longer your business manager and adviser, your own and your husband's early friend, who stands before you. It is the priest—the priest who stood before you in the moment of your life when you had gone farthest astray.

MRS. ALVING. And what has the priest to say to me?

MANDERS. I will first stir up your memory a little. The moment is well chosen. To-morrow will be the tenth anniversary of your husband's death. To-morrow the memorial in his honour will be unveiled. To-morrow I shall have to speak to the whole assembled multitude. But to-day I will speak to you alone.

MRS. ALVING. Very well, Pastor Manders. Speak.

MANDERS. Do you remember that after less than a year of married life you stood on the verge of an abyss? That you forsook your house and home? That you fled from your husband? Yes, Mrs. Alving—fled, fled, and refused to return to him, however much he begged and prayed you?

MRS. ALVING. Have you forgotten how infinitely miserable I was in that first year?

MANDERS. It is the very mark of the spirit of rebellion to crave for happiness in this life. What right have we human beings to happiness? We have simply to do our duty, Mrs. Alving! And your duty was to hold firmly to the man you had once chosen, and to whom you were bound by the holiest ties.

MRS. ALVING. You know very well what sort of life Alving was leading—what excesses he was guilty of.

MANDERS. I know very well what rumours there were about him; and I am the last to approve the life he led in his young days, if report did not wrong him. But a wife is not appointed to be her husband's judge. It was your duty to bear with humility the cross which a Higher Power had, in its wisdom, laid upon you. But instead of that you rebelliously throw away the cross, desert the backslider whom you should have supported, go and risk your good name and reputation, and—nearly succeed in ruining other people's reputation into the bargain.

MRS. ALVING. Other people's? One other person's, you mean.

MANDERS. It was incredibly reckless of you to seek refuge with me.

MRS. ALVING. With our clergyman? With our intimate friend?

MANDERS. Just on that account. Yes, you may thank God that I possessed the necessary firmness; that I succeeded in dissuading you from your wild designs; and that it was vouchsafed me to lead you back to the path of duty, and home to your lawful husband.

MRS. ALVING. Yes, Pastor Manders, that was certainly your work.

MANDERS. I was but a poor instrument in a Higher Hand. And what a blessing has it not proved to you, all the days of your life, that I induced you to resume the yoke of duty and obedience! Did not everything happen as I foretold? Did not Alving turn his back on his errors, as a man should? Did he not live with you from that time, lovingly and blamelessly all his days? Did he not become a benefactor to the whole district? And did he not help you to rise to his own level, so that you, little by little, became his assistant in all his undertakings? And a capital assistant, too—oh, I know, Mrs. Alving, that praise is due to you.—But now I come to the next great error in your life.

MRS. ALVING. What do you mean?

MANDERS. Just as you once disowned a wife's duty, so you have since disowned a mother's.

MRS. ALVING. Ah——!

MANDERS. You have been all your life under the dominion of a pestilent spirit of self-will. The whole bias of your mind has been towards insubordination and lawlessness. You have never known how to endure any bond. Everything that has weighed upon you in life you have cast away without care or conscience, like a burden you were free to throw off at will. It did not please you to be a wife any longer, and you left your husband. You found it troublesome to be a mother, and you sent your child forth among strangers.

MRS. ALVING. Yes, that is true. I did so.

MANDERS. And thus you have become a stranger to him.

MRS. ALVING. No! no! I am not.

MANDERS. Yes, you are; you must be. And in what state of mind has he returned to you? Bethink yourself well, Mrs. Alving. You sinned greatly against your husband;—that you recognise by raising yonder memorial to him. Recognise now, also, how you have sinned against your son—there may yet be time to lead him back from the paths of error. Turn back yourself, and save what may yet be saved in him. For *[With uplifted forefinger.]* verily, Mrs. Alving, you are a guilt-laden mother!—This I have thought it my duty to say to you.   *[Silence.]*

MRS. ALVING. *[Slowly and with self-control.]* You have now spoken out, Pastor Manders; and to-morrow you are to speak publicly in memory of my husband. I shall not speak to-morrow. But now I will speak frankly to you, as you have spoken to me.

MANDERS. To be sure; you will plead excuses for your conduct——

MRS. ALVING. No. I will only tell you a story.

MANDERS. Well——?

MRS. ALVING. All that you have just said about my husband and me, and our life after you had brought me back to the path of duty—as you called it—about all that you know nothing from personal observation. From that moment you, who had been our intimate friend, never set foot in our house again.

MANDERS. You and your husband left the town immediately after.

MRS. ALVING. Yes; and in my husband's lifetime you never came to see us. It was business that forced you to visit me when you undertook the affairs of the Orphanage.

MANDERS. *[Softly and hesitatingly.]* Helen—if that is meant as a reproach, I would beg you to bear in mind——

MRS. ALVING. ——the regard you owed to your position, yes; and that I was a runaway wife. One can never be too cautious with such unprincipled creatures.

MANDERS. My dear—Mrs. Alving, you know that is an absurd exaggeration——

MRS. ALVING. Well well, suppose it is. My point is that your judgment as to my married life is founded upon nothing but common knowledge and report.

MANDERS. I admit that. What then?

MRS. ALVING. Well, then, Pastor Manders—I will tell you the truth. I have sworn to myself that one day you should know it— you alone!

MANDERS. What is the truth, then?

MRS. ALVING. The truth is that my husband died just as dissolute as he had lived all his days.

MANDERS. *[Feeling after a chair.]* What do you say?

MRS. ALVING. After nineteen years of marriage, as dissolute—in his desires at any rate—as he was before you married us.

MANDERS. And those—those wild oats—those irregularities— those excesses, if you like—you call "a dissolute life"?

MRS. ALVING. Our doctor used the expression.

MANDERS. I do not understand you.

MRS. ALVING. You need not.

MANDERS. It almost makes me dizzy. Your whole married life, the seeming union of all these years, was nothing more than a hidden abyss!

MRS. ALVING. Neither more nor less. Now you know it.

MANDERS. This is—this is inconceivable to me. I cannot grasp it! I cannot realise it! But how was it possible to——? How could such a state of things be kept secret?

MRS. ALVING. That has been my ceaseless struggle, day after day. After Oswald's birth, I thought Alving seemed to be a little better. But it did not last long. And then I had to struggle twice as hard, fighting as though for life or death, so that nobody should know what sort of man my child's father was. And you know that power Alving had of winning people's hearts. Nobody seemed able to believe anything but good of him. He was one of those people whose life does not bite upon their reputation. But at last, Mr. Manders— for you must know the whole story—the most repulsive thing of all happened.

MANDERS. More repulsive than what you have told me!

MRS. ALVING. I had gone on bearing with him, although I knew very well the secrets of his life out of doors. But when he brought the scandal within our own walls——

MANDERS. Impossible! Here!

MRS. ALVING. Yes; here in our own home. It was there, *[Pointing towards the first door on the right.]* in the dining-room, that I first came to know of it. I was busy with something in there, and the door was standing ajar. I heard our housemaid come up from the garden, with water for those flowers.

MANDERS. Well——?

MRS. ALVING. Soon after, I heard Alving come in too. I heard him say something softly to her. And then I heard— *[With a short laugh.]* —oh! it still sounds in my ears, so hateful and yet so ludicrous—I heard my own servant-maid whisper, "Let me go, Mr. Alving! Let me be!"

MANDERS. What unseemly levity on his part! But it cannot have been more than levity, Mrs. Alving; believe me, it cannot.

MRS. ALVING. I soon knew what to believe. Mr. Alving had his way with the girl; and that connection had consequences, Mr. Manders.

MANDERS. *[As though petrified.]* Such things in this house; in this house!

MRS. ALVING. I had borne a great deal in this house. To keep him at home in the evenings, and at night, I had to make myself his boon companion in his secret orgies up in his room. There I have had to sit alone with him, to clink glasses and drink with him, and to listen to his ribald, silly talk. I have had to fight with him to get him dragged to bed——

MANDERS. *[Moved.]* And you were able to bear all this!

MRS. ALVING. I had to bear it for my little boy's sake. But when the last insult was added; when my own servant-maid——; then I swore to myself: This shall come to an end! And so I took the reins into my own hand—the whole control—over him and everything else. For now I had a weapon against him, you see; he dared not oppose me. It was then I sent Oswald away from home. He was nearly seven years old, and was beginning to observe and ask questions, as children do. That I could not bear. It seemed to me the child must be poisoned by merely breathing the air of this polluted home. That was why I sent him away. And now you can see, too, why he was never allowed to set foot inside his home so long as his father lived. No one knows what that cost me.

MANDERS. You have indeed had a life of trial.

MRS. ALVING. I could never have borne it if I had not had my work. For I may truly say that I have worked! All the additions to the estate—all the improvements—all the labour-saving appliances, that Alving was so much praised for having introduced—do you suppose he had energy for anything of the sort?—he, who lay all day on the sofa, reading an old Court Guide! No; but I may tell you this too: when he had his better intervals, it was I who urged him on; it was I who had to drag the whole load when he relapsed into his evil ways, or sank into querulous wretchedness.

MANDERS. And it is to this man that you raise a memorial?

MRS. ALVING. There you see the power of an evil conscience.

MANDERS. Evil——? What do you mean?

MRS. ALVING. It always seemed to me impossible but that the truth must come out and be believed. So the Orphanage was to deaden all rumours and set every doubt at rest.

MANDERS. In that you have certainly not missed your aim, Mrs. Alving.

MRS. ALVING. And besides, I had one other reason. I was determined that Oswald, my own boy, should inherit nothing whatever from his father.

MANDERS. Then it is Alving's fortune that——?

MRS. ALVING. Yes. The sums I have spent upon the Orphanage, year by year, make up the amount—I have reckoned it up precisely— the amount which made Lieutenant Alving "a good match" in his day.

MANDERS. I don't understand——

MRS. ALVING. It was my purchase-money. I do not choose that that money should pass into Oswald's hands. My son shall have everything from me—everything.

[Oswald Alving enters through the second door to the right; he has taken off his hat and overcoat in the hall.]

MRS. ALVING. *[Going towards him.]* Are you back again already? My dear, dear boy!

OSWALD. Yes. What can a fellow do out of doors in this eternal rain? But I hear dinner is ready. That's capital!

REGINA. *[With a parcel, from the dining-room.]* A parcel has come for you, Mrs. Alving.   *[Hands it to her.]*

MRS. ALVING. *[With a glance at Mr. Manders.]* No doubt copies of the ode for to-morrow's ceremony.

MANDERS. H'm——

REGINA. And dinner is ready.

MRS. ALVING. Very well. We will come directly. I will just——
                              [Begins to open the parcel.]

REGINA. *[To Oswald.]* Would Mr. Alving like red or white wine?

OSWALD. Both, if you please.

REGINA. *Bien.* Very well, sir.   *[She goes into the dining-room.]*

OSWALD. I may as well help to uncork it.

[He also goes into the dining-room, the door of which swings half open behind him.]

MRS. ALVING. *[Who has opened the parcel.]* Yes, I thought so. Here is the Ceremonial Ode, Pastor Manders.

MANDERS. *[With folded hands.]* With what countenance I am to deliver my discourse to-morrow——!

MRS. ALVING. Oh, you will get through it somehow.

MANDERS. *[Softly, so as not to be heard in the dining-room.]* Yes; it would not do to provoke scandal.

MRS. ALVING. *[Under her breath, but firmly.]* No. But then this long, hateful comedy will be ended. From the day after to-morrow, I shall act in every way as though he who is dead had never lived in this house. There shall be no one here but my boy and his mother.

[From the dining-room comes the noise of a chair overturned, and at the same moment is heard:]

REGINA. *[Sharply, but in a whisper.]* Oswald! take care! are you mad? Let me go!

MRS. ALVING. *[Starts in terror.]* Ah——!

[She stares wildly towards the half-open door. Oswald is heard laughing and humming. A bottle is uncorked.]

MANDERS. *[Agitated.]* What can be the matter? What is it, Mrs. Alving?

MRS. ALVING. *[Hoarsely.]* Ghosts! The couple from the conservatory—risen again!

MANDERS. Is it possible! Regina——? Is she——?

MRS. ALVING. Yes. Come. Not a word——!

[She seizes Pastor Manders by the arm, and walks unsteadily towards the dining-room.]

CURTAIN

ACT 2

The same room. The mist still lies heavy over the landscape. Manders and Mrs. Alving enter from the dining-room.

MRS. ALVING. *[Still in the doorway.]* Velbekomme,[1] Mr. Manders. *[Turns back towards the dining-room.]* Aren't you coming too, Oswald?

OSWALD. *[From within.]* No, thank you. I think I shall go out a little.

MRS. ALVING. Yes, do. The weather seems a little brighter now. *[She shuts the dining-room door, goes to the hall door, and calls:]* Regina!

REGINA. *[Outside.]* Yes, Mrs. Alving?

MRS. ALVING. Go down to the laundry, and help with the garlands.

REGINA. Yes, Mrs. Alving.

[Mrs. Alving assures herself that Regina goes; then shuts the door.]

MANDERS. I suppose he cannot overhear us in there?

MRS. ALVING. Not when the door is shut. Besides, he's just going out.

MANDERS. I am still quite upset. I don't know how I could swallow a morsel of dinner.

MRS. ALVING. *[Controlling her nervousness, walks up and down.]*

1 *Velbekomme:* a courteous expression, which may be translated "May good digestion wait on appetite."

Nor I. But what is to be done now?

MANDERS. Yes; what is to be done? I am really quite at a loss. I am so utterly without experience in matters of this sort.

MRS. ALVING. I feel sure that, so far, no mischief has been done.

MANDERS. No; heaven forbid! But it is an unseemly state of things, nevertheless.

MRS. ALVING. It is only an idle fancy on Oswald's part; you may be sure of that.

MANDERS. Well, as I say, I am not accustomed to affairs of the kind. But I should certainly think——

MRS. ALVING. Out of the house she must go, and that immediately. That is as clear as daylight——

MANDERS. Yes, of course she must.

MRS. ALVING. But where to? It would not be right to——

MANDERS. Where to? Home to her father, of course.

MRS. ALVING. To whom did you say?

MANDERS. To her—— But then, Engstrand is not——? Good God, Mrs. Alving, it's impossible! You must be mistaken after all.

MRS. ALVING. Unfortunately there is no possibility of mistake. Johanna confessed everything to me; and Alving could not deny it. So there was nothing to be done but to get the matter hushed up.

MANDERS. No, you could do nothing else.

MRS. ALVING. The girl left our service at once, and got a good sum of money to hold her tongue for the time. The rest she managed for herself when she got to town. She renewed her old acquaintance with Engstrand, no doubt let him see that she had money in her purse, and told him some tale about a foreigner who put in here with a yacht that summer. So she and Engstrand got married in hot haste. Why, you married them yourself.

MANDERS. But then how to account for——? I recollect distinctly Engstrand coming to give notice of the marriage. He was quite overwhelmed with contrition, and bitterly reproached himself for the misbehaviour he and his sweetheart had been guilty of.

MRS. ALVING. Yes; of course he had to take the blame upon himself.

MANDERS. But such a piece of duplicity on his part! And towards me too! I never could have believed it of Jacob Engstrand. I shall not fail to take him seriously to task; he may be sure of that.—And then the immorality of such a connection! For money——! How much did the girl receive?

MRS. ALVING. Three hundred dollars.

MANDERS. Just think of it—for a miserable three hundred dollars, to go and marry a fallen woman!

MRS. ALVING. Then what have you to say of me? I went and married a fallen man.

MANDERS. Why—good heavens!—what are you talking about! A fallen man!

MRS. ALVING. Do you think Alving was any purer when I went with him to the altar than Johanna was when Engstrand married her?

MANDERS. Well, but there is a world of difference between the two cases——

MRS. ALVING. Not so much difference after all—except in the price:—a miserable three hundred dollars and a whole fortune.

MANDERS. How can you compare such absolutely dissimilar cases? You had taken counsel with your own heart and with your natural advisers.

MRS. ALVING. *[Without looking at him.]* I thought you understood where what you call my heart had strayed to at the time.

MANDERS. *[Distantly.]* Had I understood anything of the kind, I should not have been a daily guest in your husband's house.

MRS. ALVING. At any rate, the fact remains that with myself I took no counsel whatever.

MANDERS. Well then, with your nearest relatives—as your duty bade you—with your mother and your two aunts.

MRS. ALVING. Yes, that is true. Those three cast up the account for me. Oh, it's marvellous how clearly they made out that it would be downright madness to refuse such an offer. If mother could only see me now, and know what all that grandeur has come to!

MANDERS. Nobody can be held responsible for the result. This, at least, remains clear: your marriage was in full accordance with law and order.

MRS. ALVING. *[At the window.]* Oh, that perpetual law and order! I often think that is what does all the mischief in this world of ours.

MANDERS. Mrs. Alving, that is a sinful way of talking.

MRS. ALVING. Well, I can't help it; I must have done with all this constraint and insincerity. I can endure it no longer. I must work my way out to freedom.

MANDERS. What do you mean by that?

MRS. ALVING. *[Drumming on the window-frame.]* I ought never to have concealed the facts of Alving's life. But at that time I dared not do anything else—I was afraid, partly on my own account. I was such a coward.

MANDERS. A coward?

MRS. ALVING. If people had come to know anything, they would have said—"Poor man! with a runaway wife, no wonder he kicks over the traces."

MANDERS. Such remarks might have been made with a certain show of right.

MRS. ALVING. *[Looking steadily at him.]* If I were what I ought to be, I should go to Oswald and say, "Listen, my boy: your father led a vicious life——"

MANDERS. Merciful heavens——!

MRS. ALVING. ——and then I should tell him all I have told you— every word of it.

MANDERS. You shock me unspeakably, Mrs. Alving.

MRS. ALVING. Yes; I know that. I know that very well. I myself am shocked at the idea. *[Goes away from the window.]* I am such a coward.

MANDERS. You call it "cowardice" to do your plain duty? Have you forgotten that a son ought to love and honour his father and mother?

MRS. ALVING. Do not let us talk in such general terms. Let us ask: Ought Oswald to love and honour Chamberlain Alving?

MANDERS. Is there no voice in your mother's heart that forbids you to destroy your son's ideals?

MRS. ALVING. But what about the truth?

MANDERS. But what about the ideals?

MRS. ALVING. Oh—ideals, ideals! If only I were not such a coward!

MANDERS. Do not despise ideals, Mrs. Alving; they will avenge themselves cruelly. Take Oswald's case: he, unfortunately, seems to have few enough ideals as it is; but I can see that his father stands before him as an ideal.

MRS. ALVING. Yes, that is true.

MANDERS. And this habit of mind you have yourself implanted and fostered by your letters.

MRS. ALVING. Yes; in my superstitious awe for duty and the proprieties, I lied to my boy, year after year. Oh, what a coward— what a coward I have been!

MANDERS. You have established a happy illusion in your son's heart, Mrs. Alving; and assuredly you ought not to undervalue it.

MRS. ALVING. H'm; who knows whether it is so happy after all——? But, at any rate, I will not have any tampering with Regina. He shall not go and wreck the poor girl's life.

MANDERS. No; good God—that would be terrible!

MRS. ALVING. If I knew he was in earnest, and that it would be for his happiness——

MANDERS. What? What then?

MRS. ALVING. But it couldn't be; for unfortunately Regina is not the right sort of woman.

MANDERS. Well, what then? What do you mean?

MRS. ALVING. If I weren't such a pitiful coward, I should say to him, "Marry her, or make what arrangement you please, only let us have nothing underhand about it."

MANDERS. Merciful heavens, would you let them marry! Anything so dreadful——! so unheard of——

MRS. ALVING. Do you really mean "unheard of"? Frankly, Pastor Manders, do you suppose that throughout the country there are not plenty of married couples as closely akin as they?

MANDERS. I don't in the least understand you.

MRS. ALVING. Oh yes, indeed you do.

MANDERS. Ah, you are thinking of the possibility that——Alas! yes, family life is certainly not always so pure as it ought to be. But in such a case as you point to, one can never know—at least with any certainty. Here, on the other hand—that you, a mother, can think of letting your son——!

MRS. ALVING. But I cannot—I wouldn't for anything in the world; that is precisely what I am saying.

MANDERS. No, because you are a "coward," as you put it. But if you were not a "coward," then——? Good God! a connection so shocking!

MRS. ALVING. So far as that goes, they say we are all sprung from connections of that sort. And who is it that arranged the world so, Pastor Manders?

MANDERS. Questions of that kind I must decline to discuss with you, Mrs. Alving; you are far from being in the right frame of mind for them. But that you dare to call your scruples "cowardly"——!

MRS. ALVING. Let me tell you what I mean. I am timid and faint-hearted because of the ghosts that hang about me, and that I can never quite shake off.

MANDERS. What do you say hangs about you?

MRS. ALVING. Ghosts! When I heard Regina and Oswald in there, it was as though ghosts rose up before me. But I almost think we are all of us ghosts, Pastor Manders. It is not only what we have inherited from our father and mother that "walks" in us. It is all sorts of dead ideas, and lifeless old beliefs, and so forth. They have no vitality, but they cling to us all the same, and we cannot shake them off. Whenever I take up a newspaper, I seem to see ghosts gliding between the lines. There must be ghosts all the country over, as thick as the sands of the sea. And then we are, one and all, so piti-fully afraid of the light.

MANDERS. Aha—here we have the fruits of your reading. And pretty fruits they are, upon my word! Oh, those horrible, revolu-tionary, freethinking books!

MRS. ALVING. You are mistaken, my dear Pastor. It was you your-self who set me thinking; and I thank you for it with all my heart.

MANDERS. I!

MRS. ALVING. Yes—when you forced me under the yoke of what you called duty and obligation; when you lauded as right and proper what my whole soul rebelled against as something loathsome. It was then that I began to look into the seams of your doctrines. I wanted only to pick at a single knot; but when I had got that undone, the whole thing ravelled out. And then I understood that it was all machine-sewn.

MANDERS. [Softly, with emotion.] And was that the upshot of my life's hardest battle?

MRS. ALVING. Call it rather your most pitiful defeat.

MANDERS. It was my greatest victory, Helen—the victory over myself.

MRS. ALVING. It was a crime against us both.

MANDERS. When you went astray, and came to me crying, "Here I am; take me!" I commanded you, saying, "Woman, go home to your lawful husband." Was that a crime?

MRS. ALVING. Yes, I think so.

MANDERS. We two do not understand each other.

MRS. ALVING. Not now, at any rate.

MANDERS. Never—never in my most secret thoughts have I regarded you otherwise than as another's wife.

MRS. ALVING. Oh—indeed?

MANDERS. Helen——!

MRS. ALVING. People so easily forget their past selves.

MANDERS. I do not. I am what I always was.

MRS. ALVING. [Changing the subject.] Well well well; don't let us talk of old times any longer. You are now over head and ears in Boards and Committees, and I am fighting my battle with ghosts, both within me and without.

MANDERS. Those without I shall help you to lay. After all the terrible things I have heard from you today, I cannot in conscience permit an unprotected girl to remain in your house.

MRS. ALVING. Don't you think the best plan would be to get her provided for?—I mean, by a good marriage.

MANDERS. No doubt. I think it would be desirable for her in every respect. Regina is now at the age when—— Of course I don't know much about these things, but——

MRS. ALVING. Regina matured very early.

MANDERS. Yes, I thought so. I have an impression that she was remarkably well developed, physically, when I prepared her for confirmation. But in the meantime, she ought to be at home, under her father's eye—— Ah! but Engstrand is not—— That he—that he—could so hide the truth from me!   [A knock at the door.]

MRS. ALVING. Who can this be? Come in!

ENGSTRAND. [In his Sunday clothes, in the doorway.] I humbly beg your pardon, but——

MANDERS. Aha! H'm——

MRS. ALVING. Is that you, Engstrand?

ENGSTRAND. ——there was none of the servants about, so I took the great liberty of just knocking.

MRS. ALVING. Oh, very well. Come in. Do you want to speak to me?

ENGSTRAND. [Comes in.] No, I'm obliged to you, ma'am; it was with his Reverence I wanted to have a word or two.

MANDERS. [Walking up and down the room.] Ah—indeed! You want to speak to me, do you?

ENGSTRAND. Yes, I'd like so terrible much to——

MANDERS. [Stops in front of him.] Well; may I ask what you want?

ENGSTRAND. Well, it was just this, your Reverence: we've been paid off down yonder—my grateful thanks to you, ma'am,—and now everything's finished, I've been thinking it would be but right and proper if we, that have been working so honestly together all this time—well, I was thinking we ought to end up with a little prayer-meeting to-night.

MANDERS. A prayer-meeting? Down at the Orphanage?

ENGSTRAND. Oh, if your Reverence doesn't think it proper——

MANDERS. Oh yes, I do; but—h'm—

ENGSTRAND. I've been in the habit of offering up a little prayer in the evenings, myself——

MRS. ALVING. Have you?

ENGSTRAND. Yes, every now and then—just a little edification, in a manner of speaking. But I'm a poor, common man, and have little enough gift, God help me!—and so I thought, as the Reverend Mr. Manders happened to be here, I'd——

MANDERS. Well, you see, Engstrand, I have a question to put to you first. Are you in the right frame of mind for such a meeting! Do you feel your conscience clear and at ease?

ENGSTRAND. Oh, God help us, your Reverence! we'd better not talk about conscience.

MANDERS. Yes, that is just what we must talk about. What have you to answer?

ENGSTRAND. Why—a man's conscience—it can be bad enough now and then.

MANDERS. Ah, you admit that. Then perhaps you will make a clean breast of it, and tell me—the real truth about Regina?

MRS. ALVING. [Quickly.] Mr. Manders!

MANDERS. [Reassuringly.] Please allow me——

ENGSTRAND. About Regina! Lord, what a turn you gave me! [Looks at Mrs. Alving.] There's nothing wrong about Regina, is there?

MANDERS. We will hope not. But I mean, what is the truth about you and Regina? You pass for her father, eh!

ENGSTRAND. [Uncertain.] Well—h'm—your Reverence knows all about me and poor Johanna.

MANDERS. Come now, no more prevarication! Your wife told Mrs. Alving the whole story before quitting her service.

ENGSTRAND. Well, then, may——! Now, did she really?

MANDERS. You see we know you now, Engstrand.

ENGSTRAND. And she swore and took her Bible oath——

MANDERS. Did she take her Bible oath?

ENGSTRAND. No; she only swore; but she did it that solemnlike.

MANDERS. And you have hidden the truth from me all these years?

Hidden it from me, who have trusted you without reserve, in everything.

ENGSTRAND. Well, I can't deny it.

MANDERS. Have I deserved this of you, Engstrand? Have I not always been ready to help you in word and deed, so far as it lay in my power? Answer me. Have I not?

ENGSTRAND. It would have been a poor look-out for me many a time but for the Reverend Mr. Manders.

MANDERS. And this is how you reward me! You cause me to enter falsehoods in the Church Register, and you withhold from me, year after year, the explanations you owed alike to me and to the truth. Your conduct has been wholly inexcusable, Engstrand; and from this time forward I have done with you!

ENGSTRAND. [With a sigh.] Yes! I suppose there's no help for it.

MANDERS. How can you possibly justify yourself?

ENGSTRAND. Who could ever have thought she'd have gone and made bad worse by talking about it? Will your Reverence just fancy yourself in the same trouble as poor Johanna——

MANDERS. I!

ENGSTRAND. Lord bless you, I don't mean just exactly the same. But I mean, if your Reverence had anything to be ashamed of in the eyes of the world, as the saying goes. We menfolk oughtn't to judge a poor woman too hardly, your Reverence.

MANDERS. I am not doing so. It is you I am reproaching.

ENGSTRAND. Might I make so bold as to ask your Reverence a bit of a question?

MANDERS. Yes, if you want to.

ENGSTRAND. Isn't it right and proper for a man to raise up the fallen?

MANDERS. Most certainly it is.

ENGSTRAND. And isn't a man bound to keep his sacred word?

MANDERS. Why, of course he is; but——

ENGSTRAND. When Johanna had got into trouble through that Englishman—or it might have been an American or a Russian, as they call them—well, you see, she came down into the town. Poor thing, she'd sent me about my business once or twice before: for she couldn't bear the sight of anything as wasn't handsome; and I'd got this damaged leg of mine. Your Reverence recollects how I ventured up into a dancing saloon, where seafaring men was carrying on with drink and devilry, as the saying goes. And then, when I was for giving them a bit of an admonition to lead a new life——

MRS. ALVING. [At the window.] H'm——

MANDERS. I know all about that, Engstrand; the ruffians threw you downstairs. You have told me of the affair already. Your infirmity is an honour to you.

ENGSTRAND. I'm not puffed up about it, your Reverence. But what

I wanted to say was, that when she came and confessed all to me, with weeping and gnashing of teeth, I can tell your Reverence I was sore at heart to hear it.

MANDERS. Were you indeed, Engstrand? Well, go on.

ENGSTRAND. So I says to her, "The American, he's sailing about on the boundless sea. And as for you, Johanna," says I, "you've committed a grievous sin, and you're a fallen creature. But Jacob Engstrand," says I, "he's got two good legs to stand upon, he has——" You see, your Reverence, I was speaking figurative-like.

MANDERS. I understand quite well. Go on.

ENGSTRAND. Well, that was how I raised her up and made an honest woman of her, so as folks shouldn't get to know how as she'd gone astray with foreigners.

MANDERS. In all that you acted very well. Only I cannot approve of your stooping to take money——

ENGSTRAND. Money? I? Not a farthing!

MANDERS. [Inquiringly to Mrs. Alving.] But——

ENGSTRAND. Oh, wait a minute!—now I recollect. Johanna did have a trifle of money. But I would have nothing to do with that. "No," says I, "that's mammon; that's the wages of sin. This dirty gold—or notes, or whatever it was—we'll just fling that back in the American's face," says I. But he was off and away, over the stormy sea, your Reverence.

MANDERS. Was he really, my good fellow?

ENGSTRAND. He was indeed, sir. So Johanna and I, we agreed that the money should go to the child's education; and so it did, and I can account for every blessed farthing of it.

MANDERS. Why, this alters the case considerably.

ENGSTRAND. That's just how it stands, your Reverence. And I make so bold as to say as I've been an honest father to Regina, so far as my poor strength went; for I'm but a weak vessel, worse luck!

MANDERS. Well, well, my good fellow——

ENGSTRAND. All the same, I bear myself witness as I've brought up the child, and lived kindly with poor Johanna, and ruled over my own house, as the Scripture has it. But it couldn't never enter my head to go to your Reverence and puff myself up and boast because even the likes of me had done some good in the world. No, sir; when anything of that sort happens to Jacob Engstrand, he holds his tongue about it. It don't happen so terrible often, I daresay. And when I do come to see your Reverence, I find a mortal deal that's wicked and weak to talk about. For I said it before and I says it again—a man's conscience isn't always as clean as it might be.

MANDERS. Give me your hand, Jacob Engstrand.

ENGSTRAND. Oh, Lord! your Reverence——

MANDERS. Come, no nonsense [wrings his hand]. There we are!

ENGSTRAND. And if I might humbly beg your Reverence's pardon——

MANDERS. You? On the contrary, it is I who ought to beg your pardon——

ENGSTRAND. Lord, no, sir!

MANDERS. Yes, assuredly. And I do it with all my heart. Forgive me for misunderstanding you. I only wish I could give you some proof of my hearty regret, and of my good-will towards you——

ENGSTRAND. Would your Reverence do it?

MANDERS. With the greatest pleasure.

ENGSTRAND. Well then, here's the very chance. With the bit of money I've saved here, I was thinking I might set up a Sailors' Home down in the town.

MRS. ALVING. You?

ENGSTRAND. Yes; it might be a sort of Orphanage, too, in a manner of speaking. There's such a many temptations for seafaring folk ashore. But in this Home of mine, a man might feel like as he was under a father's eye, I was thinking.

MANDERS. What do you say to this, Mrs. Alving?

ENGSTRAND. It isn't much as I've got to start with, Lord help me! But if I could only find a helping hand, why——

MANDERS. Yes, yes; we will look into the matter more closely. I entirely approve of your plan. But now, go before me and make everything ready, and get the candles lighted, so as to give the place an air of festivity. And then we will pass an edifying hour together, my good fellow; for now I quite believe you are in the right frame of mind.

ENGSTRAND. Yes, I trust I am. And so I'll say good-bye, ma'am, and thank you kindly; and take good care of Regina for me— *[Wipes a tear from his eye.]*—poor Johanna's child. Well, it's a queer thing, now; but it's just like as if she'd growd into the very apple of my eye. It is, indeed. *[He bows and goes out through the hall.]*

MANDERS. Well, what do you say of that man now, Mrs. Alving? That was a very different account of matters, was it not?

MRS. ALVING. Yes, it certainly was.

MANDERS. It only shows how excessively careful one ought to be in judging one's fellow creatures. But what a heartfelt joy it is to ascertain that one has been mistaken! Don't you think so?

MRS. ALVING. *[Laying her two hands upon his shoulders.]* And I say that I have half a mind to put my arms round your neck, and kiss you.

MANDERS. *[Stepping hastily back.]* No, no! God bless me! What an idea!

MRS. ALVING. *[With a smile.]* Oh, you needn't be afraid of me.

MANDERS. *[By the table.]* You have sometimes such an exaggerated way of expressing yourself. Now, let me just collect all the documents, and put them in my bag. *[He does so.]* There, that's all right. And now, good-bye for the present. Keep your eyes open when Oswald comes back. I shall look in again later.

[He takes his hat and goes out through the hall door. Mrs. Alving sighs, looks for a moment out of the window, sets the room in order a little, and is about to go into the dining-room, but stops at the door with a half-suppressed cry.]

MRS. ALVING. Oswald, are you still at table?

OSWALD. *[In the dining room.]* I'm only finishing my cigar.

MRS. ALVING. I thought you had gone for a little walk.

OSWALD. In such weather as this?

[A glass clinks. Mrs. Alving leaves the door open, and sits down with her knitting on the sofa by the window.]

OSWALD. Wasn't that Pastor Manders that went out just now?

MRS. ALVING. Yes; he went down to the Orphanage.

OSWALD. H'm.   *[The glass and decanter clink again.]*

MRS. ALVING. *[With a troubled glance.]* Dear Oswald, you should take care of that liqueur. It is strong.

OSWALD. It keeps out the damp.

MRS. ALVING. Wouldn't you rather come in here, to me?

OSWALD. I mayn't smoke in there.

MRS. ALVING. You know quite well you may smoke cigars.

OSWALD. Oh, all right then; I'll come in. Just a tiny drop more first.—There! *[He comes into the room with his cigar, and shuts the door after him. A short silence.]* Where has the pastor gone to?

MRS. ALVING. I have just told you; he went down to the Orphanage.

OSWALD. Oh, yes; so you did.

MRS. ALVING. You shouldn't sit so long at table, Oswald.

OSWALD. *[Holding his cigar behind him.]* But I find it so pleasant, mother. *[Strokes and caresses her.]* Just think what it is for me to come home and sit at mother's own table, in mother's room, and eat mother's delicious dishes.

MRS. ALVING. My dear, dear boy!

OSWALD. *[Somewhat impatiently, walks about and smokes.]* And what else can I do with myself here? I can't set to work at anything.

MRS. ALVING. Why can't you?

OSWALD. In such weather as this? Without a single ray of sunshine the whole day? *[Walks up the room.]* Oh, not to be able to work——!

MRS. ALVING. Perhaps it was not quite wise of you to come home?

OSWALD. Oh, yes, mother; I had to.

MRS. ALVING. You know I would ten times rather forgo the joy of having you here, than let you——

OSWALD. *[Stops beside the table.]* Now just tell me, mother: does it really make you so very happy to have me home again.

MRS. ALVING. Does it make me happy!

OSWALD. *[Crumpling up a newspaper.]* I should have thought it must be pretty much the same to you whether I was in existence or not.

MRS. ALVING. Have you the heart to say that to your mother, Oswald?

OSWALD. But you've got on very well without me all this time.

MRS. ALVING. Yes; I have got on without you. That is true.

[A silence. Twilight slowly begins to fall. Oswald paces to and fro across the room. He has laid his cigar down.]

OSWALD. *[Stops beside Mrs. Alving.]* Mother, may I sit on the sofa beside you?

MRS. ALVING. *[Makes room for him.]* Yes, do, my dear boy.

OSWALD. *[Sits down.]* There is something I must tell you, mother.

MRS. ALVING. *[Anxiously.]* Well?

OSWALD. *[Looks fixedly before him.]* For I can't go on hiding it any longer.

MRS. ALVING. Hiding what? What is it?

OSWALD. *[As before.]* I could never bring myself to write to you about it; and since I've come home——

MRS. ALVING. *[Seizes him by the arm.]* Oswald, what is the matter?

OSWALD. Both yesterday and to-day I have tried to put the thoughts away from me—to cast them off; but it's no use.

MRS. ALVING. *[Rising.]* Now you must tell me everything, Oswald!

OSWALD. *[Draws her down to the sofa again.]* Sit still; and then I will try to tell you.—I complained of fatigue after my journey——

MRS. ALVING. Well? What then?

OSWALD. But it isn't that that is the matter with me; not any ordinary fatigue——

MRS. ALVING. *[Tries to jump up.]* You are not ill, Oswald?

OSWALD. *[Draws her down again.]* Sit still, mother. Do take it quietly. I'm not downright ill, either; not what is commonly called "ill." *[Clasps his hands above his head.]* Mother, my mind is broken down—ruined—I shall never be able to work again!

[With his hands before his face, he buries his head in her lap, and breaks into bitter sobbing.]

MRS. ALVING. *[White and trembling.]* Oswald! Look at me! No, no; it's not true.

OSWALD. *[Looks up with despair in his eyes.]* Never to be able to work again! Never!—never! A living death! Mother, can you imagine anything so horrible?

MRS. ALVING. My poor boy! How has this horrible thing come upon you?

OSWALD. *[Sitting upright again.]* That's just what I cannot possibly grasp or understand. I have never led a dissipated life—never, in any respect. You mustn't believe that of me, mother! I've never done that.

MRS. ALVING. I am sure you haven't, Oswald.

OSWALD. And yet this has come upon me just the same—this awful misfortune!

MRS. ALVING. Oh, but it will pass over, my dear, blessëd boy.

It's nothing but over-work. Trust me, I am right.

OSWALD. *[Sadly.]* I thought so too, at first; but it isn't so.

MRS. ALVING. Tell me everything, from beginning to end.

OSWALD. Yes, I will.

MRS. ALVING. When did you first notice it?

OSWALD. It was directly after I had been home last time, and had got back to Paris again. I began to feel the most violent pains in my head—chiefly in the back of my head, they seemed to come. It was as though a tight iron ring was being screwed round my neck and upwards.

MRS. ALVING. Well, and then?

OSWALD. At first I thought it was nothing but the ordinary headache I had been so plagued with while I was growing up——

MRS. ALVING. Yes, yes——

OSWALD. But it wasn't that. I soon found that out. I couldn't work any more. I wanted to begin upon a big new picture, but my powers seemed to fail me; all my strength was crippled; I could form no definite images; everything swam before me—whirling round and round. Oh, it was an awful state! At last I sent for a doctor—and from him I learned the truth.

MRS. ALVING. How do you mean?

OSWALD. He was one of the first doctors in Paris. I told him my symptoms; and then he set to work asking me a string of questions which I thought had nothing to do with the matter. I couldn't imagine what the man was after——

MRS. ALVING. Well?

OSWALD. At last he said: "There has been something worm-eaten in you from your birth." He used that very word—*vermoulu.*

MRS. ALVING. *[Breathlessly.]* What did he mean by that?

OSWALD. I didn't understand either, and begged him to explain himself more clearly. And then the old cynic said—*[Clenching his fist.]* Oh——!

MRS. ALVING. What did he say?

OSWALD. He said, "The sins of the fathers are visited upon the children."

MRS. ALVING. *[Rising slowly.]* The sins of the fathers——!

OSWALD. I very nearly struck him in the face——

MRS. ALVING. *[Walks away across the room.]* The sins of the fathers——

OSWALD. *[Smiles sadly.]* Yes; what do you think of that? Of course I assured him that such a thing was out of the question. But do you think he gave in? No, he stuck to it; and it was only when I produced your letters and translated the passages relating to father——

MRS. ALVING. But then——?

OSWALD. Then of course he had to admit that he was on the wrong track; and so I learned the truth—the incomprehensible truth! I ought not to have taken part with my comrades in that light-hearted, glorious life of theirs. It had been too much for my strength. So I had brought it upon myself!

MRS. ALVING. Oswald! No, no; do not believe it!

OSWALD. No other explanation was possible, he said. That's the awful part of it. Incurably ruined for life—by my own heedlessness! All that I meant to have done in the world—I never dare think of it again—I'm not able to think of it. Oh! if I could only live over again, and undo all I have done! *[He buries his face in the sofa.]*

[Mrs. Alving wrings her hands and walks, in silent struggle, backwards and forwards.]

OSWALD. *[After a while, looks up and remains resting upon his elbow.]* If it had only been something inherited—something one wasn't responsible for! But this! To have thrown away so shamefully, thoughtlessly, recklessly, one's own happiness, one's own health, everything in the world—one's future, one's very life——!

MRS. ALVING. No, no, my dear, darling boy; this is impossible! *[Bends over him.]* Things are not so desperate as you think.

OSWALD. Oh, you don't know—— *[Springs up.]* And then, mother, to cause you all this sorrow! Many a time I have almost wished and hoped that at bottom you didn't care so very much about me.

MRS. ALVING. I, Oswald? My only boy! You are all I have in the world! The only thing I care about!

OSWALD. *[Seizes both her hands and kisses them.]* Yes, yes, I see it. When I'm at home, I see it, of course; and that's almost the hardest part for me.—But now you know the whole story; and now we won't talk any more about it to-day. I daren't think of it for long together. *[Goes up the room.]* Get me something to drink, mother.

MRS. ALVING. To drink? What do you want to drink now?

OSWALD. Oh, anything you like. You have some cold punch in the house.

MRS. ALVING. Yes, but my dear Oswald——

OSWALD. Don't refuse me, mother. Do be kind, now! I must have something to wash down all these gnawing thoughts. *[Goes into the conservatory.]* And then——it's so dark here! *[Mrs. Alving pulls a bell-rope on the right.]* And this ceaseless rain! It may go on week after week, for months together. Never to get a glimpse of the sun! I can't recollect ever having seen the sun shine all the times I've been at home.

MRS. ALVING. Oswald—you are thinking of going away from me.

OSWALD. H'm—*[Drawing a heavy breath.]*—I'm not thinking of anything. I cannot think of anything! *[In a low voice.]* I let thinking alone.

REGINA. *[From the dining-room.]* Did you ring, ma'am?

MRS. ALVING. Yes; let us have the lamp in.

REGINA. Yes, ma'am. It's ready lighted. *[Goes out.]*

MRS. ALVING. *[Goes across to Oswald.]* Oswald, be frank with me.

OSWALD. Well, so I am, mother. *[Goes to the table.]* I think I have told you enough.

[Regina brings the lamp and sets it upon the table.]

MRS. ALVING. Regina, you may bring us a small bottle of champagne.

REGINA. Very well, ma'am. *[Goes out.]*

OSWALD. *[Puts his arm round Mrs. Alving's neck.]* That's just what I wanted. I knew mother wouldn't let her boy go thirsty.

MRS. ALVING. My own, poor, darling Oswald; how could I deny you anything now?

OSWALD. *[Eagerly.]* Is that true, mother? Do you mean it?

MRS. ALVING. How? What?

OSWALD. That you couldn't deny me anything.

MRS. ALVING. My dear Oswald——

OSWALD. Hush!

[Regina brings a tray with a half-bottle of champagne and two glasses, which she sets on the table.]

REGINA. Shall I open it?

OSWALD. No, thanks. I will do it myself.

[Regina goes out again.]

MRS. ALVING. *[Sits down by the table.]* What was it you meant—that I musn't deny you?

OSWALD. *[Busy opening the bottle.]* First let us have a glass—or two.

[The cork pops; he pours wine into one glass, and is about to pour it into the other.]

MRS. ALVING. *[Holding her hand over it.]* Thanks; not for me.

OSWALD. Oh! won't you? Then I will!

[He empties the glass, fills, and empties it again; then he sits down by the table.]

MRS. ALVING. *[In expectancy.]* Well?

OSWALD. *[Without looking at her.]* Tell me—I thought you and Pastor Manders seemed so odd—so quiet—at dinner to-day.

MRS. ALVING. Did you notice it?

OSWALD. Yes. H'm——*[After a short silence.]* Tell me: what do you think of Regina?

MRS. ALVING. What do I think?

OSWALD. Yes; isn't she splendid?

MRS. ALVING. My dear Oswald, you don't know her as I do——

OSWALD. Well?

MRS. ALVING. Regina, unfortunately, was allowed to stay at home too long. I ought to have taken her earlier into my house.

OSWALD. Yes, but isn't she splendid to look at, mother?

[*He fills his glass.*]

MRS. ALVING. Regina has many serious faults——

OSWALD. Oh, what does that matter? [*He drinks again.*]

MRS. ALVING. But I am fond of her, nevertheless, and I am responsible for her. I wouldn't for all the world have any harm happen to her.

OSWALD. [*Springs up.*] Mother, Regina is my only salvation!

MRS. ALVING. [*Rising.*] What do you mean by that?

OSWALD. I cannot go on bearing all this anguish of soul alone.

MRS. ALVING. Have you not your mother to share it with you?

OSWALD. Yes; that's what I thought; and so I came home to you. But that will not do. I see it won't do. I cannot endure my life here.

MRS. ALVING. Oswald!

OSWALD. I must live differently, mother. That is why I must leave you. I will not have you looking on at it.

MRS. ALVING. My unhappy boy! But, Oswald, while you are so ill as this——

OSWALD. If it were only the illness, I should stay with you, mother, you may be sure; for you are the best friend I have in the world.

MRS. ALVING. Yes, indeed I am, Oswald; am I not?

OSWALD. [*Wanders restlessly about.*] But it's all the torment, the gnawing remorse—and then, the great, killing dread. Oh—that awful dread!

MRS. ALVING. [*Walking after him.*] Dread? What dread? What do you mean?

OSWALD. Oh, you mustn't ask me any more. I don't know. I can't describe it. [*Mrs. Alving goes over to the right and pulls the bell.*]

OSWALD. What is it you want?

MRS. ALVING. I want my boy to be happy—that is what I want. He sha'n't go on brooding over things. [*To Regina, who appears at the door:*] More champagne—a large bottle. [*Regina goes.*]

OSWALD. Mother!

MRS. ALVING. Do you think we don't know how to live here at home?

OSWALD. Isn't she splendid to look at? How beautifully she's built! And so thoroughly healthy!

MRS. ALVING. [*Sits by the table.*] Sit down, Oswald; let us talk quietly together. ·

OSWALD. [*Sits.*] I daresay you don't know, mother, that I owe Regina some reparation.

MRS. ALVING. You!

OSWALD. For a bit of thoughtlessness, or whatever you like to call it—very innocent, at any rate. When I was home last time——

MRS. ALVING. Well?

OSWALD. She used often to ask me about Paris, and I used to tell her one thing and another. Then I recollect I happened to say to her one day, "Shouldn't you like to go there yourself?"

MRS. ALVING. Well?

OSWALD. I saw her face flush, and then she said, "Yes, I should like it of all things." "Ah, well," I replied, "it might perhaps be managed"—or something like that.

MRS. ALVING. And then?

OSWALD. Of course I had forgotten all about it; but the day before yesterday I happened to ask her whether she was glad I was to stay at home so long——

MRS. ALVING. Yes?

OSWALD. And then she gave me such a strange look, and asked, "But what's to become of my trip to Paris?"

MRS. ALVING. Her trip!

OSWALD. And so it came out that she had taken the thing seriously; that she had been thinking of me the whole time, and had set to work to learn French——

MRS. ALVING. So that was why——!

OSWALD. Mother—when I saw that fresh, lovely, splendid girl standing there before me—till then I had hardly noticed her—but when she stood there as though with open arms ready to receive me——

MRS. ALVING. Oswald!

OSWALD. ——then it flashed upon me that in her lay my salvation; for I saw that she was full of the joy of life.

MRS. ALVING. [Starts.] The joy of life——? Can there be salvation in that?

REGINA. [From the dining-room, with a bottle of champagne.] I'm sorry to have been so long, but I had to go to the cellar.

[Places the bottle on the table.]

OSWALD. And now bring another glass.

REGINA. [Looks at him in surprise.] There is Mrs. Alving's glass, Mr. Alving.

OSWALD. Yes, but bring one for yourself, Regina. [Regina starts and gives a lightning-like side glance at Mrs. Alving.] Why do you wait?

REGINA. [Softly and hesitatingly.] Is it Mrs. Alving's wish?

MRS. ALVING. Bring the glass, Regina.

[Regina goes out into the dining-room.]

OSWALD. [Follows her with his eyes.] Have you noticed how she walks?—so firmly and lightly?

MRS. ALVING. This can never be, Oswald!

OSWALD. It's a settled thing. Can't you see that? It's no use saying anything against it.

[Regina enters with an empty glass, which she keeps in her hand.]

OSWALD. Sit down, Regina.

[Regina looks inquiringly at Mrs. Alving.]

MRS. ALVING. Sit down. *[Regina sits on a chair by the dining-room door, still holding the empty glass in her hand.]* Oswald—what were you saying about the joy of life?

OSWALD. Ah, the joy of life, mother—that's a thing you don't know much about in these parts. I have never felt it here.

MRS. ALVING. Not when you are with me?

OSWALD. Not when I'm at home. But you don't understand that.

MRS. ALVING. Yes, yes; I think I almost understand it—now.

OSWALD. And then, too, the joy of work! At bottom, it's the same thing. But that, too, you know nothing about.

MRS. ALVING. Perhaps you are right. Tell me more about it, Oswald.

OSWALD. I only mean that here people are brought up to believe that work is a curse and a punishment for sin, and that life is something miserable, something it would be best to have done with, the sooner the better.

MRS. ALVING. "A vale of tears," yes; and we certainly do our best to make it one.

OSWALD. But in the great world people won't hear of such things. There, nobody really believes such doctrines any longer. There, you feel it a positive bliss and ecstasy merely to draw the breath of life. Mother, have you noticed that everything I have painted has turned upon the joy of life?—always, always upon the joy of life?—light and sunshine and glorious air—and faces radiant with happiness. That is why I'm afraid of remaining at home with you.

MRS. ALVING. Afraid? What are you afraid of here, with me?

OSWALD. I'm afraid lest all my instincts should be warped into ugliness.

MRS. ALVING. *[Looks steadily at him.]* Do you think that is what would happen?

OSWALD. I know it. You may live the same life here as there, and yet it won't be the same life.

MRS. ALVING. *[Who has been listening eagerly, rises, her eyes big with thought, and says:]* Now I see the sequence of things.

OSWALD. What is it you see?

MRS. ALVING. I see it now for the first time. And now I can speak.

OSWALD. *[Rising.]* Mother, I don't understand you.

REGINA. *[Who has also risen.]* Perhaps I ought to go?

MRS. ALVING. No. Stay here. Now I can speak. Now, my boy, you shall know the whole truth. And then you can choose. Oswald! Regina!

OSWALD. Hush! The Pastor——

MANDERS. *[Enters by the hall door.]* There! We have had a most edifying time down there.

OSWALD. So have we.

MANDERS. We must stand by Engstrand and his Sailors' Home. Regina must go to him and help him——

REGINA. No thank you, sir.

MANDERS. *[Noticing her for the first time.]* What——? You here? And with a glass in your hand!

REGINA. *[Hastily putting the glass down.]* Pardon!

OSWALD. Regina is going with me, Mr. Manders.

MANDERS. Going! With you!

OSWALD. Yes; as my wife—if she wishes it.

MANDERS. But, merciful God——!

REGINA. I can't help it, sir.

OSWALD. Or she'll stay here, if I stay.

REGINA. *[Involuntarily.]* Here!

MANDERS. I am thunderstruck at your conduct, Mrs. Alving.

MRS. ALVING. They will do neither one thing nor the other; for now I can speak out plainly.

MANDERS. You surely will not do that! No, no, no!

MRS. ALVING. Yes, I can speak and I will. And no ideals shall suffer after all.

OSWALD. Mother—what is it you are hiding from me?

REGINA. *[Listening.]* Oh, ma'am, listen! Don't you hear shouts outside?   *[She goes into the conservatory and looks out.]*

OSWALD. *[At the window on the left.]* What's going on? Where does that light come from?

REGINA. *[Cries out.]* The Orphanage is on fire!

MRS. ALVING. *[Rushing to the window.]* On fire!

MANDERS. On fire! Impossible! I've just come from there.

OSWALD. Where's my hat? Oh, never mind it—Father's Orpha-nage——!   *[He rushes out through the garden door.]*

MRS. ALVING. My shawl, Regina! The whole place is in a blaze!

MANDERS. Terrible! Mrs. Alving, it is a judgment upon this abode of lawlessness.

MRS. ALVING. Yes, of course. Come, Regina.

[She and Regina hasten out through the hall.]

MANDERS. *[Clasps his hands together.]* And we left it uninsured!
                 [He goes out the same way.]

CURTAIN

ACT 3

The room as before. All the doors stand open. The lamp is still burning on the table. It is dark out of doors; there is only a faint glow from the conflagration in the background to the left.

[Mrs. Alving, with a shawl over her head, stands in the conservatory, looking out. Regina, also with a shawl on, stands a little behind her.]

MRS. ALVING. The whole thing burnt!—burnt to the ground!

REGINA. The basement is still burning.

MRS. ALVING. How is it Oswald doesn't come home? There's nothing to be saved.

REGINA. Should you like me to take down his hat to him?

MRS. ALVING. Has he not even got his hat on?

REGINA. *[Pointing to the hall.]* No; there it hangs.

MRS. ALVING. Let it be. He must come up now. I shall go and look for him myself.

> *[She goes out through the garden door.]*

MANDERS. *[Comes in from the hall.]* Is not Mrs. Alving here?

REGINA. She has just gone down the garden.

MANDERS. This is the most terrible night I ever went through.

REGINA. Yes; isn't it a dreadful misfortune, sir?

MANDERS. Oh, don't talk about it! I can hardly bear to think of it.

REGINA. How can it have happened——?

MANDERS. Don't ask me, Miss Engstrand! How should *I* know? Do you, too——? Is it not enough that your father——?

REGINA. What about him?

MANDERS. Oh, he has driven me distracted——

ENGSTRAND. *[Enters through the hall.]* Your Reverence——

MANDERS. *[Turns round in terror.]* Are you after me here, too?

ENGSTRAND. Yes, strike me dead, but I must——! Oh, Lord! what am I saying? But this is a terrible ugly business, your Reverence.

MANDERS. *[Walks to and fro.]* Alas! alas!

REGINA. What's the matter?

ENGSTRAND. Why, it all came of this here prayer-meeting, you see. *[Softly.]* The bird's limed, my girl. *[Aloud.]* And to think it should be my doing that such a thing should be his Reverence's doing!

MANDERS. But I assure you, Engstrand——

ENGSTRAND. There wasn't another soul except your Reverence as ever laid a finger on the candles down there.

MANDERS. *[Stops.]* So you declare. But I certainly cannot recollect that I ever had a candle in my hand.

ENGSTRAND. And I saw as clear as daylight how your Reverence took the candle and snuffed it with your fingers, and threw away the snuff among the shavings.

MANDERS. And you stood and looked on?

ENGSTRAND. Yes; I saw it as plain as a pike-staff, I did.

MANDERS. It's quite beyond my comprehension. Besides, it has never been my habit to snuff candles with my fingers.

ENGSTRAND. And terrible risky it looked, too, that it did! But is there such a deal of harm done after all, your Reverence?

MANDERS. *[Walks restlessly to and fro.]* Oh, don't ask me!

ENGSTRAND. *[Walks with him.]* And your Reverence hadn't insured it, neither?

MANDERS. *[Continuing to walk up and down.]* No, no, no; I have told you so.

ENGSTRAND. *[Following him.]* Not insured! And then to go straight away down and set light to the whole thing! Lord, Lord, what a misfortune!

MANDERS *[Wipes the sweat from his forehead.]* Ay, you may well say that, Engstrand.

ENGSTRAND. And to think that such a thing should happen to a benevolent Institution, that was to have been a blessing both to town and country, as the saying goes! The newspapers won't be for handling your Reverence very gently, I expect.

MANDERS. No; that is just what I am thinking of. That is almost the worst of the whole matter. All the malignant attacks and inputations——! Oh, it makes me shudder to think of it!

MRS. ALVING. *[Comes in from the garden.]* He is not to be persuaded to leave the fire.

MANDERS. Ah, there you are, Mrs. Alving.

MRS. ALVING. So you have escaped your Inaugural Address, Pastor Manders.

MANDERS. Oh, I should so gladly——

MRS. ALVING. *[In an undertone.]* It is all for the best. That Orphanage would have done no one any good.

MANDERS. Do you think not?

MRS. ALVING. Do you think it would?

MANDERS. It is a terrible misfortune, all the same.

MRS. ALVING. Let us speak of it plainly, as a matter of business.— Are you waiting for Mr. Manders, Engstrand?

ENGSTRAND. *[At the hall door.]* That's just what I'm a-doing of, ma'am.

MRS. ALVING. Then sit down meanwhile.

ENGSTRAND. Thank you, ma'am; I'd as soon stand.

MRS. ALVING. *[To Manders.]* I suppose you are going by the steamer?

MANDERS. Yes; it starts in an hour.

MRS. ALVING. Then be so good as to take all the papers with you. I won't hear another word about this affair. I have other things to think of——

MANDERS. Mrs. Alving——

MRS. ALVING. Later on I shall send you a Power of Attorney to settle everything as you please.

MANDERS. That I will very readily undertake. The original destination of the endowment must now be completely changed, alas!

MRS. ALVING. Of course it must.

MANDERS. I think, first of all, I shall arrange that the Solvik property shall pass to the parish. The land is by no means without value. It can always be turned to account for some purpose or other. And the interest of the money in the Bank I could, perhaps, best apply for the benefit of some undertaking of acknowledged value to the town.

MRS. ALVING. Do just as you please. The whole matter is now completely indifferent to me.

ENGSTRAND. Give a thought to my Sailors' Home, your Reverence.

MANDERS. Upon my word, that is not a bad suggestion. That must be considered.

ENGSTRAND. Oh, devil take considering—Lord forgive me!

MANDERS. *[With a sigh.]* And unfortunately I cannot tell how long I shall be able to retain control of these things—whether public opinion may not compel me to retire. It entirely depends upon the result of the official inquiry into the fire——

MRS. ALVING What are you talking about?

MANDERS. And the result can by no means be foretold.

ENGSTRAND. *[Comes close to him.]* Ay, but it can though. For here stands old Jacob Engstrand.

MANDERS. Well well, but——?

ENGSTRAND. *[More softly.]* And Jacob Engstrand isn't the man to desert a noble benefactor in the hour of need, as the saying goes.

MANDERS. Yes, but my good fellow—how——?

ENGSTRAND. Jacob Engstrand may be likened to a sort of a guardian angel, he may, your Reverence.

MANDERS. No, no; I really cannot accept that.

ENGSTRAND. Oh, that'll be the way of it, all the same. I know a man as has taken others' sins upon himself before now, I do.

MANDERS. Jacob! *[Wrings his hand.]* Yours is a rare nature. Well, you shall be helped with your Sailors' Home. That you may rely upon.

[Engstrand tries to thank him, but cannot for emotion.]

MANDERS. *[Hangs his travelling-bag over his shoulder.]* And now let us set out. We two will go together.

ENGSTRAND. *[At the dining-room door, softly to Regina.]* You come along too, my lass. You shall live as snug as the yolk in an egg.

REGINA. *[Tosses her head.]* Merci!

[She goes out into the hall and fetches Manders overcoat.]

MANDERS. Good-bye, Mrs. Alving! and may the spirit of Law and Order descend upon this house, and that quickly.

MRS. ALVING. Good-bye, Pastor Manders.

[She goes up towards the conservatory, as she sees Oswald coming in through the garden door.]

ENGSTRAND. *[While he and Regina help Manders to get his coat* on.] Good-bye, my child. And if any trouble should come to you, you know where Jacob Engstrand is to be found. [*Softly.*] Little Harbour Street, h'm——! [*To Mrs. Alving and Oswald.*] And the refuge for wandering mariners shall be called "Chamberlain Alving's Home," that it shall! And if so be as I'm spared to carry on that house in my own way, I make so bold as to promise that it shall be worthy of the Chamberlain's memory.

MANDERS. [*In the doorway.*] H'm—h'm!—Come along, my dear Engstrand. Good-bye! Good-bye!

[*He and Engstrand go out through the hall.*]

OSWALD. [*Goes towards the table.*] What house was he talking about?

MRS. ALVING. Oh, a kind of Home that he and Pastor Manders want to set up.

OSWALD. It will burn down like the other.

MRS. ALVING. What makes you think so?

OSWALD. Everything will burn. All that recalls father's memory is doomed. Here am I, too, burning down.

[*Regina starts and looks at him.*]

MRS. ALVING. Oswald! You oughtn't to have remained so long down there, my poor boy.

OSWALD. [*Sits down by the table.*] I almost think you are right.

MRS. ALVING. Let me dry your face, Oswald; you are quite wet.

[*She dries his face with her pocket-handkerchief.*]

OSWALD. [*Stares indifferently in front of him.*] Thanks, mother.

MRS. ALVING. Are you not tired, Oswald? Should you like to sleep?

OSWALD. [*Nervously.*] No, no—not to sleep! I never sleep. I only pretend to. [*Sadly.*] That will come soon enough.

MRS. ALVING. [*Looking sorrowfully at him.*] Yes, you really are ill, my blessëd boy.

REGINA. [*Eagerly.*] Is Mr. Alving ill?

OSWALD. [*Impatiently.*] Oh, do shut all the doors! This killing dread——

MRS. ALVING. Close the doors, Regina.

[*Regina shuts them and remains standing by the hall door. Mrs. Alving takes her shawl off. Regina does the same. Mrs. Alving draws a chair across to Oswald's, and sits by him.*]

MRS. ALVING. There now! I am going to sit beside you——

OSWALD. Yes, do. And Regina shall stay here too. Regina shall be with me always. You will come to the rescue, Regina, won't you?

REGINA. I don't understand——

MRS. ALVING. To the rescue?

OSWALD. Yes—when the need comes.

MRS. ALVING. Oswald, have you not your mother to come to the rescue?

OSWALD. You? [*Smiles.*] No, mother; that rescue you will never bring me. *[Laughs sadly.]* You! ha ha! *[Looks earnestly at her.]* Though, after all, who ought to do it if not you? *[Impetuously.]* Why can't you say "thou"[1] to me, Regina? Why do'n't you call me "Oswald"?

REGINA. *[Softly.]* I don't think Mrs. Alving would like it.

MRS. ALVING. You shall have leave to, presently. And meanwhile sit over here beside us.

[Regina seats herself demurely and hesitatingly at the other side of the table.]

MRS. ALVING. And now, my poor suffering boy, I am going to take the burden off your mind——

OSWALD. You, mother?

MRS. ALVING. ——all the gnawing remorse and self-reproach you speak of.

OSWALD. And you think you can do that?

MRS. ALVING. Yes, now I can, Oswald. A little while ago you spoke of the joy of life; and at that word a new light burst for me over my life and everything connected with it.

OSWALD. *[Shakes his head.]* I don't understand you.

MRS. ALVING. You ought to have known your father when he was a young lieutenant. He was brimming over with the joy of life!

OSWALD. Yes, I know he was.

MRS. ALVING. It was like a breezy day only to look at him. And what exuberant strength and vitality there was in him!

OSWALD. Well——?

MRS. ALVING. Well then, child of joy as he was—for he was like a child in those days—he had to live at home here in a half-grown town, which had no joys to offer him—only dissipations. He had no object in life—only an official position. He had no work into which he could throw himself heart and soul; he had only business. He had not a single comrade that could realise what the joy of life meant— only loungers and boon-companions——

OSWALD. Mother——!

MRS. ALVING. So the inevitable happened.

OSWALD. The inevitable?

MRS. ALVING. You told me yourself, this evening, what would become of you if you stayed at home.

OSWALD. Do you mean to say that father——?

MRS. ALVING. Your poor father found no outlet for the over-powering joy of life that was in him. And I brought no brightness into his home.

OSWALD. Not even you?

MRS. ALVING. They had taught me a great deal about duties and so forth, which I went on obstinately believing in. Everything was marked out into duties—into my duties, and his duties, and—I am

1 *"thou"*: an informal, intimate form of address. *You* is more formal.

afraid I made his home intolerable for your poor father, Oswald.

OSWALD. Why have you never spoken of this in writing to me?

MRS. ALVING. I have never before seen it in such a light that I could speak of it to you, his son.

OSWALD. In what light did you see it, then?

MRS. ALVING. [Slowly.] I saw only this one thing: that your father was a broken-down man before you were born.

OSWALD. [Softly.] Ah——!

> [He rises and walks away to the window.]

MRS. ALVING. And then, day after day, I dwelt on the one thought that by rights Regina should be at home in this house—just like my own boy.

OSWALD. [Turning round quickly.] Regina——!

REGINA. [Springs up and asks, with bated breath.] I——?

MRS. ALVING. Yes, now you know it, both of you.

OSWALD. Regina!

REGINA. [To herself.] So mother was that kind of woman.

MRS. ALVING. Your mother had many good qualities, Regina.

REGINA. Yes, but she was one of that sort, all the same. Oh, I've often suspected it; but—— And now, if you please, ma'am, may I be allowed to go away at once?

MRS. ALVING. Do you really wish it, Regina?

REGINA. Yes, indeed I do.

MRS. ALVING. Of course you can do as you like; but——

OSWALD. [Goes towards Regina.] Go away now? Your place is here.

REGINA. *Merci,* Mr. Alving!—or now, I suppose, I may say Oswald. But I can tell you this wasn't at all what I expected.

MRS. ALVING. Regina, I have not been frank with you——

REGINA. No, that you haven't indeed. If I'd known that Oswald was an invalid, why—— And now, too, that it can never come to anything serious between us—— I really can't stop out here in the country and wear myself out nursing sick people.

OSWALD. Not even one who is so near to you?

REGINA. No, that I can't. A poor girl must make the best of her young days, or she'll be left out in the cold before she knows where she is. And I, too, have the joy of life in me, Mrs. Alving!

MRS. ALVING. Unfortunately, you have. But don't throw yourself away, Regina.

REGINA. Oh, what must be, must be. If Oswald takes after his father, I take after my mother, I daresay.—May I ask, ma'am, if Pastor Manders knows all this about me?

MRS. ALVING. Pastor Manders knows all about it.

REGINA. [Busied in putting on her shawl.] Well then, I'd better make haste and get away by this steamer. The Pastor is such a nice man to deal with; and I certainly think I've as much right to a little of that money as he has—that brute of a carpenter.

MRS. ALVING. You are heartily welcome to it, Regina.

REGINA. *[Looks hard at her.]* I think you might have brought me up as a gentleman's daughter, ma'am; it would have suited me better. *[Tosses her head.]* But pooh—what does it matter! *[With a bitter side glance at the corked bottle.]* I may come to drink champagne with gentlefolks yet.

MRS. ALVING. And if you ever need a home, Regina, come to me.

REGINA. No, thank you, ma'am. Pastor Manders will look after me, I know. And if the worst comes to the worst, I know of one house where I've every right to a place.

MRS. ALVING. Where is that?

REGINA. "Chamberlain Alving's Home."

MRS. ALVING. Regina—now I see it—you are going to your ruin.

REGINA. Oh, stuff! Good-bye.

[She nods and goes out through the hall.]

OSWALD. *[Stands at the window and looks out.]* Is she gone?

MRS. ALVING. Yes.

OSWALD. *[Murmuring aside to himself.]* I think it was a mistake, this.

MRS. ALVING. *[Goes up behind him and lays her hands on his shoulders.]* Oswald, my dear boy—has it shaken you very much?

OSWALD. *[Turns his face towards her.]* All that about father, do you mean?

MRS. ALVING. Yes, about your unhappy father. I am so afraid it may have been too much for you.

OSWALD. Why should you fancy that? Of course it came upon me as a great surprise; but it can make no real difference to me.

MRS. ALVING. *[Draws her hands away.]* No difference! That your father was so infinitely unhappy!

OSWALD. Of course I can pity him, as I would anybody else; but——

MRS. ALVING. Nothing more! Your own father!

OSWALD. *[Impatiently.]* Oh, "father,"—"father"! I never knew anything of father. I remember nothing about him, except that he once made me sick.

MRS. ALVING. This is terrible to think of! Ought not a son to love his father, whatever happens?

OSWALD. When a son has nothing to thank his father for? has never known him? Do you really cling to that old superstition?—you who are so enlightened in other ways?

MRS. ALVING. Can it be only a superstition——?

OSWALD. Yes; surely you can see that, mother. It's one of those notions that are current in the world, and so——

MRS. ALVING. *[Deeply moved.]* Ghosts!

OSWALD. *[Crossing the room.]* Yes; you may call them ghosts.

MRS. ALVING. *[Wildly.]* Oswald—then you don't love me, either!

OSWALD. You I know, at any rate——

MRS. ALVING. Yes, you know me; but is that all!

OSWALD. And, of course, I know how fond you are of me, and

I can't but be grateful to you. And then you can be so useful to me, now that I am ill.

MRS. ALVING. Yes, cannot I, Oswald? Oh, I could almost bless the illness that has driven you home to me. For I see very plainly that you are not mine: I have to win you.

OSWALD. *[Impatiently.]* Yes yes yes; all these are just so many phrases. You must remember that I am a sick man, mother. I can't be much taken up with other people; I have enough to do thinking about myself.

MRS. ALVING. *[In a low voice.]* I shall be patient and easily satisfied.

OSWALD. And cheerful too, mother!

MRS. ALVING. Yes, my dear boy, you are quite right. *[Goes towards him.]* Have I relieved you of all remorse and self-reproach now?

OSWALD. Yes, you have. But now who will relieve me of the dread?

MRS. ALVING. The dread?

OSWALD. *[Walks across the room.]* Regina could have been got to do it.

MRS. ALVING. I don't understand you. What is this about dread— and Regina?

OSWALD. Is it very late, mother?

MRS. ALVING. It is early morning. *[She looks out through the conservatory.]* The day is dawning over the mountains. And the weather is clearing, Oswald. In a little while you shall see the sun.

OSWALD. I'm glad of that. Oh, I may still have much to rejoice in and live for——

MRS. ALVING. I should think so, indeed!

OSWALD. Even if I can't work——

MRS. ALVING. Oh, you'll soon be able to work again, my dear boy—now that you haven't got all those gnawing and depressing thoughts to brood over any longer.

OSWALD. Yes, I'm glad you were able to rid me of all those fancies. And when I've got over this one thing more—— *[Sits on the sofa.]* Now we will have a little talk, mother——

MRS. ALVING. Yes, let us.

[She pushes an arm-chair towards the sofa, and sits down close to him.]

OSWALD. And meantime the sun will be rising. And then you will know all. And then I shall not feel this dread any longer.

MRS. ALVING. What is it that I am to know?

OSWALD. *[Not listening to her.]* Mother, did you not say a little while ago, that there was nothing in the world you would not do for me, if I asked you?

MRS. ALVING. Yes, indeed I said so!

OSWALD. And you'll stick to it, mother?

MRS. ALVING. You may rely on that, my dear and only boy! I have nothing in the world to live for but you alone.

OSWALD. Very well, then; now you shall hear——Mother, you have a strong, steadfast mind, I know. Now you're to sit quite still when you hear it.

MRS. ALVING. What dreadful thing can it be——?

OSWALD. You're not to scream out. Do you hear? Do you promise me that? We will sit and talk about it quietly. Do you promise me, mother?

MRS. ALVING. Yes, yes; I promise. Only speak!

OSWALD. Well, you must know that all this fatigue—and my inability to think of work—all that is not the illness itself——

MRS. ALVING. Then what is the illness itself?

OSWALD. The disease I have as my birthright— *[He points to his forehead and adds very softly]*—is seated here.

MRS. ALVING. *[Almost voiceless.]* Oswald! No—no!

OSWALD. Don't scream. I can't bear it. Yes, mother, it is seated here—waiting. And it may break out any day—at any moment.

MRS. ALVING. Oh, what horror——!

OSWALD. Now, quiet, quiet. That is how it stands with me——

MRS. ALVING. *[Springs up.]* It's not true, Oswald! It's impossible! It cannot be so!

OSWALD. I have had one attack down there already. It was soon over. But when I came to know the state I had been in, then the dread descended upon me, raging and ravening; and so I set off home to you as fast as I could.

MRS. ALVING. Then this is the dread——!

OSWALD. Yes—it's so indescribably loathsome, you know. Oh, if it had only been an ordinary mortal disease——! For I'm not so afraid of death—though I should like to live as long as I can.

MRS. ALVING. Yes, yes, Oswald, you must!

OSWALD. But this is so unutterably loathsome. To become a little baby again! To have to be fed! To have to—— Oh, it's not to be spoken of!

MRS. ALVING. The child has his mother to nurse him.

OSWALD. *[Springs up.]* No, never that! That is just what I will not have. I can't endure to think that perhaps I should lie in that state for many years—and get old and grey. And in the meantime you might die and leave me. *[Sits in Mrs. Alving's chair.]* For the doctor said it wouldn't necessarily prove fatal at once. He called it a sort of softening of the brain—or something like that. *[Smiles sadly.]* I think that expression sounds so nice. It always sets me thinking of cherry-coloured velvet—something soft and delicate to stroke.

MRS. ALVING. *[Shrieks.]* Oswald!

OSWALD. *[Springs up and paces the room.]* And now you have taken Regina from me. If I could only have had her! She would have come to the rescue, I know.

MRS. ALVING. *[Goes to him.]* What do you mean by that, my darling boy? Is there any help in the world that I would not give you?

OSWALD. When I got over my attack in Paris, the doctor told me that when it comes again—and it will come—there will be no more hope.

MRS. ALVING. He was heartless enough to——

OSWALD. I demanded it of him. I told him I had preparations to make—— *[He smiles cunningly.]* And so I had. *[He takes a little box from his inner breast pocket and opens it.]* Mother, do you see this?

MRS. ALVING. What is it?

OSWALD. Morphia.

MRS. ALVING. *[Looks at him horror-struck.]* Oswald—my boy—

OSWALD. I've scraped together twelve pilules[2]——

MRS. ALVING. *[Snatches at it.]* Give me the box, Oswald.

OSWALD. Not yet, mother. *[He hides the box again in his pocket.]*

MRS. ALVING. I shall never survive this!

OSWALD. It must be survived. Now if I'd had Regina here, I should have told her how things stood with me—and begged her to come to the rescue at the last. She would have done it. I know she would.

MRS. ALVING. Never!

OSWALD. When the horror had come upon me, and she saw me lying there helpless, like a little new-born baby, impotent, lost, hopeless—past all saving——

MRS. ALVING. Never in all the world would Regina have done this!

OSWALD. Regina would have done it. Regina was so splendidly light-hearted. And she would soon have wearied of nursing an invalid like me.

MRS. ALVING. Then heaven be praised that Regina is not here.

OSWALD. Well then, it is you that must come to the rescue, mother.

MRS. ALVING. *[Shrieks aloud.]* I!

OSWALD. Who should do it if not you?

MRS. ALVING. I! your mother!

OSWALD. For that very reason.

MRS. ALVING. I, who gave you life!

OSWALD. I never asked you for life. And what sort of a life have you given me? I will not have it! You shall take it back again!

MRS. ALVING. Help! Help!   *[She runs out into the hall.]*

OSWALD. *[Going after her.]* Do not leave me! Where are you going?

MRS. ALVING. *[In the hall.]* To fetch the doctor, Oswald! Let me pass!

OSWALD. *[Also outside.]* You shall not go out. And no one shall come in.

           [The locking of a door is heard.]

MRS. ALVING. *[Comes in again.]* Oswald! Oswald—my child!

OSWALD. *[Follows her.]* Have you a mother's heart for me—and yet can see me suffer from this unutterable dread?

MRS. ALVING. *[After a moment's silence, commands herself, and says:]* Here is my hand upon it.

OSWALD. Will you——?

---

2 *pilules:* capsules.

MRS. ALVING. If it should ever be necessary. But it will never be necessary. No, no; it is impossible.

OSWALD. Well, let us hope so. And let us live together as long as we can. Thank you, mother.

[He seats himself in the arm-chair which Mrs. Alving has moved to the sofa. Day is breaking. The lamp is still burning on the table.]

MRS. ALVING. *[Drawing near cautiously.]* Do you feel calm now?

OSWALD. Yes.

MRS. ALVING. *[Bending over him.]* It has been a dreadful fancy of yours, Oswald—nothing but a fancy. All this excitement has been too much for you. But now you shall have a long rest; at home with your mother, my own blessëd boy. Everything you point to you shall have, just as when you were a little child.—There now. The crisis is over. You see how easily it passed! Oh, I was sure it would. —And do you see, Oswald, what a lovely day we are going to have? Brilliant sunshine! Now you can really see your home.

[She goes to the table and puts out the lamp. Sunrise. The glacier and the snow-peaks in the background glow in the morning light.]

OSWALD. *[Sits in the arm-chair with his back towards the landscape, without moving. Suddenly he says:]* Mother, give me the sun.

MRS. ALVING. *[By the table, starts and looks at him.]* What do you say?

OSWALD. *[Repeats, in a dull, toneless voice.]* The sun. The sun.

MRS. ALVING. *[Goes to him.]* Oswald, what is the matter with you?

[Oswald seems to shrink together in the chair; all his muscles relax; his face is expressionless, his eyes have a glassy stare.]

MRS. ALVING. *[Quivering with terror.]* What is this? *[Shrieks.]* Oswald! what is the matter with you? *[Falls on her knees beside him and shakes him.]* Oswald! Oswald! look at me! Don't you know me?

OSWALD. *[Tonelessly as before.]* The sun.—The sun.

[Mrs. Alving springs up in despair, entwines her hands in her hair and shrieks.]

MRS. ALVING. I cannot bear it! *[Whispers, as though petrified];* I cannot bear it! Never! *[Suddenly.]* Where has he got them? *[Fumbles hastily in his breast.]* Here! *[Shrinks back a few steps and screams.]* No; no; no!—Yes!—No; no!

[She stands a few steps away from him with her hands twisted in her hair, and stares at him in speechless horror.]

OSWALD. *[Sits motionless as before and says.]* The sun.—The sun.

THE END

The Glass Menagerie

Introduction

Thomas Lanier (Tennessee) Williams was born in Columbus, Mississippi, in 1914, and moved with his family to St. Louis in 1927. He first became interested in the theater when he saw a performance of Ibsen's *Ghosts*. *The Glass Menagerie*, first produced in 1944, became a notable success, won the Drama Critics Circle Award for 1944–1945, and established Williams as one of the most important dramatists in modern America.

Although *The Glass Menagerie* is by no means completely autobiographical, the personal element constitutes an important influence on Williams. Anyone visiting St. Louis today would recognize many apartments like that of the Wingfields, apartments which Williams says "are always burning with the slow and implacable fires of human desperation." Famous and Barr, where Amanda worked for a while, is still an important department store chain in the city. Continental Shoemakers, where Tom worked, has merged with other shoe manufacturers, but Soldan High School, which Laura attended, is still very much a part of the St. Louis school system, and Tom's *Post Dispatch* appears each day. The Wabash Depot, unvisited now by even a train a day, still stands at the corner of Delmar and Des Peres Avenues. Williams' own sister owned a glass menagerie, which he has said "came to represent in my memory all the softest emotions that belong to the recollection of things past. They stood for all the tender things that relieve the austere pattern of life and make it endurable to the sensitive." Williams writes of a limited area which he knows intimately, but in this small segment he sees the world problems common to all humanity.

The influence of Ibsen shows very clearly in *The Glass Menagerie*. Amanda, the mother in this four-character play, is an incurable romantic living in the past, a past in which she was—or visualizes herself as—a charming and enchanting southern belle. It is the "ghost" of this lost past on which she dwells so insistently that brings about her own tragic situation, even though, as Williams says, "she has endurance and a kind of heroism, and though her foolishness makes her unwittingly cruel at times, there is tenderness in her." She is deserted by her husband; she drives her crippled and exceptionally shy daughter, Laura, "till she is like a piece of her own glass collection"; and she finally drives Tom to follow in his father's footsteps and desert her and Laura.

The final irony comes when, after losing her husband, handicapping her already crippled daughter, and forcing Tom to act without pity to escape from her trap, she cries after her departing son, "Go, then! Then go to the moon—you selfish dreamer!" She never completely faces the ghost of the past which has caused so much of her trouble.

THE AUTHOR'S PRODUCTION NOTES

Being a "memory play," *The Glass Menagerie* can be presented with unusual freedom of convention. Because of its considerably delicate or tenuous material, atmospheric touches and subtleties of direction play a particularly important part. Expressionism and all other unconventional techniques in drama have only one valid aim, and that is a closer approach to truth. When a play employs unconventional techniques, it is not, or certainly shouldn't be, trying to escape its responsibility of dealing with reality, or interpreting experience, but is actually or should be attempting to find a closer approach, a more penetrating and vivid expression of things as they are. The straight realistic play with its genuine frigidaire and authentic ice-cubes, its characters that speak exactly as its audience speaks, corresponds to the academic landscape and has the same virtue of a photographic likeness. Everyone should know nowadays the unimportance of the photographic in art: that truth, life, or reality is an organic thing which the poetic imagination can represent or suggest, in essence, only through transformation, through changing into other forms than those which were merely present in appearance.

These remarks are not meant as a preface only to this particular play. They have to do with a conception of a new, plastic theatre which must take the place of the exhausted theatre of realistic conventions if the theatre is to resume vitality as a part of our culture.

THE SCREEN DEVICE. There is *only one important difference between the original and acting version of the play* and that is the *omission* in the latter of the device which I tentatively included in my *original* script. This device was the use of a screen on which were projected magic-lantern slides bearing images or titles. I do not regret the omission of this device from the present Broadway production. The extraordinary power of Miss Taylor's performance made it suitable to have the utmost simplicity in the physical production. But I think it may be interesting to some readers to see how this device was conceived. So I am putting it into the published manuscript. These images and legends, projected from behind, were cast on a section of wall between the front-room and dining-room areas, which should be indistinguishable from the rest when not in use.

The purpose of this will probably be apparent. It is to give accent to certain values in each scene. Each scene contains a particular point (or several) which is structurally the most important. In an episodic play, such as this, the basic structure or narrative line may be obscured from the audience; the effect may seem fragmentary rather than architectural. This may not be the fault of the play so much as a lack of attention in the audience. The legend or image upon the screen will strengthen the effect of what is merely allusion in the writing and allow the primary point to be made more simply and lightly than if the entire responsibility were on the spoken lines. Aside from this structural value, I think the screen will have a definite emotional appeal, less definable but just as important. An imaginative producer or director may invent many other uses for this device than those indicated in the present script. In fact the possibilities of the device seem much larger to me than the instance of this play can possibly utilize.

THE MUSIC. Another extra-literary accent in this play is provided by the use of music. A single recurring tune, "The Glass Menagerie," is used to give emotional emphasis to suitable passages. This tune is like circus music, not when you are on the grounds or in the immediate vicinity of the parade, but when you are at some distance and very likely thinking of something else. It seems under those circumstances to continue almost interminably and it weaves in and out of your preoccupied consciousness; then it is the lightest, most delicate music in the world and perhaps the saddest. It expresses the surface vivacity of life with the underlying strain of immutable and inexpressible sorrow. When you look at a piece of delicately spun glass you think of two things: how beautiful it is and how easily it can be broken. Both of those ideas should be woven into the recurring tune, which dips in and out of the play as if it were carried on a wind that changes. It serves as a thread of connection and allusion between the narrator with his separate point in time and space and the subject of his story. Between each episode it returns as reference to the emotion, nostalgia, which is the first condition of the play. It is primarily Laura's music and therefore comes out most clearly when the play focuses upon her and the lovely fragility of glass which is her image.

THE LIGHTING. The lighting in the play is not realistic. In keeping with the atmosphere of memory, the stage is dim. Shafts of light are focused on selected areas or actors, sometimes in contradistinction to what is the apparent center. For instance, in the quarrel scene between Tom and Amanda, in which Laura has no active part, the clearest pool of light is on her figure. This is also true of the supper scene, when her silent figure on the sofa should remain the visual center. The light upon Laura should be distinct from the others, having a peculiar pristine clarity such as light used in early religious portraits of female saints or madonnas. A certain correspondence to light in religious paintings, such as El Greco's, where the figures are radiant in atmosphere that is relatively dusky, could be effectively used throughout the play. (It will also permit a more effective use of the screen.) A free, imaginative use of light can be of enormous value in giving a mobile, plastic quality to plays of a more or less static nature.

The Glass Menagerie

TENNESSEE WILLIAMS

Characters

AMANDA WINGFIELD *(the mother)*   *A little woman of great but confused vitality clinging frantically to another time and place. Her characterization must be carefully created, not copied from type. She is not paranoiac, but her life is paranoia. There is much to admire in Amanda, and as much to love and pity as there is to laugh at. Certainly she has endurance and a kind of heroism, and though her foolishness makes her unwittingly cruel at times, there is tenderness in her slight person.*

LAURA WINGFIELD *(her daughter)*   *Amanda, having failed to establish contact with reality, continues to live vitally in her illusions, but Laura's situation is even graver. A childhood illness has left her crippled, one leg slightly shorter than the other, and held in a brace. This defect need not be more than suggested on the stage. Stemming from this, Laura's separation increases till she is like a piece of her own glass collection, too exquisitely fragile to move from the shelf.*

TOM WINGFIELD *(her son)*   *And the narrator of the play. A poet with a job in a warehouse. His nature is not remorseless, but to escape from a trap he has to act without pity.*

JIM O'CONNOR *(the gentleman caller)*   *A nice, ordinary, young man.*

SCENE

An Alley in St. Louis
PART I: Preparation for a Gentleman Caller.
PART II: The Gentleman calls.
TIME: Now and the Past.

SCENE 1

The Wingfield apartment is in the rear of the building, one of those
   vast hive-like conglomerations of cellular living-units that flower
   as warty growths in overcrowded urban centers of lower middle-
   class population and are symptomatic of the impulse of this
   largest and fundamentally enslaved section of American society to
   avoid fluidity and differentiation and to exist and function as
   one interfused mass of automatism.
The apartment faces an alley and is entered by a fire-escape,
   a structure whose name is a touch of accidental poetic truth, for
   all of these huge buildings are always burning with the slow and
   implacable fires of human desperation. The fire-escape is
   included in the set—that is, the landing of it and steps
   descending from it.
The scene is memory and is therefore nonrealistic. Memory takes a
   lot of poetic license. It omits some details; others are exaggerated,
   according to the emotional value of the articles it touches, for
   memory is seated predominantly in the heart. The interior is
   therefore rather dim and poetic.
At the rise of the curtain, the audience is faced with the dark, grim
   rear wall of the Wingfield tenement. This building, which runs
   parallel to the footlights, is flanked on both sides by dark,
   narrow alleys which run into murky canyons of tangled
   clotheslines, garbage cans and the sinister lattice-work of
   neighboring fire-escapes. It is up and down these side alleys
   that exterior entrances and exits are made, during the play. At
   the end of Tom's opening commentary, the dark tenement wall
   slowly reveals (by means of a transparency) the interior of the
   ground floor Wingfield apartment.
Downstage is the living room, which also serves as a sleeping room
   for Laura, the sofa unfolding to make her bed. Upstage, center,
   and divided by a wide arch or second proscenium with transparent
   faded portieres (or second curtain), is the dining room. In an
   old-fashioned what-not in the living room are seen scores of
   transparent glass animals. A blown-up photograph of the
   father hangs on the wall of the living room, facing the audience,

*to the left of the archway. It is the face of a very handsome young
man in a doughboy's First World War cap. He is gallantly
smiling, ineluctably smiling, as if to say, "I will be smiling
forever."*
*The audience hears and sees the opening scene in the dining room
through both the transparent fourth wall of the building and the
transparent gauze portieres of the dining-room arch. It is during
this revealing scene that the fourth wall slowly ascends, out
of sight. This transparent exterior wall is not brought down again
until the very end of the play, during Tom's final speech.*
*The narrator is an undisguised convention of the play. He takes
whatever license with dramatic convention as is convenient to his
purposes.*
*Tom enters dressed as a merchant sailor from alley, stage left, and
strolls across the front of the stage to the fire-escape. There
he stops and lights a cigarette. He addresses the audience.*

TOM. Yes, I have tricks in my pocket, I have things up my sleeve.
But I am the opposite of a stage magician. He gives you illusion that
has the appearance of truth. I give you truth in the pleasant disguise
of illusion.

To begin with, I turn back time. I reverse it to that quaint period,
the thirties, when the huge middle class of America was matriculat-
ing in a school for the blind. Their eyes had failed them, or they had
failed their eyes, and so they were having their fingers pressed
forcibly down on the fiery Braille alphabet of a dissolving economy.

In Spain there was revolution. Here there was only shouting and
confusion.

In Spain there was Guernica.[1] Here there were disturbances of
labor, sometimes pretty violent, in otherwise peaceful cities such as
Chicago, Cleveland, Saint Louis . . .

This is the social background of the play.

MUSIC

The play is memory.

Being a memory play, it is dimly lighted, it is sentimental, it is
not realistic.

In memory everything seems to happen to music. That explains
the fiddle in the wings.

I am the narrator of the play, and also a character in it.

The other characters are my mother, Amanda, my sister, Laura,
and a gentleman caller who appears in the final scenes.

He is the most realistic character in the play, being an emissary
from a world of reality that we were somehow set apart from.

---

1 *Guernica:* Basque town in northern Spain which was bombed by the forces of
General Franco in the Spanish Civil War.

But since I have a poet's weakness for symbols, I am using this character also as a symbol; he is the long delayed but always expected something that we live for.

There is a fifth character in the play who doesn't appear except in this larger-than-life-size photograph over the mantel.

This is our father who left us a long time ago.

He was a telephone man who fell in love with long distances; he gave up his job with the telephone company and skipped the light fantastic out of town . . .

The last we heard of him was a picture post-card from Mazatlan, on the Pacific coast of Mexico, containing a message of two words— "Hello— Good-bye!" and no address.

I think the rest of the play will explain itself. . . .

Amanda's voice becomes audible through the portieres

LEGEND ON SCREEN: *"Où sont les neiges"*[2]

[He divides the portieres and enters the upstage area. Amanda and Laura are seated at the drop-leaf table. Eating is indicated by gestures without food or utensils. Amanda faces the audience. Tom and Laura are seated in profile. The interior has lit up softly and through the scrim we see Amanda and Laura seated at the table in the upstage area.]

AMANDA. *[Calling.]* Tom!
TOM. Yes, Mother.
AMANDA. We can't say grace until you come to the table!
TOM. Coming, Mother.

[He bows slightly and withdraws, reappearing a few moments later in his place at the table.]

AMANDA. *[To her son.]* Honey, don't *push* with your *fingers*. If you have to push with something, the thing to push with is a crust of bread. And chew—chew! Animals have sections in their stomachs which enable them to digest food without mastication, but human beings are supposed to chew their food before they swallow it down. Eat food leisurely, son, and really enjoy it. A well-cooked meal has lots of delicate flavors that have to be held in the mouth for appreciation. So chew your food and give your salivary glands a chance to function!

[Tom deliberately lays his imaginary fork down and pushes his chair back from the table.]

TOM. I haven't enjoyed one bite of this dinner because of your constant directions on how to eat it. It's you that make me rush through meals with your hawk-like attention to every bite I take. Sickening—spoils my appetite—all this discussion of—animals' secretion—salivary glands—mastication!

2 *Où . . . neiges:* Where are the snows (of days past).

AMANDA. *[Lightly]* Temperament like a Metropolitan star! *[He rises and crosses downstage.]* You're not excused from the table.

TOM. I'm getting a cigarette.

AMANDA. You smoke too much. *[Laura rises.]*

LAURA. I'll bring in the blanc mange.

[He remains standing with his cigarette by the portieres during the following.]

AMANDA. *[Rising.]* No, sister, no, sister—you be the lady this time and I'll be the darky.

LAURA. I'm already up.

AMANDA. Resume your seat, little sister—I want you to stay fresh and pretty—for gentlemen callers!

LAURA. I'm not expecting any gentlemen callers.

AMANDA. *[Crossing out to kitchenette. Airily]* Sometimes they come when they are least expected! Why, I remember one Sunday afternoon in Blue Mountain— *[Enters kitchenette.]*

TOM. I know what's coming!

LAURA. Yes. But let her tell it.

TOM. Again?

LAURA. She loves to tell it.

[Amanda returns with bowl of dessert.]

AMANDA. One Sunday afternoon in Blue Mountain—your mother received—*seventeen*—gentlemen callers! Why, sometimes there weren't chairs enough to accommodate them all. We had to send the nigger over to bring in folding chairs from the parish house.

TOM. *[Remaining at portieres.]* How did you entertain those gentlemen callers?

AMANDA. I understood the art of conversation!

TOM. I bet you could talk.

AMANDA. Girls in those days *knew* how to talk, I can tell you.

TOM. Yes?

IMAGE: *Amanda as a girl on a porch, greeting callers*

AMANDA. They knew how to entertain their gentlemen callers. It wasn't enough for a girl to be possessed of a pretty face and a graceful figure—although I wasn't slighted in either respect. She also needed to have a nimble wit and a tongue to meet all occasions.

TOM. What did you talk about?

AMANDA. Things of importance going on in the world! Never anything coarse or common or vulgar.

[She addresses Tom as though he were seated in the vacant chair at the table though he remains by portieres. He plays this scene as though he held the book.[3]]

3 *book:* the prompter's script.

My callers were gentlemen—all! Among my callers were some of the most prominent young planters of the Mississippi Delta—planters and sons of planters!

[Tom motions for music and a spot of light on Amanda. Her eyes lift, her face glows, her voice becomes rich and elegiac.]

SCREEN LEGEND: *"Où sont les neiges"*

There was young Champ Laughlin who later became vice-president of the Delta Planters Bank.

Hadley Stevenson who was drowned in Moon Lake and left his widow one hundred and fifty thousand in Government bonds.

There were the Cutrere brothers, Wesley and Bates. Bates was one of my bright particular beaux! He got in a quarrel with that wild Wainwright boy. They shot it out on the floor of Moon Lake Casino. Bates was shot through the stomach. Died in the ambulance on his way to Memphis. His widow was also well-provided for, came into eight or ten thousand acres, that's all. She married him on the rebound—never loved her—carried my picture on him the night he died!

And there was that boy that every girl in the Delta had set her cap for! That beautiful, brilliant young Fitzhugh boy from Greene County!

TOM. What did he leave his widow?

AMANDA. He never married! Gracious, you talk as though all of my old admirers had turned up their toes to the daisies!

TOM. Isn't this the first you've mentioned that still survives?

AMANDA. That Fitzhugh boy went North and made a fortune—came to be known as the Wolf of Wall Street! He had the Midas touch, whatever he touched turned to gold!

And I could have been Mrs. Duncan J. Fitzhugh, mind you! But—I picked your *father!*

LAURA. *[Rising.]* Mother, let me clear the table.

AMANDA. No, dear, you go in front and study your typewriter chart. Or practice your shorthand a little. Stay fresh and pretty!—It's almost time for our gentlemen callers to start arriving. *[She flounces girlishly toward the kitchenette.]* How many do you suppose we're going to entertain this afternoon?

[Tom throws down the paper and jumps up with a groan.]

LAURA. *[Alone in the dining room.]* I don't believe we're going to receive any, Mother.

AMANDA. *[Reappearing; airily.]* What? No one—not one? You must be joking!

[Laura nervously echoes her laugh. She slips in a fugitive manner through the half-open portieres and draws them gently behind her. A shaft of very clear light is thrown on her face against the faded tapestry of the curtains.]

MUSIC: *"The Glass Menagerie" under faintly.*

[*Lightly.*] Not one gentleman caller? It can't be true! There must be a flood, there must have been a tornado!

LAURA. It isn't a flood, it's not a tornado, Mother. I'm just not popular like you were in Blue Mountain. . . . [*Tom utters another groan. Laura glances at him with a faint, apologetic smile. Her voice catching a little*] Mother's afraid I'm going to be an old maid.

THE SCENE DIMS OUT WITH "GLASS MENAGERIE" MUSIC

SCENE 2

"Laura, Haven't You Ever Liked Some Boy?"

On the dark stage the screen is lighted with the image of blue roses. Gradually Laura's figure becomes apparent and the screen goes out. The music subsides.

Laura is seated in the delicate ivory chair at the small clawfoot table. She wears a dress of soft violet material for a kimono— her hair tied back from her forehead with a ribbon. She is washing and polishing her collection of glass.

Amanda appears on the fire-escape steps. At the sound of her ascent, Laura catches her breath, thrusts the bowl of ornaments away and seats herself stiffly before the diagram of the typewriter keyboard as though it held her spellbound. Something has happened to Amanda. It is written in her face as she climbs to the landing: a look that is grim and hopeless and a little absurd. She has on one of those cheap or imitation velvety-looking cloth coats with imitation fur collar. Her hat is five or six years old, one of those dreadful cloche hats that were worn in the late twenties and she is clasping an enormous black patent-leather pocketbook with nickel clasps and initials. This is her full-dress outfit, the one she usually wears to the D. A. R. Before entering she looks through the door. She purses her lips, opens her eyes very wide, rolls them upward and shakes her head. Then she slowly lets herself in the door. Seeing her mother's expression, Laura touches her lips with a nervous gesture.

LAURA. Hello, Mother, I was—

[*She makes a nervous gesture toward the chart on the wall. Amanda leans against the shut door and stares at Laura with a martyred look.*]

AMANDA. Deception? Deception?

[She slowly removes her hat and gloves, continuing the sweet suffering stare. She lets the hat and gloves fall on the floor—a bit of acting.]

LAURA. *[Shakily]* How was the D.A.R. meeting?

[Amanda slowly opens her purse and removes a dainty white hand-kerchief which she shakes out delicately and delicately touches to her lips and nostrils.]

Didn't you go to the D.A.R. meeting, Mother?

AMANDA. *[Faintly, almost inaudibly.]*—No.—No. *[Then more forcibly]* I did not have the strength—to go to the D.A.R. In fact, I did not have the courage! I wanted to find a hole in the ground and hide myself in it forever!

[She crosses slowly to the wall and removes the diagram of the typewriter keyboard. She holds it in front of her for a second, staring at it sweetly and sorrowfully—then bites her lips and tears it in two pieces.]

LAURA. *[Faintly]* Why did you do that, Mother? *[Amanda repeats the same procedure with the chart of the Gregg Alphabet.]* Why are you—

AMANDA. Why? Why? How old are you, Laura?

LAURA. Mother, you know my age.

AMANDA. I thought that you were an adult; it seems that I was mistaken.

[She crosses slowly to the sofa and sinks down and stares at Laura.]

LAURA. Please don't stare at me, Mother.

[Amanda closes her eyes and lowers her head. Count ten.]

AMANDA. What are we going to do, what is going to become of us, what is the future? *[Count ten.]*

LAURA. Has something happened, Mother! *[Amanda draws a long breath and takes out the handkerchief again. Dabbing process.]* Mother, has—something happened?

AMANDA. I'll be all right in a minute, I'm just bewildered—*[Count five.]*—by life. . . .

LAURA. Mother, I wish that you would tell me what's happened!

AMANDA. As you know, I was supposed to be inducted into my office at the D.A.R. this afternoon.

IMAGE: *A swarm of typewriters*

But I stopped off at Rubicam's Business College to speak to your teachers about your having a cold and ask them what progress they thought you were making down there.

LAURA. Oh. . . .

AMANDA. I went to the typing instructor and introduced myself as your mother. She didn't know who you were. Wingfield, she said. We don't have any such student enrolled at the school!

I assured her she did, that you have been going to classes since early in January.

"I wonder," she said, "if you could be talking about that terribly shy little girl who dropped out of school after only a few days' attendance?"

"No," I said, "Laura, my daughter, has been going to school every day for the past six weeks!"

"Excuse me," she said. She took the attendance book out and there was your name, unmistakably printed, and all the dates you were absent until they decided that you had dropped out of school.

I still said, "No, there must have been some mistake! There must have been some mix-up in the records!"

And she said, "No—I remember her perfectly now. Her hands shook so that she couldn't hit the right keys! The first time we gave a speed-test, she broke down completely—was sick at the stomach and almost had to be carried into the wash-room! After that morning she never showed up any more. We phoned the house but never got any answer"—while I was working at Famous and Barr, I suppose, demonstrating those— Oh!

I felt so weak I could barely keep on my feet!

I had to sit down while they got me a glass of water!

Fifty dollars' tuition, all of our plans—my hopes and ambitions for you—just gone up the spout, just gone up the spout like that.

[Laura draws a long breath and gets awkwardly to her feet. She crosses to the victrola and winds it up.]

What are you doing?

LAURA. Oh! *[She releases the handle and returns to her seat.]*

AMANDA. Laura, where have you been going when you've gone out pretending that you were going to business college?

LAURA. I've just been going out walking.

AMANDA. That's not true.

LAURA. It is, I just went walking.

AMANDA. Walking? Walking? In winter? Deliberately courting pneumonia in that light coat? Where did you walk to, Laura?

LAURA. All sorts of places—mostly in the park.

AMANDA. Even after you'd started catching that cold?

LAURA. It was the lesser of two evils, Mother.

IMAGE: *Winter scene in park*

I couldn't go back up. I—threw up—on the floor!

AMANDA. From half past seven till after five every day you mean to tell me you walked around in the park, because you wanted to make me think that you were still going to Rubicam's Business College?

LAURA. It wasn't as bad as it sounds. I went inside places to get warmed up.

AMANDA. Inside where?

LAURA. I went in the art museum and the birdhouses at the Zoo. I visited the penguins every day! Sometimes I did without lunch and went to the movies. Lately I've been spending most of my afternoons in the Jewel-box, that big glass house where they raise the tropical flowers.

AMANDA. You did all this to deceive me, just for deception? *[Laura looks down.]* Why?

LAURA. Mother, when you're disappointed, you get that awful suffering look on your face, like the picture of Jesus' mother in the museum!

AMANDA. Hush!

LAURA. I couldn't face it.

Pause. A whisper of strings

LEGEND: *"The crust of humility"*

AMANDA. *[Hopelessly fingering the huge pocketbook.]* So what are we going to do the rest of our lives? Stay home and watch the parades go by? Amuse ourselves with the glass menagerie, darling? Eternally play those worn-out phonograph records your father left as a painful reminder of him?

We won't have a business career—we've given that up because it gave us nervous indigestion! *[Laughs wearily.]* What is there left but dependency all our lives? I know so well what becomes of unmarried women who aren't prepared to occupy a position. I've seen such pitiful cases in the South—barely tolerated spinsters living upon the grudging patronage of sister's husband or brother's wife!—stuck away in some little mouse-trap of a room—encouraged by one in-law to visit another—little birdlike women without any nest—eating the crust of humility all their life!

Is that the future that we've mapped out for ourselves?

I swear it's the only alternative I can think of!

It isn't a very pleasant alternative, is it?

Of course—some girls *do* marry.

[Laura twists her hands nervously.]

Haven't you ever liked some boy?

LAURA. Yes. I liked one once. *[Rises.]* I came across his picture a while ago.

AMANDA. *[With some interest.]* He gave you his picture?

LAURA. No, it's in the year-book.

AMANDA. *[Disappointed.]* Oh—a high-school boy.

SCREEN IMAGE: *Jim as high-school hero bearing a silver cup*

LAURA. Yes. His name was Jim. *[Laura lifts the heavy annual from the claw-foot table.]* Here he is in *The Pirates of Penzance*.

AMANDA. *[Absently]* The what?

LAURA. The operetta the senior class put on. He had a wonderful voice and we sat across the aisle from each other Mondays, Wednesdays and Fridays in the Aud. Here he is with the silver cup for debating! See his grin?

AMANDA. *[Absently]* He must have had a jolly disposition.

LAURA. He used to call me—Blue Roses.

IMAGE: *Blue Roses*

AMANDA. Why did he call you such a name as that?

LAURA. When I had that attack of pleurosis—he asked me what was the matter when I came back. I said pleurosis—he thought that I said Blue Roses! So that's what he always called me after that. Whenever he saw me, he'd holler, "Hello, Blue Roses!" I didn't care for the girl that he went out with. Emily Meisenback. Emily was the best-dressed girl at Soldan. She never struck me, though, as being sincere . . . It says in the Personal Section—they're engaged. That's—six years ago! They must be married by now.

AMANDA. Girls that aren't cut out for business careers usually wind up married to some nice man. *[Gets up with a spark of revival.]* Sister, that's what you'll do!

[Laura utters a startled, doubtful laugh. She reaches quickly for a piece of glass.]

LAURA. But, Mother—

AMANDA. Yes? *[Crossing to photograph.]*

LAURA. *[In a tone of frightened apology.]* I'm—crippled!

IMAGE: *Screen*

AMANDA. Nonsense, Laura, I've told you never, never to use that word. Why, you're not crippled, you just have a little defect—hardly noticeable, even! When people have some slight disadvantage like that, they cultivate other things to make up for it—develop charm—and vivacity—and—*charm!* That's all you have to do! *[She turns again to the photograph.]* One thing your father had *plenty of*—was *charm!*

Tom motions to the fiddle in the wings

THE SCENE FADES OUT WITH MUSIC

SCENE 3

LEGEND ON SCREEN: *"After the fiasco—"*

[Tom speaks from the fire-escape landing.]

TOM. After the fiasco at Rubicam's Business College, the idea of getting a gentleman caller for Laura began to play a more and more important part in mother's calculations.

It became an obsession. Like some archetype of the universal unconscious, the image of the gentleman caller haunted our small apartment. . . .

IMAGE: *young man at door with flowers*

An evening at home rarely passed without some allusion to this image, this spectre, this hope. . . .

Even when he wasn't mentioned, his presence hung in Mother's preoccupied look and in my sister's frightened, apologetic manner— hung like a sentence passed upon the Wingfields!

Mother was a woman of action as well as words.

She began to take logical steps in the planned direction.

Late that winter and in the early spring—realizing that extra money would be needed to properly feather the nest and plume the bird— she conducted a vigorous campaign on the telephone, roping in subscribers to one of those magazines for matrons called *The Home-maker's Companion,* the type of journal that features the serialized sublimations of ladies of letters who think in terms of delicate cup-like breasts, slim, tapering waists, rich, creamy thighs, eyes like wood-smoke in autumn, fingers that soothe and caress like strains of music, bodies as powerful as Etruscan sculpture.

SCREEN IMAGE: *glamor magazine cover*

[Amanda enters with phone on long extension cord. She is spotted in the dim stage.]

AMANDA. Ida Scott? This is Amanda Wingfield. We *missed* you at the D. A. R. last Monday!

I said to myself: She's probably suffering with that sinus condition! How is that sinus condition?

Horrors! Heaven have mercy!—You're a Christian martyr, yes, that's what you are, a Christian martyr!

Well, I just now happened to notice that your subscription to the *Companion's* about to expire! Yes, it expires with the next issue, honey!—just when that wonderful new serial by Bessie Mae Hopper is getting off to such an exciting start. Oh, honey, it's something that you can't miss! You remember how *Gone With the Wind* took every-body by storm? You simply couldn't go out if you hadn't read it. All everybody *talked* was Scarlett O'Hara. Well, this is a book that critics already compare to *Gone With the Wind.* It's the *Gone With the Wind* of the post-World War generation!—What?—Burning?— Oh, honey, don't let them burn, go take a look in the oven and I'll hold the wire! Heavens—I think she's hung up!

DIM OUT

LEGEND ON SCREEN: *"You think I'm in love with
Continental Shoemakers?"*

*[Before the stage is lighted, the violent voices of Tom and Amanda are
heard. They are quarreling behind the portieres. In front of them stands
Laura with clenched hands and panicky expression. A clear pool of light
on her figure throughout this scene.]*

TOM. What in Christ's name am I—

AMANDA. *[Shrilly]* Don't you use that—

TOM. Supposed to do!

AMANDA. Expression! Not in my—

TOM. Ohhh!

AMANDA. Presence! Have you gone out of your senses?

TOM. I have, that's true, *driven* out!

AMANDA. What is the matter with you, you—big—big—IDIOT!

TOM. Look!—I've got *no thing,* no single thing—

AMANDA. Lower your voice!.

TOM. In my life here that I can call my OWN! Everything is—

AMANDA. Stop that shouting!

TOM. Yesterday you confiscated my books! You had the nerve to—

AMANDA. I took that horrible novel back to the library—yes!
That hideous book by that insane Mr. Lawrence. *[Tom laughs wildly.]*
I cannot control the output of diseased minds or people who cater
to them—*[Tom laughs still more wildly.]* BUT I WON'T ALLOW SUCH
FILTH BROUGHT INTO MY HOUSE! No, no, no, no, no!

TOM. House, house! Who pays rent on it, who makes a slave of
himself to—

AMANDA. *[Fairly screeching]* Don't you DARE to—

TOM. No, no, *I* mustn't say things! *I've* got to just—

AMANDA. Let me tell you—

TOM. I don't want to hear any more!

*[He tears the portieres open. The upstage area is lit with a turgid smoky
red glow. Amanda's hair is in metal curlers and she wears a very old
bathrobe, much too large for her slight figure, a relic of the faithless
Mr. Wingfield. An upright typewriter and a wild disarray of manu-
scripts is on the drop-leaf table. The quarrel was probably precipitated
by Amanda's interruption of his creative labor. A chair lying overthrown on the floor. Their gesticulating shadows are cast on the ceiling
by the fiery glow.]*

AMANDA. You *will* hear more, you—

TOM. No, I won't hear more, I'm going out!

AMANDA. You come right back in—

TOM. Out, out, out! Because I'm—

AMANDA. Come back here, Tom Wingfield! I'm not through talking to you!

TOM. Oh, go—

LAURA. *[Desperately]*—Tom!

AMANDA. You're going to listen, and no more insolence from
you! I'm at the end of my patience!

[He comes back toward her.]

TOM. What do you think I'm at? Aren't I supposed to have any
patience to reach the end of, Mother? I know, I know. It seems
unimportant to you, what I'm *doing*—what I *want* to do—having a
little *difference* between them! You don't think that—

AMANDA. I think you've been doing things that you're ashamed
of. That's why you act like this. I don't believe that you go every
night to the movies. Nobody goes to the movies night after night.
Nobody in their right minds goes to the movies as often as you
pretend to. People don't go to the movies at nearly midnight, and
movies don't let out at two A.M. Come in stumbling. Muttering to
yourself like a maniac! You get three hours' sleep and then go to
work. Oh, I can picture the way you're doing down there. Moping,
doping, because you're in no condition.

TOM. *[Wildly]* No, I'm in no condition!

AMANDA. What right have you got to jeopardize your job? Jeopardize the security of us all? How do you think we'd manage if you
were—

TOM. Listen! You think I'm crazy *about* the *warehouse?* *[He bends
fiercely toward her slight figure.]* You think I'm in love with the
Continental Shoemakers? You think I want to spend fifty-five *years*
down there in that—*celotex interior!* with—*fluorescent—tubes!*
Look! I'd rather somebody picked up a crowbar and battered out my
brains—than go back mornings! I *go!* Every time you come in yelling that God damn *"Rise and Shine!" "Rise and Shine!"* I say to
myself, "How *lucky dead* people are!" But I get up. I *go!* For sixty-
five dollars a month I give up all that I dream of doing and being
ever! And you say self—*self's* all I ever think of. Why, listen, if self
is what I thought of, Mother, I'd be where he is—GONE! *[Pointing
to father's picture.]* As far as the system of transportation reaches!
[He starts past her. She grabs his arm.] Don't grab at me, Mother!

AMANDA. Where are you going?

TOM. I'm going to the *movies!*

AMANDA. I don't believe that lie!

TOM. *[Crouching toward her, overtowering her tiny figure. She
backs away, gasping.]* I'm going to opium dens! Yes, opium dens,
dens of vice and criminals' hang-outs, Mother. I've joined the Hogan
gang, I'm a hired assassin, I carry a tommy-gun in a violin case! I
run a string of cat-houses in the Valley! They call me Killer, Killer
Wingfield, I'm leading a double-life, a simple, honest warehouse
worker by day, by night a dynamic *czar* of the *underworld, Mother.*
I go to gambling casinos, I spin away fortunes on the roulette table!

I wear a patch over one eye and a false mustache, sometimes I put on green whiskers. On those occasions they call me—*El Diablo!* Oh, I could tell you things to make you sleepless! My enemies plan to dynamite this place. They're going to blow us all sky-high some night! I'll be glad, very happy, and so will you! You'll go up, up on a broomstick, over Blue Mountain with seventeen gentlemen callers! You ugly—babbling old—*witch.* . . .

[*He goes through a series of violent, clumsy movements, seizing his overcoat, lunging to the door, pulling it fiercely open. The women watch him, aghast. His arm catches in the sleeve of the coat as he struggles to pull it on. For a moment he is pinioned by the bulky garment. With an outraged groan he tears the coat off again, splitting the shoulder of it, and hurls it across the room. It strikes against the shelf of Laura's glass collection, there is a tinkle of shattering glass. Laura cries out as if wounded.*]

MUSIC. LEGEND: *"The Glass Menagerie"*

LAURA. [*Shrilly*] My glass!—menagerie. . . .

[*She covers her face and turns away. But Amanda is still stunned and stupefied by the "ugly witch" so that she barely notices this occurrence. Now she recovers her speech.*]

AMANDA. [*In an awful voice.*] I won't speak to you—until you apologize!

[*She crosses through portieres and draws them together behind her. Tom is left with Laura. Laura clings weakly to the mantel with her face averted. Tom stares at her stupidly for a moment. Then he crosses to shelf. Drops awkwardly on his knees to collect the fallen glass, glancing at Laura as if he would speak but couldn't.*]

"The Glass Menagerie" steals in as

THE SCENE DIMS OUT

SCENE 4

[*The interior is dark. Faint light in the alley. A deep-voiced bell in a
  church is tolling the hour of five as the scene commences.
  Tom appears at the top of the alley. After each solemn boom of
  the bell in the tower, he shakes a little noise-maker or rattle as if to
  express the tiny spasm of man in contrast to the sustained power
  and dignity of the Almighty. This and the unsteadiness of his
  advance make it evident that he has been drinking. As he climbs
  the few steps to the fire-escape landing light steals up inside.*

Laura appears in night-dress, observing Tom's empty bed in the front room. Tom fishes in his pockets for door-key, removing a motley assortment of articles in the search, including a perfect shower of movie-ticket stubs and an empty bottle. At last he finds the key, but just as he is about to insert it, it slips from his fingers. He strikes a match and crouches below the door.

TOM. *[Bitterly]* One crack—and it falls through!

> *[Laura opens the door.]*

LAURA. Tom! Tom, what are you doing?

TOM. Looking for a door-key.

LAURA. Where have you been all this time?

TOM. I have been to the movies.

LAURA. All this time at the movies?

TOM. There was a very long program. There was a Garbo picture and a Mickey Mouse and a travelogue and a newsreel and a preview of coming attractions. And there was an organ solo and a collection for the milk-fund—simultaneously—which ended up in a terrible fight between a fat lady and an usher!

LAURA. *[Innocently]* Did you have to stay through everything?

TOM. Of course! And, oh, I forgot! There was a big stage show! The headliner on this stage show was Malvolio the Magician. He performed wonderful tricks, many of them, such as pouring water back and forth between pitchers. First it turned to wine and then it turned to beer and then it turned to whiskey. I know it was whiskey it finally turned into because he needed somebody to come up out of the audience to help him, and I came up—both shows! It was Kentucky Straight Bourbon. A very generous fellow, he gave souvenirs. *[He pulls from his back pocket a shimmering rainbow-colored scarf.]* He gave me this. This is his magic scarf. You can have it, Laura. You wave it over a canary cage and you get a bowl of gold-fish. You wave it over the gold-fish bowl and they fly away canaries. . . . But the wonderfullest trick of all was the coffin trick. We nailed him into a coffin and he got out of the coffin without removing one nail. *[He has come inside.]* There is a trick that would come in handy for me—get me out of this 2 by 4 situation.

> *[Flops onto bed and starts removing shoes.]*

LAURA. Tom—Shhh!

TOM. What're you shushing me for?

LAURA. You'll wake up Mother.

TOM. Goody, goody! Pay 'er back for all those "Rise an' Shines." *[Lies down, groaning.]* You know it don't take much intelligence to get yourself into a nailed-up coffin, Laura. But who in hell ever got himself out of one without removing one nail?

> *As if in answer, the father's grinning photograph*
> *lights up*

SCENE DIMS OUT

[Immediately following: The church bell is heard striking six. At the sixth stroke the alarm clock goes off in Amanda's room, and after a few moments we hear her calling: "Rise and Shine! Rise and Shine! Laura, go tell your brother to rise and shine!"]

TOM. *[Sitting up slowly.]* I'll rise—but I won't shine.

The light increases

AMANDA. Laura, tell your brother his coffee is ready.
                              [Laura slips into front room.]
LAURA. Tom!—It's nearly seven. Don't make Mother nervous. *[He stares at her stupidly. Beseechingly.]* Tom, speak to Mother this morning. Make up with her, apologize, speak to her!

TOM. She won't to me. It's her that started not speaking.

LAURA. If you just say you're sorry she'll start speaking.

TOM. Her not speaking—is that such a tragedy?

LAURA. Please—please!

AMANDA. *[Calling from kitchenette.]* Laura, are you going to do what I asked you to do, or do I have to get dressed and go out myself?

LAURA. Going, going—soon as I get on my coat!

[She pulls on a shapeless felt hat with nervous, jerky movement, pleadingly glancing at Tom. Rushes awkwardly for coat. The coat is one of Amanda's, inaccurately made-over, the sleeves too short for Laura.]

Butter and what else?

AMANDA. *[Entering upstage.]* Just butter. Tell them to charge it.

LAURA. Mother, they make such faces when I do that.

AMANDA. Sticks and stones can break our bones, but the expression on Mr. Garfinkel's face won't harm us! Tell your brother his coffee is getting cold.

LAURA. *[At door.]* Do what I asked you, will you, will you, Tom?
                              [He looks sullenly away.]
AMANDA. Laura, go now or just don't go at all!

LAURA. *[Rushing out.]* Going—going!

[A second later she cries out. Tom springs up and crosses to door. Amanda rushes anxiously in. Tom opens the door.]

TOM. Laura?

LAURA. I'm all right. I slipped, but I'm all right.

AMANDA. *[Peering anxiously after her.]* If anyone breaks a leg on those fire-escape steps, the landlord ought to be sued for every cent he possesses!

[She shuts door. Remembers she isn't speaking and returns to other room as Tom enters listlessly for his coffee, she turns her back to him and stands rigidly facing the window on the gloomy gray vault of the areaway. Its light on her face with its aged but childish features is cruelly sharp, satirical as a Daumier print.]

MUSIC UNDER: *"Ave Maria"*

[Tom glances sheepishly but sullenly at her averted figure and slumps at the table. The coffee is scalding hot; he sips it and gasps and spits it back in the cup. At his gasp, Amanda catches her breath and half turns. Then catches herself and turns back to window. Tom blows on his coffee, glancing sidewise at his mother. She clears her throat. Tom clears his. He starts to rise. Sinks back down again, scratches his head, clears his throat again. Amanda coughs. Tom raises his cup in both hands to blow on it, his eyes staring over the rim of it at his mother for several moments. Then he slowly sets the cup down and awkwardly and hesitantly rises from the chair.]

TOM. *[Hoarsely]* Mother. I—I apologize, Mother.

[Amanda draws a quick, shuddering breath. Her face works grotesquely. She breaks into childlike tears.]

I'm sorry for what I said, for everything that I said, I didn't mean it.

AMANDA. *[Sobbingly]* My devotion has made me a witch and so I make myself hateful to my children!

TOM. *No,* you *don't.*

AMANDA. I worry so much, don't sleep, it makes me nervous!

TOM. *[Gently]* I understand that.

AMANDA. I've had to put up a solitary battle all these years. But you're my right-hand bower! Don't fall down, don't fail!

TOM. *[Gently]* I try, Mother.

AMANDA. *[With great enthusiasm.]* Try and you will SUCCEED! *[The notion makes her breathless.]* Why, you—you're just *full* of natural endowments! Both of my children—they're *unusual* children! Don't you think I know it? I'm so—*proud!* Happy and—feel I've—so much to be thankful for but— Promise me one thing, Son!

TOM. What, Mother?

AMANDA. Promise, son, you'll—never be a drunkard!

TOM. *[Turns to her grinning.]* I will never be a drunkard, Mother.

AMANDA. That's what frightened me so, that you'd be drinking! Eat a bowl of Purina!

TOM. Just coffee, Mother.

AMANDA. Shredded wheat biscuit?

TOM. No. No, Mother, just coffee.

AMANDA. You can't put in a day's work on an empty stomach. You've got ten minutes—don't gulp! Drinking too-hot liquids makes cancer of the stomach. . . . Put cream in.

TOM. No, thank you.

AMANDA. To cool it.

TOM. No! No, thank you, I want it black.

AMANDA. I know, but it's not good for you. We have to do all that we can to build ourselves up. In these trying times we live in, all that we have to cling to is—each other. . . . That's why it's so important to— Tom, I— I sent out your sister so I could discuss something with you. If you hadn't spoken I would have spoken to you. *[Sits down.]*

TOM. *[Gently]* What is it, Mother, that you want to discuss?

AMANDA. *Laura!*

> *[Tom puts his cup down slowly.]*

LEGEND ON SCREEN: *"Laura"*

MUSIC: *"The Glass Menagerie"*

TOM. —Oh.—Laura . . .

AMANDA. *[Touching his sleeve.]* You know how Laura is. So quiet but—still water runs deep! She notices things and I think she— broods about them. *[Tom looks up.]* A few days ago I came in and she was crying.

TOM. What about?

AMANDA. You.

TOM. Me?

AMANDA. She has an idea that you're not happy here.

TOM. What gave her that idea?

AMANDA. What gives her any idea? However, you do act strangely. I—I'm not criticizing, understand *that!* I know your ambitions do not lie in the warehouse, that like everybody in the whole wide world —you've had to—make sacrifices, but—Tom—Tom—life's not easy, it calls for—Spartan endurance! There's so many things in my heart that I cannot describe to you! I've never told you but I—*loved* your father. . . .

TOM. *[Gently]* I know that, Mother.

AMANDA. And you—when I see you taking after his ways! Staying out late—and—well, you *had* been drinking the night you were in that—terrifying condition! Laura says that you hate the apartment and that you go out nights to get away from it! Is that true, Tom?

TOM. No. You say there's so much in your heart that you can't describe to me. That's true of me, too. There's so much in my heart that I can't describe to *you!* So let's respect each other's—

AMANDA. But, why—*why,* Tom—are you always so *restless?* Where do you *go* to, nights?

TOM. I—go to the movies.

AMANDA. Why do you go to the movies so much, Tom?

TOM. I go to the movies because—I like adventure. Adventure is something I don't have much of at work, so I go to the movies.

AMANDA. But, Tom, you go to the movies *entirely too much!*

TOM. I like a lot of adventure.

[Amanda looks baffled, then hurt. As the familiar inquisition resumes he becomes hard and impatient again. Amanda slips back into her querulous attitude toward him.]

IMAGE ON SCREEN: *Sailing vessel with Jolly*
Roger

AMANDA. Most young men find adventure in their careers.

TOM. Then most young men are not employed in a warehouse.

AMANDA. The world is full of young men employed in warehouses
and offices and factories.

TOM. Do all of them find adventure in their careers?

AMANDA. They do or they do without it! Not everybody has a craze
for adventure.

TOM. Man is by instinct a lover, a hunter, a fighter, and none of
those instincts are given much play at the warehouse!

AMANDA. Man is by instinct! Don't quote instinct to me! Instinct
is something that people have got away from! It belongs to animals!
Christian adults don't want it!

TOM. What do Christian adults want, then, Mother?

AMANDA. Superior things! Things of the mind and the spirit!
Only animals have to satisfy instincts! Surely your aims are somewhat higher than theirs! Than monkeys—pigs—

TOM. I reckon they're not.

AMANDA. You're joking. However, that isn't what I wanted to
discuss.

TOM. *[Rising.]* I haven't much time.

AMANDA. *[Pushing his shoulders.]* Sit down.

TOM. You want me to punch in red at the warehouse, Mother?

AMANDA. You have five minutes. I want to talk about Laura.

LEGEND: *"Plans and provisions"*

TOM. All right! What about Laura?

AMANDA. We have to be making some plans and provisions for
her. She's older than you, two years, and nothing has happened.
She just drifts along doing nothing. It frightens me terribly how she
just drifts along.

TOM. I guess she's the type that people call home girls.

AMANDA. There's no such type, and if there is, it's a pity! That
is unless the home is hers, with a husband!

TOM. What?

AMANDA. Oh, I can see the handwriting on the wall as plain as
I see the nose in front of my face! It's terrifying! More and more
you remind me of your father! He was out all hours without explanation!—Then *left! Good-bye!* And me with the bag to hold. I saw
that letter you got from the Merchant Marine. I know what you're
dreaming of. I'm not standing here blindfolded. Very well, then.
Then *do* it! But not till there's somebody to take your place.

TOM. What do you mean?

AMANDA. I mean that as soon as Laura has got somebody to take
care of her, married, a home of her own, independent—why, then

you'll be free to go wherever you please, on land, on sea, whichever way the wind blows you! But until that time you've got to look out for your sister. I don't say me because I'm old and don't matter! I say for your sister because she's young and dependent. I put her in business college—a dismal failure! Frightened her so it made her sick at the stomach. I took her over to the Young People's League at the church. Another fiasco. She spoke to nobody, nobody spoke to her. Now all she does is fool with those pieces of glass and play those wornout records. What kind of a life is that for a girl to lead?

TOM. What can I do about it?

AMANDA. Overcome selfishness! Self, self, self is all that you ever think of!

[Tom springs up and crosses to get his coat. It is ugly and bulky. He pulls on a cap with earmuffs.]

Where is your muffler? Put your wool muffler on!

[He snatches it angrily from the closet and tosses it around his neck and pulls both ends tight.]

Tom! I haven't said what I had in mind to ask you.

TOM. I'm too late to—

AMANDA.

[Catching his arm—very importunately. Then shyly.]

Down at the warehouse, aren't there some—nice young men?

TOM. No!

AMANDA. There *must* be—*some* . . .

TOM. Mother—   *[Gesture.]*

AMANDA. Find out one that's clean-living—doesn't drink and—ask him out for sister!

TOM. What?

AMANDA. For *sister!* To *meet!* Get *acquainted!*

TOM. *[Stamping to door.]* Oh, my go-osh!

AMANDA. Will you? *[He opens door. Imploringly]* Will you? *[He starts down.]* Will you? *Will* you, dear?

TOM. *[Calling back.]* YES!

[Amanda closes the door hesitantly and with a troubled but faintly hopeful expression.]

SCREEN IMAGE: *Glamor Magazine Cover*

Spot Amanda at phone

AMANDA. Ella Cartwright? This is Amanda Wingfield! How are you, honey? How is that kidney condition? *[Count five]* Horrors! *[Count five]* You're a Christian martyr, yes, honey, that's what you are, a Christian martyr! Well, I just now happened to notice in my little red book that your subscription to the *Companion* has just run out! I knew that you wouldn't want to miss out on the wonderful serial starting in this new issue. It's by Bessie Mae Hopper, the first thing she's written since *Honeymoon for Three.* Wasn't that a strange and interesting story? Well, this one is even lovelier, I believe. It has a sophisticated, society background. It's all about the horsey set on Long Island!

FADE OUT

SCENE 5

LEGEND ON SCREEN: *"Annunciation." Fade*
with music.

It is early dusk of a spring evening. Supper has just been finished in the Wingfield apartment. Amanda and Laura in light-colored dresses are removing dishes from the table, in the upstage area, which is shadowy, their movements formalized almost as a dance or ritual, their moving forms as pale and silent as moths. Tom, in white shirt and trousers, rises from the table and crosses toward the fire-escape.

AMANDA. *[As he passes her.]* Son, will you do me a favor?
TOM. What?
AMANDA. Comb your hair! You look so pretty when your hair is combed!

[Tom slouches on sofa with evening paper. Enormous caption "Franco Triumphs."]

There is only one respect in which I would like you to emulate your father.
TOM. What respect is that?
AMANDA. The care he always took of his appearance. He never allowed himself to look untidy.

[He throws down the paper and crosses to fire-escape.]

Where are you going?
TOM. I'm going out to smoke.
AMANDA. You smoke too much. A pack a day at fifteen cents a pack. How much would that amount to in a month? Thirty times fifteen is how much, Tom? Figure it out and you will be astounded at what you could save. Enough to give you a night-school course

in accounting at Washington U! Just think what a wonderful thing that would be for you, Son!

[*Tom is unmoved by the thought.*]

TOM. I'd rather smoke. [*He steps out on landing, letting the screen door slam.*]

AMANDA. [*Sharply*] I know! That's the tragedy of it. . . .

[*Alone, she turns to look at her husband's picture.*]

> DANCE MUSIC: *"All the world is waiting for the sunrise!"*

TOM. [*To the audience.*] Across the alley from us was the Paradise Dance Hall. On evenings in spring the windows and doors were open and the music came outdoors. Sometimes the lights were turned out except for a large glass sphere that hung from the ceiling. It would turn slowly about and filter the dusk with delicate rainbow colors. Then the orchestra played a waltz or a tango, something that had a slow and sensuous rhythm. Couples would come outside, to the relative privacy of the alley. You could see them kissing behind ash-pits and telephone poles. This was the compensation for lives that passed like mine, without any change or adventure. Adventure and change were imminent in this year. They were waiting around the corner for all these kids. Suspended in the mist over Berchtesgaden,[1] caught in the folds of Chamberlain's umbrella[2]—In Spain there was Guernica! But here there was only hot swing music and liquor, dance halls, bars, and movies, and sex that hung in the gloom like a chandelier and flooded the world with brief, deceptive rainbows. . . . All the world was waiting for bombardments!

> [*Amanda turns from the picture and comes outside*]

AMANDA. [*Sighing*] A fire-escape landing's a poor excuse for a porch.

[*She spreads a newspaper on a step and sits down, gracefully and demurely as if she were settling into a swing on a Mississippi veranda.*]

What are you looking at?

TOM. The moon.

AMANDA. Is there a moon this evening?

TOM. It's rising over Garfinkel's Delicatessen.

AMANDA. So it is! A little silver slipper of a moon. Have you made a wish on it yet?

TOM. Um-hum.

AMANDA. What did you wish for?

TOM. That's a secret.

AMANDA. A secret, huh? Well, I won't tell mine either. I will be just as mysterious as you.

---

1 *Berchtesgaden:* mountain retreat of Adolph Hitler.
2 *Chamberlain's umbrella:* Neville Chamberlain, elderly Conservative prime minister of England before World War II, habitually carried an umbrella.

TOM. I bet I can guess what yours is.

AMANDA. Is my head so transparent?

TOM. You're not a sphinx.

AMANDA. No, I don't have secrets. I'll tell you what I wished for on the moon. Success and happiness for my precious children! I wish for that whenever there's a moon, and when there isn't a moon, I wish for it, too.

TOM. I thought perhaps you wished for a gentleman caller.

AMANDA. Why do you say that?

TOM. Don't you remember asking me to fetch one?

AMANDA. I remember suggesting that it would be nice for your sister if you brought home some nice young man from the warehouse. I think that I've made that suggestion more than once.

TOM. Yes, you have made it repeatedly.

AMANDA. Well?

TOM. We are going to have one.

AMANDA. *What?*

TOM. A gentleman caller!

The annunciation is celebrated with music

[Amanda rises]

IMAGE ON SCREEN: *caller with bouquet*

AMANDA. You mean you have asked some nice young man to come over?

TOM. Yep. I've asked him to dinner.

AMANDA. You really did?

TOM. I did!

AMANDA. You did, and did he—*accept?*

TOM. He did!

AMANDA. Well, well—well, well! That's—lovely!

TOM. I thought that you would be pleased.

AMANDA. It's definite, then?

TOM. Very definite.

AMANDA. Soon?

TOM. Very soon.

AMANDA. For heaven's sake, stop putting on and tell me some things, will you?

TOM. What things do you want me to tell you?

AMANDA. *Naturally* I would like to know when he's *coming!*

TOM. He's coming tomorrow.

AMANDA. *Tomorrow?*

TOM. Yep. Tomorrow.

AMANDA. But, Tom?

TOM. Yes, Mother?

AMANDA. Tomorrow gives me no time!

TOM. Time for what?

AMANDA. Preparations! Why didn't you phone me at once, as

soon as you asked him, the minute that he accepted? Then, don't you see, I could have been getting ready!

TOM. You don't have to make any fuss.

AMANDA. Oh, Tom, Tom, Tom, of course I have to make a fuss! I want things nice, not sloppy! Not thrown together. I'll certainly have to do some fast thinking, won't I?

TOM. I don't see why you have to think at all.

AMANDA. You just don't know. We can't have a gentleman caller in a pig-sty. All my wedding silver has to be polished, the monogrammed table linen ought to be laundered! The windows have to be washed and fresh curtains put up. And how about clothes? We have to *wear* something, don't we?

TOM. Mother, this boy is no one to make a fuss over!

AMANDA. Do you realize he's the first young man we've introduced to your sister? It's terrible, dreadful, disgraceful that poor little sister has never received a single gentleman caller! Tom, come inside!

[She opens the screen door.]

TOM. What for?

AMANDA. I want to ask you some things.

TOM. If you're going to make such a fuss, I'll call it off, I'll tell him not to come!

AMANDA. You certainly won't do anything of the kind. Nothing offends people worse than broken engagements. It simply means I'll have to work like a Turk! We won't be brilliant, but we will pass inspection. Come on inside. *[Tom follows, groaning.]* Sit down.

TOM. Any particular place you would like me to sit?

AMANDA. Thank heavens I've got that new sofa! I'm also making payments on a floor lamp I'll have sent out! And put the chintz covers on, they'll brighten things up! Of course I'd hoped to have these walls re-papered. . . . What is the young man's name?

TOM. His name is O'Connor.

AMANDA. That, of course, means fish—tomorrow is Friday! I'll have that salmon loaf—with Durkee's dressing! What does he do? He works at the warehouse?

TOM. Of course! How else would I—

AMANDA. Tom, he—doesn't drink?

TOM. Why do you ask me that?

AMANDA. Your father *did!*

TOM. Don't get started on that!

AMANDA. He *does* drink, then?

TOM. Not that I know of!

AMANDA. Make sure, be certain! The last thing I want for my daughter's a boy who drinks!

TOM. Aren't you being a little bit premature? Mr. O'Connor has not yet appeared on the scene!

AMANDA. But will tomorrow. To meet your sister, and what do

I know about his character? Nothing! Old maids are better off than wives of drunkards!

TOM. Oh, my God!

AMANDA. Be still!

TOM. *[Leaning forward to whisper.]* Lots of fellows meet girls whom they don't marry!

AMANDA. Oh, talk sensibly, Tom—and don't be sarcastic! *[She has gotten a hairbrush.]*

TOM. What are you doing?

AMANDA. I'm brushing that cow-lick down! What is this young man's position at the warehouse?

TOM. *[Submitting grimly to the brush and the interrogation.]* This young man's position is that of a shipping clerk, Mother.

AMANDA. Sounds to me like a fairly responsible job, the sort of a job *you* would be in if you just had more *get-up.*
What is his salary? Have you any idea?

TOM. I would judge it to be approximately eighty-five dollars a month.

AMANDA. Well—not princely, but—

TOM. Twenty more than I make.

AMANDA. Yes, how well I know! But for a family man, eighty-five dollars a month is not much more than you can just get by on. . . .

TOM. Yes, but Mr. O'Connor is not a family man.

AMANDA. He might be, mightn't he? Some time in the future?

TOM. I see. Plans and provisions.

AMANDA. You are the only young man that I know of who ignores the fact that the future becomes the present, the present the past, and the past turns into everlasting regret if you don't plan for it!

TOM. I will think that over and see what I can make of it.

AMANDA. Don't be supercilious with your mother! Tell me some more about this—what do you call him?

TOM. James D. O'Connor. The *D.* is for Delaney.

AMANDA. Irish on *both* sides! *Gracious!* And doesn't drink?

TOM. Shall I call him up and ask him right this minute?

AMANDA. The only way to find out about those things is to make discreet inquiries at the proper moment. When I was a girl in Blue Mountain and it was suspected that a young man drank, the girl whose attentions he had been receiving, if any girl *was,* would sometimes speak to the minister of his church, or rather her father would if her father was living, and sort of feel him out on the young man's character. That is the way such things are discreetly handled to keep a young woman from making a tragic mistake!

TOM. Then how did you happen to make a tragic mistake?

AMANDA. That innocent look of your father's had everyone fooled! He *smiled*—the world was *enchanted!* No girl can do worse than put herself at the mercy of a handsome appearance! I hope that Mr. O'Connor is not too good-looking.

TOM. No, he's not too good-looking. He's covered with freckles and hasn't too much of a nose.

AMANDA. He's not right-down homely, though?

TOM. Not right-down homely. Just medium homely, I'd say.

AMANDA. Character's what to look for in a man.

TOM. That's what I've always said, Mother.

AMANDA. You've never said anything of the kind and I suspect you would never give it a thought.

TOM. Don't be so suspicious of me.

AMANDA. At least I hope he's the type that's up and coming.

TOM. I think he really goes in for self-improvement.

AMANDA. What reason have you to think so?

TOM. He goes to night school.

AMANDA. *[Beaming.]* Splendid! What does he do, I mean study?

TOM. Radio engineering and public speaking!

AMANDA. Then he has visions of being advanced in the world! Any young man who studies public speaking is aiming to have an executive job some day! And radio engineering? A thing for the future! Both of these facts are very illuminating. Those are the sort of things that a mother should know concerning any young man who comes to call on her daughter. Seriously or—not.

TOM. One little warning. He doesn't know about Laura. I didn't let on that we had dark ulterior motives. I just said, why don't you come and have dinner with us? He said okay and that was the whole conversation.

AMANDA. I bet it was! You're eloquent as an oyster. However, he'll know about Laura when he gets here. When he sees how lovely and sweet and pretty she is, he'll thank his lucky stars he was asked to dinner.

TOM. Mother, you mustn't expect too much of Laura.

AMANDA. What do you mean?

TOM. Laura seems all those things to you and me because she's ours and we love her. We don't even notice she's crippled any more.

AMANDA. Don't say crippled. You know that I never allow that word to be used!

TOM. But face facts, Mother. She is and—that's not all—

AMANDA. What do you mean "not all"?

TOM. Laura is very different from other girls.

AMANDA. I think the difference is all to her advantage.

TOM. Not quite all—in the eyes of others—strangers—she's terribly shy and lives in a world of her own and those things make her seem a little peculiar to people outside the house.

AMANDA. Don't say peculiar.

TOM. Face the facts. She is.

> *The dance-hall music changes to a tango that has*
> *a minor and somewhat ominous tone*

AMANDA. In what way is she peculiar—may I ask?

TOM. *[Gently]* She lives in a world of her own—a world of—little glass ornaments, Mother. . . .

[Gets up. Amanda remains holding brush, looking at him, troubled.]

She plays old phonograph records and—that's about all—

      [He glances at himself in the mirror and crosses to door.]

AMANDA. *[Sharply]* Where are you going?

TOM. I'm going to the movies. *[Out screen door.]*

AMANDA. Not to the movies, every night to the movies! *[Follows quickly to screen door.]* I don't believe you always go to the movies! *[He is gone. Amanda looks worriedly after him for a moment. Then vitality and optimism return and she turns from the door. Crossing to portieres.]* Laura! Laura!

LAURA. *[Answers from kitchenette.]* Yes, Mother.

AMANDA. Let those dishes go and come in front! *[Laura appears with dish towel. Gaily]* Laura, come here and make a wish on the moon!

SCREEN IMAGE: *moon*

LAURA. *[Entering.]* Moon—moon?

AMANDA. A little silver slipper of a moon. Look over your left shoulder, Laura, and make a wish!

[Laura looks faintly puzzled as if called out of sleep. Amanda seizes her shoulders and turns her at an angle by the door.]

Now! Now, darling, *wish!*

LAURA. What shall I wish for, Mother?

AMANDA. *[Her voice trembling and her eyes suddenly filling with tears.]* Happiness, Good fortune!

      The violin rises and the stage dims out

CURTAIN

SCENE 6

IMAGE: *high school hero*

TOM. And so the following evening I brought Jim home to dinner. I had known Jim slightly in high school. In high school Jim was a hero. He had tremendous Irish good nature and vitality with the scrubbed and polished look of white chinaware. He seemed to move in a continual spotlight. He was a star in basketball, captain of the debating club, president of the senior class and the glee club and he sang the male lead in the annual light operas. He was always running or bounding, never just walking. He seemed always at the point of defeating the law of gravity. He was shooting with such velocity through his adolescence that you would logically expect him to arrive at nothing short of the White House by the time he was thirty. But Jim apparently ran into more interference after his graduation from Soldan. His speed had definitely slowed. Six years after he left high school he was holding a job that wasn't much better than mine.

IMAGE: *clerk*

He was the only one at the warehouse with whom I was on friendly terms. I was valuable to him as someone who could remember his former glory, who had seen him win basketball games and the silver cup in debating. He knew of my secret practice of retiring to a cabinet of the wash-room to work on poems when business was slack in the warehouse. He called me Shakespeare. And while the other boys in the warehouse regarded me with suspicious hostility, Jim took a humorous attitude toward me. Gradually his attitude affected the others, their hostility wore off and they also began to smile at me as people smile at an oddly fashioned dog who trots across their path at some distance.

I knew that Jim and Laura had known each other at Soldan, and I had heard Laura speak admiringly of his voice. I didn't know if Jim remembered her or not. In high school Laura had been as unobtrusive as Jim had been astonishing. If he did remember Laura, it was not as my sister, for when I asked him to dinner, he grinned and said, "You know, Shakespeare, I never thought of you as having folks!"

He was about to discover that I did. . . .

Light up stage

LEGEND ON SCREEN: *"the accent of a coming
foot"*

[Friday evening. It is about five o'clock of a late spring evening which comes "scattering poems in the sky." A delicate lemony light is in the Wingfield apartment. Amanda has worked like a Turk in preparation for the gentleman caller. The results are astonishing. The new floor lamp with its rose-silk shade is in place, a colored paper lantern conceals the broken light-fixture in the ceiling, new billowing white curtains are at the windows, chintz covers are on chairs and sofa, a pair of new sofa pillows make their initial appearance. Open boxes and tissue paper are scattered on the floor. Laura stands in the middle with lifted arms while Amanda crouches before her, adjusting the hem of the new dress, devout and ritualistic. The dress is colored and designed by memory. The arrangement of Laura's hair is changed; it is softer *and more becoming. A fragile, unearthly prettiness has come out in Laura; she is like a piece of translucent glass touched by light, given a momentary radiance, not actual, not lasting.]*

AMANDA. *[Impatiently.]* Why are you trembling?

LAURA. Mother, you've made me so nervous!

AMANDA. How have I made you nervous?

LAURA. By all this fuss! You make it seem so important!

AMANDA. I don't understand you, Laura. You couldn't be satisfied with just sitting home, and yet whenever I try to arrange something for you, you seem to resist it. *[She gets up.]* Now take a look at yourself. No, wait! Wait just a moment—I have an idea!

LAURA. What is it now?

[Amanda produces two powder puffs which she wraps in handkerchiefs and stuffs in Laura's bosom.]

LAURA. Mother, what are you doing?

AMANDA. They call them "Gay Deceivers"!

LAURA. I won't wear them!

AMANDA. You will!

LAURA. Why should I?

AMANDA. Because, to be painfully honest, your chest is flat.

LAURA. You make it seem like we were setting a trap.

AMANDA. All pretty girls are a trap, a pretty trap, and men expect them to be.

LEGEND: *"a pretty trap"*

Now look at yourself, young lady. This is the prettiest you will ever be! I've got to fix myself now! You're going to be surprised by your mother's appearance!

[She crosses through portieres, humming gaily. Laura moves slowly to the long mirror and stares solemnly at herself. A wind blows the white curtains inward in a slow, graceful motion and with a faint, sorrowful sighing.]

AMANDA. *[Off stage.]* It isn't dark enough yet.

[She turns slowly before the mirror with a troubled look.]

LEGEND ON SCREEN: *"This is my sister: celebrate her with strings!"*

MUSIC

AMANDA. *[Laughing, off.]* I'm going to show you something. I'm going to make a spectacular appearance!

LAURA. What is it, Mother?

AMANDA. Possess your soul in patience—you will see! Something I've resurrected from that old trunk! Styles haven't changed so terribly much after all. . . . *[She parts the portieres.]* Now just look at your mother! [She wears a girlish frock of yellowed voile with a blue* *silk sash. She carries a bunch of jonquils—the legend of her youth is nearly revived. Feverishly]* This is the dress in which I led the cotillion. Won the cakewalk twice at Sunset Hill, wore one spring to the Governor's ball in Jackson! See how I sashayed around the ballroom, Laura? *[She raises her skirt and does a mincing step around the room.]* I wore it on Sundays for my gentlemen callers! I had it on the day I met your father—I had malaria fever all that spring. The change of climate from East Tennessee to the Delta—weakened resistance—I had a little temperature all the time—not enough to be serious—just enough to make me restless and giddy!—Invitations poured in—parties all over the Delta!—"Stay in bed," said Mother, "you have fever!"—but I just wouldn't.—I took quinine but kept on going, going!—Evenings, dances!—Afternoons, long, long rides! Picnics—lovely!—So lovely, that country in May.—All lacy with dogwood, literally flooded with jonquils!—That was the spring I had the craze for jonquils. Jonquils became an absolute obsession. Mother said "Honey, there's no more room for jonquils." And still I kept on bringing in more jonquils. Whenever, wherever I saw them, I'd say, "Stop! Stop! I see jonquils!" I made the young men help me gather the jonquils! It was a joke, Amanda and her jonquils! Finally there were no more vases to hold them, every available space was filled with jonquils. No vases to hold them? All right, I'll hold them myself! And then I—*[She stops in front of the picture.]*

MUSIC

met your father! Malaria fever and jonquils and then—this— boy. . . . *[She switches on the rose-colored lamp.]* I hope they get here before it starts to rain. *[She crosses upstage and places the jonquils in bowl on table.]* I gave your brother a little extra change so he and Mr. O'Connor could take the service car home.

LAURA. *[With altered look.]* What did you say his name was?
AMANDA. O'Connor.
LAURA. What is his first name?
AMANDA. I don't remember. Oh, yes, I do. It was—Jim!
    [Laura sways slightly and catches hold of a chair.]

LEGEND ON SCREEN: *"Not Jim!"*

LAURA. *[Faintly]* Not—Jim!
AMANDA. Yes, that was it, it was Jim! I've never known a Jim that wasn't nice!

MUSIC: *Ominous*

LAURA. Are you sure his name is Jim O'Connor?
AMANDA. Yes. Why?
LAURA. Is he the one that Tom used to know in high school?

AMANDA. He didn't say so. I think he just got to know him at the warehouse.

LAURA. There was a Jim O'Connor we both knew in high school— *[Then, with effort.]* If that is the one that Tom is bringing to dinner— you'll have to excuse me, I won't come to the table.

AMANDA. What sort of nonsense is this?

LAURA. You asked me once if I'd ever liked a boy. Don't you remember I showed you this boy's picture?

AMANDA. You mean the boy you showed me in the year book?

LAURA. Yes, that boy.

AMANDA. Laura, Laura, were you in love with that boy?

LAURA. I don't know, Mother. All I know is I couldn't sit at the table if it was him!

AMANDA. It won't be him! It isn't the least bit likely. But whether it is or not, you will come to the table. You will not be excused.

LAURA. I'll have to be, Mother.

AMANDA. I don't intend to humor your silliness, Laura. I've had too much from you and your brother, both! So just sit down and compose yourself till they come. Tom has forgotten his key so you'll have to let them in, when they arrive.

LAURA. *[Panicky]* Oh, Mother—*you* answer the door!

AMANDA. *[Lightly]* I'll be in the kitchen—busy!

LAURA. Oh, Mother, please answer the door, don't make me do it!

AMANDA. *[Crossing into kitchenette.]* I've got to fix the dressing for the salmon. Fuss, fuss—silliness!—over a gentleman caller!

> *[Door swings shut. Laura is left alone.]*

LEGEND: *"Terror!"*

[She utters a low moan and turns off the lamp—sits stiffly on the edge of the sofa, knotting her fingers together.]

LEGEND ON SCREEN: *"The opening of a door!"*

[Tom and Jim appear on the fire-escape steps and climb to landing. Hearing their approach, Laura rises with a panicky gesture. She retreats to the portieres. The doorbell. Laura catches her breath and touches her throat. Low drums.]

AMANDA. *[Calling.]* Laura, sweetheart! The door!

> *[Laura stares at it without moving.]*

JIM. I think we just beat the rain.

TOM. Uh-huh.

[He rings again, nervously. Jim whistles and fishes for a cigarette.]

AMANDA. *[Very, very gaily]* Laura, that is your brother and Mr. O'Connor! Will you let them in, darling?

> *[Laura crosses toward kitchenette door.]*

LAURA. *[Breathlessly]* Mother—you go to the door!

[Amanda steps out of kitchenette and stares furiously at Laura. She points imperiously at the door.]

LAURA. Please, please!

AMANDA. *[In a fierce whisper.]* What is the matter with you, you silly thing?

LAURA. *[Desperately]* Please, you answer it, *please?*

AMANDA. I told you I wasn't going to humor you, Laura. Why have you chosen this moment to lose your mind?

LAURA. Please, please, please, you go!

AMANDA. You'll have to go to the door because I can't!

LAURA. *[Despairingly]* I can't either!

AMANDA. *Why?*

LAURA. I'm *sick!*

AMANDA. I'm sick, too—of your nonsense! Why can't you and your brother be normal people? Fantastic whims and behavior! *[Tom gives a long ring.]* Preposterous goings on! Can you give me one reason— *[Calls out lyrically]* Coming! Just one second!—why you should be afraid to open a door? Now you answer it, Laura!

LAURA. Oh, oh, oh . . .

[She returns through the portieres. Darts to the victrola and winds it frantically and turns it on.]

AMANDA. Laura Wingfield, you march right to that door!

LAURA. Yes—yes, Mother!

[A faraway, scratchy rendition of "Dardanella" softens the air and gives her strength to move through it. She slips to the door and draws it cautiously open. Tom enters with the caller, Jim O'Connor.]

TOM. Laura, this is Jim. Jim, this is my sister, Laura.

JIM. *[Stepping inside.]* I didn't know that Shakespeare had a sister!

LAURA. *[Retreating stiff and trembling from the door.]* How—how do you do?

JIM. *[Heartily extending his hand.]* Okay!

                      [Laura touches it hesitantly with hers.]

JIM. Your hand's *cold*, Laura!

LAURA. Yes, well—I've been playing the victrola. . . .

JIM. Must have been playing classical music on it! You ought to play a little hot swing music to warm you up!

LAURA. Excuse me—I haven't finished playing the victrola. . . .

[She turns awkwardly and hurries into the front room. She pauses a second by the victrola. Then catches her breath and darts through the portieres like a frightened deer.]

JIM. *[Grinning]* What was the matter?

TOM. Oh—with Laura? Laura is—terribly shy.

JIM. Shy, huh? It's unusual to meet a shy girl nowadays. I don't believe you ever mentioned you had a sister.

TOM. Well, now you know. I have one. Here is the *Post Dispatch.* You want a piece of it?

JIM. Un-huh.

TOM. What piece? The comics?

JIM. Sports! *[Glances at it.]* Ole Dizzy Dean is on his bad behavior.

TOM. *[Disinterest.]* Yeah?

               [Lights cigarette and crosses back to fire-escape door.]

JIM. Where are *you* going?

TOM. I'm going out on the terrace.

JIM. *[Goes after him.]* You know, Shakespeare—I'm going to sell you a bill of goods!

TOM. What goods?

JIM. A course I'm taking.

TOM. Huh?

JIM. In public speaking! You and me, we're not the warehouse type.

TOM. Thanks—that's good news. But what has public speaking got to do with it?

JIM. It fits you for—executive positions!

TOM. Awww.

JIM. I tell you it's done a helluva lot for me.

IMAGE: Executive at desk

TOM. In what respect?

JIM. In every! Ask yourself what is the difference between you an' me and men in the office down front? Brains?—No!—Ability?—No! Then what? Just one little thing—

TOM. What is that one little thing?

JIM. Primarily it amounts to—social poise! Being able to square up to people and hold your own on any social level!

AMANDA. *[Off stage.]* Tom?

TOM. Yes, Mother?

AMANDA. Is that you and Mr. O'Connor?

TOM. Yes, Mother.

AMANDA. Well, you just make yourselves comfortable in there.

TOM. Yes, Mother.

AMANDA. Ask Mr. O'Connor if he would like to wash his hands.

JIM. Aw, no—no—thank you—I took care of that at the warehouse. Tom—

TOM. Yes?

JIM. Mr. Mendoza was speaking to me about you.

TOM. Favorably?

JIM. What do you think?

TOM. Well—

JIM. You're going to be out of a job if you don't wake up.

TOM. I am waking up—

JIM. You show no signs.

TOM. The signs are interior.

> IMAGE ON SCREEN: *The sailing vessel with Jolly Roger again*

TOM. I'm planning to change.

[He leans over the rail speaking with quiet exhilaration. The incandescent marquees and signs of the first-run movie houses light his face from across the alley. He looks like a voyager.]

I'm right at the point of committing myself to a future that doesn't include the warehouse and Mr. Mendoza or even a night-school course in public speaking.

JIM. What are you gassing about?

TOM. I'm tired of the movies.

JIM. Movies!

TOM. Yes, movies! Look at them—*[A wave toward the marvels of Grand Avenue.]* All of those glamorous people—having adventures—hogging it all, gobbling the whole thing up! You know what happens? People go to the *movies* instead of *moving!* Hollywood characters are supposed to have all the adventures for everybody in America, while everybody in America sits in a dark room and watches them have them! Yes, until there's a war. That's when adventure becomes available to the masses! *Everyone's* dish, not only Gable's! Then the people in the dark room come out of the dark room to have some adventures themselves—Goody, goody!—It's our turn now, to go to the South Sea Island—to make a safari—to be exotic, far-off!—but I'm not patient. I don't want to wait till then. I'm tired of the *movies* and I am *about* to *move!*

JIM. *[Incredulously]* Move?

TOM. Yes.

JIM. When?

TOM. Soon!

JIM. Where? Where?

[Theme three music seems to answer the question, while Tom thinks it over. He searches among his pockets.]

TOM. I'm starting to boil inside. I know I seem dreamy, but inside—well, I'm boiling!—Whenever I pick up a shoe, I shudder a little thinking how short life is and what I am doing!—Whatever that means, I know it doesn't mean shoes—except as something to wear on a traveler's feet! *[Finds paper]* Look—

JIM. What?

TOM. I'm a member.

JIM. *[Reading.]* The Union of Merchant Seamen.

TOM. I paid my dues this month, instead of the light bill.

JIM. You will regret it when they turn the lights off.

TOM. I won't be here.

JIM. How about your mother?

TOM. I'm like my father. The bastard son of a bastard! See how he grins? And he's been absent going on sixteen years!

JIM. You're just talking, you drip. How does your mother feel about it?

TOM. Shhh!—Here comes Mother! Mother is not acquainted with my plans!

AMANDA. *[Enters portieres.]* Where are you all?

TOM. On the terrace, Mother.

[They start inside. She advances to them. Tom is distinctly shocked at her appearance. Even Jim blinks a little. He is making his first contact with girlish Southern vivacity and in spite of the night-school course in public speaking is somewhat thrown off the beam by the unexpected outlay of social charm. Certain responses are attempted by Jim but are swept aside by Amanda's gay laughter and chatter. Tom is embarrassed but after the first shock Jim reacts very warmly. Grins and chuckles, is altogether won over.]

IMAGE: *Amanda as a girl*

AMANDA. *[Coyly smiling, shaking her girlish ringlets.]* Well, well, well, so this is Mr. O'Connor. Introductions entirely unnecessary. I've heard so much about you from my boy. I finally said to him, Tom —good gracious!—why don't you bring this paragon to supper? I'd like to meet this nice young man at the warehouse!—Instead of just hearing him sing your praises so much!

I don't know why my son is so stand-offish—that's not Southern behavior!

Let's sit down and—I think we could stand a little more air in here! Tom, leave the door open. I felt a nice fresh breeze a moment ago. Where has it gone to?

Mmm, so warm already! And not quite summer, even. We're going to burn up when summer really gets started.

However, we're having—we're having a very light supper. I think light things are better fo' this time of year. The same as light clothes are. Light clothes an' light food are what warm weather calls fo'. You know our blood gets so thick during th' winter—it takes a while fo' us to *adjust* ou'selves!—when the season changes . . .

It's come so quick this year. I wasn't prepared. All of a sudden— heavens! Already summer!—I ran to the trunk an' pulled out this light dress—Terribly old! Historical almost! But feels so good—so good an' co-ol, y'know. . . .

TOM. Mother—

AMANDA. Yes, honey?

TOM. How about—supper?

AMANDA. Honey, you go ask Sister if supper is ready! You know that Sister is in full charge of supper!

Tell her you hungry boys are waiting for it. *[To Jim]* Have you met Laura?

JIM. She—

AMANDA. Let you in? Oh, good, you've met already! It's rare for a girl as sweet an' pretty as Laura to be domestic! But Laura is, thank heavens, not only pretty but also very domestic. I'm not at all. I never was a bit. I never could make a thing but angel-food cake. Well, in the South we had so many servants. Gone, gone, gone. All vestige of gracious living! Gone completely! I wasn't prepared for what the future brought me. All of my gentlemen callers were sons of planters and so of course I assumed that I would be married to one and raise my family on a large piece of land with plenty of servants. But man proposes—and woman accepts the proposal!—To vary that old, old saying a little bit—I married no planter! I married a man who worked for the telephone company!—That gallantly smiling gentleman over there! *[Points to the picture.]* A telephone man who—fell in love with long-distance!—Now he travels and I don't even know where!— But what am I going on for about my tribulations? Tell me yours— I hope you don't have any! Tom?

TOM. *[Returning.]* Yes, Mother?

AMANDA. Is supper nearly ready?

TOM. It looks to me like supper is on the table.

AMANDA. Let me look—

> *[She rises prettily and looks through portieres.]*

Oh, lovely!—But where is Sister?

TOM. Laura is not feeling well and she says that she thinks she'd better not come to the table.

AMANDA. What?—Nonsense!—Laura? Oh, Laura!

LAURA. *[Off stage, faintly]* Yes, Mother.

AMANDA. You really must come to the table. We won't be seated until you come to the table! Come in, Mr. O'Connor. You sit over there, and I'll—Laura? Laura Wingfield! You're keeping us waiting, honey! We can't say grace until you come to the table!

[The back door is pushed weakly open and Laura comes in. She is obviously quite faint, her lips trembling, her eyes wide and staring. She moves unsteadily toward the table.]

LEGEND: *"Terror!"*

[Outside a summer storm is coming abruptly. The white curtains billow inward at the windows and there is a sorrowful murmur and deep blue dusk. Laura suddenly stumbles—she catches at a chair with a faint moan.]

TOM. Laura!

AMANDA. Laura!

There is a clap of thunder

LEGEND: *"Ah!"*

[*Despairingly*] Why, Laura, you *are* sick, darling! Tom, help your sister into the living room, dear! Sit in the living room, Laura—rest on the sofa. Well! [*To the gentleman caller*] Standing over the hot stove made her ill!—I told her that it was just too warm this evening, but —[*Tom comes back in. Laura is on the sofa.*] Is Laura all right now?

TOM. Yes.

AMANDA. What *is* that? Rain? A nice cool rain has come up! [*She gives the gentleman caller a frightened look.*] I think we may—have grace—now . . . [*Tom looks at her stupidly.*] Tom, honey—you say grace!

TOM. Oh . . . "For these and all thy mercies—"

[*They bow their heads, Amanda stealing a nervous glance at Jim. In the living room Laura, stretched on the sofa, clenches her hand to her lips, to hold back a shuddering sob.*]

God's Holy Name be praised—

THE SCENE DIMS OUT

SCENE 7

A Souvenir.

*Half an hour later. Dinner is just being finished in the upstage
    area which is concealed by the drawn portieres. As the curtain rises
    Laura is still huddled upon the sofa, her feet drawn under her,
    her head resting on a pale blue pillow, her eyes wide and mysteriously
    watchful. The new floor lamp with its shade of rose-colored silk
    gives a soft, becoming light to her face, bringing out the fragile,
    unearthly prettiness which usually escapes attention. There is
    a steady murmur of rain, but it is slackening and stops soon after
    the scene begins; the air outside becomes pale and luminous as
    the moon breaks out. A moment after the curtain rises, the lights
    in both rooms flicker and go out.*

JIM. Hey, there, Mr. Light Bulb!

[*Amanda laughs nervously.*]

LEGEND: *"Suspension of a public service"*

AMANDA. Where was Moses when the lights went out? Ha-ha. Do you know the answer to that one, Mr. O'Connor?

JIM. No, Ma'am, what's the answer?

AMANDA. In the dark! *[Jim laughs appreciatively.]* Everybody sit still. I'll light the candles. Isn't it lucky we have them on the table? Where's a match? Which of you gentlemen can provide a match?

JIM. Here.

AMANDA. Thank you, sir.

JIM. Not at all, Ma'am!

AMANDA. I guess the fuse has burnt out. Mr. O'Connor, can you tell a burnt-out fuse? I know I can't and Tom is a total loss when it comes to mechanics.

*Sound: Getting up: Voices recede a little to
kitchenette*

Oh, be careful you don't bump into something. We don't want our gentleman caller to break his neck. Now wouldn't that be a fine howdy-do?

JIM. Ha-ha! Where is the fuse-box?

AMANDA. Right here next to the stove. Can you see anything?

JIM. Just a minute.

AMANDA. Isn't electricity a mysterious thing? Wasn't it Benjamin Franklin who tied a key to a kite? We live in such a mysterious universe, don't we? Some people say that science clears up all the mysteries for us. In my opinion it only creates more!

Have you found it yet?

JIM. No, Ma'am. All these fuses look okay to me.

AMANDA. Tom!

TOM. Yes, Mother?

AMANDA. That light bill I gave you several days ago. The one I told you we got the notices about?

LEGEND: *"Ha!"*

TOM. Oh.—Yeah.

AMANDA. You didn't neglect to pay it by any chance?

TOM. Why, I—

AMANDA. Didn't! I might have known it!

JIM. Shakespeare probably wrote a poem on that light bill, Mrs. Wingfield.

AMANDA. I might have known better than to trust him with it! There's such a high price for negligence in this world!

JIM. Maybe the poem will win a ten-dollar prize.

AMANDA. We'll just have to spend the remainder of the evening in the nineteenth century, before Mr. Edison made the Mazda lamp!

JIM. Candlelight is my favorite kind of light.

AMANDA. That shows you're romantic! But that's no excuse for Tom. Well, we got through dinner. Very considerate of them to let us get through dinner before they plunged us into everlasting darkness, wasn't it, Mr. O'Connor?

JIM. Ha-ha!

AMANDA. Tom, as a penalty for your carelessness you can help me with the dishes.

JIM. Let me give you a hand.

AMANDA. Indeed you will not!

JIM. I ought to be good for something.

AMANDA. Good for something? *[Her tone is rhapsodic.]* You? Why, Mr. O'Connor, nobody, *nobody's* given me this much entertainment in years—as you have!

JIM. Aw, now, Mrs. Wingfield!

AMANDA. I'm not exaggerating, not one bit! But Sister is all by her lonesome. You go keep her company in the parlor!

I'll give you this lovely old candelabrum that used to be on the altar at the church of the Heavenly Rest. It was melted a little out of shape when the church burnt down. Lightning struck it one spring. Gypsy Jones was holding a revival at the time and he intimated that the church was destroyed because the Episcopalians gave card parties.

JIM. Ha-ha.

AMANDA. And how about you coaxing Sister to drink a little wine? I think it would be good for her! Can you carry both at once?

JIM. Sure. I'm Superman!

AMANDA. Now, Thomas, get into this apron!

[The door of the kitchenette swings closed on Amanda's gay laughter; the flickering light approaches the portieres. Laura sits up nervously as he enters. Her speech at first is low and breathless from the almost intolerable strain of being alone with a stranger.]

     THE LEGEND: *"I don't suppose you remember*
                 me at all!"

[In her first speeches in this scene, before Jim's warmth overcomes her paralyzing shyness, Laura's voice is thin and breathless as though she has just run up a steep flight of stairs. Jim's attitude is gently humorous. In playing this scene it should be stressed that while the incident is apparently unimportant, it is to Laura the climax of her secret life.]

JIM. Hello, there, Laura.

LAURA. *[Faintly]* Hello. *[She clears her throat.]*

JIM. How are you feeling now? Better?

LAURA. Yes, Yes, thank you.

JIM. This is for you. A little dandelion wine.
         [He extends it toward her with extravagant gallantry.]

LAURA. Thank you.

JIM. Drink it—but don't get drunk!

[He laughs heartily. Laura takes the glass uncertainly; laughs shyly.]

Where shall I set the candles?

LAURA. Oh—oh, anywhere . . .

JIM. How about here on the floor? Any objections?

LAURA. No.

JIM. I'll spread a newspaper under to catch the drippings. I like to sit on the floor. Mind if I do?

LAURA. Oh, no.

JIM. Give me a pillow?

LAURA. What?

JIM. A pillow!

LAURA. Oh . . . *[Hands him one quickly.]*

JIM. How about you? Don't you like to sit on the floor?

LAURA. Oh—yes.

JIM. Why don't you then?

LAURA. I—will.

JIM. Take a pillow!

[Laura does. Sits on the other side of the candelabrum. Jim crosses his legs and smiles engagingly at her.]

I can't hardly see you sitting way over there.

LAURA. I can—see you.

JIM. I know, but that's not fair, I'm in the limelight. *[Laura moves her pillow closer.]* Good! Now I can see you! Comfortable?

LAURA. Yes.

JIM. So am I. Comfortable as a cow! Will you have some gum?

LAURA. No, thank you.

JIM. I think that I will indulge, with your permission. *[Musingly unwraps it and holds it up.]* Think of the fortune made by the guy that invented the first piece of chewing gum. Amazing, huh? The Wrigley Building is one of the sights of Chicago.—I saw it summer before last when I went up to the Century of Progress.[1] Did you take in the Century of Progress?

LAURA. No, I didn't.

JIM. Well, it was quite a wonderful exposition. What impressed me most was the Hall of Science. Gives you an idea of what the future will be in America, even more wonderful than the present time is! *[Pause. Smiling at her.]* Your brother tells me you're shy. Is that right, Laura?

LAURA. I—don't know.

JIM. I judge you to be an old-fashioned type of girl. Well, I think that's a pretty good type to be. Hope you don't think I'm being too personal—do you?

LAURA. *[Hastily, out of embarrassment]* I believe I *will* take a piece of gum, if you—don't mind. *[Clearing her throat]* Mr. O'Connor, have you—kept up with your singing?

JIM. Singing? Me?

LAURA. Yes. I remember what a beautiful voice you had.

JIM. When did you hear me sing?

1 *Century of Progress:* World's Fair in Chicago (1933-1934).

Voice off stage in the pause

VOICE.

> O blow, ye winds, heigh-ho,
> A-roving I will go!
>   I'm off to my love
>   With a boxing glove—
> Ten thousand miles away!

JIM. You say you've heard me sing?

LAURA. Oh, yes! Yes, very often . . . I—don't suppose—you remember me—at all?

JIM. *[Smiling doubtfully.]* You know I have an idea I've seen you before. I had that idea as soon as you opened the door. It seemed almost like I was about to remember your name. But the name I started to call you—wasn't a name! And so I stopped myself before I said it.

LAURA. Wasn't it—Blue Roses?

JIM. *[Springs up. Grinning.]* Blue Roses!—My gosh, yes—Blue Roses! That's what I had on my tongue when you opened the door! Isn't it funny what tricks your memory plays? I didn't connect you with high school somehow or other. But that's where it was; it was high school. I didn't even know you were Shakespeare's sister! Gosh, I'm sorry.

LAURA. I didn't expect you to. You—barely knew me!

JIM. But we did have a speaking acquaintance, huh?

LAURA. Yes, we spoke to each other.

JIM. When did you recognize me?

LAURA. Oh, right away!

JIM. Soon as I came in the door?

LAURA. When I heard your name I thought it was probably you. I knew that Tom used to know you a little in high school. So when you came in the door—Well, then I was—sure.

JIM. Why didn't you *say* something, then?

LAURA. *[Breathlessly]* I didn't know what to say, I was—too surprised!

JIM. For goodness' sakes! You know, this sure is funny!

LAURA. Yes! Yes, isn't it, though . . .

JIM. Didn't we have a class in something together?

LAURA. Yes, we did.

JIM. What class was that?

LAURA. It was—singing—Chorus!

JIM. Aw!

LAURA. I sat across the aisle from you in the Aud.

JIM. Aw.

LAURA. Mondays, Wednesdays and Fridays.

JIM. Now I remember—you always came in late.

LAURA. Yes, it was so hard for me, getting upstairs. I had that brace on my leg—it clumped so loud!

JIM. I never heard any clumping.

LAURA. *[Wincing at the recollection.]* To me it sounded like—thunder!

JIM. Well, well, well, I never even noticed.

LAURA. And everybody was seated before I came in. I had to walk in front of all those people. My seat was in the back row. I had to go clumping all the way up the aisle with everyone watching!

JIM. You shouldn't have been self-conscious.

LAURA. I know, but I was. It was always such a relief when the singing started.

JIM. Aw, yes, I've placed you now! I used to call you Blue Roses. How was it that I got started calling you that?

LAURA. I was out of school a little while with pleurosis. When I came back you asked me what was the matter. I said I had pleurosis —you thought I said Blue Roses. That's what you always called me after that!

JIM. I hope you didn't mind.

LAURA. Oh, no—I liked it. You see, I wasn't acquainted with many—people. . . .

JIM. As I remember you sort of stuck by yourself.

LAURA. I—I—never have had much luck at—making friends.

JIM. I don't see why you wouldn't.

LAURA. Well, I—started out badly.

JIM. You mean being—

LAURA. Yes, it sort of—stood between me—

JIM. You shouldn't have let it!

LAURA. I know, but it did, and—

JIM. You were shy with people!

LAURA. I tried not to be but never could—

JIM. Overcome it?

LAURA. No, I—I never could!

JIM. I guess being shy is something you have to 'work out of kind of gradually.

LAURA. *[Sorrowfully]* Yes—I guess it—

JIM. Takes time!

LAURA. Yes—

JIM. People are not so dreadful when you know them. That's what you have to remember! And everybody has problems, not just you, but practically everybody has got some problems. You think of yourself as having the only problems, as being the only one who is disappointed. But just look around you and you will see lots of people as disappointed as you are. For instance, I hoped when I was going to high school that I would be further along at this time, six years later, than I am now—You remember that wonderful write-up I had in *The Torch?*

LAURA. Yes!   *[She rises and crosses to table.]*
JIM. It said I was bound to succeed in anything I went into!
[Laura returns with the annual.] Holy Jeez! The Torch!

*[He accepts it reverently. They smile across it with mutual wonder.
Laura crouches beside him and they begin to turn through it. Laura's
shyness is dissolving in his warmth.]*

LAURA. Here you are in *The Pirates of Penzance!*
JIM. *[Wistfully]* I sang the baritone lead in that operetta.
LAURA. *[Raptly]* So—*beautifully!*
JIM. *[Protesting]* Aw—
LAURA. Yes, yes—beautifully—beautifully!
JIM. You heard me?
LAURA. All three times!
JIM. No!
LAURA. Yes!
JIM. All three performances?
LAURA. I—wanted to ask you to—autograph my program.
JIM. Why didn't you ask me to?
LAURA. You were always surrounded by your own friends so
much that I never had a chance to.
JIM. You should have just—
LAURA. Well, I—thought you might think I was—
JIM. Thought I might think you was—what?
LAURA. Oh—
JIM. *[With reflective relish.]* I was beleaguered by females in
those days.
LAURA. You were terribly popular!
JIM. Yeah—
LAURA. You had such a—friendly way—
JIM. I was spoiled in high school.
LAURA. Everybody—liked you!
JIM. Including you?
LAURA. I—yes, I—I did, too—
                    [She gently closes the book in her lap.]
JIM. Well, well, well!—Give me that program, Laura. *[She hands
it to him. He signs it with a flourish.]* There you are—better late
than never!
LAURA. Oh, I—what a—surprise!
JIM. My signature isn't worth very much right now. But some
day—maybe—it will increase in value! Being disappointed is one
thing and being discouraged is something else. I am disappointed
but I am not discouraged. I'm twenty-three years old. How old
are you?
LAURA. I'll be twenty-four in June.
JIM. That's not old age!
LAURA. No, but—

JIM. You finished high school?

LAURA. *[With difficulty.]* I didn't go back.

JIM. You mean you dropped out?

LAURA. I made bad grades in my final examinations. *[She rises and replaces the book and the program. Her voice strained.]* How is— Emily Meisenbach getting along?

JIM. Oh, that kraut-head!

LAURA. Why do you call her that?

JIM. That's what she was.

LAURA. You're not still—going with her?

JIM. I never see her.

LAURA. It said in the Personal Section that you were—engaged!

JIM. I know, but I wasn't impressed by that—propaganda!

LAURA. It wasn't—the truth?

JIM. Only in Emily's optimistic opinion!

LAURA. Oh—

> LEGEND: *"What have you done since high school?"*

[Jim lights a cigarette and leans indolently back on his elbows smiling at Laura with a warmth and charm which lights her inwardly with altar candles. She remains by the table and turns in her hands a piece of glass to cover her tumult.]

JIM. *[After several reflective puffs on a cigarette.]* What have you done since high school? *[She seems not to hear him.]* Huh? *[Laura looks up.]* I said what have you done since high school, Laura?

LAURA. Nothing much.

JIM. You must have been doing something these six long years.

LAURA. Yes.

JIM. Well, then, such as what?

LAURA. I took a business course at business college—

JIM. How did that work out?

LAURA. Well, not very—well—I had to drop out, it gave me— indigestion—

> *[Jim laughs gently.]*

JIM. What are you doing now?

LAURA. I don't do anything—much. Oh, please don't think I sit around doing nothing! My glass collection takes up a good deal of time. Glass is something you have to take good care of.

JIM. What did you say—about glass?

LAURA. Collection I said—I have one—*[She clears her throat and turns away again, acutely shy.]*

JIM. *[Abruptly]* You know what I judge to be the trouble with you? Inferiority complex! Know what that is? That's what they call it when someone lowrates himself! I understand it because I had it, too. Although my case was not so aggravated as yours seems to be. I had it until I took up public speaking, developed my voice, and learned that I had an aptitude for science. Before that time I never thought of myself as being outstanding in any way whatsoever! Now I've never made a regular study of it, but I have a friend who says I can analyze people better than doctors that make a profession of it. I don't claim that to be necessarily true, but I can sure guess a person's psychology, Laura! *[Takes out his gum.]* Excuse me, Laura. I always take it out when the flavor is gone. I'll use this scrap of paper to wrap it in. I know how it is to get it stuck on a shoe. Yep—that's what I judge to be your principal trouble. A lack of confidence in yourself as a person. You don't have the proper amount of faith in yourself. I'm basing that fact on a number of your remarks and also on certain observations I've made. For instance that clumping you thought was so awful in high school. You say you even dreaded to walk into class. You see what you did? You dropped out of school, you gave up an education because of a clump, which as far as I know was practically non-existent! A little physical defect is what you have. Hardly noticeable even! Magnified thousands of times by imagination! You know what my strong advice to you is? Think of yourself as *superior* in some way!

LAURA. In what way would I think?

JIM. Why, man alive, Laura! Just look about you a little. What do you see? A world full of common people! All of 'em born and all of 'em going to die! Which of them has one-tenth of your good points! Or mine! Or anyone else's, as far as that goes—Gosh! Everybody excels in some one thing. Some in many! *[Unconsciously glances at himself in the mirror.]* All you've got to do is discover in *what!* Take me, for instance. *[He adjusts his tie at the mirror.]* My interest happens to lie in electro-dynamics. I'm taking a course in radio engineering at night school, Laura, on top of a fairly responsible job at the warehouse. I'm taking that course and studying public speaking.

LAURA. Ohhhh.

JIM. Because I believe in the future of television! *[Turning back to her.]* I wish to be ready to go up right along with it. Therefore I'm planning to get in on the ground floor. In fact I've already made the right connections and all that remains is for the industry to get under way! Full steam—*[His eyes are starry.]* Knowledge—Zzzzzp! *Money* —Zzzzzp!—*Power!* That's the cycle democracy is built on!

[His attitude is convincingly dynamic. Laura stares at him, even her shyness eclipsed in her absolute wonder. He suddenly grins.]

I guess you think I think a lot of myself!

LAURA. No—o-o-o, I—

JIM. Now how about you? Isn't there something you take more interest in than anything else?

LAURA. Well, I do—as I said—have my—glass collection—

A peal of girlish laughter from the kitchen

JIM. I'm not right sure I know what you're talking about. What kind of glass is it?

LAURA. Little articles of it, they're ornaments mostly! Most of them are little animals made out of glass, the tiniest little animals in the world. Mother calls them a glass menagerie! Here's an example of one, if you'd like to see it! This is one of the oldest. It's nearly thirteen.

MUSIC: *"The Glass Menagerie"*

[He stretches out his hand.]

Oh, be careful—if you breathe, it breaks!

JIM. I'd better not take it. I'm pretty clumsy with things.

LAURA. Go on, I trust you with him! *[Places it in his palm.]* There now—you're holding him gently! Hold him over the light, he loves the light! You see how the light shines through him?

JIM. It sure does shine!

LAURA. I shouldn't be partial, but he is my favorite one.

JIM. What kind of a thing is this one supposed to be?

LAURA. Haven't you noticed the single horn on his forehead?

JIM. A unicorn, huh?

LAURA. Mmm-hmmm!

JIM. Unicorns, aren't they extinct in the modern world?

LAURA. I know!

JIM. Poor little fellow, he must feel sort of lonesome.

LAURA. *[Smiling.]* Well, if he does he doesn't complain about it. He stays on a shelf with some horses that don't have horns and all of them seem to get along nicely together.

JIM. How do you know?

LAURA. *[Lightly]* I haven't heard any arguments among them!

JIM. *[Grinning.]* No arguments, huh? Well, that's a pretty good sign! Where shall I set him?

LAURA. Put him on the table. They all like a change of scenery once in a while!

JIM. *[Stretching.]* Well, well, well, well—Look how big my shadow is when I stretch!

LAURA. Oh, oh, yes—it stretches across the ceiling!

JIM. *[Crossing to door.]* I think it's stopped raining. *[Opens fire-escape door.]* Where does the music come from?

LAURA. From the Paradise Dance Hall across the alley.

JIM. How about cutting the rug a little, Miss Wingfield?

LAURA. Oh, I—

JIM. Or is your program filled up? Let me have a look at it. *[Grasps imaginary card.]* Why, every dance is taken! I'll just have to scratch some out.

WALTZ MUSIC: *"La Golondrina"*

Ahhh, a waltz!

[He executes some sweeping turns by himself then holds his arms toward Laura.]

LAURA. *[Breathlessly]* I—can't dance!

JIM. There you go, that inferiority stuff!

LAURA. I've never danced in my life!

JIM. Come on, try!

LAURA. Oh, but I'd step on you!

JIM. I'm not made out of glass.

LAURA. How—how—how do we start?

JIM. Just leave it to me. You hold your arms out a little.

LAURA. Like this?

JIM. A little bit higher. Right. Now don't tighten up, that's the main thing about it—relax.

LAURA. *[Laughing breathlessly]* It's hard not to.

JIM. Okay.

LAURA. I'm afraid you can't budge me.

JIM. What do you bet I can't?

> *[He swings her into motion.]*

LAURA. Goodness, yes, you can!

JIM. Let yourself go, now, Laura, just let yourself go.

LAURA. I'm—

JIM. Come on!

LAURA. Trying!

JIM. Not so stiff—Easy does it!

LAURA. I know but I'm—

JIM. Loosen th' backbone! There now, that's a lot better.

LAURA. Am I?

JIM. Lots, lots better!

> *[He moves her about the room in a clumsy waltz.]*

LAURA. Oh, my!

JIM. Ha-ha!

LAURA. Oh, my goodness!

JIM. Ha-ha-ha! *[They suddenly bump into the table. Jim stops.]* What did we hit on?

LAURA. Table.

JIM. Did something fall off it? I think—

LAURA. Yes.

JIM. I hope that it wasn't the little glass horse with the horn!

LAURA. Yes.

JIM. Aw, aw, aw. Is it broken?

LAURA. Now it is just like all the other horses.

JIM. It's lost its—

LAURA. Horn! It doesn't matter. Maybe it's a blessing in disguise.

JIM. You'll never forgive me. I bet that that was your favorite piece of glass.

LAURA. I don't have favorites much. It's no tragedy, Freckles. Glass breaks so easily. No matter how careful you are. The traffic jars the shelves and things fall off them.

JIM. Still I'm awfully sorry that I was the cause.

LAURA. *[Smiling]* I'll just imagine he had an operation. The horn was removed to make him feel less—freakish! *[They both laugh.]* Now he will feel more at home with the other horses, the ones that don't have horns . . .

JIM. Ha-ha that's very funny! *[Suddenly serious.]* I'm glad to see that you have a sense of humor.

You know—you're—well—very different! Surprisingly different from anyone else I know! *[His voice becomes soft and hesitant with a genuine feeling.]* Do you mind me telling you that? *[Laura is abashed beyond speech.]* I mean it in a nice way . . . *[Laura nods shyly, looking away.]* You make me feel sort of—I don't know how to put it! I'm usually pretty good at expressing things, but—This is something that I don't know how to say! *[Laura touches her throat and clears it— turns the broken unicorn in her hands.]* *[Even softer.]* Has anyone ever told you that you were pretty?

PAUSE: *Music*

[Laura looks up slowly, with wonder, and shakes her head.]

Well, you are! In a very different way from anyone else. And all the nicer because of the difference too.

[His voice becomes low and husky. Laura turns away, nearly faint with the novelty of her emotions.] I wish that you were my sister. I'd teach you to have some confidence in yourself. The different people are not like other people, but being different is nothing to be ashamed of. Because other people are not such wonderful people. They're one hundred times one thousand. You're one times one! They walk all over the earth. You just stay here. They're common as—weeds, but—you—well, your're—*Blue Roses!*

IMAGE ON SCREEN: *Blue Roses*

Music Changes

LAURA. But blue is wrong for—roses . . .

JIM. It's right for you!—You're—pretty!

LAURA. In what respect am I pretty?

JIM. In all respects—believe me! Your eyes—your hair—are pretty! Your hands are pretty! *[He catches hold of her hand.]* You think I'm making this up because I'm invited to dinner and have to be nice. Oh, I could do that! I could put on an act for you, Laura, and say lots of things without being very sincere. But this time I am. I'm talking to you sincerely. I happened to notice you had this inferiority complex that keeps you from feeling comfortable with people. Somebody needs to build your confidence up and make you proud instead of shy and turning away and—blushing—Somebody—ought to—ought to—kiss you, Laura! *[His hand slips slowly up her arm to her shoulder.]*

Music swells tumultuously

[He suddenly turns her about and kisses her on the lips. When he releases her, Laura sinks on the sofa with a bright, dazed look. Jim backs away and fishes in his pocket for a cigarette.]

LEGEND ON SCREEN: *"Souvenir"*

Stumble-john!

[He lights the cigarette, avoiding her look. There is a peal of girlish laughter from Amanda in the kitchen. Laura slowly raises and opens her hand. It still contains the little broken glass animal. She looks at it with a tender, bewildered expression.]

Stumble-john! I shouldn't have done that—That was way off the beam. You don't smoke, do you?

[She looks up, smiling, not hearing the question. He sits beside her a little gingerly. She looks at him speechlessly—waiting. He coughs decorously and moves a little farther aside as he considers the situation and senses her feelings, dimly, with perturbation. Gently.]

Would you—care for a—mint?

[She doesn't seem to hear him but her look grows brighter even.]

Peppermint—Life-Saver? My pocket's a regular drug store—wherever I go . . .

[He pops a mint in his mouth. Then gulps and decides to make a clean breast of it. He speaks slowly and gingerly.]

Laura, you know, if I had a sister like you, I'd do the same thing as Tom. I'd bring out fellows and—introduce her to them. The right type of boys of a type to—appreciate her. Only—well—he made a mistake about me. Maybe I've got no call to be saying this. That may not have been the idea in having me over. But what if it was? There's nothing wrong about that. The only trouble is that in my case —I'm not in a situation to—do the right thing.

   I can't take down your number and say I'll phone. I can't call up next week and—ask for a date. I thought I had better explain the situation in case you—misunderstood it and—hurt your feelings. . . .

[Pause. Slowly, very slowly, Laura's look changes, her eyes returning slowly from his to the ornament in her palm. Amanda utters another gay laugh in the kitchen.]

   LAURA. *[Faintly]* You—won't—call again?

   JIM. No, Laura, I can't. *[He rises from the sofa.]* As I was just explaining, I've—got strings on me. Laura, I've—been going steady! I go out all of the time with a girl named Betty. She's a home-girl like you, and Catholic, and Irish, and in a great many ways we—get along fine. I met her last summer on a moonlight boat trip up the river to Alton, on the *Majestic*. Well—right away from the start it was—love!

LEGEND: *Love!*

[Laura sways slightly forward and grips the arm of the sofa. He fails to notice, now enrapt in his own comfortable being.]

Being in love has made a new man of me!

[Leaning stiffly forward, clutching the arm of the sofa, Laura struggles visibly with her storm. But Jim is oblivious, she is a long way off.]

The power of love is really pretty tremendous! Love is something that —changes the whole world, Laura!

[The storm abates a little and Laura leans back. He notices her again.]

It happened that Betty's aunt took sick, she got a wire and had to go to Centralia. So Tom—when he asked me to dinner—I naturally just accepted the invitation, not knowing that you—that he—that I— *[He stops awkwardly.]* Huh—I'm a stumble-john!

[He flops back on the sofa. The holy candles in the altar of Laura's face have been snuffed out. There is a look of almost infinite desolation. Jim glances at her uneasily.]

I wish that you would—say something.

[She bites her lip which was trembling and then bravely smiles. She opens her hand again on the broken glass ornament. Then she gently takes his hand and raises it level with her own. She carefully places the unicorn in the palm of his hand, then pushes his fingers closed upon it.]

What are you—doing that for? You want me to have him?—Laura? *[She nods.]* What for?

LAURA. A—souvenir . . .

[She rises unsteadily and crouches beside the victrola to wind it up.]

LEGEND ON SCREEN: *"Things Have a Way of
Turning Out So Badly!"*
or
IMAGE: *"Gentleman Caller Waving Goodbye!—
Gaily"*

[At this moment Amanda rushes brightly back in the front room. She bears a pitcher of fruit punch in an old-fashioned cut-glass pitcher and a plate of macaroons. The plate has a gold border and poppies painted on it.]

AMANDA. Well, well, well! Isn't the air delightful after the shower? I've made you children a little liquid refreshment. *[Turns gaily to the gentleman caller.]* Jim, do you know that song about lemonade?

> Lemonade, lemonade
> Made in the shade and stirred with a spade—
> Good enough for any old maid!

JIM. *[Uneasily]* Ha-ha! No—I never heard it.

AMANDA. Why, Laura! You look so serious!

JIM. We were having a serious conversation.

AMANDA. Good! Now you're better acquainted!

JIM. *[Uncertainly]* Ha-ha! Yes.

AMANDA. You modern young people are much more serious-minded than my generation. I was so gay as a girl!

JIM. You haven't changed, Mrs. Wingfield.

AMANDA. Tonight I'm rejuvenated! The gaiety of the occasion, Mr. O'Connor! *[She tosses her head with a peal of laughter. Spills lemonade.]* Oooo! I'm baptizing myself!

JIM. Here—let me—

AMANDA. *[Setting the pitcher down.]* There now. I discovered we had some maraschino cherries. I dumped them in, juice and all!

JIM. You shouldn't have gone to that trouble, Mrs. Wingfield.

AMANDA. Trouble, trouble? Why, it was loads of fun! Didn't you hear me cutting up in the kitchen? I bet your ears were burning! I told Tom how outdone with him I was for keeping you to himself so long a time! He should have brought you over much, much sooner! Well, now that you've found your way, I want you to be a very frequent caller! Not just occasional but all the time. Oh, we're going to have a lot of gay times together! I see them coming! Mmmm, just breathe that air! So fresh, and the moon's so pretty! I'll skip back out—I know where my place is when young folks are having a—serious conversation!

JIM. Oh, don't go out, Mrs. Wingfield. The fact of the matter is I've got to be going.

AMANDA. Going, now? You're joking! Why, it's only the shank of the evening, Mr. O'Connor!

JIM. Well, you know how it is.

AMANDA. You mean you're a young workingman and have to keep workingmen's hours. We'll let you off early tonight. But only on the condition that next time you stay later. What's the best night for you? Isn't Saturday night the best night for you workingmen?

JIM. I have a couple of time-clocks to punch, Mrs. Wingfield. One at morning, another one at night!

AMANDA. My, but you *are* ambitious! You work at night, too?

JIM. No, Ma'am, not work but—Betty! *[He crosses deliberately to pick up his hat.]*

*The band at the Paradise Dance Hall goes into
a tender waltz*

AMANDA. Betty? Betty? Who's—Betty!

There is an ominous cracking sound in the sky

JIM. Oh, just a girl. The girl I go steady with! *[He smiles
charmingly.]*

The sky falls

LEGEND: *"The Sky Falls"*

AMANDA. *[A long-drawn exhalation.]* Ohhhh . . . Is it a serious
romance, Mr. O'Connor?

JIM. We're going to be married the second Sunday in June.

AMANDA. Ohhh—how nice! Tom didn't mention that you were
engaged to be married.

JIM. The cat's not out of the bag at the warehouse yet. You
know how they are. They call you Romeo and stuff like that.

*[He stops at the oval mirror to put on his hat. He carefully shapes
the brim and the crown to give a discreetly dashing effect.]*

It's been a wonderful evening, Mrs. Wingfield. I guess this is what
they mean by Southern hospitality.

AMANDA. It really wasn't anything at all.

JIM. I hope it don't seem like I'm rushing off. But I promised
Betty I'd pick her up at the Wabash depot, an' by the time I get my
jalopy down there her train'll be in. Some women are pretty upset if you keep 'em waiting.

AMANDA. Yes, I know—The tyranny of women! *[Extends her
hand.]* Good-bye, Mr. O'Connor. I wish you luck—and happiness
—and success! All three of them, and so does Laura!—Don't you,
Laura!

LAURA. Yes!

JIM. *[Taking her hand.]* Good-bye, Laura. I'm certainly going to
treasure that souvenir. And don't forget the good advice I gave you.
[Raises his voice to a cheery shout.] So long, Shakespeare! Thanks
again, ladies—Good night!

*[He grins and ducks jauntily out. Still bravely grimacing, Amanda
closes the door on the gentleman caller. Then she turns back to the
room with a puzzled expression. She and Laura don't dare to face
each other. Laura crouches beside the victrola to wind it.]*

AMANDA. *[Faintly]* Things have a way of turning out so badly.
I don't believe that I would play the victrola. Well, well—well—
Our gentleman caller was engaged to be married! Tom!

TOM. *[From back.]* Yes, Mother?

AMANDA. Come in here a minute. I want to tell you something awfully funny.

TOM. *[Enters with macaroon and a glass of the lemonade.]* Has the gentleman caller gotten away already?

AMANDA. The gentleman caller has made an early departure. What a wonderful joke you played on us!

TOM. How do you mean?

AMANDA. You didn't mention that he was engaged to be married.

TOM. Jim? Engaged?

AMANDA. That's what he just informed us.

TOM. I'll be jiggered! I didn't know about that.

AMANDA. That seems very peculiar.

TOM. What's peculiar about it?

AMANDA. Didn't you call him your best friend down at the warehouse?

TOM. He is, but how did I know?

AMANDA. It seems extremely peculiar that you wouldn't know your best friend was going to be married!

TOM. The warehouse is where I work, not where I know things about people!

AMANDS. You don't know things anywhere! You live in a dream; you manufacture illusions! *[He crosses to door.]* Where are you going?

TOM. I'm going to the movies.

AMANDA. That's right, now that you've had us make such fools of ourselves. The effort, the preparations, all the expense! The new floor lamp, the rug, the clothes for Laura! All for what? To entertain some other girl's fiancé! Go to the movies, go! Don't think about us, a mother deserted, an unmarried sister who's crippled and has no job! Don't let anything interfere with your selfish pleasure! Just go, go, go—to the movies!

TOM. All right, I will! The more you shout about my selfishness to me the quicker I'll go, and I won't go to the movies!

AMANDA. Go, then! Then go to the moon—you selfish dreamer!

[Tom smashes his glass on the floor. He plunges out on the fire-escape, slamming the door. Laura screams—cut by door. Dance-hall music up. Tom goes to the rail and grips it desperately, lifting his face in the chill white moonlight penetrating the narrow abyss of the alley.]

LEGEND ON SCREEN: *"And So Good-bye . . ."*

[Tom's closing speech is timed with the interior pantomine. The interior scene is played as though viewed through soundproof glass. Amanda appears to be making a comforting speech to Laura who is huddled upon the sofa. Now that we cannot hear the mother's speech, her silliness is gone and she has dignity and tragic beauty. Laura's dark hair hides her face until at the end of the speech she lifts it to

smile at her mother. Amanda's gestures are slow and graceful, almost dance-like, as she comforts the daughter. At the end of her speech she glances a moment at the father's picture—then withdraws through the portieres. At close of Tom's speech, Laura blows out the candles, ending the play.]

TOM. I didn't go to the moon, I went much further—for time is the longest distance between two places—Not long after that I was fired for writing a poem on the lid of a shoe-box. I left Saint Louis. I descended the steps of this fire-escape for a last time and followed, from then on, in my father's footsteps, attempting to find in motion what was lost in space—I traveled around a great deal. The cities swept about me like dead leaves, leaves that were brightly colored but torn away from the branches. I would have stopped, but I was pursued by something. It always came upon me unawares, taking me altogether by surprise. Perhaps it was a familiar bit of music. Perhaps it was only a piece of transparent glass—Perhaps I am walking along a street at night, in some strange city, before I have found companions. I pass the lighted window of a shop where perfume is sold. The window is filled with pieces of colored glass, tiny transparent bottles in delicate colors, like bits of a shattered rainbow. Then all at once my sister touches my shoulder. I turn around and look into her eyes . . . Oh, Laura, Laura, I tried to leave you behind me, but I am more faithful than I intended to be! I reach for a cigarette, I cross the street, I run into the movies or a bar, I buy a drink, I speak to the nearest stranger—anything that can blow your candles out! *[Laura bends over the candles.]*—for nowadays the world is lit by lightning! Blow out your candles, Laura—and so good-bye. . . .

[She blows the candles out.]

THE SCENE DISSOLVES

All My Sons

1941 - 1945

Introduction

In 1947, *All My Sons* won for Arthur Miller the Drama Critics Circle Award for the best play of the season. In *All My Sons* Miller attempted to accomplish what he has stated to be the purpose of all modern tragic writers: the portrayal of representative men, who, through pain, evaluate themselves justly and who, by facing themselves and their responsibilities, gain their true place in society. Although *All My Sons* takes for its subject matter the lives of a small group of people during the last years of World War II and the three years following, it succeeds admirably in making its few people stand for man. In addition, the play successfully develops the theme of its title—the duty of all men to accept their responsibilities and to face themselves honestly.

In spite of this success, Miller was apparently unaware that the play itself had accomplished its purpose; he has Jim Bayless state the theme explicitly.

> *Theme*
>
> Oh, no, he'll come back. We all come back, Kate. These private little revolutions always die. The compromise is always made. In a peculiar way, Frank is right—every man does have a star. The star of one's honesty. And you spend your life groping for it, but once it's out it never lights again. I don't think he went very far. He probably just wanted to be alone to watch his star go out.

Miller has Chris, who seems to serve as Miller's spokesman as well as society's conscience, tell his father:

> You can be better! Once and for all you can know there's a universe of people outside and you're responsible to it.

When Joe Keller realizes this, he is unable to face his responsibilities to society and kills himself. It is apparent Miller feels compelled to repeat again and again the basic theme of his play.

Ten years after he wrote *All My Sons,* Miller said of it, "I wanted to make the moral world as real and evident as the immoral one so splendidly is."

All My Sons
A Play in Three Acts

ARTHUR MILLER

The Characters:

JOE KELLER   DR. JIM BAYLISS

KATE KELLER   SUE BAYLISS

CHRIS KELLER   FRANK LUBEY

ANN DEEVER   LYDIA LUBEY

GEORGE DEEVER   BERT

332

ACT 1

*The back yard of the Keller home in the outskirts of an American town. August
of our era.*

*The stage is hedged on right and left by tall, closely planted poplars which
lend the yard a secluded atmosphere. Upstage is filled with the back of
the house and its open, unroofed porch which extends into the yard
some six feet. The house is two stories high and has seven rooms. It would
have cost perhaps fifteen thousand in the early twenties when it was
built. Now it is nicely painted, looks tight and comfortable, and the yard
is green with sod, here and there plants whose season is gone. At the
right, beside the house, the entrance of the driveway can be seen, but the
poplars cut off view of its continuation downstage. In the left corner,
downstage, stands the four-foot-high stump of a slender apple tree whose
upper trunk and branches lie toppled beside it, fruit still clinging to its
branches.*

*Downstage right is a small, trellised arbor, shaped like a sea shell, with a
decorative bulb hanging from its forward-curving roof. Garden chairs
and a table are scattered about. A garbage pail on the ground next to the
porch steps, a wire leaf-burner near it.*

[*On the rise: It is early Sunday morning. Joe Keller is sitting in the sun reading the want ads of the Sunday paper, the other sections of which lie neatly
on the ground beside him. Behind his back, inside the arbor, Doctor Jim
Bayliss is reading part of the paper at the table.*

*Keller is nearing sixty. A heavy man of stolid mind and build, a business
man these many years, but with the imprint of the machine-shop worker and
boss still upon him. When he reads, when he speaks, when he listens, it is
with the terrible concentration of the uneducated man for whom there is still
wonder in many commonly known things, a man whose judgments must be
dredged out of experience and a peasant-like common sense. A man among
men.*

*Doctor Bayliss is nearly forty. A wry self-controlled man, an easy talker,
but with a wisp of sadness that clings even to his self-effacing humor.*

*At curtain, Jim is standing at left, staring at the broken tree. He taps a
pipe on it, blows through the pipe, feels in his pockets for tobacco, then
speaks.*]

JIM. Where's your tobacco?

KELLER. I think I left it on the table. *[Jim goes slowly to table on the arbor, finds a pouch, and sits there on the bench, filling his pipe.]* Gonna rain tonight.

JIM. Paper says so?

KELLER. Yeah, right here.

JIM. Then it can't rain.

[Frank Lubey enters, through a small space between the poplars. Frank is thirty-two but balding. A pleasant, opinionated man, uncertain of himself, with a tendency toward peevishness when crossed, but always wanting it pleasant and neighborly. He rather saunters in, leisurely, nothing to do. He does not notice Jim in the arbor. On his greeting, Jim does not bother looking up.]

FRANK. Hya.

KELLER. Hello, Frank. What's doin'?

FRANK. Nothin'. Walking off my breakfast. *[Looks up at the sky.]* That beautiful? Not a cloud.

KELLER. *[Looking up.]* Yeah, nice.

FRANK. Every Sunday ought to be like this.

KELLER. *[Indicating the sections beside him.]* Want the paper?

FRANK. What's the difference, it's all bad news. What's today's calamity?

KELLER. I don't know, I don't read the news part any more. It's more interesting in the want ads.

FRANK. Why, you trying to buy something?

KELLER. No, I'm just interested. To see what people want, y'know? For instance, here's a guy is lookin' for two Newfoundland dogs. Now what's he want with two Newfoundland dogs?

FRANK. That is funny.

KELLER. Here's another one. Wanted—old dictionaries. High prices paid. Now what's a man going to do with an old dictionary?

FRANK. Why not? Probably a book collector.

KELLER. You mean he'll make a living out of that?

FRANK. Sure, there's a lot of them.

KELLER. *[Shaking his head.]* All the kind of business goin' on. In my day, either you were a lawyer, or a doctor, or you worked in a shop. Now—

FRANK. Well, I was going to be a forester once.

KELLER. Well, that shows you; in my day, there was no such thing. *[Scanning the page, sweeping it with his hand.]* You look at a page like this you realize how ignorant you are. *[Softly, with wonder, as he scans page.]* Psss!

FRANK. *[Noticing tree.]* Hey, what happened to your tree?

KELLER. Ain't that awful? The wind must've got it last night. You heard the wind, didn't you?

FRANK. Yeah, I got a mess in my yard, too. *[Goes to tree.]* What a pity. *[Turning to Keller]* What'd Kate say?

KELLER. They're all asleep yet. I'm just waiting for her to see it.

FRANK. *[Struck.]* You know?—it's funny.

KELLER. What?

FRANK. Larry was born in August. He'd been twenty-seven this month. And his tree blows down.

KELLER. *[Touched.]* I'm surprised you remember his birthday, Frank. That's nice.

FRANK. Well, I'm working on his horoscope.

KELLER. How can you make him a horoscope? That's for the future, ain't it?

FRANK. Well, what I'm doing is this, see. Larry was reported missing on November twenty-fifth, right?

KELLER. Yeah?

FRANK. Well, then, we assume that if he was killed it was on November twenty-fifth. Now, what Kate wants—

KELLER. Oh, Kate asked you to make a horoscope?

FRANK. Yeah, what she wants to find out is whether November twenty-fifth was a favorable day for Larry.

KELLER. What is that, favorable day?

FRANK. Well, a favorable day for a person is a fortunate day, according to his stars. In other words it would be practically impossible for him to have died on his favorable day.

KELLER. Well, was that his favorable day?—November twenty-fifth?

FRANK. That's what I'm working on to find out. It takes time! See, the point is, if November twenty-fifth was his favorable day, then it's completely possible he's alive somewhere, because—I mean it's possible. *[He notices Jim now. Jim is looking at him as though at an idiot. To Jim—with an uncertain laugh]* I didn't even see you.

KELLER. *[To Jim.]* Is he talkin' sense?

JIM. Him? He's all right. He's just completely out of his mind, that's all.

FRANK. *[Peeved.]* The trouble with you is, you don't *believe* in anything.

JIM. And your trouble is that you believe in *anything*. *You* didn't see my kid this morning, did you?

FRANK. No.

KELLER. Imagine? He walked off with his thermometer. Right out of his bag.

JIM. *[Getting up.]* What a problem. One look at a girl and he takes her temperature. *[Goes to driveway, looks upstage toward street.]*

FRANK. That boy's going to be a real doctor; he's smart.

JIM. Over my dead body he'll be a doctor. A good beginning, too.

FRANK. Why? It's an honorable profession.

JIM. *[Looking at him tiredly.]* Frank, will you stop talking like a civics book? *[Keller laughs.]*

FRANK. Why, I saw a movie a couple of weeks ago, reminded me of you. There was a doctor in that picture—

KELLER. Don Ameche!

FRANK. I think it was, yeah. And he worked in his basement discovering things. That's what you ought to do; you could help humanity, instead of—

JIM. I would love to help humanity on a Warner Brothers salary.

KELLER. *[Pointing at him, laughing.]* That's very good, Jim.

JIM. *[Looking toward house.]* Well, where's the beautiful girl was supposed to be here?

FRANK. *[Excited.]* Annie came?

KELLER. Sure, sleepin' upstairs. We picked her up on the one o'clock train last night. Wonderful thing. Girl leaves here, a scrawny kid. Couple of years go by, she's a regular woman. Hardly recognized her, and she was running in and out of this yard all her life. That was a very happy family used to live in your house, Jim.

JIM. Like to meet her. The block can use a pretty girl. In the whole neighborhood there's not a damned thing to look at. *[Sue, Jim's wife, enters. She is rounding forty, an overweight woman who fears it. On seeing her, Jim wryly adds]* Except my wife, of course.

SUE. *[In same spirit.]* Mrs. Adams is on the phone, you dog.

JIM *[To Keller.]* Such is the condition which prevails— *[Going to his wife.]* my love, my light.

SUE. Don't sniff around me. *[Pointing to their house.]* And give her a nasty answer. I can smell her perfume over the phone.

JIM. What's the matter with her now?

SUE. I don't know, dear. She sounds like she's in terrible pain—unless her mouth is full of candy.

JIM. Why don't you just tell her to lay down?

SUE. She enjoys it more when you tell her to lay down. And when are you going to see Mr. Hubbard?

JIM. My dear; Mr. Hubbard is not sick, and I have better things to do than to sit there and hold his hand.

SUE. It seems to me that for ten dollars you could hold his hand.

JIM. *[To Keller.]* If your son wants to play golf tell him I'm ready. Or if he'd like to take a trip around the world for about thirty years.

[He exits.]

KELLER. Why do you needle him? He's a doctor, women are supposed to call him up.

SUE. All I said was Mrs. Adams is on the phone. Can I have some of your parsley?

KELLER. Yeah, sure. *[She goes to parsley box and pulls some parsley.]* You were a nurse too long, Susie. You're too . . . too . . . realistic.

SUE. *[Laughing, pointing at him.]* Now you said it!

[Lydia Lubey enters. She is a robust, laughing girl of twenty-seven.]

LYDIA. Frank, the toaster— *[Sees the others.]* Hya.

KELLER. Hello!

LYDIA. *[To Frank.]* The toaster is off again.

FRANK. Well, plug it in, I just fixed it.

LYDIA. *[Kindly, but insistently.]* Please, dear, fix it back like it was before.

FRANK. I don't know why you can't learn to turn on a simple thing like a toaster! *[He exits.]*

SUE. *[Laughing.]* Thomas Edison.

LYDIA. *[Apologetically.]* He's really very handy. *[She sees broken tree.]* Oh, did the wind get your tree?

KELLER. Yeah, last night.

LYDIA. Oh, what a pity. Annie get in?

KELLER. She'll be down soon. Wait'll you meet her, Sue, she's a knockout.

SUE. I should've been a man. People are always introducing me to beautiful women. *[To Joe.]* Tell her to come over later: I imagine she'd like to see what we did with her house. And thanks. *[She exits.]*

LYDIA. Is she still unhappy, Joe?

KELLER. Annie? I don't suppose she goes around dancing on her toes, but she seems to be over it.

LYDIA. She going to get married? Is there anybody—?

KELLER. I suppose—say, it's a couple years already. She can't mourn a boy forever.

LYDIA. It's so strange—Annie's here and not even married. And I've got three babies. I always thought it'd be the other way around.

KELLER. Well, that's what a war does. I had two sons, now I got one. It changed all the tallies. In my day when you had sons it was an honor. Today a doctor could make a million dollars if he could figure out a way to bring a boy into the world without a trigger finger.

LYDIA. You know, I was just reading—

[Enter Chris Keller from house, stands in doorway.]

LYDIA. Hya, Chris.

[Frank shouts from offstage.]

FRANK. Lydia, come in here! If you want the toaster to work don't plug in the malted mixer.

LYDIA. *[Embarrassed, laughing.]* Did I?

FRANK. And the next time I fix something don't tell me I'm crazy! Now come in here!

LYDIA. *[To Keller.]* I'll never hear the end of this one.

KELLER. *[Calling to Frank.]* So what's the difference? Instead of toast have a malted!

LYDIA. Sh! sh! *[She exits, laughing.]*

*[Chris watches her off. He is thirty-two; like his father, solidly built, a
listener. A man capable of immense affection and loyalty. He has a cup of
coffee in one hand, part of a doughnut in the other.]*

KELLER. You want the paper?

CHRIS. That's all right, just the book section. *[He bends down
and pulls out part of paper on porch floor.]*

KELLER. You're always reading the book section and you never
buy a book.

CHRIS. *[Coming down to settee.]* I like to keep abreast of my ignorance. *[He sits on settee.]*

KELLER. What is that, every week a new book comes out?

CHRIS. Lot of new books.

KELLER. All different.

CHRIS. All different.

*[Keller shakes his head, puts knife down on bench, takes oilstone up to the
cabinet.]*

KELLER. Psss! Annie up yet?

CHRIS. Mother's giving her breakfast in the dining room.

KELLER. *[Looking at broken tree.]* See what happened to the tree?

CHRIS. *[Without looking up.]* Yeah.

KELLER. What's Mother going to say?

*[Bert runs on from driveway. He is about eight. He jumps on stool, then on
Keller's back.]*

BERT. You're finally up.

KELLER. *[Swinging him around and putting him down.]* Ha! Bert's
here! Where's Tommy? He's got his father's thermometer again.

BERT. He's taking a reading.

CHRIS. What!

BERT. But it's only oral.

KELLER. Oh, well, there's no harm in oral. So what's new this
morning, Bert?

BERT. Nothin'. *[He goes to broken tree, walks around it.]*

KELLER. Then you couldn't've made a complete inspection of the
block. In the beginning, when I first made you a policeman you
used to come in every morning with something new. Now, nothin's
ever new.

BERT. Except some kids from Thirtieth Street. They started kick-
ing a can down the block, and I made them go away because you
were sleeping.

KELLER. Now you're talkin', Bert. Now you're on the ball. First
thing you know I'm liable to make you a detective.

BERT. *[Pulling him down by the lapel and whispering in his ear.]* Can
I see the jail now?

KELLER. Seein' the jail ain't allowed, Bert. You know that.

BERT. Aw, I betcha there isn't even a jail. I don't see any bars on the cellar windows.

KELLER. Bert, on my word of honor there's a jail in the basement. I showed you my gun, didn't I?

BERT. But that's a hunting gun.

KELLER. That's an arresting gun!

BERT. Then why don't you ever arrest anybody? Tommy said another dirty word to Doris yesterday, and you didn't even demote him.

[*Keller chuckles and winks at Chris, who is enjoying all this.*]

KELLER. Yeah, that's a dangerous character, that Tommy. [*Beckons him closer.*] What word does he say?

BERT. [*Backing away quickly in great embarrassment.*] Oh, I can't say that.

KELLER. [*Grabbing him by the shirt and pulling him back.*] Well, gimme an idea.

BERT. I can't. It's not a nice word.

KELLER. Just whisper it in my ear. I'll close my eyes. Maybe I won't even hear it.

[*Bert, on tiptoe, puts his lips to Keller's ear, then in unbearable embarrassment steps back.*]

BERT. I can't, Mr. Keller.

CHRIS. [*Laughing.*] Don't make him do that.

KELLER. Okay, Bert. I take your word. Now go out, and keep both eyes peeled.

BERT. [*Interested.*] For what?

KELLER. For what! Bert, the whole neighborhood is depending on you. A policeman don't ask questions. Now peel them eyes!

BERT. [*Mystified, but willing.*] Okay. [*He runs off stage back of arbor.*]

KELLER. [*Calling after him.*] And mum's the word, Bert.

[*Bert stops and sticks his head through the arbor.*]

BERT. About what?

KELLER. Just in general. Be v-e-r-y careful.

BERT. [*Nodding in bewilderment.*] Okay. [*He exits.*]

KELLER. [*Laughing.*] I got all the kids crazy!

CHRIS. One of these days, they'll all come in here and beat your brains out.

KELLER. What's she going to say? Maybe we ought to tell her before she sees it.

CHRIS. She saw it.

KELLER. How could she see it? I was the first one up. She was still in bed.

CHRIS. She was out here when it broke.

KELLER. When?

CHRIS. About four this morning. *[Indicating window above them.]* I heard it cracking and I woke up and looked out. She was standing right here when it cracked.

KELLER. What was she doing out here four in the morning?

CHRIS. I don't know. When it cracked she ran back into the house and cried in the kitchen.

KELLER. Did you talk to her?

CHRIS. No, I—I figured the best thing was to leave her alone. *[Pause]*

KELLER. *[Deeply touched.]* She cried hard?

CHRIS. I could hear her right through the floor of my room.

KELLER. *[After slight pause.]* What was she doing out here at that hour? *[Chris silent. With an undertone of anger showing.]* She's dreaming about him again. She's walking around at night.

CHRIS. I guess she is.

KELLER. She's getting just like after he died. *[Slight pause.]* What's the meaning of that?

CHRIS. I don't know the meaning of it. *[Slight pause.]* But I know one thing, Dad. We've made a terrible mistake with Mother.

KELLER. What?

CHRIS. Being dishonest with her. That kind of thing always pays off, and now it's paying off.

KELLER. What do you mean, dishonest?

CHRIS. You know Larry's not coming back and I know it. Why do we allow her to go on thinking that we believe with her?

KELLER. What do you want to do, argue with her?

CHRIS. I don't want to argue with her, but it's time she realized that nobody believes Larry is alive any more. *[Keller simply moves away, thinking, looking at the ground.]* Why shouldn't she dream of him, walk the nights waiting for him? Do we contradict her? Do we say straight out that we have no hope any more? That we haven't had any hope for years now?

KELLER. *[Frightened at the thought.]* You can't say that to her.

CHRIS. We've got to say it to her.

KELLER. How're you going to prove it? Can you prove it?

CHRIS. For God's sake, three years! Nobody comes back after three years. It's insane.

KELLER. To you it is, and to me. But not to her. You can talk yourself blue in the face, but there's no body and there's no grave, so where are you?

CHRIS. Sit down, Dad. I want to talk to you.

[Keller looks at him searchingly a moment.]

KELLER. The trouble is the Goddam newspapers. Every month some boy turns up from nowhere, so the next one is going to be Larry, so—

CHRIS. All right, all right, listen to me. *[Slight pause. Keller sits on settee.]* You know why I asked Annie here, don't you?

KELLER. *[He knows, but—]* Why?

CHRIS. You know.

KELLER. Well, I got an idea, but— What's the story?

CHRIS. I'm going to ask her to marry me. *[Slight pause. Keller nods.]*

KELLER. Well, that's only your business, Chris.

CHRIS. You know it's not only my business.

KELLER. What do you want me to do? You're old enough to know your own mind.

CHRIS. *[Asking, annoyed.]* Then it's all right, I'll go ahead with it?

KELLER. Well, you want to be sure Mother isn't going to—

CHRIS. Then it isn't just my business.

KELLER. I'm just sayin'—

CHRIS. Sometimes you infuriate me, you know that? Isn't it your business, too, if I tell this to Mother and she throws a fit about it? You have such a talent for ignoring things.

KELLER. I ignore what I gotta ignore. The girl is Larry's girl.

CHRIS. She's not Larry's girl.

KELLER. From Mother's point of view he is not dead and you have no right to take his girl. *[Slight pause.]* Now you can go on from there if you know where to go, but I'm tellin' you I don't know where to go. See? I don't know. Now what can I do for you?

CHRIS. I don't know why it is, but every time I reach out for something I want, I have to pull back because other people will suffer. My whole bloody life, time after time after time.

KELLER. You're a considerate fella, there's nothing wrong in that.

CHRIS. To hell with that.

KELLER. Did you ask Annie yet?

CHRIS. I wanted to get this settled first.

KELLER. How do you know she'll marry you? Maybe she feels the same way Mother does?

CHRIS. Well, if she does, then that's the end of it. From her letters I think she's forgotten him. I'll find out. And then we'll thrash it out with Mother? Right? Dad, don't avoid me.

KELLER. The trouble is, you don't see enough women. You never did.

CHRIS. So what? I'm not fast with women.

KELLER. I don't see why it has to be Annie.

CHRIS. Because it is.

KELLER. That's a good answer, but it don't answer anything. You haven't seen her since you went to war. It's five years.

CHRIS. I can't help it. I know her best. I was brought up next door to her. These years when I think of someone for my wife, I think of Annie. What do you want, a diagram?

KELLER. I don't want a diagram . . . I—I'm— She thinks he's

coming back, Chris. You marry that girl and you're pronouncing him dead. Now what's going to happen to Mother? Do you know? I don't! *[Pause.]*

CHRIS. All right, then, Dad.

KELLER. *[Thinking Chris has retreated.]* Give it some more thought.

CHRIS. I've given it three years of thought. I'd hoped that if I waited, Mother would forget Larry and then we'd have a regular wedding and everything happy. But if that can't happen here, then I'll have to get out.

KELLER. What the hell is *this?*

CHRIS. I'll get out. I'll get married and live some place else. Maybe in New York.

KELLER. Are you crazy?

CHRIS. I've been a good son too long, a good sucker. I'm through with it.

KELLER. You've got a business here, what the hell is this?

CHRIS. The business! The business doesn't inspire me.

KELLER. Must you be inspired?

CHRIS. Yes. I like it an hour a day. If I have to grub for money all day long at least at evening I want it beautiful. I want a family, I want some kids, I want to build something I can give myself to. Annie is in the middle of that. Now . . . where do I find it?

KELLER. You mean— *[Goes to him.]* Tell me something, you mean you'd leave the business?

CHRIS. Yes. On this I would.

KELLER. *[After a pause.]* Well . . . you don't want to think like that.

CHRIS. Then help me stay here.

KELLER. All right, but—but don't think like that. Because what the hell did I work for? That's only for you, Chris, the whole shootin' match is for you!

CHRIS. I know that, Dad. Just you help me stay here.

KELLER. *[Putting a fist up to Chris's jaw]* But don't think that way, you hear me?

CHRIS. I am thinking that way.

KELLER. *[Lowering his hand.]* I don't understand you, do I?

CHRIS. No, you don't. I'm a pretty tough guy.

KELLER. Yeah. I can see that.

[Mother appears on porch. She is in her early fifties, a woman of uncontrolled inspirations and an overwhelming capacity for love.]

MOTHER. Joe?

CHRIS. *[Going toward porch.]* Hello, Mom.

MOTHER. *[Indicating house behind her; to Keller.]* Did you take a bag from under the sink?

KELLER. Yeah, I put it in the pail.

MOTHER. Well, get it out of the pail. That's my potatoes.

[Chris bursts out laughing—goes up into alley.]

KELLER. *[Laughing.]* I thought it was garbage.

MOTHER. Will you do me a favor, Joe? Don't be helpful.

KELLER. I can afford another bag of potatoes.

MOTHER. Minnie scoured that pail in boiling water last night. It's cleaner than your teeth.

KELLER. And I don't understand why, after I worked forty years and I got a maid, why I have to take out the garbage.

MOTHER. If you would make up your mind that every bag in the kitchen isn't full of garbage you wouldn't be throwing out my vege= tables. Last time it was the onions.

[Chris comes on, hands her bag.]

KELLER. I don't like garbage in the house.

MOTHER. Then don't eat. *[She goes into the kitchen with bag.]*

CHRIS. That settles you for today.

KELLER. Yeah, I'm in last place again. I don't know, once upon a time I used to think that when I got money again I would have a maid and my wife would take it easy. Now I got money, and I got a maid, and my wife is workin' for the maid. *[He sits in one of the chairs.]*

[Mother comes out on last line. She carries a pot of string beans.]

MOTHER. It's her day off, what are you crabbing about?

CHRIS. *[To Mother.]* Isn't Annie finished eating?

MOTHER. *[Looking around preoccupiedly at yard.]* She'll be right out. *[Moves.]* That wind did some job on this place. *[Of the tree.]* So much for that, thank God.

KELLER. *[Indicating chair beside him.]* Sit down, take it easy.

MOTHER. *[Pressing her hand to top of her head.]* I've got such a funny pain on the top of my head.

CHRIS. Can I get you an aspirin?

[Mother picks a few petals off ground, stands there smelling them in her hand, then sprinkles them over plants.]

MOTHER. No more roses. It's so funny . . . everything decides to happen at the same time. This month is his birthday; his tree blows down, Annie comes. Everything that happened seems to be coming back. I was just down the cellar, and what do I stumble over? His baseball glove. I haven't seen it in a century.

CHRIS. Don't you think Annie looks well?

MOTHER. Fine. There's no question about it. She's a beauty . . . I still don't know what brought her here. Not that I'm not glad to see her, but—

CHRIS. I just thought we'd all like to see each other again. *[Mother just looks at him, nodding ever so slightly—almost as though admitting something.]* And I wanted to see her myself.

MOTHER. *[As her nods halt, to Keller.]* The only thing is I think her nose got longer. But I'll always love that girl. She's one that didn't jump into bed with somebody else as soon as it happened with her fella.

KELLER. *[As though that were impossible for Annie.]* Oh, what're you—?

MOTHER. Never mind. Most of them didn't wait till the telegrams were opened. I'm just glad she came, so you can see I'm not *completely* out of my mind. *[Sits, and rapidly breaks string beans in the pot.]*

CHRIS. Just because she isn't married doesn't mean she's been mourning Larry.

MOTHER. *[With an undercurrent of observation.]* Why then isn't she?

CHRIS. *[A little flustered.]* Well . . . it could've been any number of things.

MOTHER. *[Directly at him.]* Like what, for instance?

CHRIS. *[Embarrassed, but standing his ground.]* I don't know. Whatever it is. Can I get you an aspirin?

[Mother puts her hand to her head. She gets up and goes aimlessly toward the trees on rising.]

MOTHER. It's not like a headache.

KELLER. You don't sleep, that's why. She's wearing out more bedroom slippers than shoes.

MOTHER. I had a terrible night. *[She stops moving.]* I never had a night like that.

CHRIS. *[Looking at Keller.]* What was it, Mom? Did you dream?

MOTHER. More, more than a dream.

CHRIS. *[Hesitantly.]* About Larry?

MOTHER. I was fast asleep, and— *[Raising her arm over the audience.]* Remember the way he used to fly low past the house when he was in training? When we used to see his face in the cockpit going by? That's the way I saw him. Only high up. Way, way up, where the clouds are. He was so real I could reach out and touch him. And suddenly he started to fall. And crying, crying to me . . . Mom, Mom! I could hear him like he was in the room. Mom! . . . it was his voice! If I could touch him I knew I could stop him, if I could only— *[Breaks off, allowing her outstretched hand to fall.]* I woke up and it was so funny— The wind . . . it was like the roaring of his engine. I came out here . . . I must've still been half asleep. I could hear that roaring like he was going by. The tree snapped right in front of me—and I like—came awake. *[She is looking at tree. She suddenly realizes something, turns with a reprimanding finger shaking slightly at Keller.]* See? We should never have planted that tree. I said so in the first place; it was too soon to plant a tree for him.

CHRIS. *[Alarmed.]* Too soon!

MOTHER. *[Angering.]* We rushed into it. Everybody was in such a hurry to bury him. I *said* not to plant it yet. *[To Keller.]* I *told* you to—!

CHRIS. Mother, Mother! *[She looks into his face.]* The wind blew it down. What significance has that got? What are you talking about? Mother, please . . . Don't go through it all again, will you? It's no good, it doesn't accomplish anything. I've been thinking, y'know?— maybe we ought to put our minds to forgetting him?

MOTHER. That's the third time you've said that this week.

CHRIS. Because it's not right; we never took up our lives again. We're like at a railroad station waiting for a train that never comes in.

MOTHER. *[Pressing top of her head.]* Get me an aspirin, heh?

CHRIS. Sure, and let's break out of this, heh, Mom? I thought the four of us might go out to dinner a couple of nights, maybe go dancing out at the shore.

MOTHER. Fine. *[To Keller.]* We can do it tonight.

KELLER. Swell with me!

CHRIS. Sure, let's have some fun. *[To Mother]* You'll start with this aspirin. *[He goes up and into house with new spirit. Her smile vanishes.]*

MOTHER. *[With an accusing undertone.]* Why did he invite her here?

KELLER. Why does that bother you?

MOTHER. She's been in New York three and a half years, why all of a sudden—?

KELLER. Well, maybe—maybe he just wanted to see her.

MOTHER. Nobody comes seven hundred miles "just to see."

KELLER. What do you mean? He lived next door to the girl all his life, why shouldn't he want to see her again? *[Mother looks at him critically.]* Don't look at me like that, he didn't tell me any more than he told you.

MOTHER. *[A warning and a question.]* He's not going to marry her.

KELLER. How do you know he's even thinking of it?

MOTHER. It's got that about it.

KELLER. *[Sharply watching her reaction.]* Well? So what?

MOTHER. *[Alarmed.]* What's going on here, Joe?

KELLER. Now listen, kid—

MOTHER. *[Avoiding contact with him.]* She's not his girl, Joe; she knows she's not.

KELLER. You can't read her mind.

MOTHER. Then why is she still single? New York is full of men, why isn't she married? *[Pause.]* Probably a hundred people told her she's foolish, but she's waited.

KELLER. How do you know why she waited?

MOTHER. She knows what I know, that's why. She's faithful as a rock. In my worst moments, I think of her waiting, and I know again that I'm right.

KELLER. Look, it's a nice day. What are we arguing for?

MOTHER. *[Warningly.]* Nobody in this house dast take her faith away, Joe. Strangers might. But not his father, not his brother.

KELLER. *[Exasperated.]* What do you want me to do? What do you want?

MOTHER. I want you to act like he's coming back. Both of you. Don't think I haven't noticed you since Chris invited her. I won't stand for any nonsense.

KELLER. But, Kate—

MOTHER. Because if he's not coming back, then I'll kill myself! Laugh. Laugh at me. *[She points to tree.]* But why did that happen the very night she came back? Laugh, but there are meanings in such things. She goes to sleep in his room and his memorial breaks in pieces. Look at it; look. *[She sits on bench.]* Joe—

KELLER. Calm yourself.

MOTHER. Believe with me, Joe. I can't stand all alone.

KELLER. Calm yourself.

MOTHER. Only last week a man turned up in Detroit, missing longer than Larry. You read it yourself.

KELLER. All right, all right, calm yourself.

MOTHER. You above all have got to believe, you—

KELLER. *[Rising.]* Why me above all?

MOTHER. Just don't stop believing.

KELLER. What does that mean, me above all?

[Bert comes rushing on.]

BERT. Mr. Keller! Say, Mr. Keller . . . *[Pointing up driveway.]* Tommy just said it again!

KELLER. *[Not remembering any of it.]* Said what? Who?

BERT. The dirty word.

KELLER. Oh. Well—

BERT. Gee, aren't you going to arrest him? I warned him.

MOTHER. *[With suddenness.]* Stop that, Bert. Go home. *[Bert backs up, as she advances.]* There's no jail here.

KELLER. *[As though to say, "Oh-what-the-hell-let-him-believe-there-is"]* Kate—

MOTHER. *[Turning on Keller furiously.]* There's no jail here! I want you to stop that jail business! *[He turns, shamed, but peeved.]*

BERT. *[Past her to Keller.]* He's right across the street.

MOTHER. Go home, Bert. *[Bert turns around and goes up driveway. She is shaken. Her speech is bitten off, extremely urgent.]* I want you to stop that, Joe. That whole jail business!

KELLER. *[Alarmed, therefore angered.]* Look at you, look at you shaking.

MOTHER. *[Trying to control herself, moving about clasping her hands.]* I can't help it.

KELLER. What have I got to hide? What the hell is the matter with you, Kate?

MOTHER. I didn't say you had anything to hide, I'm just telling you to stop it! Now stop it!

[Ann and Chris appear on porch. Ann is twenty-six, gentle but despite herself capable of holding fast to what she knows. Chris opens door for her.]

ANN. Hya, Joe! *[She leads off a general laugh that is not self-conscious because they know one another too well.]*

CHRIS. *[Bringing Ann down, with an outstretched, chivalric arm.]* Take a breath of that air, kid. You never get air like that in New York.

MOTHER. *[Genuinely overcome with it.]* Annie, where did you get that dress!

ANN. I couldn't resist. I'm taking it right off before I ruin it. *[Swings around.]* How's that for three weeks' salary?

MOTHER. *[To Keller.]* Isn't she the most—? *[To Ann.]* It's gorgeous, simply gor—

CHRIS. *[To mother.]* No kidding, now, isn't she the prettiest gal you ever saw?

MOTHER. *[Caught short by his obvious admiration, she finds herself reaching out for a glass of water and aspirin in his hand, and—]* You gained a little weight, didn't you, darling? *[She gulps pill and drinks.]*

ANN. It comes and goes.

KELLER. Look how nice her legs turned out!

ANN. *[As she runs to fence.]* Boy, the poplars got thick, didn't they?

[Keller moves to settee and sits.]

KELLER. Well, it's three years, Annie. We're gettin' old, kid.

MOTHER. How does Mom like New York? *[Ann keeps looking through trees.]*

ANN. *[A little hurt.]* Why'd they take our hammock away?

KELLER. Oh, no, it broke. Couple of years ago.

MOTHER. What broke? He had one of his light lunches and flopped into it.

ANN. *[Laughs and turns back toward Jim's yard.]* Oh, excuse me!

[Jim has come to fence and is looking over it. He is smoking a cigar. As she cries out, he comes on around on stage.]

JIM. How do you do. *[To Chris.]* She looks very intelligent!

CHRIS. Ann, this is Jim—Doctor Bayliss.

ANN. *[Shaking Jim's hand.]* Oh, sure, he writes a lot about you.

JIM. Don't you believe it. He likes everybody. In the battalion he was known as Mother McKeller.

ANN. I can believe it. You know—? *[To Mother.]* It's so strange seeing him come out of that yard. *[To Chris.]* I guess I never grew up. It almost seems that Mom and Pop are in there now. And you and my brother doing algebra, and Larry trying to copy my home-work. Gosh, those dear dead days beyond recall.

JIM. Well, I hope that doesn't mean you want me to move out?

sue. *[Calling from off stage.]* Jim, come in here! Mr. Hubbard is on the phone!

jim. I told you I don't want—

sue. *[Commandingly sweet.]* Please, dear! Please!

jim. *[Resigned.]* All right, Susie. *[Trailing off.]* All right, all right . . . *[To Ann.]* I've only met you, Ann, but if I may offer you a piece of advice— When you marry, never—even in your mind—never count your husband's money.

sue. *[From offstage.]* Jim?

jim. At once! *[Turns and goes off.]* At once. *[He exits.]*

mother. *[Ann is looking at her. She speaks meaningfully.]* I told her to take up the guitar. It'd be a common interest for them. *[They laugh.]* Well, he loves the guitar!

[Ann, as though to overcome Mother, becomes suddenly lively, crosses to Keller on settee, sits on his lap.]

ann. Let's eat at the shore tonight! Raise some hell around here, like we used to before Larry went!

mother. *[Emotionally.]* You think of him! You see? *[Triumphantly.]* She thinks of him!

ann. *[With an uncomprehending smile.]* What do you mean, Kate?

mother. Nothing. Just that you—remember him, he's in your thoughts.

ann. That's a funny thing to say; how could I help remembering him?

mother. *[It is drawing to a head the wrong way for her; she starts anew. She rises and comes to Ann.]* Did you hang up your things?

ann. Yeah . . . *[To Chris.]* Say, you've sure gone in for clothes. I could hardly find room in the closet.

mother. No, don't you remember? That's Larry's room.

ann. You mean . . . they're Larry's?

mother. Didn't you recognize them?

ann. *[Slowly rising, a little embarrassed.]* Well, it never occurred to me that you'd—I mean the shoes are all shined.

mother. Yes, dear. *[Slight pause. Ann can't stop staring at her. Mother breaks it by speaking with the relish of gossip, putting her arm around Ann and walking with her.]* For so long I've been aching for a nice conversation with you, Annie. Tell me something.

ann. What?

mother. I don't know. Something nice.

chris. *[Wryly.]* She means do you go out much?

mother. Oh, shut up.

keller. And are any of them serious?

mother. *[Laughing, sits in her chair.]* Why don't you both choke?

keller. Annie, you can't go into a restaurant with that woman any more. In five minutes thirty-nine strange people are sitting at the table telling her their life story.

MOTHER. If I can't ask Annie a personal question—

KELLER. Askin' is all right, but don't beat her over the head. You're beatin' her, you're beatin' her. *[They are laughing.]*

[Ann takes pan of beans off stool, puts them on floor under chair and sits.]

ANN. *[To Mother.]* Don't let them bulldoze you. Ask me anything you like. What do you want to know, Kate? Come on, let's gossip.

MOTHER. *[To Chris and Keller.]* She's the only one is got any sense. *[To Ann.]* Your mother—she's not getting a divorce, heh?

ANN. No, she's calmed down about it now. I think when he gets out they'll probably live together. In New York, of course.

MOTHER. That's fine. Because your father is still—I mean he's a decent man after all is said and done.

ANN. I don't care. She can take him back if she likes.

MOTHER. And you? *[Shakes her head negatively]* go out much? *[Slight pause.]*

ANN. *[Delicately.]* You mean am I still waiting for him?

MOTHER. Well, no. I don't expect you to wait for him but—

ANN. *[Kindly.]* But that's what you mean, isn't it?

MOTHER. Well . . . yes.

ANN. Well, I'm not, Kate.

MOTHER. *[Faintly.]* You're not?

ANN. Isn't it ridiculous? You don't really imagine he's—?

MOTHER. I know, dear, but don't say it's ridiculous, because the papers were full ot it; I don't know about New York, but there was half a page about a man missing even longer than Larry, and he turned up from Burma.

CHRIS. *[Coming to Ann.]* He couldn't have wanted to come home very badly, Mom.

MOTHER. Don't be so smart.

CHRIS. You can have a helluva time in Burma.

ANN. *[Rises and swings around in back of Chris.]* So I've heard.

CHRIS. Mother, I'll bet you money that you're the only woman in the country who after three years is still—

MOTHER. You're sure?

CHRIS. Yes, I am.

MOTHER. Well, if you're sure then your're sure. *[She turns her head away an instant.]* They don't say it on the radio but I'm sure that in the dark at night they're still waiting for their sons.

CHRIS. Mother, you're absolutely—

MOTHER. *[Waving him off.]* Don't be so damned smart! Now stop it! *[Slight pause.]* There are just a few things you *don't* know. All of you. And I'll tell you one of them, Annie. Deep, deep in your heart you've always been waiting for him.

ANN. *[Resolutely.]* No, Kate.

MOTHER. *[With increasing demand.]* But deep in your heart, Annie!

CHRIS. She ought to know, shouldn't she?

MOTHER. Don't let them tell you what to think. Listen to your heart. Only your heart.

ANN. Why does your heart tell you he's alive?

MOTHER. Because he has to be.

ANN. But why, Kate?

MOTHER. [*Going to her.*] Because certain things have to be, and certain things can never be. Like the sun has to rise, it has to be. That's why there's God. Otherwise anything could happen. But there's God, so certain things can never happen. I would know, Annie—just like I knew the day he [*indicates Chris*] went into the terrible battle. Did he write me? Was it in the papers? No, but that morning I couldn't raise my head off the pillow. Ask Joe. Suddenly, I knew. I knew! And he was nearly killed that day. Ann, you *know* I'm right!

[*Ann stands there in silence, then turns trembling, going upstage.*]

ANN. No, Kate.

MOTHER. I have to have some tea.

[*Frank appears, carrying ladder.*]

FRANK. Annie! [*Coming down.*] How are you, gee whiz!

ANN. [*Taking his hand.*] Why, Frank, you're losing your hair.

KELLER. He's got responsibility.

FRANK. Gee whiz!

KELLER. Without Frank the stars wouldn't know when to come out.

FRANK. [*Laughs; to Ann.*] You look more womanly. You've matured. You—

KELLER. Take it easy, Frank, you're a married man.

ANN. [*As they laugh.*] You still haberdashering?

FRANK. Why not? Maybe I too can get to be president.[1] How's your brother? Got his degree, I hear.

ANN. Oh, George has his own office now!

FRANK. Don't say! [*Funereally.*] And your dad? Is he—?

ANN. [*Abruptly.*] Fine. I'll be in to see Lydia.

FRANK. [*Sympathetically.*] How about it, does Dad expect a parole soon?

ANN. [*With growing ill-ease.*] I really don't know, I—

FRANK. [*Staunchly defending her father for her sake.*] I mean because I feel, y'know, that if an intelligent man like your father is put in prison, there ought to be a law that says either you execute him, or let him go after a year.

CHRIS. [*Interrupting.*] Want a hand with that ladder, Frank?

FRANK. [*Taking cue.*] That's all right, I'll— [*Picks up ladder.*] I'll finish the horoscope tonight, Kate. [*Embarrassed.*] See you later, Ann, you look wonderful. [*He exits. They look at Ann.*]

1 President Harry S Truman (1945–1953) owned a hat business, or haberdashery, earlier in his life.

ANN. *[To Chris, as she sits slowly on stool.]* Haven't they stopped talking about Dad?

CHRIS. *[Comes down and sits on arm of chair.]* Nobody talks about him any more.

KELLER. *[Rises and comes to her.]* Gone and forgotten, kid.

ANN. Tell me. Becuase I don't want to meet anybody on the block if they're going to—

CHRIS. I don't want you to worry about it.

ANN. *[To Keller.]* Do they still remember the case, Joe? Do they talk about you?

KELLER. The only one still talks about it is my wife.

MOTHER. That's because you keep on playing policeman with the kids. All their parents hear out of you is jail, jail, jail.

KELLER. Actually what happened was that when I got home from the penitentiary the kids got very interested in me. You know kids. I was *[Laughs.]* like the expert on the jail situation. And as time passed they got it confused and . . . I ended up a detective. *[Laughs.]*

MOTHER. Except that *they* didn't get it confused. *[To Ann.]* He hands out police badges from the Post Toasties boxes. *[They laugh.]*

[Ann rises and comes to Keller, putting her arm around his shoulder.]

ANN. *[Wondrously at them, happy.]* Gosh, it's wonderful to hear you laughing about it.

CHRIS. Why, what'd you expect?

ANN. The last thing I remember on this block was one word— "Murderers!" Remember that, Kate?—Mrs. Hammond standing in front of our house and yelling that word? She's still around, I suppose?

MOTHER. They're all still around.

KELLER. Don't listen to her. Every Saturday night the whole gang is playin' poker in this arbor. All the ones who yelled murderer takin' my money now.

MOTHER. Don't, Joe; she's a sensitive girl, don't fool her. *[To Ann.]* They still remember about Dad. It's different with him. *[Indicates Joe.]* He was exonerated, your father's still there. That's why I wasn't so enthusiastic about your coming. Honestly, I know how sensitive you are, and I told Chris, I said—

KELLER. Listen, you do like I did and you'll be all right. The day I come home, I got out of my car—but not in front of the house . . . on the corner. You should've been here, Annie, and you too, Chris; you'd-a seen something. Everybody knew I was getting out that day; the porches were loaded. Picture it now; none of them believed I was innocent. The story was, I pulled a fast one getting myself exonerated. So I get out of my car, and I walk down the street. But very slow. And with a smile. The beast! I was the beast; the guy who sold cracked cylinder heads to the Army Air Force; the guy who made twenty-one P-40s crash in Australia. Kid, walkin' down the street that day I was guilty as hell. Except I wasn't, and there was a court paper in my pocket to prove I wasn't, and I walked . . . past . . . the porches. Result? Fourteen months later I had one of the best shops in the state again, a respected man again; bigger than ever.

CHRIS. *[With admiration.]* Joe McGuts.

KELLER. *[Now with great force.]* That's the only way you lick 'em is guts! *[To Ann.]* The worst thing you did was to move away from here. You made it tough for your father when he gets out. That's why I tell you, I like to see him move back right on this block.

MOTHER. *[Pained.]* How could they move back?

KELLER. It ain't gonna end *till* they move back! *[To Ann.]* Till people play cards with him again, and talk with him, and smile with him—you play cards with a man you know he can't be a murderer. And the next time you write him I like you to tell him just what I said. *[Ann simply stares at him.]* You hear me?

ANN. *[Surprised.]* Don't you hold anything against him?

KELLER. Annie, I never believed in crucifying people.

ANN. *[Mystified.]* But he was your partner, he dragged you through the mud.

KELLER. Well, he ain't my sweetheart, but you gotta forgive, don't you?

ANN. You, either, Kate? Don't you feel any—?

KELLER. *[To Ann.]* The next time you write Dad—

ANN. I don't write him.

KELLER. *[Struck.]* Well, every now and then you—

ANN. *[A little shamed, but determined.]* No, I've *never* written to him. Neither has my brother. *[To Chris.]* Say, do you feel this way, too?

CHRIS. He murdered twenty-one pilots.

KELLER. What the hell kinda talk is that?

MOTHER. That's not a thing to say about a man.

ANN. What else can you say? When they took him away I followed him, went to him every visiting day. I was crying all the time. Until the news came about Larry. Then I realized. It's wrong to pity a man like that. Father or no father, there's only one way to look at him. He knowingly shipped out parts that would crash an airplane. And how do you know Larry wasn't one of them?

MOTHER. I was waiting for that. *[Going to her.]* As long as you're here, Annie, I want to ask you never to say that again.

ANN. You surprise me. I thought you'd be mad at him.

MOTHER. What your father did had nothing to do with Larry. Nothing.

ANN. But we can't know that.

MOTHER. *[Striving for control.]* As long as you're here!

ANN. *[Perplexed.]* But, Kate—

MOTHER. Put that out of your head!

KELLER. Because—

MOTHER. *[Quickly to Keller.]* That's all, that's enough. *[Places her* hand on her head.] Come inside now, and have some tea with me. *[She turns and goes up steps.]*

KELLER. *[To Ann.]* The one thing you—

MOTHER. *[Sharply.]* He's not dead, so there's no argument! Now come!

KELLER. *[Angrily.]* In a minute! *[Mother turns and goes into house.]* Now look, Annie—

CHRIS. All right, Dad, forget it.

KELLER. No, she dasn't feel that way. Annie—

CHRIS. I'm sick of the whole subject, now cut it out.

KELLER. You want her to go on like this? *[To Ann.]* Those cylinder heads went into P-40s only. What's the matter with you? You know Larry never flew a P-40.

CHRIS. So who flew those P-40s, pigs?

KELLER. The man was a fool, but don't make a murderer out of him. You got no sense? Look what it does to her! *[To Ann.]* Listen, you gotta appreciate what was doin' in that shop in the war. The both of you! It was a madhouse. Every half hour the Major callin' for cylinder heads, they were whippin' us with the telephone. The trucks were hauling them away hot, damn near. I mean just try to see it human, see it human. All of a sudden a batch comes out with a crack. That happens, that's the business. A fine, hairline crack. All right, so— so he's a little man, your father, always scared of loud voices. What'll the Major say?—Half a day's production shot. . . . What'll I say? You know what I mean? Human. *[He pauses.]* So he takes out his tools and he—covers over the cracks. All right—that's bad, it's wrong, but that's what a little man does. If I could have gone in that day I'd told him—junk 'em, Steve, we can afford it. But alone he was afraid. But I know he meant no harm. He believed they'd hold up a hundred per cent. That's a mistake, but it ain't murder. You mustn't feel that way about him. You understand me? It ain't right.

ANN. *[She regards him a moment.]* Joe, let's forget it.

KELLER. Annie, the day the news came about Larry he was in the next cell to mine—Dad. And he cried, Annie—he cried half the night.

ANN. *[Touched.]* He shoulda cried all night. *[Slight pause.]*

KELLER. *[Almost angered.]* Annie, I do not understand why you—!

CHRIS. *[Breaking in—with nervous urgency.]* Are you going to stop it?

ANN. Don't yell at him. He just wants everybody happy.

KELLER. *[Clasps her around waist, smiling.]* That's my sentiments. Can you stand steak?

CHRIS. And champagne!

KELLER. Now you're operatin'! I'll call Swanson's for a table! Big time tonight, Annie!

ANN. Can't scare me.

KELLER. *[To Chris, pointing at Ann.]* I like that girl. Wrap her up.

[They laugh. Goes up porch.] You got nice legs, Annie! . . . I want to see everybody drunk tonight. *[Pointing to Chris.]* Look at him, he's blushin'! *[He exits, laughing, into house.]*

CHRIS. *[Calling after him.]* Drink your tea, Casanova. *[He turns to Ann.]* Isn't he a great guy?

ANN. You're the only one I know who loves his parents.

CHRIS. I know. It went out of style, didn't it?

ANN. *[With a sudden touch of sadness.]* It's all right. It's a good thing. *[She looks about.]* You know? It's lovely here. The air is sweet.

CHRIS. *[Hopefully.]* You're not sorry you came?

ANN. Not sorry, no. But I'm—not going to stay.

CHRIS. Why?

ANN. In the first place, your mother as much as told me to go.

CHRIS. Well—

ANN. You saw that—and then you—you've been kind of—

CHRIS. What?

ANN. Well . . . kind of embarrassed ever since I got here.

CHRIS. The trouble is I planned on kind of sneaking up on you over a period of a week or so. But they take it for granted that we're all set.

ANN. I knew they would. Your mother anyway.

CHRIS. How did you know?

ANN. From *her* point of view, why else would I come?

CHRIS. Well . . . would you want to? *[Ann still studies him.]* I guess you know this is why I asked you to come.

ANN. I guess this is why I came.

CHRIS. Ann, I love you. I love you a great deal. *[Finally.]* I love you. *[Pause. She waits.]* I have no imagination . . . that's all I know to tell you. *[Ann is waiting, ready.]* I'm embarrassing you. I didn't want to tell it to you here. I wanted some place we'd never been; a place where we'd be brand new to each other. . . . You feel it's wrong here, don't you? This yard, this chair? I want you to be ready for me. I don't want to win you away from anything.

ANN. *[Putting her arms around him.]* Oh, Chris, I've been ready a long, long time!

CHRIS. Then he's gone forever. You're sure.

ANN. I almost got married two years ago.

CHRIS. Why didn't you?

ANN. You started to write to me—*[Slight pause.]*

CHRIS. You felt something that far back?

ANN. Every day since!

CHRIS. Ann, why didn't you let me know?

ANN. I was waiting for you, Chris. Till then you never wrote. And when you did, what did you say? You sure can be ambiguous, you know.

CHRIS. *[Looks toward house, then at her, trembling.]* Give me a kiss, Ann. Give me a—*[They kiss.]* God, I kissed you, Annie, I kissed Annie. How long, how long I've been waiting to kiss you!

ANN. I'll never forgive you. Why did you wait all these years? All

I've done is sit and wonder if I was crazy for thinking of you.

CHRIS. Annie, we're going to live now! I'm going to make you so happy. *[He kisses her, but without their bodies touching.]*

ANN. *[A little embarrassed.]* Not like that you're not.

CHRIS. I kissed you . . .

ANN. Like Larry's brother. Do it like you, Chris. *[He breaks away from her abruptly.]* What is it, Chris?

CHRIS. Let's drive some place . . . I want to be alone with you.

ANN. No . . . what is it, Chris, your mother?

CHRIS. No—nothing like that.

ANN. Then what's wrong? Even in your letters, there was something ashamed.

CHRIS. Yes. I suppose I have been. But it's going from me.

ANN. You've got to tell me—

CHRIS. I don't know how to start. *[He takes her hand.]*

ANN. It wouldn't work this way. *[Slight pause.]*

CHRIS. *[Speaks quietly, factually at first.]* It's all mixed up with so many other things. . . . You remember, overseas, I was in command of a company?

ANN. Yeah, sure.

CHRIS. Well, I lost them.

ANN. How many?

CHRIS. Just about all.

ANN. Oh, gee!

CHRIS. It takes a little time to toss that off. Because they weren't just men. For instance, one time it'd been raining several days and this kid came to me, and gave me his last pair of dry socks. Put them in my pocket. That's only a little thing—but . . . that's the kind of guys I had. They didn't die; they killed themselves for each other. I mean that exactly; a little more selfish and they'd 've been here today. And I got an idea—watching them go down. Everything was being destroyed, see, but it seemed to me that one new thing was made. A kind of—responsibility. Man for man. You understand me?—To show that, to bring that onto the earth again like some kind of a monument and everyone would feel it standing there, behind him, and it would make a difference to him. *[Pause.]* And then I came home and it was incredible. I—there was no meaning in it here; the whole thing to them was a kind of a—bus accident. I went to work with Dad, and that rat-race again. I felt—what you said—ashamed somehow. Because nobody was changed at all. It seemed to make suckers out of a lot of guys. I felt wrong to be alive, to open the bankbook, to drive the new car, to see the new refrigerator. I mean you can take those things out of a war, but when you drive that car you've got to know that it came out of the love a man can have for a man, you've got to be a little better because of that. Otherwise what you have is really loot, and there's blood on it. I didn't want to take any of it. And I guess that included you.

ANN. And you still feel that way?

CHRIS. I want you now, Annie.

ANN. Because you mustn't feel that way any more. Because you have a right to whatever you have. Everything, Chris, understand that? To me, too . . . And the money, there's nothing wrong in your money. Your father put hundreds of planes in the air, you should be proud. A man should be paid for that . . .

CHRIS. Oh Annie, Annie . . . I'm going to make a fortune for you!

KELLER. *[Offstage.]* Hello . . . Yes. Sure.

ANN. *[Laughing softly.]* What'll I do with a fortune?

[They kiss. Keller enters from house.]

KELLER. *[Thumbing toward house.]* Hey, Ann, your brother— *[They step apart shyly. Keller comes down, and wryly]* What is this, Labor Day?

CHRIS. *[Waving him away, knowing the kidding will be endless.]* All right, all right.

ANN. You shouldn't burst out like that.

KELLER. Well, nobody told me it was Labor Day. *[Looks around.]* Where's the hot dogs?

CHRIS. *[Loving it.]* All right. You said it once.

KELLER. Well, as long as I know it's Labor Day from now on, I'll wear a bell around my neck.

ANN. *[Affectionately.]* He's so subtle!

CHRIS. George Bernard Shaw as an elephant.

KELLER. George!—hey, you kissed it out of my head—your brother's on the phone.

ANN. *[Surprised.]* My brother?

KELLER. Yeah, George. Long distance.

ANN. What's the matter, is anything wrong?

KELLER. I don't know, Kate's talking to him. Hurry up, she'll cost him five dollars.

ANN. *[Takes a step upstage, then comes down toward Chris.]* I wonder if we ought to tell your mother yet? I mean I'm not very good in an argument.

CHRIS. We'll wait till tonight. After dinner. Now don't get tense, just leave it to me.

KELLER. What're you telling her?

CHRIS. Go ahead, Ann. *[With misgivings, Ann goes up and into house.]* We're getting married, Dad. *[Keller nods indecisively.]* Well, don't you say anything?

KELLER. *[Distracted.]* I'm glad, Chris, I'm just—George is calling from Columbus.

CHRIS. Columbus!

KELLER. Did Annie tell you he was going to see his father today?

CHRIS. No, I don't think she knew anything about it.

KELLER. *[Asking uncomfortably.]* Chris! You—you think you know her pretty good?

CHRIS. *[Hurt and apprehensive.]* What kind of a question?

KELLER. I'm just wondering. All these years George don't go to see his father. Suddenly he goes . . . and she comes here.

CHRIS. Well, what about it?

KELLER. It's crazy, but it comes to my mind. She don't hold nothin' against me, does she?

CHRIS. *[Angry.]* I don't know what you're talking about.

KELLER. *[A little more combatively.]* I'm just talkin'. To his last day in court the man blamed it all on me; and this is his daughter. I mean if she was sent here to find out something?

CHRIS. *[Angered.]* Why? What is there to find out?

ANN. *[On phone, offstage.]* Why are you so excited, George? What happened there?

KELLER. I mean if they want to open up the case again, for the nuisance value, to hurt us?

CHRIS. Dad . . . how could you think that of her?

ANN. *[Still on phone.]* But what did he say to you, for God's sake?   *[Together.]*

KELLER. It couldn't be, heh. You know.

CHRIS. Dad, you amaze me . . .

KELLER. *[Breaking in.]* All right, forget it, forget it. *[With great force, moving about.]* I want a clean start for you, Chris. I want a new sign over the plant—Christopher Keller, Incorporated.

CHRIS. *[A little uneasily.]* J. O. Keller is good enough.

KELLER. We'll talk about it. I'm going to build you a house, stone, with a driveway from the road. I want you to spread out, Chris, I want you to use what I made for you. *[He is close to him now.]* I mean, with joy, Chris, without shame . . . with joy.

CHRIS. *[Touched.]* I will, Dad.

KELLER. *[With deep emotion.]* Say it to me.

CHRIS. Why?

KELLER. Because sometimes I think you're . . . ashamed of the money.

CHRIS. No, don't feel that.

KELLER. Because it's good money, there's nothing wrong with that money.

CHRIS. *[A little frightened.]* Dad, you don't have to tell me this.

KELLER. *[With overriding affection and self-confidence now. He grips Chris by the back of the neck, and with laughter between his determined jaws.]* Look, Chris, I'll go to work on Mother for you. We'll get her so drunk tonight we'll all get married! *[Steps away, with a wide gesture of his arm.]* There's gonna be a wedding, kid, like there never was seen! Champagne, tuxedos—!

[He breaks off as Ann's voice comes out loud from the house where she is still talking on phone.]

ANN. Simply because when you get excited you don't control yourself. . . . *[Mother comes out of house.]* Well, what did he tell you for God's sake? *[Pause.]* All right, come then. *[Pause.]* Yes, they'll all be here. Nobody's running away from you. And try to get hold of yourself, will you? *[Pause.]* All right, all right. Good-by.

[There is a brief pause as Ann hangs up receiver, then comes out of kitchen.]

CHRIS. Something happen?

KELLER. He's coming here?

ANN. On the seven o'clock. He's in Columbus. *[To Mother.]* I told him it would be all right.

KELLER. Sure, fine! Your father took sick?

ANN. *[Mystified.]* No, George didn't say he was sick. I— *[Shaking it off.]* I don't know, I suppose it's something stupid, you know my brother— *[She comes to Chris.]* Let's go for a drive, or something . . .

CHRIS. Sure. Give me the keys, Dad.

MOTHER. Drive through the park. It's beautiful now.

CHRIS. Come on, Ann. *[To them.]* Be back right away.

ANN. *[As she and Chris exit up drive way.]* See you.

[Mother comes down toward Keller, her eyes fixed on him.]

KELLER. Take your time. *[To Mother.]* What does George want?

MOTHER. He's been in Columbus since this morning with Steve. He's gotta see Annie right away, he says.

KELLER. What for?

MOTHER. I don't know. *[She speaks with warning.]* He's a lawyer now, Joe. George is a lawyer. All these years he never even sent a postcard to Steve. Since he got back from the war, not a postcard.

KELLER. So what?

MOTHER. *[Her tension breaking out.]* Suddenly he takes an airplane from New York to see him. An airplane!

KELLER. Well? So?

MOTHER. *[Trembling.]* Why?

KELLER. I don't read minds. Do you?

MOTHER. Why, Joe? What has Steve suddenly got to tell him that he takes an airplane to see him?

KELLER. What do I care what Steve's got to tell him?

MOTHER. You're sure, Joe?

KELLER. *[Frightened, but angry.]* Yes, I'm sure.

MOTHER. *[Sits stiffly in a chair.]* Be smart now, Joe. The boy is coming. Be smart.

KELLER. *[Desperately.]* Once and for all, did you hear what I said? I said I'm sure!

MOTHER. *[Nods weakly.]* All right, Joe. *[He straightens up.]* Just . . . be smart.

[Keller, in hopeless fury, looks at her, turns around, goes up to porch and into house, slamming screen door violently behind him. Mother sits in chair down-

stage, stiffly, staring, seeing.]

CURTAIN

ACT 2

As twilight falls, that evening.

On the rise, Chris is discovered sawing the broken-off tree, leaving stump standing alone. He is dressed in good pants, white shoes, but without a shirt. He disappears with tree up the alley when Mother appears on porch. She comes down and stands watching him. She has on a dressing gown, carries a tray of grape-juice drink in a pitcher, and glasses with sprigs of mint in them.

MOTHER. *[Calling up alley.]* Did you have to put on good pants to do that? *[She comes downstage and puts tray on table in the arbor. Then looks around uneasily, then feels pitcher for coolness. Chris enters from alley brushing off his hands.]* You notice there's more light with that thing gone?

CHRIS. Why aren't you dressing?

MOTHER. It's suffocating upstairs. I made a grape drink for Georgie. He always liked grape. Come and have some.

CHRIS. *[Impatiently.]* Well, come on, get dressed. And what's Dad sleeping so much for? *[He goes to table and pours a glass of juice.]*

MOTHER. He's worried. When he's worried he sleeps. *[Pauses. Looks into his eyes.]* We're dumb, Chris. Dad and I are stupid people. We don't know anything. You've got to protect us.

CHRIS. You're silly; what's there to be afraid of?

MOTHER. To his last day in court Steve never gave up the idea that Dad made him do it. If they're going to open the case again I won't live through it.

CHRIS. George is just a damn fool, Mother. How can you take him seriously?

MOTHER. That family hates us. Maybe even Annie—

CHRIS. Oh, now, Mother . . .

MOTHER. You think just because you like everybody, they like you!

CHRIS. All right, stop working yourself up. Just leave everything to me.

MOTHER. When George goes home tell her to go with him.

CHRIS. *[Noncommittally.]* Don't worry about Annie.

MOTHER. Steve is her father, too.

CHRIS. Are you going to cut it out? Now, come.

MOTHER. *[Going upstage with him.]* You don't realize how people can hate, Chris, they can hate so much they'll tear the world to pieces.

[Ann, dressed up, appears on porch.]

CHRIS. Look! She's dressed already. *[As he and Mother mount porch.]* I've just got to put on a shirt.

ANN. *[In a preoccupied way.]* Are you feeling well, Kate?

MOTHER. What's the difference, dear. There are certain people, y'know, the sicker they get the longer they live. *[She goes into house.]*

CHRIS. You look nice.

ANN. We're going to tell her tonight.

CHRIS. Absolutely, don't worry about it.

ANN. I wish we could tell her now. I can't stand scheming. My stomach gets hard.

CHRIS. It's not scheming, we'll just get her in a better mood.

MOTHER. *[Offstage, in the house.]* Joe, are you going to sleep all day!

ANN. *[Laughing.]* The only one who's relaxed is your father. He's fast asleep.

CHRIS. I'm relaxed.

ANN. Are you?

CHRIS. Look. *[He holds out his hand and makes it shake.]* Let me know when George gets here.

[He goes into the house. Ann moves aimlessly, and then is drawn toward tree stump. She goes to it, hesitantly touches broken top in the hush of her thoughts. Offstage Lydia calls, "Johnny! Come get your supper!" Sue enters, and halts, seeing Ann.]

SUE. Is my husband—?

ANN. *[Turns, startled.]* Oh!

SUE. I'm terribly sorry.

ANN. It's all right, I—I'm a little silly about the dark.

SUE. *[Looks about.]* It is getting dark.

ANN. Are you looking for your husband?

SUE. As usual. *[Laughs tiredly.]* He spends so much time here, they'll be charging him rent.

ANN. Nobody was dressed so he drove over to the depot to pick up my brother.

SUE. Oh, your brother's in?

ANN. Yeah, they ought to be here any minute now. Will you have a cold drink?

SUE. I will, thanks. *[Ann goes to table and pours.]* My husband. Too hot to drive me to beach. Men are like little boys; for the neighbors they'll always cut the grass.

ANN. People like to do things for the Kellers. Been that way since I can remember.

SUE. It's amazing. I guess your brother's coming to give you away, heh?

ANN. *[Giving her drink.]* I don't know. I suppose.

SUE. You must be all nerved up.

ANN. It's always a problem getting yourself married, isn't it?

SUE. That depends on your shape, of course. I don't see why you should have had a problem.

ANN. I've had chances—

SUE. I'll bet. It's romantic . . . it's very unusual to me, marrying the brother of your sweetheart.

ANN. I don't know. I think it's mostly that whenever I need somebody to tell me the truth I've always thought of Chris. When he tells you something you know it's so. He relaxes me.

SUE. And he's got money. That's important, you know.

ANN. It wouldn't matter to me.

SUE. You'd be surprised. It makes all the difference. I married an intern. On my salary. And that was bad, because as soon as a woman supports a man he owes her something. You can never owe somebody without resenting them. *[Ann laughs.]* That's true, you know.

ANN. Underneath, I think the doctor is very devoted.

SUE. Oh, certainly. But it's bad when a man always sees the bars in front of him. Jim thinks he's in jail all the time.

ANN. Oh . . .

SUE. That's why I've been intending to ask you a small favor, Ann. It's something very important to me.

ANN. Certainly, if I can do it.

SUE. You can. When you take up housekeeping, try to find a place away from here.

ANN. Are you fooling?

SUE. I'm very serious. My husband is unhappy with Chris around.

ANN. How is that?

SUE. Jim's a successful doctor. But he's got an idea he'd like to do medical research. Discover things. You see?

ANN. Well, isn't that good?

SUE. Research pays twenty-five dollars a week minus laundering the hair shirt. You've got to give up your life to go into it.

ANN. How does Chris—

SUE. *[With growing feeling.]* Chris makes people want to be better than it's possible to be. He does that to people.

ANN. Is that bad?

SUE. My husband has a family, dear. Every time he has a session with Chris he feels as though he's compromising by not giving up everything for research. As though Chris or anybody else isn't compromising. It happens with Jim every couple of years. He meets a man and makes a statue out of him.

ANN. Maybe he's right. I don't mean that Chris is a statue, but—

SUE. Now darling, you know he's not right.

ANN. I don't agree with you. Chris—

SUE. Let's face it, dear. Chris is working with his father, isn't he? He's taking money out of that business every week in the year.

ANN. What of it?

SUE. You asked me what of it.

ANN. I certainly do. *[She seems about to burst out.]* You oughtn't cast aspersions like that, I'm surprised at you.

SUE. You're surprised at me!

ANN. He'd never take five cents out of that plant if there was anything wrong with it.

SUE. You know that.

ANN. I know it. I resent everything you've said.

SUE. *[Moving toward her.]* You know what I resent, dear?

ANN. Please, I don't want to argue.

SUE. I resent living next door to the Holy Family. It makes me look like a bum, you understand?

ANN. I can't do anything about that.

SUE. Who is he to ruin a man's life? Everybody knows Joe pulled a fast one to get out of jail.

ANN. That's not true!

SUE. Then why don't you go out and talk to people? Go on, talk to them. There's not a person on the block who doesn't know the truth.

ANN. That's a lie. People come here all the time for cards and—

SUE. So what? They give him credit for being smart. I do, too. I've got nothing against Joe. But if Chris wants people to put on the hair shirt let him take off his broadcloth. He's driving my husband crazy with that phony idealism of his, and I'm at the end of my rope on it! *[Chris enters on porch, wearing shirt and tie now. She turns quickly, hearing. With a smile.]* Hello, darling. How's Mother?

CHRIS. I thought George came.

SUE. No, it was just us.

CHRIS. *[Coming down to them.]* Susie, do me a favor, heh? Go up to Mother and see if you can calm her. She's all worked up.

SUE. She still doesn't know about you two?

CHRIS. *[Laughs a little.]* Well, she senses it, I guess. You know my mother.

SUE. *[Going up to porch.]* Oh, yeah, she's psychic.

CHRIS. Maybe there's something in the medicine chest.

SUE. I'll give her one of everything. *[On porch.]* Don't worry about Kate; couple of drinks, dance her around a little . . . She'll love Ann. *[To Ann.]* Because you're the female version of him. *[Chris laughs.]* Don't be alarmed, I said version. *[She goes into house.]*

CHRIS. Interesting woman, isn't she?

ANN. Yeah, she's very interesting.

CHRIS. She's a great nurse, you know, she——

ANN. *[In tension, but trying to control it.]* Are you still doing that?

CHRIS. *[Sensing something wrong, but still smiling.]* Doing what?

ANN. As soon as you get to know somebody you find a distinction for them. How do you know she's a great nurse?

CHRIS. What's the matter, Ann?

ANN. The woman hates you. She despises you!

CHRIS. Hey . . . What's hit you?

ANN. Gee, Chris——

CHRIS. What happened here?

ANN. You never—— Why didn't you tell me?

CHRIS. Tell you what?

ANN. She says they think Joe is guilty.

CHRIS. What difference does it make what they think?

ANN. I don't care what they think, I just don't understand why you took the trouble to deny it. You said it was all forgotten.

CHRIS. I didn't want you to feel there was anything wrong in you coming here, that's all. I know a lot of people think my father was guilty, and I assumed there might be some question in your mind.

ANN. But I never once said I suspected him.

CHRIS. Nobody says it.

ANN. Chris, I know how much you love him, but it could never——

CHRIS. Do you think I could forgive him if he'd done that thing?

ANN. I'm not here out of a blue sky, Chris. I turned my back on my father, if there's anything wrong here now——

CHRIS. I know that, Ann.

ANN. George is coming from Dad, and I don't think it's with a blessing.

CHRIS. He's welcome here. You've got nothing to fear from George.

ANN. Tell me that . . . Just tell me that.

CHRIS. The man is innocent, Ann. Remember he was falsely accused once and it put him through hell. How would you behave if you were faced with the same thing again? Annie, believe me, there's nothing wrong for you here, believe me, kid.

ANN. All right, Chris, all right. *[They embrace as Keller appears quietly on porch. Ann simply studies him.]*

KELLER. Every time I come out here it looks like Playland! *[They break and laugh in embarrassment.]*

CHRIS. I thought you were going to shave?

KELLER. *[Sitting on bench.]* In a minute. I just woke up, I can't see nothin'.

ANN. You look shaved.

KELLER. Oh, no. *[Massages his jaw.]* Gotta be extra special tonight. Big night, Annie. So how's it feel to be a married woman?

ANN. *[Laughs.]* I don't know, yet.

KELLER. *[To Chris.]* What's the matter, you slippin'? *[He takes a little box of apples from under the bench as they talk.]*

CHRIS. The great roué!

KELLER. What is that, roué?

CHRIS. It's French.

KELLER. Don't talk dirty. *[They laugh.]*

CHRIS. *[To Ann.]* You ever meet a bigger ignoramus?

KELLER. Well, somebody's got to make a living.

ANN. *[As they laugh.]* That's telling him.

KELLER. I don't know, everybody's gettin' so Goddam educated in this country there'll be nobody to take away the garbage. *[They laugh.]* It's gettin' so the only dumb ones left are the bosses.

ANN. You're not so dumb, Joe.

KELLER. I know, but you go into our plant, for instance. I got so many lieutenants, majors and colonels that I'm ashamed to ask somebody to sweep the floor. I gotta be careful I'll insult somebody. No kiddin.' It's a tragedy: you stand on the street today and spit, you're gonna hit a college man.

CHRIS. Well, don't spit.

KELLER. *[Breaks apple in half, passing it to Ann and Chris.]* I mean to say, it's comin' to a pass. *[He takes a breath.]* I been thinkin', Annie . . . your brother, George. I been thinkin' about your brother George. When he comes I like you to *brooch* something to him.

CHRIS. Broach.

KELLER. What's the matter with brooch?

CHRIS. *[smiling]* It's not English.

KELLER. When I went to night school it was brooch.

ANN. *[Laughing.]* Well, in day school it's broach.

KELLER. Don't surround me, will you? Seriously, Ann . . . You say he's not well. George, I been thinkin', why should he knock himself out in New York with that cut-throat competition, when I got so many friends here; I'm very friendly with some big lawyers in town. I could set George up here.

ANN. That's awfully nice of you, Joe.

KELLER. No, kid, it ain't nice of me. I want you to understand me. I'm thinking of Chris. *[Slight pause.]* See . . . this is what I mean. You get older, you want to feel that you—accomplished something. My only accomplishment is my son. I ain't brainy. That's all I accomplished. Now, a year, eighteen months, your father'll be a free man. Who is he going to come to, Annie? His baby. You. He'll come, old, mad, into your house.

ANN. That can't matter any more, Joe.

KELLER. I don't want that to come between us. *[Gestures between Chris and himself.]*

ANN. I can only tell you that that could never happen.

KELLER. You're in love now, Annie, but believe me, I'm older than you and I know—a daughter is a daughter, and a father is a father. And it could happen. *[He pauses.]* I like you and George to go to him in prison and tell him . . . "Dad, Joe wants to bring you into the business when you get out."

ANN. *[Surprised, even shocked.]* You'd have him as a partner?

KELLER. No, no partner. A good job. *[Pause. He sees she is shocked, a little mystified. He gets up, speaks more nervously.]* I want him to know, Annie . . . while he's sitting there I want him to know that when he gets out he's got a place waitin' for him. It'll take his bitterness away. To know you got a place . . . it sweetens you.

ANN. Joe, you owe him nothing.

KELLER. I owe him a good kick in the teeth, but he's your father.

CHRIS. Then kick him in the teeth! I don't want him in the plant, so that's that! You understand? And besides, don't talk about him like that. People misunderstand you!

KELLER. And I don't understand why she has to crucify the man.

CHRIS. Well, it's her father, if she feels—

KELLER. No, no.

CHRIS. *[Almost angrily.]* What's it to you? Why—?

KELLER. *[A commanding outburst in high nervousness.]* A father is a father! *[As though the outburst had revealed him, he looks about, wanting to retract it. His hand goes to his cheek.]* I better—I better shave. *[He turns and a smile is on his face. To Ann.]* I didn't mean to yell at you, Annie.

ANN. Let's forget the whole thing, Joe.

KELLER. Right. *[To Chris.]* She's likeable.

CHRIS. *[A little peeved at the man's stupidity.]* Shave, will you?

KELLER. Right again.

[As he turns to porch Lydia comes hurrying from her house.]

LYDIA. I forgot all about it. *[Seeing Chris and Ann.]* Hya. *[To Joe.]* I promised to fix Kate's hair for tonight. Did she comb it yet?

KELLER. Always a smile, hey, Lydia?

LYDIA. Sure, why not?

KELLER. *[Going up on porch.]* Come on up and comb my Katie's hair. *[Lydia goes up on porch.]* She's got a big night, make her beautiful.

LYDIA. I will.

KELLER. *[Holds door open for her and she goes into kitchen. To Chris and Ann.]* Hey, that could be a song.
      [He sings softly.]
   "Come on up and comb my Katie's hair . . .
      Oh, come on up, 'cause she's my lady fair—"
[To Ann.] How's that for one year of night school?
      [He continues singing as he goes into kitchen.]
   "Oh, come on up, come on up, and comb my lady's hair—"

[Jim Bayliss rounds corner of driveway, walking rapidly. Jim crosses to Chris, motions him and pulls him down excitedly. Keller stands just inside kitchen door, watching them.]

CHRIS. What's the matter? Where is he?

JIM. Where's your mother?

CHRIS. Upstairs, dressing.

ANN. *[Crossing to them rapidly.]* What happened to George?

JIM. I asked him to wait in the car. Listen to me now. Can you take some advice? *[They wait.]* Don't bring him in here.

ANN. Why?

JIM. Kate is in bad shape, you can't explode this in front of her.

ANN. Explode what?

JIM. You know why he's here, don't try to kid it away. There's blood in his eye; drive him somewhere and talk to him alone.

[Ann turns to go up drive, takes a couple of steps, sees Keller, and stops. He goes quietly on into house.]

CHRIS. *[Shaken, and therefore angered.]* Don't be an old lady.

JIM. He's come to take her home. What does that mean? *[To Ann.]* You know what that means. Fight it out with him some place else.

ANN. *[Comes back down toward Chris.]* I'll drive . . . him somewhere.

CHRIS. *[Goes to her.]* No.

JIM. Will you stop being an idiot?

CHRIS. Nobody's afraid of him here. Cut that out!

[He starts for driveway, but is brought up short by George, who enters there. George is Chris's age, but a paler man, now on the edge of his self-restraint. He speaks quietly, as though afraid to find himself screaming. An instant's hesitation and Chris steps up to him, hand extended, smiling.]

CHRIS. Helluva way to do; what're you sitting out there for?

GEORGE. Doctor said your mother isn't well, I—

CHRIS. So what? She'd want to see you, wouldn't she? We've been waiting for you all afternoon. *[He puts his hand on George's arm, but George pulls away, coming across toward Ann.]*

ANN. *[Touching his collar.]* This is filthy, didn't you bring another shirt?

[George breaks away from her, and moves down, examining the yard. Door opens, and he turns rapidly, thinking it is Kate, but it's Sue. She looks at him; he turns away and moves to fence. He looks over it at his former home. Sue comes downstage.]

SUE. *[Annoyed.]* How about the beach, Jim?

JIM. Oh, it's too hot to drive.

SUE. How'd you get to the station—Zeppelin?

CHRIS. This is Mrs. Bayliss, George. *[Calling, as George pays no attention, staring at house.]* George! *[George turns.]* Mrs. Bayliss.

SUE. How do you do.

GEORGE. *[Removing his hat.]* You're the people who bought our house, aren't you?

SUE. That's right. Come and see what we did with it before you leave.

GEORGE. *[Walks down and away from her.]* I liked it the way it was.

SUE. *[After a brief pause.]* He's frank, isn't he?

JIM. *[Pulling her off.]* See you later. . . . Take it easy, fella. *[They exit.]*

CHRIS. *[Calling after them.]* Thanks for driving him! *[Turning to George.]* How about some grape juice? Mother made it especially for you.

GEORGE. *[With forced appreciation.]* Good old Kate, remembered my grape juice.

CHRIS. You drank enough of it in this house. How've you been, George?—Sit down.

GEORGE. *[Keeps moving.]* It takes me a minute. *[Looking around.]* It seems impossible.

CHRIS. What?

GEORGE. I'm back here.

CHRIS. Say, you've gotten a little nervous, haven't you?

GEORGE. Yeah, toward the end of the day. What're you, big executive now?

CHRIS. Just kind of medium. How's the law?

GEORGE. I don't know. When I was studying in the hospital it seemed sensible, but outside there doesn't seem to be much of a law. The trees got thick, didn't they? *[Points to stump.]* What's that?

CHRIS. Blew down last night. We had it there for Larry. You know.

GEORGE. Why, afraid you'll forget him?

CHRIS. *[Starts for George.]* Kind of a remark is that?

ANN. *[Breaking in, putting a restraining hand on Chris.]* When did you start wearing a hat?

GEORGE. *[Discovers hat in his hand.]* Today. From now on I decided to look like a lawyer, anyway. *[He holds it up to her.]* Don't you recognize it?

ANN. Why? Where—?

GEORGE. Your father's— He asked me to wear it.

ANN. How is he?

GEORGE. He got smaller.

ANN. Smaller?

GEORGE. Yeah, little. *[Holds out his hand to measure.]* He's a little man. That's what happens to suckers, you know. It's good I went to him in time—another year there'd be nothing left but his smell.

CHRIS. What's the matter, George, what's the trouble?

GEORGE. The trouble? The trouble is when you make suckers out of people once, you shouldn't try to do it twice.

CHRIS. What does that mean?

GEORGE. *[To Ann.]* You're not married yet, are you?

ANN. George, will you sit down and stop—?

GEORGE. Are you married yet?

ANN. No, I'm not married yet.

GEORGE. You're not going to marry him.

ANN. Why am I not going to marry him?

GEORGE. Because his father destroyed your family.

CHRIS. Now look, George . . .

GEORGE. Cut it short, Chris. Tell her to come home with me. Let's not argue, you know what I've got to say.

CHRIS. George, you don't want to be the voice of God, do you?

GEORGE. I'm—

CHRIS. That's been your trouble all your life, George, you dive into things. What kind of a statement is that to make? You're a big boy now.

GEORGE. I'm a big boy now.

CHRIS. Don't come bulling in here. If you've got something to say, be civilized about it.

GEORGE. Don't civilize me!

ANN. Shhh!

CHRIS. *[Ready to hit him.]* Are you going to talk like a grown man or aren't you?

ANN. *[Quickly, to forestall an outburst.]* Sit down, dear. Don't be angry, what's the matter? *[He allows her to seat him, looking at her.]* Now what happened? You kissed me when I left, now you—

GEORGE. *[Breathlessly.]* My life turned upside down since then. I couldn't go back to work when you left. I wanted to go to Dad and tell him you were going to be married. It seemed impossible not to tell him. He loved you so much. *[He pauses.]* Annie—we did a terrible thing. We can never be forgiven. Not even to send him a card at Christmas. I didn't see him once since I got home from the war! Annie, you don't know what was done to that man. You don't know what happened.

ANN. *[Afraid.]* Of course I know.

GEORGE. You can't know, you wouldn't be here. Dad came to work that day. The night foreman came to him and showed him the cylinder heads . . . they were coming out of the process with defects. There was something wrong with the process. So Dad went directly to the phone and called here and told Joe to come down right away. But the morning passed. No sign of Joe. So Dad called again. By this time he had over a hundred defectives. The Army was screaming for stuff and Dad didn't have anything to ship. So Joe told him . . . on the phone he told him to weld, cover up the cracks in any way he could, and ship them out.

CHRIS. Are you through now?

GEORGE. *[Surging up at him.]* I'm not through now! *[Back to Ann.]* Dad was afraid. He wanted Joe there if he was going to do it. But Joe can't come down . . . He's sick. Sick! He suddenly gets the flu! Suddenly! But he promised to take responsibility. Do you understand what I'm saying? On the telephone you can't have responsibility! In a court you can always deny a phone call and that's exactly what he did. They knew he was a liar the first time, but in the appeal they believed that rotten lie and now Joe is a big shot and your father is the patsy. *[He gets up.]* Now what're you going to do? Eat his food, sleep in his bed? Answer me; what're you going to do?

CHRIS. What're you going to do, George?

GEORGE. He's too smart for me, I can't prove a phone call.

CHRIS. Then how dare you come in here with that rot?

ANN. George, the court—

GEORGE. The court didn't know your father! But you know him. You know in your heart Joe did it.

CHRIS. *[Whirling him around.]* Lower your voice or I'll throw you out of here!

GEORGE. She knows. She knows.

CHRIS. *[To Ann.]* Get him out of here, Ann. Get him out of here.

ANN. George, I know everything you've said. Dad told that whole thing in court, and they—

GEORGE. *[Almost a scream.]* The court did not know him, Annie!

ANN. Shhh!—But he'll say anything, George. You know how quick he can lie.

GEORGE. *[Turning to Chris, with deliberation.]* I'll ask you something, and look me in the eye when you answer me.

CHRIS. I'll look you in the eye.

GEORGE. You know your father—

CHRIS. I know him well.

GEORGE. And he's the kind of boss to let a hundred and twenty-one cylinder heads be repaired and shipped out of his shop without even knowing about it?

CHRIS. He's that kind of boss.

GEORGE. And that's the same Joe Keller who never left his shop without first going around to see that all the lights were out.

CHRIS *[With growing anger.]* The same Joe Keller.

GEORGE. The same man who knows how many minutes a day his workers spend in the toilet.

CHRIS. The same man.

GEORGE. And my father, that frightened mouse who'd never buy a shirt without somebody along—that man would dare do such a thing on his own?

CHRIS. On his own. And because he's a frightened mouse this is another thing he'd do—throw the blame on somebody else because he's not man enough to take it himself. He tried it in court but it didn't work, but with a fool like you it works!

GEORGE. Oh, Chris, you're a liar to yourself!

ANN. *[Deeply shaken.]* Don't talk like that!

CHRIS. *[Sits facing George.]* Tell me, George. What happened? The court record was good enough for you all these years, why isn't it good now? Why did you believe it all these years?

GEORGE. *[After a slight pause.]* Because you believed it. . . . That's the truth, Chris. I believed everything, because I thought you did. But today I heard it from his mouth. From his mouth it's altogether different than the record. Anyone who knows him, and knows your father, will believe it from his mouth. Your Dad took everything we have. I can't beat that. But she's one item he's not going to grab. *[He turns to Ann.]* Get your things. Everything they have is covered with blood. You're not the kind of a girl who can live with that. Get your things.

CHRIS. Ann . . . you're not going to believe that, are you?

ANN. *[Goes to him.]* You know it's not true, don't you?

GEORGE. How can he tell you? It's his father. *[To Chris.]* None of these things ever even cross your mind?

CHRIS. Yes, they crossed my mind. Anything can cross your mind!

GEORGE. *He knows,* Annie. He knows!

CHRIS. The voice of God!

GEORGE. Then why isn't your name on the business? Explain that to her!

CHRIS. What the hell has that got to do with—?

GEORGE. Annie, why isn't his name on it?

CHRIS. Even when I don't own it!

GEORGE. Who're you kidding? Who gets it when he dies? *[To Ann.]* Open your eyes, you know the both of them, isn't that the first thing they'd do, the way they love each other?—J. O. Keller and Son? *[Pause. Ann looks from him to Chris.]* I'll settle it. Do you want to settle it, or are you afraid to?

CHRIS. What do you mean?

GEORGE. Let me go up and talk to your father. In ten minutes you'll have the answer. Or are you afraid of the answer?

CHRIS. I'm not afraid of the answer. I know the answer. But my mother isn't well and I don't want a fight here now.

GEORGE. Let me go to him.

CHRIS. You're not going to start a fight here now.

GEORGE. *[to Ann.]* What more do you want! *[There is a sound of footsteps in the house.]*

ANN. *[Turns her head suddenly toward house.]* Someone's coming.

CHRIS. *[To George, quietly.]* You won't say anything now.

ANN. You'll go soon. I'll call a cab.

GEORGE. You're coming with me.

ANN. And don't mention marriage, because we haven't told her yet.

GEORGE. You're coming with me.

ANN. You understand? Don't— George, you're not going to start anything now! *[She hears footsteps.]* Shsh!

[Mother enters on porch. She is dressed almost formally; her hair is fixed. They are all turned toward her. On seeing George she raises both hands, comes down toward him.]

MOTHER. Georgie, Georgie.

GEORGE. *[He has always liked her.]* Hello, Kate.

MOTHER. *[Cups his face in her hands.]* They made an old man out of you. *[Touches his hair.]* Look, you're gray.

GEORGE. *[Her pity, open and unabashed, reaches into him, and he smiles sadly.]* I know, I—

MOTHER. I told you when you went away, don't try for medals.

GEORGE. *[Laughs, tiredly.]* I didn't try, Kate. They made it very easy for me.

MOTHER. *[Actually angry.]* Go on. You're all alike. *[To Ann.]* Look at him, why did you say he's fine? He looks like a ghost.

GEORGE. *[Relishing her solicitude.]* I feel all right.

MOTHER. I'm sick to look at you. What's the matter with your mother, why don't she feed you?

ANN. He just hasn't any appetite.

MOTHER. If he ate in my house he'd have an appetite. *[To Ann.]* I pity your husband! *[To George.]* Sit down. I'll make you a sandwich.

GEORGE. *[Sits with an embarrassed laugh.]* I'm really not hungry.

MOTHER. Honest to God, it breaks my heart to see what happened to all the children. How we worked and planned for you, and you end up no better than us.

GEORGE. *[With deep feeling for her.]* You . . . you haven't changed at all, you know that, Kate?

MOTHER. None of us changed, Georgie. We all love you. Joe was just talking about the day you were born and the water got shut off. People were carrying basins from a block away—a stranger would have thought the whole neighborhood was on fire! *[They laugh. She sees the juice. To Ann.]* Why didn't you give him some juice!

ANN. *[Defensively.]* I offered it to him.

MOTHER. *[Scoffingly.]* You offered it to him! *[Thrusting glass into George's hand.]* Give it to him! *[To George, who is laughing.]* And now you're going to sit here and drink some juice . . . and look like something!

GEORGE. *[Sitting.]* Kate, I feel hungry already.

CHRIS. *[Proudly.]* She could turn Mahatma Ghandi into a heavy-weight!

MOTHER. *[To Chris, with great energy.]* Listen, to hell with the restaurant! I got a ham in the icebox, and frozen strawberries, and avocados, and—

ANN. Swell, I'll help you!

GEORGE. The train leaves at eight-thirty, Ann.

MOTHER. *[To Ann.]* You're leaving?

CHRIS. No, Mother, she's not—

ANN. *[Breaking through it, going to George.]* You hardly got here; give yourself a chance to get acquainted again.

CHRIS. Sure, you don't even know us any more.

MOTHER. Well, Chris, if they can't stay, don't—

CHRIS. No, it's just a question of George, Mother, he planned on—

GEORGE. *[Gets up politely, nicely, for Kate's sake.]* Now wait a minute, Chris . . .

CHRIS. *[Smiling and full of command, cutting him off.]* If you want to go, I'll drive you to the station now, but if you're staying, no arguments while you're here.

MOTHER. *[At last confessing the tension.]* Why should he argue? *[She goes to him. With desperation and compassion, stroking his hair.]* Georgie and us have no argument. How could we have an argument, Georgie? We all got hit by the same lightning, how can you—? Did you see what happened to Larry's tree, Georgie? *[She has taken his arm, and unwillingly he moves across stage with her.]* Imagine? While I was dreaming of him in the middle of the night, the wind came along and—

[Lydia enters on porch. As soon as she sees him.]

LYDIA. Hey, Georgie! Georgie! Georgie! Georgie! Georgie! *[She comes down to him eagerly. She has a flowered hat in her hand, which Kate takes from her as she goes to George.]*

GEORGE. *[As they shake hands eagerly, warmly.]* Hello, Laughy. What'd you do, grow?

LYDIA. I'm a big girl now.

MOTHER. Look what she can do to a hat!

ANN. *[To Lydia, admiring the hat.]* Did you make that?

MOTHER. In ten minutes! *[She puts it on.]*

LYDIA. *[Fixing it on her head.]* I only rearranged it.

GEORGE. You still make your own clothes?

CHRIS. *[To Mother.]* Ain't she classy! All she needs now is a Russian wolfhound.

MOTHER. *[Moving her head.]* It feels like somebody is sitting on my head.

ANN. No, it's beautiful, Kate.

MOTHER. *[Kisses Lydia. To George.]* She's a genius! You should've married her. *[They laugh.]* This one can feed you!

LYDIA. *[Strangely embarrassed.]* Oh, stop that, Kate.

GEORGE. *[To Lydia.]* Didn't I hear you had a baby?

MOTHER. You don't hear so good. She's got three babies.

GEORGE. *[A little hurt by it—to Lydia.]* No kidding, three?

LYDIA. Yeah, it was one, two, three— You've been away a long time, Georgie.

GEORGE. I'm beginning to realize.

MOTHER. *[To Chris and George.]* The trouble with you kids is you *think* too much.

LYDIA. Well, we think, too.

MOTHER. Yes, but not all the time.

GEORGE. *[With almost obvious envy.]* They never took Frank, heh?

LYDIA. *[A little apologetically.]* No, he was always one year ahead of the draft.

MOTHER. It's amazing. When they were calling boys twenty-seven Frank was just twenty-eight, when they made it twenty-eight he was just twenty-nine. That's why he took up astrology. It's all in when you were born, it just goes to show.

CHRIS. What does it go to show?

MOTHER. *[To Chris.]* Don't be so intelligent. Some superstitions are very nice! *[To Lydia.]* Did he finish Larry's horoscope?

LYDIA. I'll ask him now, I'm going in. *[To George, a little sadly, almost embarrassed.]* Would you like to see my babies? Come on.

GEORGE. I don't think so, Lydia.

LYDIA. *[Understanding.]* All right. Good luck to you, George.

GEORGE. Thanks. And to you . . . And Frank. *[She smiles at him, turns and goes off to her house. George stands staring after her.]*

LYDIA. *[As she runs off.]* Oh, Frank!

MOTHER. *[Reading his thoughts.]* She got pretty, heh?

GEORGE. *[Sadly.]* Very pretty.

MOTHER. *[As a reprimand.]* She's beautiful, you damned fool!

GEORGE. *[Looks around longingly; and softly, with a catch in his throat.]* She makes it seem so nice around here.

MOTHER. *[Shaking her finger at him.]* Look what happened to you because you wouldn't listen to me! I told you to marry that girl and stay out of the war!

GEORGE. *[Laughs at himself.]* She used to laugh too much.

MOTHER. And you didn't laugh enough. While you were getting mad about Fascism Frank was getting into her bed.

GEORGE *[To Chris.]* He won the war, Frank.

CHRIS. All the battles.

MOTHER. *[In pursuit of this mood.]* The day they started the draft, Georgie, I told you you loved that girl.

CHRIS. *[Laughs.]* And truer love hath no man!

MOTHER. I'm smarter than any of you.

GEORGE. *[Laughing.]* She's wonderful!

MOTHER. And now you're going to listen to me, George. You had big principles, Eagle Scouts the three of you; so now I got a tree, and this one *[Indicating Chris.]* when the weather gets bad he can't stand on his feet; and that big dope *[Pointing to Lydia's house.]* next door who never reads anything but Andy Gump[2] has three children and his house is paid off. Stop being a philosopher, and look after yourself. Like Joe was just saying—you move back here, he'll help you get set, and I'll find you a girl and put a smile on your face.

GEORGE. Joe? Joe wants me here?

ANN. *[Eagerly.]* He asked me to tell you, and I think it's a good idea.

MOTHER. Certainly. Why must you make believe you hate us? Is that another principle?—that you have to hate us? You don't hate us, George, I know you, you can't fool me, I diapered you. *[Suddenly, to Ann.]* You remember Mr. Marcy's daughter?

2 *Andy Gump:* Andy Gump was a chinless character in a comic strip.

ANN. *[Laughing, to George.]* She's got you hooked already! *[George laughs, is excited.]*

MOTHER. You look her over, George; you'll see she's the most beautiful—

CHRIS. She's got warts, George.

MOTHER. *[To Chris.]* She hasn't got warts! *[To George.]* So the girl has a little beauty mark on her chin—

CHRIS. And two on her nose.

MOTHER. You remember. Her father's the retired police inspector.

CHRIS. Sergeant, George.

MOTHER. He's a very kind man!

CHRIS. He looks like a gorilla.

MOTHER. *[To George.]* He never shot anybody.

[They all burst out laughing, as Keller appears in doorway. George rises abruptly and stares at Keller, who comes rapidly down to him.]

KELLER. *[The laughter stops. With strained joviality.]* Well! Look who's here! *[Extending his hand.]* Georgie, good to see ya.

GEORGE. *[Shaking hands—somberly.]* How're you, Joe?

KELLER. So-so. Gettin' old. You comin' out to dinner with us?

GEORGE. No, got to be back in New York.

ANN. I'll call a cab for you. *[She goes up into the house.]*

KELLER. Too bad you can't stay, George. Sit down. *[To Mother.]* He looks fine.

MOTHER. He looks terrible.

KELLER. That's what I said, you look terrible, George. *[They laugh.]* I wear the pants and she beats me with the belt.

GEORGE. I saw your factory on the way from the station. It looks like General Motors.

KELLER. I wish it was General Motors, but it ain't. Sit down, George. Sit down. *[Takes a cigar out of his pocket.]* So you finally went to see your father, I hear?

GEORGE. Yes, this morning. What kind of stuff do you make now?

KELLER. Oh, little of everything. Pressure cookers, an assembly for washing machines. Got a nice, flexible plant now. So how'd you find Dad? Feel all right?

GEORGE. *[Searching Keller, speaking indecisively.]* No, he's not well, Joe.

KELLER. *[Lighting his cigar.]* Not his heart again, is it?

GEORGE. It's everything, Joe. It's his soul.

KELLER. *[Blowing out smoke.]* Uh huh—

CHRIS. How about seeing what they did with your house?

KELLER. Leave him be.

GEORGE. *[To Chris, indicating Keller.]* I'd like to talk to him.

KELLER. Sure, he just got here. That's the way they do, George. A little man makes a mistake and they hang him by the thumbs; the big ones become ambassadors. I wish you'd-a told me you were going to see Dad.

GEORGE. *[Studying him.]* I didn't know you were interested.

KELLER. In a way, I am. I would like him to know, George, that as far as I'm concerned, any time he wants, he's got a place with me. I would like him to know that.

GEORGE. He hates your guts, Joe. Don't you know that?

KELLER. I imagined it. But that can change, too.

MOTHER. Steve was never like that.

GEORGE. He's like that now. He'd like to take every man who made money in the war and put him up against a wall.

CHRIS. He'll need a lot of bullets.

GEORGE. And he'd better not get any.

KELLER. That's a sad thing to hear.

GEORGE. *[With bitterness dominant.]* Why? What'd you expect him to think of you?

KELLER. *[The force of his nature rising, but under control.]* I'm sad to see he hasn't changed. As long as I know him, twenty-five years, the man never learned how to take the blame. You know that, George.

GEORGE. *[He does.]* Well, I—

KELLER. But you do know it. Because the way you come in here you don't look like you remember it. I mean like in nineteen thirty-seven when we had the shop on Flood Street. And he damn near blew us all up with that heater he left burning for two days without water. He wouldn't admit that was his fault, either. I had to fire a mechanic to save his face. You remember that.

GEORGE. Yes, but—

KELLER. I'm just mentioning it, George. Because this is just another one of a lot of things. Like when he gave Frank that money to invest in oil stock.

GEORGE. *[Distressed.]* I know that, I—

KELLER. *[Driving in, but restrained.]* But it's good to remember those things, kid. The way he cursed Frank because the stock went down. Was that Frank's fault? To listen to him Frank was a swindler. And all the man did was give him a bad tip.

GEORGE. *[Gets up, moves away.]* I know those things . . .

KELLER. Then remember them, remember them. *[Ann comes out of house.]* There are certain men in the world who rather see everybody hung before they'll take blame. You understand me, George?

[They stand facing each other, George trying to judge him.]

ANN. *[Coming downstage.]* The cab's on its way. Would you like to wash?

MOTHER. *[With the thrust of hope.]* Why must he go? Make the midnight, George.

KELLER. Sure, you'll have dinner with us!

ANN. How about it? Why not? We're eating at the lake, we could have a swell time.

[A long pause, as George looks at Ann, Chris, Keller, then back to her.]

GEORGE. All right.

MOTHER. Now you're talking.

CHRIS. I've got a shirt that'll go right with that suit.

MOTHER. Size fifteen and a half, right, George?

GEORGE. Is Lydia—? I mean—Frank and Lydia coming?

MOTHER. I'll get you a date that'll make her look like a— *[She starts upstage.]*

GEORGE. *[Laughing.]* No, I don't want a date.

CHRIS. I know somebody just for you! Charlotte Tanner! *[He starts for the house.]*

KELLER. Call Charlotte, that's right.

MOTHER. Sure, call her up. *[Chris goes into house.]*

ANN. You go up and pick out a shirt and tie.

GEORGE. *[Stops, looks around at them and the place.]* I never felt at home anywhere but here. I feel so—*[He nearly laughs, and turns away from them.]* Kate, you look so young, you know? You didn't change at all. It . . . rings an old bell. *[Turns to Keller.]* You too, Joe, you're amazingly the same. The whole atmosphere is.

KELLER. Say, I ain't got time to get sick.

MOTHER. He hasn't been laid up in fifteen years.

KELLER. Except my flu during the war.

MOTHER. Huhh?

KELLER. My flu, when I was sick during . . . the war.

MOTHER. Well, sure . . . *[To George.]* I mean except for that flu. *[George stands perfectly still.]* Well, it slipped my mind, don't look at me that way. He wanted to go to the shop but he couldn't lift himself off the bed. I thought he had pneumonia.

GEORGE. Why did you say he's never—?

KELLER. I know how you feel, kid, I'll never forgive myself. If I could've gone in that day I'd never allow Dad to touch those heads.

GEORGE. She said you've never been sick.

MOTHER. I said he was sick, George.

GEORGE. *[Going to Ann.]* Ann, didn't you hear her say—?

MOTHER. Do you remember every time you were sick?

GEORGE. I'd remember pneumonia. Especially if I got it just the day my partner was going to patch up cylinder heads . . . What happened that day, Joe?

[Frank enters briskly from driveway, holding Larry's horoscope in his hand. He comes to Kate.]

FRANK. Kate! Kate!

MOTHER. Frank, did you see George?

FRANK. *[Extending his hand.]* Lydia told me, I'm glad to . . . you'll have to pardon me. *[Pulling Mother over.]* I've got something amazing for you, Kate, I finished Larry's horoscope.

MOTHER. You'd be interested in this, George. It's wonderful the way he can understand the—

CHRIS. *[Entering from house.]* George, the girl's on the phone—

MOTHER. *[Desperately.]* He finished Larry's horoscope!

CHRIS. Frank, can't you pick a better time than this?

FRANK. The greatest men who ever lived believed in the stars!

CHRIS. Stop filling her head with that junk!

FRANK. Is it junk to feel that there's a greater power than ourselves? I've studied the stars of his life! I won't argue with you, I'm telling you. Somewhere in this world your brother is alive!

MOTHER. *[Instantly to Chris.]* Why isn't it possible?

CHRIS. Because it's insane.

FRANK. Just a minute now. I'll tell you something and you can do as you please. Just let me say it. He was supposed to have died on November twenty-fifth. But November twenty-fifth was his favorable day.

CHRIS. Mother!

MOTHER. Listen to him!

FRANK. It was a day when everything good was shining on him, the kind of day he should've married on. You can laugh at a lot of it, I can understand you laughing. But the odds are a million to one that a man won't die on his favorable day. That's known, that's known, Chris!

MOTHER. Why isn't it possible, why isn't it possible, Chris!

GEORGE. *[To Ann.]* Don't you understand what she's saying? She just told you to go. What are you waiting for now?

CHRIS. Nobody can tell her to go. *[A car horn is heard.]*

MOTHER. *[To Frank.]* Thank you, darling, for your trouble. Will you tell him to wait, Frank?

FRANK. *[As he goes.]* Sure thing.

MOTHER. *[Calling out.]* They'll be right out, driver!

CHRIS. She's not leaving, Mother.

GEORGE. You heard her say it, he's never been sick!

MOTHER. He misunderstood me, Chris! *[Chris looks at her, struck.]*

GEORGE. *[To Ann.]* He simply told your father to kill pilots, and covered himself in bed!

CHRIS. You'd better answer him, Annie. Answer him.

MOTHER. I packed your bag, darling.

CHRIS. What?

MOTHER. I packed your bag. All you've got to do is close it.

ANN. I'm not closing anything. He asked me here and I'm staying till he tells me to go. *[To George]* Till Chris tells me!

CHRIS. That's all! Now get out of here, George!

MOTHER. *[To Chris.]* But if that's how he feels—

CHRIS. That's all, nothing more till Christ comes, about the case or Larry as long as I'm here! *[To George.]* Now get out of here, George!

GEORGE. *[To Ann.]* You tell me. I want to hear you tell me.

ANN. Go, George!

[They disappear up the driveway, Ann saying, "Don't take it that way, Georgie! Please don't take it that way."]

CHRIS. *[Turning to his mother.]* What do you mean, you packed her bag? How dare you pack her bag?

MOTHER. Chris—

CHRIS. How dare you pack her bag?

MOTHER. She doesn't belong here.

CHRIS. Then I don't belong here.

MOTHER. She's Larry's girl.

CHRIS. And I'm his brother and he's dead, and I'm marrying his girl.

MOTHER. Never, never in this world!

KELLER. You lost your mind?

MOTHER. You have nothing to say!

KELLER. *[Cruelly.]* I got plenty to say. Three and a half years you been talking like a maniac—

[Mother smashes him across the face.]

MOTHER. Nothing. You have nothing to say. Now I say. He's coming back, and everybody has got to wait.

CHRIS. Mother, Mother—

MOTHER. Wait, wait—

CHRIS. How long? How long?

MOTHER. *[Rolling out of her.]* Till he comes; forever and ever till he comes!

CHRIS. *[As an ultimatum.]* Mother, I'm going ahead with it.

MOTHER. Chris, I've never said no to you in my life, now I say no!

CHRIS. You'll never let him go till I do it.

MOTHER. I'll never let him go and you'll never let him go!

CHRIS. I've let him go. I've let him go a long—

MOTHER. *[With no less force, but turning from him.]* Then let your father go. *[Pause. Chris stands transfixed.]*

KELLER. She's out of her mind.

MOTHER. Altogether! *[To Chris, but not facing them]* Your brother's alive, darling, because if he's dead, your father killed him. Do you understand me now? As long as you live, that boy is alive. God does not let a son be killed by his father. Now you see, don't you? Now you see. *[Beyond control, she hurries up and into house.]*

KELLER. *[Chris has not moved. He speaks insinuatingly, questioningly.]* She's out of her mind.

CHRIS. *[In a broken whisper.]* Then . . . you did it?

KELLER. *[With the beginning of plea in his voice.]* He never flew a P-40—

CHRIS. *[Struck; deadly.]* But the others.

KELLER. [*Insistently.*] She's out of her mind. [*He takes a step toward Chris, pleadingly.*]

CHRIS. [*Unyielding.*] Dad . . . you did it?

KELLER. He never flew a P-40, what's the matter with you?

CHRIS. [*Still asking, and saying.*] Then you did it. To the others.

[*Both hold their voices down.*]

KELLER. [*Afraid of him, his deadly insistence.*] What's the matter with you? What the hell is the matter with you?

CHRIS. [*Quietly, incredibly.*] How could you do that? How?

KELLER. What's the matter with you!

CHRIS. Dad . . . Dad, you killed twenty-one men!

KELLER. What, killed?

CHRIS. You killed them, you murdered them.

KELLER. [*As though throwing his whole nature open before Chris.*] How could I kill anybody?

CHRIS. Dad! Dad!

KELLER. [*Trying to hush him.*] I didn't kill anybody!

CHRIS. Then explain it to me. What did you do? Explain it to me or I'll tear you to pieces!

KELLER. [*Horrified at his overwhelming fury.*] Don't, Chris, don't—

CHRIS. I want to know what you did, now what did you do? You had a hundred and twenty cracked engine-heads, now what did you do?

KELLER. If you're going to hang me then I—

CHRIS. I'm listening. God Almighty, I'm listening!

KELLER. [*Their movements now are those of subtle pursuit and escape. Keller keeps a step out of Chris's range as he talks.*] You're a boy, what could I do! I'm in business, a man is in business; a hundred and twenty cracked, you're out of business; you got a process, the process don't work you're out of business; you don't know how to operate, your stuff is no good; they close you up, they tear up your contracts, what the hell's it to them? You lay forty years into a business and they knock you out in five minutes, what could I do, let them take forty years, let them take my life away? [*His voice cracking*] I never thought they'd install them. I swear to God. I thought they'd stop 'em before anybody took off.

CHRIS. Then why'd you ship them out?

KELLER. By the time they could spot them I thought I'd have the process going again, and I could show them they needed me and they'd let it go by. But weeks passed and I got no kick-back, so I was going to tell them.

CHRIS. Then why didn't you tell them?

KELLER. It was too late. The paper, it was all over the front page, twenty-one went down, it was too late. They came with handcuffs into the shop, what could I do? [*He sits on bench.*] Chris . . . Chris, I did it for you, it was a chance and I took it for you. I'm sixty-one years old, when would I have another chance to make something for you? Sixty-one years old you don't get another chance, do ya?

CHRIS. You even knew they wouldn't hold up in the air.

KELLER. I didn't say that.

CHRIS. But you were going to warn them not to use them—

KELLER. But that don't mean—

CHRIS. It means you knew they'd crash.

KELLER. It don't mean that.

CHRIS. Then you *thought* they'd crash.

KELLER. I was afraid maybe—

CHRIS. You were afraid maybe! God in heaven, what kind of a man are you? Kids were hanging in the air by those heads. You knew that!

KELLER. For you, a business for you!

CHRIS. [*With burning fury.*] For me! Where do you live, where have you come from? For me!—I was dying every day and you were killing my boys and you did it for me? What the hell do you think I was thinking of, the Goddam business? Is that as far as your mind can see, the business? What is that, the world—the business? What the hell do you mean, you did it for me? Don't you have a country? Don't you live in the world? What the hell are you? You're not even an animal, no animal kills his own, what are you? What must I do to you? I ought to tear the tongue out of your mouth, what must I do? [*With his fist he pounds down upon his father's shoulder. He stumbles away, covering his face as he weeps.*] What must I do, Jesus God, what must I do?

KELLER. Chris . . . My Chris . . .

CURTAIN

ACT 3

Two o'clock the following morning, Mother is discovered on the rise, rocking ceaselessly in a chair, staring at her thoughts. It is an intense, slight, sort of rocking. A light shows from upstairs bedroom, lower floor windows being dark. The moon is strong and casts its bluish light.

[*Presently Jim, dressed in jacket and hat, appears, and seeing her, goes up beside her.*]

JIM. Any news?

MOTHER. No news.

JIM. *[Gently.]* You can't sit up all night, dear, why don't you go to bed?

MOTHER. I'm waiting for Chris. Don't worry about me, Jim, I'm perfectly all right.

JIM. But it's almost two o'clock.

MOTHER. I can't sleep. *[Slight pause.]* You had an emergency?

JIM. *[Tiredly.]* Somebody had a headache and thought he was dying. *[Slight pause.]* Half of my patients are quite mad. Nobody realizes how many people are walking around loose, and they're cracked as coconuts. Money. Money-money-money-money. You say it long enough it doesn't mean anything. *[She smiles, makes a silent laugh.]* Oh, how I'd love to be around when that happens!

MOTHER. *[Shaking her head.]* You're so childish, Jim! Sometimes you are.

JIM. *[Looks at her a moment.]* Kate. *[Pause.]* What happened?

MOTHER. I told you. He had an argument with Joe. Then he got in the car and drove away.

JIM. What kind of an argument?

MOTHER. An argument, Joe . . . He was crying like a child, before.

JIM. They argued about Ann?

MOTHER. *[After slight hesitation.]* No, not Ann. Imagine? *[Indicates lighted window above.]* She hasn't come out of that room since he left. All night in that room.

JIM. *[Looks at window, then at her.]* What'd Joe do, tell him?

MOTHER. *[Stops rocking.]* Tell him what?

JIM. Don't be afraid, Kate, I know. I've always known.

MOTHER. How?

JIM. It occurred to me a long time ago.

MOTHER. I always had the feeling that in the back of his head, Chris . . . almost knew. I didn't think it would be such a shock.

JIM. *[Gets up.]* Chris would never know how to live with a thing like that. It takes a certain talent—for lying. You have it, and I do. But not him.

MOTHER. What do you mean . . . He's not coming back?

JIM. Oh, no, he'll come back. We all come back, Kate. These private little revolutions always die. The compromise is always made. In a peculiar way. Frank is right—every man does have a star. The star of one's honesty. And you spend your life groping for it, but once it's out it never lights again. I don't think he went very far. He probably just wanted to be alone to watch his star go out.

MOTHER. Just as long as he comes back.

JIM. I wish he wouldn't, Kate. One year I simply took off, went to New Orleans; for two months I lived on bananas and milk, and studied a certain disease. It was beautiful. And then she came, and she cried. And I went back home with her. And now I live in the usual darkness; I can't find myself; it's even hard sometimes to remember the kind of man I wanted to be. I'm a good husband; Chris is a good son—he'll come back.

[Keller comes out on porch in dressing gown and slippers. He goes upstage— to alley. Jim goes to him.]

JIM. I have a feeling he's in the park. I'll look around for him. Put her to bed, Joe; this is no good for what she's got. *[Jim exits up driveway.]*

KELLER. *[Coming down.]* What does he want here?

MOTHER. His friend is not home.

KELLER. *[Comes down to her. His voice is husky.]* I don't like him mixing in so much.

MOTHER. It's too late, Joe. He knows.

KELLER. *[Apprehensively.]* How does he know?

MOTHER. He guessed a long time ago.

KELLER. I don't like that.

MOTHER. *[Laughs dangerously, quietly into the line.]* What you don't like.

KELLER. Yeah, what I don't like.

MOTHER. You can't bull yourself through this one, Joe, you better be smart now. This thing—this thing is not over yet.

KELLER. *[Indicating lighted window above.]* And what is she doing up there? She don't come out of the room.

MOTHER. I don't know, what is she doing? Sit down, stop being mad. You want to live? You better figure out your life.

KELLER. She don't know, does she?

MOTHER. She saw Chris storming out of here. It's one and one— she knows how to add.

KELLER. Maybe I ought to talk to her?

MOTHER. Don't ask me, Joe.

KELLER. *[Almost an outburst.]* Then who do I ask? But I don't think she'll do anything about it.

MOTHER. You're asking me again.

KELLER. I'm askin' you. What am I, a stranger? I thought I had a family here. What happened to my family?

MOTHER. You've got a family. I'm simply telling you that I have no strength to think any more.

KELLER. You have no strength. The minute there's trouble you have no strength.

MOTHER. Joe, you're doing the same thing again; all your life whenever there's trouble you yell at me and you think that settles it.

KELLER. Then what do I do? Tell me, talk to me, what do I do?

MOTHER. Joe . . . I've been thinking this way. If he comes back—

KELLER. What do you mean "if"? He's comin' back!

MOTHER. I think if you sit him down and you—explain yourself. I mean you ought to make it clear to him that you know you did a terrible thing. *[Not looking into his eyes.]* I mean if he saw that you realize what you did. You see?

KELLER. What ice does that cut?

MOTHER. *[A little fearfully.]* I mean if you told him that you want to pay for what you did.

KELLER. *[Sensing . . . quietly.]* How can I pay?

MOTHER. Tell him—you're willing to go to prison. *[Pause.]*

KELLER. *[Stuck, amazed.]* I'm willing to—?

MOTHER. *[Quickly.]* You wouldn't go, he wouldn't ask you to go. But if you told him you wanted to, if he could feel that you wanted to pay, maybe he would forgive you.

KELLER. He would forgive me! For what?

MOTHER. Joe, you know what I mean.

KELLER. I don't know what you mean! You wanted money, so I made money. What must I be forgiven! You wanted money, didn't you?

MOTHER. I didn't want it that way.

KELLER. I didn't want it that way, either! What difference is it what you want? I spoiled the both of you. I should've put him out when he was ten like I was put out, and make him earn his keep. Then he'd know how a buck is made in this world. Forgiven! I could live on a quarter a day myself, but I got a family so I—

MOTHER. Joe, Joe . . . It don't excuse it that you did it for the family.

KELLER. It's got to excuse it!

MOTHER. There's something bigger than the family to him.

KELLER. Nothin' is bigger!

MOTHER. There is to him.

KELLER. There's nothin' he could do that I wouldn't forgive. Because he's my son. Because I'm his father and he's my son.

MOTHER. Joe, I tell you—

KELLER. Nothin's bigger than that. And you're goin' to tell him, you understand? I'm his father and he's my son, and if there's something bigger than that I'll put a bullet in my head!

MOTHER. You stop that!

KELLER. You heard me. Now you know what to tell him. *[Pause. He moves from her—halts.]* But he wouldn't put me away though . . . He wouldn't do that . . . Would he?

MOTHER. He loved you, Joe, you broke his heart.

KELLER. But to put me away . . .

MOTHER. I don't know. I'm beginning to think we don't really know him. They say in the war he was such a killer. Here he was always afraid of mice. I don't know him. I don't know what he'll do.

KELLER. Goddam, if Larry was alive he wouldn't act like this. He understood the way the world is made. He listened to me. To him the world had a forty-foot front, it ended at the building line. This one, everything bothers him. You make a deal, overcharge two cents, and his hair falls out. He don't understand money. Too easy, it came too easy. Yes, sir. Larry. That was a boy we lost. Larry.

Larry. *[He slumps on chair in front of her.]* What am I gonna do, Kate?

MOTHER. Joe, Joe, please . . . You'll be all right, nothing is going to happen.

KELLER. *[Desperately, lost.]* For you, Kate, for both of you, that's all I ever lived for . . .

MOTHER. I know, darling, I know. *[Ann enters from house. They say nothing, waiting for her to speak.]*

ANN. Why do you stay up? I'll tell you when he comes.

KELLER. *[Rises, goes to her.]* You didn't eat supper, did you? *[To Mother.]* Why don't you make her something?

MOTHER. Sure, I'll—

ANN. Never mind, Kate, I'm all right. *[They are unable to speak to each other.]* There's something I want to tell you. *[She starts, then halts.]* I'm not going to do anything about it.

MOTHER. She's a good girl! *[To Keller.]* You see? She's a—

ANN. I'll do nothing about Joe, but you're going to do something for me. *[Directly to Mother.]* You made Chris feel guilty with me. Whether you wanted to or not, you've crippled him in front of me. I'd like you to tell him that Larry is dead and that you know it. You understand me? I'm not going out of here alone. There's no life for me that way. I want you to set him free. And then I promise you, everything will end, and we'll go away, and that's all.

KELLER. You'll do that. You'll tell him.

ANN. I know what I'm asking, Kate. You had two sons. But you've only got one now.

KELLER. You'll tell him.

ANN. And you've got to say it to him so he knows you mean it.

MOTHER. My dear, if the boy was dead, it wouldn't depend on my words to make Chris know it. . . . The night he gets into your bed, his heart will dry up. Because he knows and you know. To his dying day he'll wait for his brother! No, my dear, no such thing. You're going in the morning, and you're going alone. That's your life, that's your lonely life. *[She goes to porch, and starts in.]*

ANN. Larry is dead, Kate.

MOTHER. *[She stops.]* Don't speak to me.

ANN. I said he's dead. I know! He crashed off the coast of China November twenty-fifth! His engine didn't fail him. But he died. I know . . .

MOTHER. How did he die? You're lying to me. If you know, how did he die?

ANN. I loved him. You know I loved him. Would I have looked at anyone else if I wasn't sure? That's enough for you.

MOTHER. *[Moving on her.]* What's enough for me? What're you talking about? *[She grasps Ann's wrists.]*

ANN. You're hurting my wrists.

MOTHER. What are you talking about! *[Pause. She stares at Ann a moment, then turns and goes to Keller.]*

ANN. Joe, go in the house.

KELLER. Why should I—

ANN. Please go.

KELLER. Lemme know when he comes. *[Keller goes into house.]*

MOTHER. *[as she sees Ann taking a letter from her pocket.]* What's that?

ANN. Sit down. *[Mother moves left to chair, but does not sit.]* First you've got to understand. When I came, I didn't have any idea that Joe—I had nothing against him or you. I came to get married. I hoped . . . So I didn't bring this to hurt you. I thought I'd show it to you only if there was no other way to settle Larry in your mind.

MOTHER. Larry? *[Snatches letter from Ann's hand.]*

ANN. He wrote it to me just before he— *[Mother opens and begins to read letter.]* I'm not trying to hurt you, Kate. You're making me do this, now remember you're— Remember. I've been so lonely, Kate . . . I can't leave here alone again. *[A long, low moan comes from Mother's throat as she reads.]* You made me show it to you. You wouldn't believe me. I told you a hundred times, why wouldn't you believe me!

MOTHER. Oh, my God . . .

ANN. *[With pity and fear.]* Kate, please, please . . .

MOTHER. My God, my God . . .

ANN. Kate, dear, I'm so sorry . . . I'm so sorry.

[Chris enters from driveway. He seems exhausted.]

CHRIS. What's the matter—?

ANN. Where were you? . . . You're all perspired. *[Mother doesn't move.]* Where were you?

CHRIS. Just drove around a little. I thought you'd be gone.

ANN. Where do I go? I have nowhere to go.

CHRIS. *[To Mother.]* Where's Dad?

ANN. Inside lying down.

CHRIS. Sit down, both of you. I'll say what there is to say.

MOTHER. I didn't hear the car . . .

CHRIS. I left it in the garage.

MOTHER. Jim is out looking for you.

CHRIS. Mother . . . I'm going away. There are a couple of firms in Cleveland, I think I can get a place. I mean, I'm going away for good. *[To Ann alone.]* I know what you're thinking, Annie. It's true. I'm yellow. I was made yellow in this house because I suspected my father and I did nothing about it, but if I knew that night when I came home what I know now, he'd be in the district attorney's office by this time, and I'd have brought him there. Now if I look at him, all I'm able to do is cry.

MOTHER. What are you talking about? What else can you do?

CHRIS. I could jail him! I could jail him, if I were human any more. But I'm like everybody else now. I'm practical now. You made me practical.

MOTHER. But you have to be.

CHRIS. The cats in that alley are practical, the bums who ran away when we were fighting were practical. Only the dead ones weren't practical. But now I'm practical, and I spit on myself. I'm going away. I'm going now.

ANN. *[Going up to him.]* I'm coming with you.

CHRIS. No, Ann.

ANN. Chris, I don't ask you to do anything about Joe.

CHRIS. You do, you do.

ANN. I swear I never will.

CHRIS. In your heart you always will.

ANN. Then do what you have to do!

CHRIS. Do what? What is there to do? I've looked all night for a reason to make him suffer.

ANN. There's reason, there's reason!

CHRIS. What? Do I raise the dead when I put him behind bars? Then what'll I do it for? We used to shoot a man who acted like a dog, but honor was real there, you were protecting something. But here? This is the land of the great big dogs, you don't love a man here, you eat him! That's the principle; the only one we live by —it just happened to kill a few people this time, that's all. The world's that way, how can I take it out on him? What sense does that make? This is a zoo, a zoo!

ANN. *[To Mother.]* You know what he's got to do! Tell him!

MOTHER. Let him go.

ANN. I won't let him go. You'll tell him what he's got to do . . .

MOTHER. Annie!

ANN. Then I will!

[Keller enters from house. Chris sees him, goes down near arbor.]

KELLER. What's the matter with you? I want to talk to you.

CHRIS. I've got nothing to say to you.

KELLER. *[Taking his arm.]* I want to talk to you!

CHRIS. *[Pulling violently away from him.]* Don't do that, Dad. I'm going to hurt you if you do that. There's nothing to say, so say it quick.

KELLER. Exactly what's the matter? What's the matter? You got too much money? Is that what bothers you?

CHRIS. *[With an edge of sarcasm.]* It bothers me.

KELLER. If you can't get used to it, then throw it away. You hear me? Take every cent and give it to charity, throw it in the sewer. Does that settle it? In the sewer, that's all. You think I'm kidding? I'm tellin' you what to do, if it's dirty then burn it. It's your money, that's not my money. I'm a dead man, I'm an old dead man, nothing's mine. Well, talk to me! What do you want to do!

CHRIS. It's not what I want to do. It's what you want to do.

KELLER. What should I want to do? *[Chris is silent.]* Jail? You want me to go to jail? If you want me to go, say so! Is that where

I belong? Then tell me so! *[Slight pause.]* What's the matter, why can't you tell me? *[Furiously.]* You say everything else to me, say that! *[Slight pause.]* I'll tell you why you can't say it. Because you know I don't belong there. Because you know! *[With growing emphasis and passion, and a persistent tone of desperation.]* Who worked for nothin' in that war? When they work for nothin', I'll work for nothin'. Did they ship a gun or a truck outa Detroit before they got their price? Is that clean? It's dollars and cents, nickels and dimes; war and peace, it's nickles and dimes, what's clean? Half the Goddam country is gotta go if I go! That's why you can't tell me.

CHRIS. That's exactly why.

KELLER. Then . . . why am *I* bad?

CHRIS. *I* know you're no worse than most men but I thought you were better. I never saw you as a man. I saw you as my father. *[Almost breaking.]* I can't look at you this way, I can't look at myself!

[He turns away, unable to face Keller. Ann goes quickly to Mother, takes letter from her and starts for Chris. Mother instantly rushes to intercept her.]

MOTHER. Give me that!

ANN. He's going to read it! *[She thrusts letter into Chris's hand.]* Larry. He wrote it to me the day he died.

KELLER. Larry!

MOTHER. Chris, it's not for you. *[He starts to read.]* Joe . . . go away . . .

KELLER. *[Mystified, frightened.]* Why'd she say, Larry, what—?

MOTHER. *[Desperately pushes him toward alley, glancing at Chris.]* Go to the street, Joe, go to the street! *[She comes down beside Keller.]* Don't, Chris . . . *[Pleading from her whole soul.]* Don't tell him.

CHRIS. *[Quietly.]* Three and one half years . . . talking, talking. Now you tell me what you must do. . . . This is how he died, now tell me where you belong.

KELLER. *[Pleading.]* Chris, a man can't be a Jesus in this world!

CHRIS. I know all about the world. I know the whole crap story. Now listen to this, and tell me what a man's got to be! *[Reads.]* "My dear Ann: . . ." You listening? He wrote this the day he died. Listen, don't cry. . . . Listen! "My dear Ann: It is impossible to put down the things I feel. But I've got to tell you something. Yesterday they flew in a load of papers from the States and I read about Dad and your father being convicted. I can't express myself. I can't tell you how I feel—I can't bear to live any more. Last night I circled the base for twenty minutes before I could bring myself in. How could he have done that? Every day three or four men never come back and he sits back there doing business. . . . I don't know how to tell you what I feel. . . . I can't face anybody. . . . I'm going out on a mission in a few minutes. They'll probably report me missing. If they do, I want you to know that you mustn't wait for me. I tell you, Ann, if I had him there now I could kill him—" [*Keller grabs letter from Chris's hand and reads it. After a long pause.*] Now blame the world. Do you understand that letter?

KELLER. [*Speaking almost inaudibly.*] I think I do. Get the car. I'll put on my jacket. [*He turns and starts slowly for the house. Mother rushes to intercept him.*]

MOTHER. Why are you going? You'll sleep, why are you going?

KELLER. I can't sleep here. I'll feel better if I go.

MOTHER. You're so foolish. Larry was your son too, wasn't he? You know he'd never tell you to do this.

KELLER. [*Looking at letter in his hand.*] Then what is this if it isn't telling me? Sure, he was my son. But I think to him they were all my sons. And I guess they were, I guess they were. I'll be right down. [*Exits into house.*]

MOTHER. [*To Chris, with determination.*] You're not going to take him!

CHRIS. I'm taking him.

MOTHER. It's up to you, if you tell him to stay he'll stay. Go and tell him!

CHRIS. Nobody could stop him now.

MOTHER. You'll stop him! How long will he live in prison? Are you trying to kill him?

CHRIS. [*Holding out letter.*] I thought you read this!

MOTHER. [*Of Larry, the letter.*] The war is over! Didn't you hear? It's over!

CHRIS. Then what was Larry to you? A stone that fell into the water? It's not enough for him to be sorry. Larry didn't kill himself to make you and Dad sorry.

MOTHER. What more can we be!

CHRIS. You can be better! Once and for all you can know there's a universe of people outside and you're responsible to it, and unless you know that, you threw away your son because that's why he died.

[*A shot is heard in the house. They stand frozen for a brief second. Chris starts for porch, pauses at step, turns to Ann.*]

CHRIS. Find Jim! [*He goes on into the house and Ann runs up driveway. Mother stands alone, transfixed.*]

MOTHER. [*Softly, almost moaning.*] Joe . . . Joe . . . Joe . . . Joe . . . [*Chris comes out of house, down to Mother's arms.*]

CHRIS. [*Almost crying.*] Mother, I didn't mean to—

MOTHER. Don't dear. Don't take it on yourself. Forget now. Live. [*Chris stirs as if to answer.*] Shhh . . . [*She puts his arms down gently and moves toward porch.*] Shhh . . . [*As she reaches porch steps she begins sobbing.*]

CURTAIN

Appendix

The following discussion is intended to help the reader understand the preceding plays more clearly. While reading these or any other plays, the student should direct his attention to following the most important elements of each play: 1) subject matter, 2) theme, 3) structure, 4) characterization, and 5) tone. The most important of these, of course, is theme. The others are really only the means of developing the theme. In analyzing every play, one should be able to state the subject matter and theme and show how the theme is developed.

Every drama is about *something;* that is, every play is concerned with some kind of *subject matter;* and the more important the subject matter the more important are the possibilities of the play. A play which concerned itself completely with an unimportant episode in a person's life would very likely be a very unimportant play. In a word, a play, to be worth anything at all, must be about an idea that has implications beyond the individual people and events in the drama itself.

Frequently a title of a play tells its audience what its subject matter is, for example, *Everyman, Ghosts, All My Sons. Everyman,* as we have said, takes for its subject matter salvation and the moral evaluation which men in the Middle Ages thought and many men today think they must face at the time of death. *Ghosts* is not only about particular individuals, Mrs. Alving and her son, Oswald, but it is also about the influence of the past on the present. *All My Sons* is not primarily about Joe Keller and the other characters in the play, or even about his dead son, Larry. Rather, it is about the reasons behind man's evil actions and the results of such actions. As Joe says of the pilots who died because of his actions, "They were all my sons."

The subject matter of a play is the general subject with which it is concerned. The *theme* of a play, however, is what the author *thinks* about his subject matter. It is the "meaning" implied by the author; it is what the author is "saying"; it is his interpretation of the experiences he depicts. In a word, the theme of any work is the statement it makes explicitly or implicitly about its subject matter. As such, it must be set down in the form of a predication, that is, an affirmation or a denial, a declaration or an assertion. For example, in *Hamlet,* whatever else William Shakespeare says, he certainly makes the predication that at some time in every man's life, once he becomes aware of what the right action for him is, he must take that action and be indifferent to its results. Stated another way, a man must do his duty regardless of what he thinks will be the outcome of his actions. Nowhere does Shakespeare explicitly say this, but by analyzing his play we can understand the predication he is making.

One of the most important elements of any play is its *structure* (its planned framework or the organization of its parts). A brief analysis of the structure of *Everyman* will help to clarify this point.

The author

> . . . presents his actions in a more complex form than would be necessary if he were only making a point about Christian values. He has several climaxes, with resultant changes in tension and mood; he makes rather skillfull use of irony; he uses different means of suspense. In other words, he is trying in every way he can to make us become emotionally concerned; he wants his story to be effective as a story—his plot to work as plot.
>
> For the sake of the theme, all the author must do is show Everyman embracing Christian values and thus gaining everlasting life. But the author is not content with so simple a pattern: he wishes to present also Everyman's devotion to false values, and later his failure to distinguish, in the realm of sound values, between those which are only of earthly significance and those which relate directly to eternal salvation. Now these experiences have to come in a certain order, and as we observe what that order is, we really discover the structure of the play.*

As Aristotle pointed out, the plot of a play is an imitation of an action. A successful play, however, does not give the impression of a plot being acted out, but rather of being the result of what the *characters* in the play must do. By looking into a play's characters and their *motivation* (the justification of the action of a character in a plot by a convincing and compelling cause for that action), one can come to a closer understanding of a play's theme. Motivation usually consists of a combination of psychological traits and external events. Whatever else it may consist of, if it is properly worked out it leaves the audience with the recognition of those emotive and circumstantial forces in a character which made the action of the plot inevitable.

The *tone* of a play is the general effect produced by an author's selection and treatment of his materials. It is the result of his attitude (how he *feels*) toward his subject matter. It comes across to the audience through his treatment of the psychology, language, and action of his characters.

In order to understand the plays in this volume more clearly, the reader should be able to indicate for each play the *subject matter* and the *theme*. He should be able to show concretely how *structure, characterization,* and *tone* are used by the author to develop his theme.

*Brooks, Cleanth and Heilman, Robert B., *Understanding Drama*, (New York: Henry Holt and Company, 1948), p. 104.